BROUGHT TO LIGHT

BROUGHT TO LIGHT

Contemporary Freemasonry, Meaning, and Society

J. SCOTT KENNEY

WILFRID LAURIER
UNIVERSITY PRESS

This book has been published with the help of a grant from the Canadian Federation for the Humanities and Social Sciences, through the Awards to Scholarly Publications Program, using funds provided by the Social Sciences and Humanities Research Council of Canada. Wilfrid Laurier University Press acknowledges the financial support of the Government of Canada through the Canada Book Fund for its publishing activities. This work was supported by the Research Support Fund.

ONTARIO ARTS COUNCIL
CONSEIL DES ARTS DE L'ONTARIO
an Ontario government agency
un organisme du gouvernement de l'Ontario

Library and Archives Canada Cataloguing in Publication

Kenney, J. Scott (James Scott), 1961–, author
    Brought to light : contemporary freemasonry, meaning, and society / J. Scott Kenney.

Includes bibliographical references and index.
Issued in print and electronic formats.
ISBN 978-1-77112-194-1 (paperback).—ISBN 978-1-77112-195-8 (pdf).—ISBN 978-1-77112-196-5 (epub)

    1. Freemasonry—Canada. 2. Freemasons—Canada—Social conditions. 3. Free-masons—Atlantic Provinces—Interviews. 4. Kenney, J. Scott (James Scott), 1963–. 5. Freemasons—Canada—Biography. I. Title.

HS558.K45 2016   366'.10971   C2015-905581-4
                                                                   C2015-905582-2

Cover design by Angela Booth Malleau. Front-cover image © Dekanarysas I Dreamstime .com. Frontispiece image—an interpretation of a Masonic stained-glass window—created in 2015 and executed with colour markers on 8½-x-11-inch card stock. Copyright © Natalie Kenney. Text design by Angela Booth Malleau.

© 2016 Wilfrid Laurier University Press
Waterloo, Ontario, Canada
www.wlupress.wlu.ca

CONTENTS

PREFACE

W hen I was initiated into the Freemasons in September 1999, just a few months after receiving my PhD from McMaster University, I was struck by something obvious. Extensively trained in symbolic interactionist theory during my graduate studies, I saw unfolding before my eyes an organization that emphasized the use of carefully coordinated ritual actions, combined with complex, multi-layered symbolism, to socially construct meaning for its members. The desire to conduct a study was born. After all, how could I resist utilizing a sociological approach, which emphasizes the pragmatic construction of meaning through symbolic actions, as a way of studying an organization that utilizes symbolic, ritualized actions to construct meaning?

At first I moved slowly. I felt that somebody must have done this before. It was just too obvious. I did some research and found that there was, indeed, a sociological literature. Beginning with Georg Simmel's (1908) publication *Sociology of Secrecy and of Secret Societies*, which characterizes so-called secret fraternal organizations as fostering boundaries, separation, and corresponding validation such that members come to see themselves as a sort of "aristocracy," there have been many sociological works on the Freemasons and fraternal organizations. Perhaps most notably, Mark Carnes (1989) argued in *Secret Ritual and Manhood in Victorian America* that fraternal ritual provided solace and psychological guidance during young men's troubled passage to manhood. Relatedly, Mary Ann Clawson (1989) asserted that nineteenth-century fraternalism articulated a gendered vision of brotherhood in an era of class conflict, attracting a multi-class membership and organized social solidarity centred on the ambiguous symbolic figure of the artisan, the producer-proprietor, when this role was under stress and a growing assertion of a feminine vision of social and affective life threatened to undermine male institutional solidarity.

Yet these, and many other studies, while illuminating in many ways, struck me as problematic. They tended to emphasize the "big picture" (i.e., macro-level structural dynamics filtered through today's sociological preoccupations with class and gender). While these could not be ruled out entirely, relatively little emphasis was placed on the likely more diverse, pragmatic constructions of meaning engaged in by the membership. Furthermore, the vast majority of extant studies focused on the past. Little work had been done on Freemasons and the meanings that they construct in the very different social world inhabited by members today. Given the vast social changes that took place in the twentieth century, particularly from the 1960s onward, along with the decline of social capital and community organizations, there appeared to be a crying need to study the meanings constructed by contemporary Freemasons. I felt that these major theoretical and empirical gaps called for contemporary study.

Given these issues, I initially attempted to identify multiple theoretical issues germane to an interactionist study of this organization. While difficult to imagine a complete list before entering the field, I first attempted in 2005 to articulate the relevance of various "sensitizing concepts" in a paper presented at the Canonbury Masonic Research Conference in London. This was subsequently published in 2007 as "Ritual Actions and Meaning among Freemasons" in the fourth volume of *The Canonbury Papers, Freemasonry and Initiatic Traditions* (edited by R. A. Gilbert), part of which is adapted in chapter 1 of this volume.

Around this same time, I experienced a great stroke of luck. Having some years before appeared in the documentary film *Inside Freemasonry* (Arcadia Entertainment, 2004), a film about contemporary Freemasons produced by a member of my first lodge, I asked him if he still had the film footage. "Yeah," he responded, "do you want it?" This resulted in being provided with a banker's box of fifty-eight videotapes, including detailed interview data from twenty-seven individuals, all collected with written consent to disseminate their comments on television. This provided an invaluable boost to my project.

In short order I applied for research funding to conduct a more extensive qualitative study in this area. In 2006, I was awarded a $32,600 Research Development Initiatives Grant from the Social Sciences and Humanities Research Council of Canada as well as a $6,900 Vice President's Research Grant from Memorial University to fund this study. After receiving ethics clearance, I spent the autumn of 2006 to December of 2007 travelling throughout Newfoundland and Nova Scotia interviewing Freemasons about their experiences, activities, involvement, and, perhaps most importantly, the meanings they derived from their activities in the Masonic order.

Ultimately, I collected an enormous amount of data on the experiences of, and meanings constructed by, contemporary Freemasons. These came from two primary sources: interviews with 121 contemporary Canadian Freemasons (seventy-two in Nova Scotia and forty-nine in Newfoundland and Labrador), and the video footage. I also drew upon, and questioned these against, my observations and experiences in the Masonic order over the last decade and a half.

After collecting, exhaustively transcribing, critically cross-checking, and coding these data, I worked on this book and strove to maintain a happy medium between the potential information unavailable to a detached outsider and the perils of proximity in studying what is often seen as a closed institution (Bryon-Portet 2011). In the meantime I was busy giving conference presentations, getting independent feedback, and submitting the occasional paper to journals. For example, in 2008 I presented "The Social Construction of Curiosity: Dramaturgical Processes and Initiation among Contemporary Freemasons" at a conference of the Society for the Study of Symbolic Interaction in Boston. I presented "Pragmatic Constructions of History among Contemporary Freemasons" at the International Conference on the History of Freemasonry (ICHF) in Edinburgh in 2009 (which subsequently appeared in the peer-reviewed *Journal for Research into Freemasonry and Fraternalism*). In 2012, I presented "Freemasons Today: Thematic Claims of Life Changes since Becoming a Mason" at the First International Conference on Contemporary Esotericism in Stockholm. Finally, I presented a paper entitled "Paths to Masonry Today: Social Factors Behind Joining the Craft among Twentieth and Twenty-first Century Canadian Freemasons" at the 2013 ICHF in Edinburgh (which also appeared in the *Journal for Research into Freemasonry and Fraternalism*). Adaptations of the latter two appear, respectively, as chapters 2 and 7 of the current volume.

Throughout all of this, my ongoing research was highlighted in areas as diverse as Memorial University's 2007 annual *Research Report*, interviews on CBC Radio, in the St. John's *Telegram*, in the Memorial University *Gazette*, and on the local television program *Out of the Fog*. I also spent considerable time giving talks to the local Masonic community and the occasional guest lecture for other faculty. I published a number of non-peer-reviewed papers on Masonic websites and in Masonic publications. Finally, I was cast as the unofficial "social convenor" of the Memorial University of Newfoundland Masonic community and University Lodge No. 34 (which was formed in 2007 by brethren who regularly met for drinks at the campus pub).

I continue to study various aspects of the Masonic order and Freemasons' experiences in today's rapidly changing, postmodern society. I have found that this is a group that varies in many respects from its portrayal as a secretive, closed organization. Of course, like many community groups today, it hardly lacks organizational and social challenges; and while somewhat more diverse than in the past, it is not devoid of difficulties surrounding inclusion, membership, status, pseudostatus, and bureaucratization. Yet, in different ways, the lodge also provides a safe, ritualized space to socialize; increase social capital; experience supportive bonds of "brotherhood"; engage in charitable work; build character, abilities, and skills; and, ultimately, to attempt to symbolically untangle new meanings relevant to members' lives in today's increasingly perplexing world.

ACKNOWLEDGEMENTS

I would like to offer my heartfelt thanks to the many people and organizations that assisted me, in one way or another, with this book.

I would like to thank my wife, Sylvia, and my kids, Natalie and Nicholas, for their support and encouragement over the years that it took to conduct interviews and transcribe and analyze the data, along with the extensive writing, rewriting, and editing involved. Indeed, I would like to offer a special thanks to my daughter, Natalie, who contributed the artwork that appears in the frontispiece and on the back cover of this book.

I would like to thank the many Freemasons throughout Nova Scotia and Newfoundland that I interviewed for this study. Your willingness to participate, to discuss your experiences, and to offer considered insights into contemporary Freemasonry were invaluable. In many respects, I am but the messenger.

I would like to thank John Wesley Chisholm of Arcadia Entertainment for generously providing me the video footage that makes up part of this study.

I would like to thank the Grand Lodge of Nova Scotia, the Grand Lodge of Newfoundland and Labrador, and the Grand Lodge of Scotland, District Grand Lodge of Newfoundland and Labrador, for their support and assistance in this endeavour.

I would like to thank Brian Johansen and Brandt Evans for their helpful assistance in the laborious task of transcribing the data. Having done a considerable portion of this myself, I know how time-consuming, tedious, and, at times, difficult it can be to accurately capture the exact phrasing of a recording. Thank you, brethren, for your help with this invaluable task.

I would like to thank my colleague Rose Ricciardelli for putting me in contact with the wonderful people at Wilfrid Laurier University Press.

I would like to thank the staff of Wilfrid Laurier University Press for their assistance and encouragement as I prepared this book for publication—notably

Lisa Quinn, Leslie Macredie, Clare Hitchens, Rob Kohlmeier, and Mike Bechthold, as well as Margaret Crammond.

I would like to thank the Social Sciences and Humanities Research Council of Canada, along with Memorial University of Newfoundland, for granting me research funding to pursue this study.

I would like to thank my fellow researchers currently working diligently to expand the field of Masonic research in academia. Your support, suggestions, and encouragement at conferences and elsewhere have been invaluable along the way. Special thanks in this regard go to Andreas Onnerfors, Jeffrey Tyssens, Andrew Pink, and Andrew Prescott.

I would like to thank the brethren of my mother lodge, Burns #10, Grand Lodge of Nova Scotia, for first inspiring me on the journey that led to this study. Our lodge may be gone now—whether for good or perhaps just for a while—but it still shines brightly for me to this day.

I would like to thank the brethren of my current lodges, University Lodge #34, Whiteway Lodge #8, and Clift Lodge #10, Grand Lodge of Newfoundland and Labrador, for their support and encouragement. Indeed, I also thank the brethren in the various concordant bodies for their insights and inspiration.

I would like to thank my father, James L. Kenney, for being there from the very beginning, for supporting and conducting me throughout my initiation, for attending lodge with me regularly as I took my degrees, for encouraging me to move forward through the offices, and for travelling a long distance to attend my installation while he was ill. Without you, Dad, none of this would have ever happened.

CHAPTER 1

CONTEMPORARY FREEMASONRY
A Neglected Field

Freemasonry has become an increasingly controversial topic. It has been thrust into public awareness through popular books like *The Da Vinci Code* (Brown 2003), films like *National Treasure* (2004), and a host of websites and documentaries. In academia, this interest has been paralleled by a recent proliferation of research, the opening of institutes such as the Roosevelt Center for Civil Society and Masonic Studies,[1] and symposia such as the International Conference on the History of Freemasonry. Yet, the former tend to be caricatures, a playing to pervasive stereotypes for public consumption. On the other hand, academic work—especially that produced by Masonic scholars—largely emphasizes historical and philological matters (Pietre-Stones 2005; Wade 2002). Indeed, to the limited extent that a sociological focus exists in research, it largely involves study of the roles played and the meanings articulated by Freemasonry in social history (Hackett 2014; Dunbar 2012; Morrison 2012; Egel 2011; Fozdar 2011; Cano 2009; Marshall 2009; Walker 2008; Clawson 2007; Quiroz 2007; Beaurepaire 2006; Skocpol 2003; Scanlan 2002; Wade 2002; Putnam 2000; Beito 2000; Uribe-Uran 2000; Bullock 1998; Hetherington 1997; Jacob 1991; Clawson 1989; Carnes 1989; Jacob 1981). Yet, aside from a few recent forays into the area (Kaplan 2014; Mahmud 2012; Poulet 2010; Mahmud-Abdelwahib 2008), there has been a relative paucity of sociological work on the *contemporary* meaning of active participation for members themselves.

In this book I seek to address this relative theoretical and empirical neglect. With reference to the symbolic interactionist literature in sociology, and drawing upon qualitative data from contemporary Freemasons, in the pages that follow I paint a detailed theoretical and empirical picture of contemporary members of "the Craft."

FREEMASONRY: BACKGROUND AND CONTEXT

What is Freemasonry? Masonic ritual commonly defines it as "a peculiar system of morality, veiled in allegory and illustrated by symbols." As it offers no sacraments, means of salvation, nor specific theology, it explicitly claims that it is not a religion but a "fraternity" that "makes good men better." Elaborating, *Coil's Masonic Encyclopedia* states that Freemasonry

> is an oath-bound fraternal order of men; deriving from the medieval
> fraternity of operative Freemasons; adhering to many of their Ancient
> Charges, laws, customs, and legends; loyal to the civil government under
> which it exists; inculcating moral and social virtues by symbolic applica-
> tion of the working tools of the stonemasons and by allegories, lectures
> and charges; the members of which are obligated to observe principles
> of brotherly love, equality, mutual aid and assistance, secrecy and con-
> fidence; have secret modes of recognizing one another as Masons when
> abroad in the world; and meet in lodges, each governed by a Master,
> assisted by Wardens, where petitioners, after particular inquiry into their
> mental, moral and physical qualifications, are formally admitted into the
> Society in secret ceremonies based in part on old legends of the Craft.
> (Coil 1996, 164)

Coil adds that Freemasonry is a "way of life" incorporating a "broad humanitarianism" in which members are urged "to think," but "not what to think." Discussion of divisive topics like religion and politics in lodge are specifically prohibited. Open to all social, religious, and ethnic backgrounds, it encourages reflection, tolerance, self-improvement, and charitable activity (1996, 164–65).

In addition to the male order—which is by far the largest, most wide-spread, and the subject of this book—there are also women-only, "adoptive," and mixed ("co-Masonic") orders in many jurisdictions around the world (Mahmud 2012; Ormières 2011; Mahmud-Abdelwahib 2008; Allen 2003; Coil 1996; Rich 1997; Yronwode 2002). Unlike the "regular" Freemasonry of the Anglo-Saxon world (which requires belief in a Supreme Being and excludes women), many of these more "liberal" European Grand Lodges claim liberty of conscience and admit women.

Given the above, Freemasonry involves interrelated subcultural associ-ations, existing within and between societies, focusing on fostering self-improvement and charitable activity through ritual activity. Nevertheless, the Craft's well-known "secretiveness" (a.k.a. "privacy") has often led to spec-ulation.[2] Hence, there is a vast anti-Masonic literature suggesting that Free-masonry is widely involved in political conspiracies and/or organized crime, or, most frequently, attacking it from religious standpoints (de Hoyos and Morris 1997). Which characterization Masonry is *perceived* to fit often depends on insider versus outsider views, social location, and the availability and variety of interpretive resources that one brings to bear on the issue.

Freemasonry is also highly organized. Local lodges manage their own matters but are overseen by state or provincial Grand Lodges. The latter maintain legitimacy to administer lodges within their areas through mutual recognition at the international level. A trans-societal subculture (Prus 1997, 34), Freemasonry can be seen as "institutionally complete" (Best and Luckenbill 1982).

The origins of this complex, ritualistic organization are, at best, obscure, and some, like Jones (1950), distinguish between its legendary history (or histories) and that which can be more readily documented. Leaving aside fanciful legends of ancient Egypt, the kingdom of Solomon, or the medieval Knights Templar, plus long-standing claims that it originated in England, Stevenson (1990) has persuasively argued that Freemasonry originated in Scotland during the seventeenth century. Declining medieval stonemasons' guilds, in need of members and support, gradually integrated "gentlemen" deeply imbued with late Renaissance Neoplatonic, hermetic, Rosicrucian, and kabbalistic thought. The result was a growing system of lodges with rituals and secrets combining legends and practices of the building trade with European mystical traditions.

Freemasonry "went public" in London in 1717, when four lodges combined to form the Grand Lodge of England (Coil 1996). It spread rapidly across Europe and around the globe in the eighteenth century, aided by emigration, colonization, and military lodges. While linked to British imperialism (Fozdar 2011; Harland-Jacobs 2007), it also helped to ecumenically bridge social boundaries and undermine oppressive social orders by fostering enlightenment ideals and assisting in the emergence of civil society (Beaurepaire 2006; Jacob 1981, 1991).

Despite, or partially in response to, controversies such as its alleged involvement in the French and American revolutions, long-standing opposition by the Catholic church, and even persecution by the Nazis, Freemasonry grew during much of the nineteenth and well into the twentieth century throughout the Western world (Coil 1996), facilitating educational enrolment (Egel 2011) and helping to give shape to the public sphere (Hackett 2014). Indeed, despite a widespread anti-Masonic American political movement between 1826 and 1840 that negatively impacted US Grand Lodges and their membership for a time (Bullock 1998; Coil 1996), American Freemasonry experienced significant growth following the Civil War (Clawson 1989; Carnes 1989) which continued into the 20th century. Beyond the common stereotype that Freemasonry fostered business connections, growth was aided by its "social service" or "insurance" practices when public social programs were virtually non-existent (Beito 2000). Meanwhile, Masonry developed spinoff organizations ("concordant bodies") during periods of growth, typically founded by younger members unable to move up status hierarchies dominated by older brethren (Morris 2007a). Yet there were also periods of "creative destruction" (Bullock 2007), where it responded to social changes by shifting emphasis and reorganizing institutions. By the mid-twentieth century, with the development of big government, big business, and labour organizations, along with the popularity of "service clubs" like Rotary and Kiwanis, Freemasonry, particularly in the United States, shifted from a fraternity primarily emphasizing ritual and self-improvement to a highly organized, institutionalized, even bureaucratic group focused on supporting or coordinating various Masonic philanthropies (Tabbert 2007).

In terms of gross membership numbers, Freemasonry peaked between the end of WWII and 1959, and, like many community organizations, it has experienced a significant decline in overall membership since the 1960s (Masonic Service Association 2014; Belton and Harrison 2007; Belton 2004; Beito 2000; Putnam 2000). Despite a shift in emphasis and efforts to keep members' dues low, and regardless of marketing efforts to attract new members in the 1980s (Hackett 2014), membership continued to drop (Tabbert 2007). Explanations range from the gradual replacement of Freemasonry's social service and insurance functions (Beito 2000) and the undermining of social capital (Putnam 2000) to the thesis that a relatively long period of prosperity fostered a "culture of contentment" among the "middle classes," the relative lack of economic crisis undercutting the feeling of "uncertainty" traditionally conducive to membership growth (Belton and Harrison 2007). By the 1990s, Freemasonry suffered from over-institutionalization, bureaucratization, and an aging and declining membership. Moreover, rather than the organized opposition of the past, Freemasonry, like other community organizations, was at times confronted with relative indifference (Putnam 2000).

Surprisingly, however, in some areas there has been a recent resurgence of interest in Freemasonry, notably among younger men in their thirties and forties (Hackett 2014; Tschorn 2008). Thus, California experienced seven straight years of increases in initiations by 2008, the average age of members dropped (Tschorn 2008), and new lodges were being formed (Hackett 2014; Tschorn 2008). Indeed, I have been provided with statistics documenting a 17.9 percent increase in initiations in Scottish Rite Freemasonry in the United States since its low point in 2004 (Morris 2007b). *Initiations* grew three years in a row. Moreover, the median age of these initiates has dropped to forty-five years, with 25 percent now under thirty-five (Alban 2007). While not enough to offset *overall* declining membership figures—reflecting ongoing deaths among a relatively large cohort of older members (Hackett 2014)—larger classes of new initiates appeared to be relatively common in the last decade (Hackett 2014; Tschorn 2008; Morris 2007b; Alban 2007). Indeed in Canada I have also witnessed unusual numbers of relatively young initiates in parts of two jurisdictions, and I personally helped to form a new lodge in 2007. Curiosity is afoot. As one colleague with access to a provincial membership database put it, "Something is going on."

Some argue this reflects popular culture—movies and books that paint the fraternity positively or link it to mysterious alternate histories (Morris 2007b). Others credit the Internet (Tschorn 2008) and a recently "more open" public relations stance. It may also reflect less of a culture of contentment than in previous generations. With the "disappearance of the sacred" (Meštrović 1997, 101–22), the relative absence of emotionally meaningful rites in the Durkheimian sense, there may also be a search for authenticity, for "collective effervescence" in today's mass-mediated cultural terrain, where interpersonal hazing rituals and rites of passage have been making a comeback as ways to set groups apart and make members feel special (113). Indeed Hackett (2014) calls attention to the potential role of ritualistic movements like the Masonic Restoration Foundation in this respect. Whatever the basis, this presents an opportune time to take a closer look at Freemasonry.

SOCIOLOGICAL RESEARCH ON FREEMASONRY

Sociologists have been studying Freemasonry for over a century, beginning with Georg Simmel's classic theoretical work (1908) in which he suggests that the separation involved in the necessary inclusion/exclusion in "secret societies" translates into a form of validation whereby members come to see themselves as a sort of aristocracy (Simmel 1908; Hazelrigg 1969). More specifically, from a neo-functionalist perspective, it has been argued that Freemasonry serves various purposes including social recognition, intellectual information, spiritual liberation, social assistance, psychosocial development, and the provision of psychological, social, and cultural connectedness for members (Bolle de Bal 1989). Much is made of the rhetoric of "brotherhood" versus the reality of exclusion (Davis 2000; Schmidt 1987). Nevertheless, it is commonly argued that secrecy enables members a form of sociability, solace, and emotional connectedness centred around civility, enlightenment, and moral improvement (Morrison 2012; Hoffman 2001; Carnes 1989), in some eyes perhaps even constituting a "civil religion" in relation to political ideals (Fozdar 2011; Jolicoeur and Knowles 1978).

Since the elaborate symbolic rituals utilized by these groups lend themselves to varying interpretations (Poulet 2010; Carnes 1989; Dierickx 1989), various writers have attempted to elaborate or empirically contextualize them. In this respect, it is important to consider issues of the relation of "secret societies"—and their members—to the broader society. As Erickson (1981) points out, the relative risk involved in being a member of such groups in some societies is very important, and it affects both who is recruited and the social makeup of members. In many societies, for example, it is largely dominant groups that make up the membership, and, in such contexts, Freemasonry has been characterized as a historical aspect of British imperial hegemony (Fozdar 2011; Griggs 1994), a ritualistic way of transmitting and sustaining imperial ideology, identity, and even prevailing ideals of masculinity (Fozdar 2011; Greene 2002; Harland-Jacobs 2000), as well as a way of fostering patriarchal social relations (Morrison 2012; Clawson 1989; Carnes 1989; Papademas 1991; Schmidt 1987). In these respects, some have noted that Masonic fraternalism played a key role in relation to gender and class formations in nineteenth-century America (Clawson 1989; Carnes 1989), the membership of the British business elite (Jeremy 1984), the aristocracy of the nineteenth-century Hawaiian Kingdom (Karpiel 1998), political elites in Italy (Mahmud-Abdelwahib 2008) and in Gabon (Auge 2007), the liberal elite in nineteenth-century Colombia (Cano 2009), and the "educated classes" in eighteenth-century Russia (Smith 1996). It has even been suggested that Freemasonry, as such, has a select appeal to certain segments of the population such as academics, police, and the military (Doan 1993; Combes 1989). Nevertheless, focusing on such examples is only part of the picture.

For example, in some societies it has been very dangerous to belong to a Masonic order. Masons were ruthlessly persecuted by the Nazis and in several Fascist states, such as in Vichy France (Cools 2012; Hellman 2001), in Mussolini's Italy (Gramsci 2007), and in interwar Romania (R. Clark 2012). Indeed, in some countries even today conspiracy theories linger, while suspicion and surveillance lead Masons to see themselves as unfairly persecuted (Mahmud 2012; Mahmud-Abdelwahib 2008). All the same, Hazelrigg argues that "the greater the tendency toward political oppression and totalitarian regimentation in the larger society, the greater the tendency toward development of secret societies within the larger society" (1969, 327). This observation naturally underscores the radical role that Freemasons, among others, played in undermining oppressive social orders by fostering enlightenment ideals and assisting in the historical emergence of civil society, both in Europe (Jacob 1991, 1981) and in Latin America (Cano 2009; Quiroz 2007; Uribe-Uran 2000).

But beyond such broad political matters, some have pointed out the key integrative role at times played by Freemasonry in socially marginalized contexts. For example, there have been studies of the historic role played by African-American Freemasonry (a.k.a. "Prince Hall" Masonry) in African-American community, identity construction, and activism in the context of a racist culture (Dunbar 2012; Walker 2008; Wallace 1995); the role of Freemasonry in the transnational production of Black middle-class masculinity in Africa (Summers 2003); the impact of historic female lodges on the identities and actions of members (Burke 1989); the close historical ties between an Italian-language lodge and its ethnic community in San Francisco before

WWII (Canepa 1990); the comfort Freemasonry afforded to nineteenth-century Chinese immigrants to Western Canada (Marshall 2009); and the key role played by Masonry in a nineteenth-century American mining community (de Los Reyes and Lara 1999). As such, Freemasonry can play a role among marginalized groups much like that suggested for "deviant identity" (Rubington and Weinberg 1987), enabling them to manage their identities with the support and rationalizations of other subcultural members. Thus this is no mere ritualism (Merton 1968), engaging in rituals for their own sake, but a meaningful activity that is identified with by marginalized groups, warranting further investigation.

Ultimately, in the words of Clawson (1989, 244), Freemasonry

> has never, then, been a simple phenomenon; rather, it has been distinguished by the many uses to which it was put, the differing interpretations its adherents placed on their membership, and the various satisfactions that they derived from their participation. Consequently, there are many ways to understand it.

THEORETICAL MECHANISMS: EXPLAINING THE IMPACT OF RITUAL

Despite the apparent wealth of material above, something is missing. It is relatively clear from the literature that involvement in Freemasonry has some impact on its members, particularly their identities in a particular social context. However, the mechanisms are often insufficiently elaborated. In other words, *how* this occurs—particularly in the *present*—often remains unclear. Simmel's theoretical formulation is far too general, and the potentially tautological nature of the neo-functionalist accounts above is logically problematic. Of course, there have been piecemeal papers suggesting, for example, that researchers need to consider the dramaturgical elements in ritual, such as specialized clothing (McBride 2000), and the "alternate space" provided by the fraternity in which an ideal world can be imagined (Hetherington 1997), and to focus on the distinction between sign and signal in the symbolic language of secret societies (Petitat 1998). Yet, these are insufficient to comprehensively account for this effect.

One is also reminded of structured theoretical accounts that focus on the relationship between ritual, identity, and emotion and attempt to make connections between emotional outcomes and social structural relationships of power and status (Collins 1990). While suggestive, such work is problematic in that it appears to limit the possible outcomes of a ritual interaction to particular meanings such as one's relative power, status, or degree of inclusion/exclusion. Given the multi-faceted nature of symbols generally, and ritual contexts in particular, such ideas serve best as suggestive starting points, little more.

More recently a few sociologists have sought to employ more ethnographic approaches to flesh out these issues. Thus Kaplan (2014), in a study of contemporary Israeli Freemasonry, considers how the logic of friendship and intimacy is extended into a broader organizational and societal context such that, in members' ritual activities and everyday lives, distinctions between interpersonal, public, and collective intimacy are partially collapsed into a deeper solidarity. Mahmud-Abdelwahib (2008), in a study of Italian female and mixed-gender lodges, emphasizes pedagogy of knowledge transmission, secrecy, prestige, cultural capital, and perceptions of persecution as key components in the ritual and social processes by which "Mason" becomes a core identity category. Finally, Poulet (2010) looks at the relationship between prior dispositions, the process of apprenticeship, and a tacit pedagogy of analogical reasoning in the integration of a socially diverse, less traditionally elite population into the French Masonic order.

While certainly highlighting a number of important issues, these do not provide as comprehensive and consistent a picture of the relevant theoretic mechanisms involved as one would like. To date, the best attempts to elaborate these matters have contextually employed historical data, comparing ritual and outcome in relation to practitioners' comments. For example, Carnes (1989) argues for the significance of "liminal rituals" containing symbols standing in opposition to existing social hierarchies and rules (i.e., mediating between unstated psychological concerns and social structures in societies experiencing cultural change). He argues that "successful rituals intuitively summon up the symbols that addressed member anxieties without raising them explicitly" (1989, 36). In effect, "by encompassing many different meanings, symbols make it possible to express indirectly conflicts within society" (1989, 63). He particularly notes, for example, how Masonic rituals of birth, struggle, death, and resurrection implicitly articulated gender conflicts in Victorian society, particularly death to the "emotional culture" of women and the reality of distant fathers to rebirth as an adult man. In this, the lodge, whether articulated in terms of "brotherly love" or in feminine terms (e.g., "Mother lodge"), promoted a space and social form that "could literally give voice to sentiments that would otherwise remain unexpressed" (1989, 123). Ultimately, he argues that the symbolic rituals

> brought into the lodge many of the conflicts of the outside world, first transforming them into metaphors and symbols so that members could more effectively confront them.... The ritualists in a sense served as psychological lightening rods, intensifying and channeling widely shared anxieties and then discharging them harmlessly through the medium of liminal ritual. (1989, 144–46)

Clawson largely agrees, noting that "the power of a cultural product may depend precisely upon its ability to engage people at different levels of meaning, to resolve symbolically the contradictory experiences of everyday life" (1989, 12). However, she defines this in political terms, noting that the selectivity involved in ritual "draws people's attention to certain forms of relationship and activity—and at the same time, therefore, deflects their attention from other forms, since every form of seeing is also a way of not seeing. It thus defines as authoritative certain ways of seeing society" (1989, 13). She feels that the "truth" involved is confirmed through aesthetic appeal and the character of the social relations "cemented" by the ritual experience (1989,13). Substantively, she argues that, in nineteenth-century America, by dramatically fusing apparently irreconcilable relations of social life through the vivid portrayal of a central symbol (e.g., kinship), Masonic ritual

> articulated a vision of the social world that spoke to some of the culture's most troubling questions about relations between the sexes and the classes. Through its ritual, it constructed bonds of loyalty across class lines and thus demonstrated the possibility of a social order founded on harmonious class relations. And, as a cultural institution that maintained and idealized solidarity among White men, it offered gender and race as the most logical and legitimate categories for the organization of collective identity. (1989, 254–55)

Other writers have also made significant contributions to the study of ritual symbolism. For example, Van Gennep (1960) writes of how "rites of passage" revolving around symbolic separation, transition, and incorporation provide humans with sacred connections during turbulent times of passage in their lives. Hetherington contends that, historically, Masonic symbolism mingled, in a changing society, "the search for moral stability through tolerance and reason with that of arcane mystery and ritual in a heterotopic public/private space of reason and emotion" (1997, 104). As part of the "civilizing process," where formerly isolated strangers were emotively transformed into trustworthy brothers, Masons not only were provided with the symbolic means to increase their sense of security and stability in their own lives but allowed the interests of civil society to develop (Hetherington 1997, 198). Finally, Hoffman (2001) echoes many of these themes (e.g., the civilizing process, providing a sense of security) but particularly emphasizes how the metaphor of brotherhood enabled intimacy and the satisfaction of "emotional needs" that could not be met elsewhere in nineteenth-century society, premised on a metaphor of equality among the initiated and exclusivity, even elitism, in relation to outsiders. Indeed, some have seen the symbolic activities of Freemasonry as a "perpetual morality play," a sort of WASP "civil religion" (Wilson 1980, 134).

So what should be made of all this? Again, while certainly suggestive of interesting hypotheses and evocative themes, I would suggest that these works cannot be simply translated without modification into current research. My reasoning is as follows. First, I must stress that the vast majority of these writers were discussing the role of symbolism in relation to *historical* studies of Freemasonry (i.e., the nineteenth century). While their research is often well sourced and articulately presented, the fact is that they are speaking about the significance of Freemasonry either in a far different time, or, in other cases, in cultures quite different from that found in, for example, contemporary North America. Gender, race, and class relations have changed greatly, while cultural change and variation raise questions of easy comparability. Hence while things like the ability of symbolism to meaningfully reconcile difficult structural relations during times of social change remain interesting, new times, new cleavages, new changes, and new contexts necessitate a fresh investigation of the processes involved. Secondly, several of these writers have pointed to the inherent mutability of Masonic symbolism (Jacob 1991; Carnes 1989; Clawson 1989), and linguistic analysis of both contemporary (Dierickx 1989) and historical Masonic ritual (Jacob 1991) back this up. Indeed, as noted, Masonic ritual has been embraced by both conservatives and radicals alike at various times, each selecting what they like from the symbolism and backgrounding the rest. Thus, it will be interesting to examine what contemporary Masons stress about these matters today. Thirdly, from an interactionist perspective (Hewitt 2003), making broad structural generalizations about the *overall* meaning of Masonic symbolism, even in historical periods, is dismissive of emergent meaning. Rather than focus so extensively on structural conditions in the wider society and generalize about how they play themselves out in ritual, it would be better methodologically to start with the meanings that emerge in practice and then attempt to connect them with structural concerns as expressed by respondents themselves. Of course, not all of these will be the same, as members will be involved for different reasons, come from different backgrounds, and so on. Thus, I feel that it would be best to take Masonic symbolism as mutable, *inductively* examine how individual Masons both construct their actions and emergent meanings, and then consider how these might relate to broader societal concerns—not the other way around (Glaser and Strauss 1967).

Ultimately, most studies remain *historical* pieces. Indeed, Clawson implies that Freemasonry is no longer an important topic, and Carnes that it has not been sufficiently studied in the present. Thus Clawson goes so far as to claim that, today, Freemasons are commonly seen as "anachronisms," even "the stuff of comedy" (1989, 263), while Carnes's only suggestion in relation to contemporary Masonry comes almost as an afterthought. His words, in a concluding chapter, not only exemplify this problem, they suggest that further investigation is needed:

> Masons with whom I have spoken are moved by the [initiation] experience. Conceivably these rituals, though greatly abbreviated, may still address psychological needs much like those of a hundred years ago but now a consequence perhaps, of high rates of divorce and fatherless families or of a contemporary religious experience often devoid of faith. It is more likely, as the differences between the Victorian era and the present are greater than the similarities, that current members have rearranged the symbols and motifs of Freemasonry and conferred upon them new and different meanings. (1989, 156)

In the chapters that follow, I intend to begin correcting this theoretical and empirical imbalance. However, before getting into my research methodology and sample, I want to go further. Specifically, I want to introduce and highlight the relevance of the symbolic interactionist literature in social psychology (Hewitt 2003) for the study of contemporary Freemasonry. In the following sections I elaborate a series of significant theoretical bases for the ritualistic enactment of meaning and identity that are, at best, only implicit in the literature above. Given that Freemasonry emphasizes the learning by rote and ritualistic enactment of carefully scripted rites carrying varying, complex, and interconnected symbolic meanings, I explore the possible relevance of key interactionist themes, including: (1) the interplay between symbol, act, and emergent meaning; (2) dramaturgical analysis; (3) gender, emotion, and emotion management; (4) the phenomenological, lived experiences of participants; (5) ethnomethodological concepts such as indexicality, reflexivity, and the maintenance of social reality by accounting practices; and (6) the implications of all of the above for the self and identity of participants.[3]

The Interplay between Symbol, Act, and Emergent Meaning

American philosopher George Herbert Mead (1934) sought to address the problem of the "meaning of meaning." Influenced by the thought of C. S. Pierce, William James, and his colleague John Dewey, Mead argued that meaning is pragmatically created in the interplay of social activity and significant symbols: sometimes reinforcing, other times creatively innovating new understandings. In this process, meaning is not fixed, but emergent from symbols, actions, and what individuals bring to a given situation. Significantly, he argued that many encounters can go on unreflectively, but, should there be a disruption of one's previous activity, a search for, and construction of, meaning goes hand in hand with endeavours toward a practical solution.

A key element in all of this is Mead's theory of action. Briefly, an act begins with impulse, which arises when a pre-existing adjustment or line of activity is disturbed, followed by the stages of perception, manipulation, and consummation (Hewitt 2003, 44). In this process, in which individuals take social attitudes toward self and toward other and turn the imagined attitude of other toward self, there is much interpretation, sub-vocal talking to oneself, and engaging in "aligning actions." Ultimately, an interactional outcome emerges that constitutes *anew* the meaning of the act (Mead 1934, 81). In this, meaning is so closely intertwined with social action as to be inseparable. Moreover, given the fluid, interactional, and creative nature of this process, meanings may be enacted that either reinforce traditional interpretations or synthesize new and innovative takes on what is going on.

It is fairly obvious that this approach is relevant to understanding the emergent meanings derived by Freemasons today (e.g., candidates during initiation experience something radically unfamiliar, a disruption of their previous adjustment requiring reflective interpretation and the construction of meaning in relation to the symbolic ritual). The beauty is that this approach takes the meaning of symbols not as fixed but as emergent of the interplay of symbols and actions. It allows far more room for meanings to emerge than, say, the more fixed models revolving around power and status outcomes (Collins 1990). Moreover, while it may be socially contextualized, it is not so structurally limited as to suggest that gender, class, and other meanings emerge consistently across the board; rather, they variously emerge out of the background that each member brings to the interaction, as well as the performance of ritual actions. In perhaps a broader sense than it is usually intended, this exemplifies a common aphorism in Freemasonry that "you get out of it what you put into it."

Hence, I feel that the Meadian focus on emergent meaning—and the inductive, grounded theory approach that goes with it (Glaser and Strauss 1967)—has obvious advantages for approaching the symbolism and ritual actions of contemporary Freemasons. It simply makes sense to examine an institution that actively employs symbols to construct meaning through a perspective that focuses on how meaning is interpretively constructed through symbolic communication and action.

Dramaturgical Analysis

Perhaps no other issue was as obvious as the neat fit between dramaturgical analysis and the practices of Freemasons. Goffman (1959), and others who followed in his wake, drew interactionists' attention to the importance of impression management in negotiating social encounters in everyday life. Utilizing the metaphor of the theatre, he notes that it is important to consider the impressions that individuals may give, which they may manipulate in a situation in order to smoothly facilitate encounters—such impressions thereby working to the practical advantage of the actor(s) in question. As is

well known, he elaborates on this theatrical metaphor to discuss individuals'
use, in everyday interactional life, of "front" and "backstage" areas, "props,"
"parts," "teamwork," and so on. As such, Goffman's ideas provide a rich
mine of material for analysis of Freemasonry.

To begin with the most obvious parallels, not only do Freemasons conduct elaborate, staged rituals—from initiations on through a graded series of
"degrees"—they often do so with elaborate costumes, props, manipulation
of "front" and "backstage" areas, and careful attention to lighting, dramatic
effect, and so on (Clawson 2007). Generally, when a Masonic lodge is preparing to portray a "degree" (i.e., ritual drama) for candidates, officers meet
several times in the preceding weeks to practise their "parts." In between, in
most lodges, key participants work to memorize their "lines" in the ritual in
the same fashion as actors preparing for a play. Indeed, not to put too fine a
point on it, one Masonic body I have witnessed encompasses *all* the accoutrements of the conventional theatre—including a full stage area, elaborate
lighting, dressing rooms, costume and prop storage areas, even special areas
where makeup is applied! While not all Masonic lodges have such elaborate
facilities, it is fair to say that great care often goes into presenting rituals,
into portraying the "ideal heterotopic space" in which a perfect world may
be imagined (Hetherington 1997). Thus the theatrical metaphor popularized
by Goffman is powerfully relevant in this context.

However, aside from the obvious, there are other important considerations. First of all, Iain Mangham and Michael Overington have taken such
themes even further by elaborating the idea of *organizations as theatre*. They
take a dramaturgical approach to the study of organizations in contrast to traditional, systematically rational paradigms that implicitly deny human agency
and creativity, an approach enabling the study of organizational activity with
methods similar to those that "theatre-goers bring to their appreciation of
drama" (1987, 25–26). They assert that "theatre is *the* metaphor for studying
social *action*, how it can be staged and how it can be explained" (1987, 52).
By considering realities by staging experiences, theatre provides "an affective
interpretation of the how, what, when, where and why of any social action,"
the source of the "metaphorical resources that we want for the conceptualization of social conduct" (1987, 52).

It is my contention that just such an approach to the Masonic order, as
a *dramaturgically organized* institution—one that exists both inside *and* outside of the lodge room—is particularly apt. My only concern in this respect
is that, unlike the senior managers studied by Mangham and Overington
in occupational organizations, in which dramaturgical elements are not as
openly in the forefront and actors are somewhat freer to adjust their comments
and lines of action, Freemasonry is frequently a much more openly theatrical enterprise, where an explicitly scripted ritual drama is used to illustrate

important philosophic and moral lessons. Mangham and Overington's work, on the other hand, emphasizes social and organizational life in its mundane, taken-for-granted, repetitive, and, strategic aspects. In this respect, one may perhaps characterize the former somewhat more in terms of "life as theatre," and the latter "theatre as life." What I am saying is that the idea of utilizing theatrical metaphors as tools for understanding Freemasonry in organizational terms is quite apt, but there may be important differences in emphasis that need to be taken into account to reflect the often scripted, ritual-driven nature of its organization.

As noted, other writers have attempted to discern the broad symbolic meanings of Masonic dramas of spiritual birth, work, death, and "resurrection" typically as they were inculcated and broadly affected participants in earlier historical times (i.e., the eighteenth and nineteenth centuries). Be that as it may, I feel that a more micro-level dramaturgical analysis is needed to identify important differences, variations, and patterns of impact of such ritual devices for contemporary participants (both initiates and actors in the dramas themselves) to shed a fresh—and, I might add—a relatively inductive light on participants' experiences today. Yes, conscious reflection arises when dramatic rituals and their associated metaphors make problematic previous understandings of life (Mangham and Overington 1987, 48). Yet times have changed, and understandings may emerge today that are different from those of the past. Investigating these is one of the tasks of this book.

Gender, Emotion, and Emotion Management

Issues of gender, emotion, and emotion management are important for understanding Freemasonry, and they are often so closely interrelated as to be virtually inseparable. Nevertheless, for analytic purposes at least, it will be instructive to review and comment upon some of the key themes that may be fruitful for the study of the Craft today.

The first thing to be aware of is that Freemasonry, with certain limited exceptions such as the Order of the Eastern Star, several European Grand Lodges (e.g., La Grande Loge Féminine de France), "lodges of adoption," specific historic female initiates, and the emergence of co-Masonry, remains primarily a men's organization (Mahmud 2012; Ormières 2011; Mahmud-Abdelwahib 2008; Allen 2003; Coil 1996; Rich 1997; Yronwode 2002; Burke 1989). Women have been traditionally excluded from mainstream Freemasonry on the basis of the "historical landmark" that the members of the stonemasons' guilds upon which "the Craft" is based were all men. Whether true or not, admitting women has not been on the formal agenda in the "regular" Freemasonry of the Anglo-Saxon world—including Canada. This effectively means that Freemasonry provides one of the ultimate opportunities for male bonding in society (Morrison 2012; Hoffman 2001; Carnes 1989;

Clawson 1989).[4] As it remains by far the predominant type of Freemasonry (particularly in the jurisdictions under study), except where otherwise noted it is the male order that is addressed in this book.

Several writers have commented on this traditional exclusion, from feminists who rail at sexism (Mahmud 2012; Schmidt 1987), even in Masons' philanthropic activities (Papademas 1991), to writers that attempt to carefully analyze the gender dynamics that explain men's involvement in the past (Clawson 2007; Hoffman 2001; Carnes 1989). It is important to consider what has been written—even if much of it is pitched largely in relation to history—to see how this may help shed light on the key gender issues surrounding Freemasonry today.

There have been three extended historical treatments of gender in relation to male Freemasonry, all of which agree on a number of particulars. Mark Carnes (1989) argues that Freemasonry in Victorian America served as a source of stability and support amid the chaos of life. At the time, young men faced a difficult passage to manhood. Gender distinctions were very sharply drawn, and fathers tended to be absent, thereby depriving young men of "psychological guides to their core masculinity" (Carnes 1989, 114). Young men often experienced a prolonged period of dependence before they could be in a sufficient position to marry, and, through all of this, were generally taught the emotional sensibilities, moral values, and increasingly evangelical form of religiosity associated with adult women. As such, young men were often anxious about how they would fit into the world of adult men. Masonic ritual squarely addressed these concerns:

> Ritual developed each of the following themes: (1) an initiate at the outset of his task was portrayed as immature or unmasculine; (2) he overcame obstacles as he embarked on a difficult journey through the stages of childhood and adolescence; (3) this journey or ordeal reached a climax when he was killed (or nearly killed) by angry father figures; (4) he was reborn as a man into a new family of approving brethren and patriarchs. In this way the emotional orientations instilled by maternal nurture would give way to lessons of ancient patriarchs.... In contrast to a "feminized Protestantism," the rituals emphasized man's inherent deficiencies, offered the transformatory magic of a sudden and emotional conversion, and invoked an impersonal and foreboding deity. (Carnes 1989, 125–26)

Carnes states these rituals implied that "though women gave birth to man's body, initiation gave birth to his soul, surrounding him with 'brothers' who would lavish on him the utmost affection and kindness" (1989, 119–20). Much of this process also involved the idea that one had to die to feminine identifications to be reborn as a man, thereby being able to come to terms with the unpleasant realities of life. Most significantly, he adds that

having learned to control their emotions and to affect a "manly" deportment, Victorian fathers may have been incapable of articulating affection
to their own sons. The ritual could literally give voice to sentiments that
would otherwise remain unexpressed. Its dramaturgical devices enabled
elderly patriarchs to adopt and to love as their own the younger brethren
of the order, who were in turn assured of paternal approval and affection.
(1989, 123)

Similarly, Mary Ann Clawson has argued that Freemasonry articulated an
egalitarian vision of *brotherhood* in an era of social change, not only paying
homage to traditional male working ideals of the artisan in a capitalist society
where such socio-economic forms were on the decline, but implicitly articulating a moral vision of social life in opposition to women's increasingly vocal
articulation of emotional and moral positions (e.g., the temperance movement,
emotional forms of Protestantism).

Fraternal mutuality was inspired by a vision of masculine camaraderie
derived from the workshop and the tavern. In late nineteenth-century
America this collective identity was subject to assault from two directions. Industrial development and the growing assertion of a feminine
vision of social and affective life threatened to undermine major institutions of male solidarity, thus making fraternal institutions doubly attractive. (Clawson 1989, 14)

But perhaps the most explicit articulation of such themes comes from the
work of Stefan-Ludwig Hoffman, who writes of the experiences of German
Freemasons in the nineteenth century. He asserts that church, marriage, and
work could not fill the "emptiness of the soul" that many middle class men
experienced at the time:

Secrecy and the emotional cult of brotherhood promised solace from
the conflicts of professional everyday life. At the same time, they also
created—to formulate this pointedly—their own "male world of love and
ritual" beyond marriage. This flight from domesticity is one of the reasons for the increasing popularity of all-male associations and secret societies which developed in the middle of the nineteenth century.... While,
both in public and private spheres, men increasingly sought to accord
with the ideal of a man ruled by reason, emotional relations between men
attained increasing significance in locations which were removed from
the family and from the public. Within these spaces, emotional relations
between men were by no means taboo. (2001, 225)

Hoffman adds that the secluded nature of these meetings offered participants
a drama of self-exploration in which fears, hopes, and desires for which there
appeared to be no legitimate place outside of the lodge could be articulated

dramatically. Secrecy and formal ritual made it possible for men to open themselves to this emotional world and at the same time protect it from the "profane" world outside (1989, 232). Indeed, he even likens it to modern "group therapy" for "stressed executives" (1989, 230).

So what can be taken from these historical accounts for the contemporary study of Freemasonry? There are a number of possibilities. While gender lines are certainly not as sharply drawn today as in Victorian times, it may be that such institutions operate in a similar fashion, especially among traditional men, as a refuge from the stresses and strains of postmodern life. Moreover, given that we now live in a period of far greater social change (in Carnes's words "of high rates of divorce, fatherless families and religious institutions devoid of meaning" (1989, 156)), along with rampant consumerism, social isolation, and mass-mediated disenchantment, perhaps the lodge could be seen by many more as a source of stability in a sea of change. In Durkheimian terms, we have moved from an era of essentialist ideas of gender relations, in which social regulation was so high as to be almost fatalistic, to one where they are undergoing an anomic process of change (accelerating rapidly since the 1960s). The idea that the lodge can, for contemporary reasons, serve as a refuge seems worthy of investigation, but it will be important to keep these differences in mind as specific themes emerge.

But there is a related direction that could be investigated as well. The sociology of emotion has become prominent in the past several decades, and sociological work in this vein has greatly expanded our understanding of emotion in social life (Kemper 1990). I have already mentioned, for example, Collins's (1990) neo-Durkheimian discussion of the relation between ritual, "emotional energy," and social solidarity, particularly as it relates to establishing and reinforcing relationships of power, status, and inclusion/exclusion. However, despite its obvious utility in considering *some* of the emotional *outcomes* of ritual, we must not be blinded to other possibilities. For example, it would also be helpful to consider the work of authors like Arlie Hochschild (1990), Peggy Thoits (1990), and Candace Clark (1990), who have each produced ideas relevant to the study of Freemasonry.

Each of these writers speaks of emotion not only in terms of what *happens* to us, but as something we *do* as well. Hochschild notes, for example, how our experience of emotion, as well as our emotional activities, are influenced by "feeling rules" and "expression rules" in particular contexts, and that we engage in various strategies such as "surface acting" and "deep acting" to bring either our expression or our actual feelings in line with such situational emotional norms (1990, 122–24). Hochschild has elaborated her ideas in relation to studies of service workers such as flight attendants and bill collectors, as well as in relation to the "gender ideologies" that married couples adhere to and attempt to emotionally manage when issues arise over tasks, responsibilities, and involvement. Thoits (1990) elaborates on Hochschild's ideas, indicating that particular emotions may be, and often are, out of line with such emotional norms, and therefore "deviant." Finally, Candace Clark (1990) considers emotions almost as tactical weapons that individuals may use, through various "micropolitical strategies," to enhance their position or "place" in a particular interaction.

Such ideas suggest a number of potentially fruitful avenues for the study of contemporary Freemasonry. Thus, one could examine the gendered feeling rules and expression rules implicit in the ritual and situated practices of Freemasonry where brethren ritualistically learn to "subdue their passions." One thing I have often noticed, for example, is the profound sense not only that one should adhere to the appropriate etiquette, titles, and forms of address in lodge, but almost that there is an expressive norm requiring that members speak to one another in a *positive* way (e.g., welcoming visitors; being positive, welcoming, and supportive of each other; politely encouraging visiting dignitaries to speak; thanking speakers for their helpful comments, etc.). This may relate to the idea of the lodge as a refuge from the struggles and concerns of outside life, as well as representing a self-interested form of public relations. Yet not everyone is necessarily feeling that positive (e.g., at a late meeting, when everyone is tired and wants to get downstairs for a snack and a drink, hearing the fifth or sixth dignitary ramble on his thanks for a wonderful meeting takes some effort at "emotion management" among those present).

The above example also serves to highlight what happens when negative or discordant emotions are expressed. In my experience, the expression of negative feelings in open lodge (as opposed to in committees, for example) is frowned upon, and such incidents stand out. In fact, I would go so far as to say that they may be a particular form of "emotional deviance" in relation to the feeling and expression rules implicit in lodge ritual and practice (Thoits 1990).

Of course, that is not to say that there are no politics at work in Freemasonry. Like other institutions such as workplaces, schools, churches, and sociology departments, Freemasonry has not only official, formal hierarchies but a lively tradition of office politics behind the scenes (e.g., in committees). As such, Candace Clark's (1990) ideas on the use of emotions as tools to enhance place may be a useful concept to apply to the various tactics used by various parties to push their positions, have access to resources, and the like.

Finally, I must again bring all of this back to the issue of gender. First, because we are dealing with men, there is likely to be a strong emphasis on individual participants "managing their feelings"—just as, for example, we see in the bereavement literature (Cook 1988). Indeed, the heavy emphasis on ritual—and individual, thoughtful reflection on its meaning—may represent male ways of eliciting, or "doing," some emotions (Hochschild 1983) while simultaneously "managing" others in their own right (Hochschild 1990). Practising Masonry may itself be a method.

Secondly, it is clear from the historical literature that women in the nineteenth century were not always happy about extensive male involvement in Freemasonry (Clawson 1989). I expect that it may be quite revealing to look at the contemporary issues Freemasons face, navigate, and try to manage in relation to their involvement in Masonic activities today.

Thus, I feel that Freemasonry is not only a potentially fruitful site for the examination of contemporary gender issues and their interplay with the wider society but a wonderful site for reviewing specifically male emotional experiences and practices.

The Phenomenological, Lived Experiences of Participants

Proceeding from the above discussion are two broader philosophical issues related to the lived experiences of Freemasons. First, I consider the relevance of phenomenology, outlining how social processes enabling various constructions of reality may be relevant to Masonic ritual. Next, I discuss the bodily and emotional aspects as they may relate to the realities constructed.

Phenomenology focuses on multiple realities and the construction of knowledge (Schutz 1962; Berger and Luckmann 1966). Schutz's general position, derived from Husserl, is that the world is an inherently complex place, with numerous ways that even the simplest situations can be interpreted. As such, individuals must develop and employ many working assumptions (i.e., typical recipes for understanding) to interact effectively. Without the interpretive resources made available through the processes of typification and objectification—which necessarily highlight some features of encounters and background others—we will be frustrated in our efforts and accomplish little. Berger and Luckmann broaden this approach by outlining how these processes serve to underpin shared conceptions of knowledge. They argue that reality itself is socially constructed, and they attempt to understand both its subjective and objective aspects in terms of the central mechanism of externalization, objectification, and internalization of symbolic typifications in human group life (1966, 129). Language is central in these social interactional processes for constituting and circumscribing meaningful realities (1966, 39–40).

I would suggest that several elements here are exceptionally relevant to Freemasonry. First of all, Masonic ritual is very complex, and its symbolism carries multiple levels of meaning for the most basic of terms (e.g., even the simple term "lodge" may refer to the organization, the meeting place, the individual Mason, the universe, and the afterlife, among other things, depending on its use). Moreover, the "secrecy" surrounding Freemasonry means that new initiates are quite unable to understand what is going on around them, and the language "reveals as well as conceals" (e.g., I once recall speaking with another Mason briefly while a non-Masonic individual looked on; this person commented afterwards that he could not really make sense of our conversation). Hence, without careful observation and internalization of the interpretive resources of other participants, as well as testing their own externalizations in practice, new initiates will not have access to the typifications, working assumptions, or recipes enabling them to effectively understand and participate in "the Craft."

Secondly, initiates must also learn the specialized language, and observe its meaning in relation to actions and objects, in order to "appresent" or bring back the "realities" they have learned in lodge when "talking to themselves" in solitary thought. This is particularly relevant, not only because we are dealing with men (who may not be quite so open when they are uncertain about something) but also because Masonic initiates are required to *memorize*, in succession, several portions of the ritual, and be *tested* on them in open lodge before they can be accepted as full members of the Craft. This means that initiates who want to proceed inevitably feel a certain amount of social pressure (e.g., from helpful brethren who invariably offer to assist them) as well as put pressure on themselves so as not to later look foolish before the group. This continues as Masons progress through their career, often memorizing parts in various ritual dramas they will portray. Here, the *mnemonic* aspect of what I call the "deep internalization" of these realities is accomplished—sometimes alone, sometimes with others—which can encourage reflection upon the symbolic meanings—and realities—of the ritual. This may intensify the construction of a shared intersubjective reality for the Masonic community, a set of typifications that smooth social interchange, stimulate thought and reflection, and carry social meanings that may be applied to other areas of one's life.

Ultimately, it will be important to consider these reality construction processes to provide a sufficient account of Freemasonry in the contemporary world. Nevertheless, the social background of initiates, when combined with ritual processes and reflective activity, may well result in very different constructions of reality than in the past (i.e., new "legitimations"), perhaps even varying between generations. It is these lived realities, against the backdrop of the postmodern world, that will be most interesting to consider today.

But there remains another aspect of phenomenological sociology that may be usefully employed in the study of Freemasonry. Supplementing the predominantly normative approaches above, Norman Denzin (1982, 1984, 1985, 1990) articulates a parallel phenomenological approach to emotion that is useful in two respects. First, he elaborates an *interpretive* model of emotion that outlines the ongoing social processes involved in both interpersonal and intrapersonal interaction. Secondly, he attempts to link this model to various aspects of the *body* experienced by the emoting individual that serve to ratify socially constructed realities. Both are significant to the study of Freemasonry.

First, Denzin (1982, 1984) argues that emotional social encounters between individuals in the "interactional stream" (e.g., conversations, visible gestures, actions) are internalized and dealt with subjectively by individuals through reflection in the "phenomenological stream" (i.e., sub-vocal thought). Emotion arises out of inhibited, interpreted social acts in which the subject inserts self-conversations between the perception of experience and the organization of action. In these conversations, feelings directed to the self mediate action and interpretation. The individual takes his or her attitude toward self and toward other, and the imagined attitude of the other toward self, into the process of responding emotionally (1984, 54–57). The other responds in turn. At times, the balance of emotional interaction is more sub-vocal, at other times, more interpersonal. Naturally, in the confusion and unfamiliar process of being initiated as a Freemason, not only will there be cognitive attempts at understanding, but the emotional content, operating in the above fashion, is highly relevant to the "reality" of interpretations.

Secondly, and related to his phenomenological commitment to studying emotion *from within* as lived experience, Denzin draws attention to the role of the body (1985, 224). He feels that the body is the heart of embodied experience, providing the explicit "point of reference" for all meaningful, lived emotional experience. According to Denzin, it has a fourfold structure:

> It is a *physical body* for the person; a *lived presence* for the subject in his *inner field of experience*; an *enacted ensemble of embodied action for others*; and an ensemble of moving action *for the subject. Each of these four forms of emotion's lived body provides a distinctly different mode of lived emotion*: (1) sensible feelings of sensations; (2) feelings of the lived body; (3) intentional value feelings; and (4) moral feelings of self. (1990, 88) [emphasis added]

Denzin devotes much work elaborating these four modes of lived emotion, which are rooted in the phenomenological *expansion of the concept "self,"* to include different dimensions of the "lived body." Each serves to underpin the reality of constructed interpretations.

First, according to Denzin, *sensible feelings* refer to sensations located in the body, as physical pain is, for example, but they do not originate in the self-conversations of the subject. They are part of the lived body that others cannot share or know how they are felt by the person. They are not the emotion, but they *ratify* for the subject the emotionality that is felt (1985, 228–29). For the purposes of the topic at hand, I should note that certain aspects of Masonic ritual affect parts of the body *directly*, sometimes vividly, unexpectedly, and dramatically and, as such sensible feelings may play a powerful role in ratifying the emotion—and the reality—felt by initiates.

Next, Denzin considers *feelings of the lived body*. These, while accompanied by sensible feelings, are not found in a particular part or section of the subject's body but throughout its total extension as a "unitary field of experience" (e.g., profound sorrow, sadness, happiness, or anger). Significantly, because these express an orientation to the interactional world of experience, they are accessible to others and they can furnish the foundations for socially shared feelings. Once expressed, others are able to vicariously share in the subject's feelings (1985, 230). For present purposes, it has been my experience—and that of some others I have known—that profound bodily emotions may be experienced during initiation. Moreover, just as Denzin articulates, others observing may vicariously share in the experience—waiting with great anticipation for dramatic moments, actions, and emotions portrayed in a degree, for example, and physically experiencing moments of sadness or laughter, as the case may be.

Third, Denzin discusses *intentional value feelings*. These, quite simply, are "feelings about feelings," where "the subject seeks to isolate the core meanings an instance of emotionality has for him" (1985, 230). In doing so, he interprets the feelings he has in relation to values rooted in his culture or group that transcend the specific instance in question (1985, 230). For example, among Freemasons, initiates and brethren not only have feelings, they wonder if they *should* feel that way (e.g., amused or bored when presented with a particular ritual incident). Some who are between degrees may wonder why they are still nervous about their next degree or whether their expectations are unrealistic. Some facing the impending examination in open lodge on their memory work may become nervous and then express emotions about their nerves, questioning whether they will "go blank" or be able to "use that energy" to perform well. Brethren portraying degrees might wonder if they've done a good job, if they've presented the emotions appropriately, or whether degrees should be performed with more fervour. Some brethren wonder whether the experience is emotionally meaningful, some agreeing, others moving on because "they don't get what they expected." Thus, intentional value feelings are an important consideration.

Finally, Denzin discusses *feelings of the self and the moral person*. These involve "inner moral feelings the person directs toward herself as a moral object in her own world and in the world of others. Feelings of self are central, for the subject reveals herself to herself through the feeling of these feelings (1985, 232). Significantly, in these overall moral assessments Denzin distinguishes two levels of the self—the surface and the deep:

> The surface, public self is given to others through the subject's communicative acts, and managed through emotion management rules. The deep, inner, moral self is revealed through self and moral feelings which involve a feeling for the self as a distinct moral object and subject in the world.

The self of the moral person is the self that has dignity, self-respect, self-responsibility, and an inner sense of moral worth. Moral self-consciousness or value awareness is at the core of the person at this deep level. The moral feelings of the morally self-reflective subject involve a respect for the moral codes of the everyday lifeworld. By subjecting himself to this moral code the subject gains self-dignity and self-respect. This internalized self-respect, which comes from the inner and outer moral codes of the world of daily interactional life, constitutes the inner meanings of the moral person. (1985, 232–33)

I feel that this latter aspect of Denzin's formulation is of key significance. Because Freemasonry uses symbol and ritual essentially to articulate a system of morality, it inculcates values and provides members with symbolic moral "tools" with which to engage life. For example, one is taught that one is akin to a rough stone and must use the various symbolic "working tools" of the Craft, such as the gavel, gauge, plumb, level, and square to break off the rough edges to make a perfect stone and fit harmoniously—that is, morally—into the "spiritual temple" of society. Such imagery can have a profound impact on initiates' and participants' feelings of self and the moral person. Moreover, given the mnemonic practices mentioned earlier—practices that persist throughout one's Masonic career as one takes various offices and memorizes various aspects of ritual—the moral lessons for self gradually *sedimentize*, as it were, from the surface to the deep level of one's emotional self. One might find members, for example, drawing upon Masonic symbolism when discussing moral incidents or dilemmas (e.g., saying someone is not acting "on the level," or engaging in "square dealing"). As such, consideration of Denzin's formulation will be of great help when examining the experiences of contemporary Freemasons.

In sum, I feel that these phenomenological approaches, often associated with interactionism, may be usefully employed when studying members' experiences in contemporary Freemasonry. They will be useful in studying not only the typifications that adherents utilize to facilitate their activities but also the constructions of reality that emerge. Moreover, Denzin's phenomenological approach to emotion, particularly his integration of the "lived body" to all of this, suggests further fruitful avenues of investigation when studying initiation and the identities that may emerge from ritual processes.

Ethnomethodology: Accounting Practices, Indexicality, and Reflexivity

Ethnomethodology takes phenomenology's focus on multiple realities and attention to necessary background assumptions and radically problematizes them. Indeed, it asserts that these seen-but-unnoticed background expectancies are nothing short of ongoing *accomplishments*, and it provides a more methodological focus for how individuals make sense of social activities.

As propounded by its founder, Harold Garfinkel, a number of concepts have emerged as core elements in this approach: (1) breaching and accounting practices, (2) indexicality, (3) reflexivity, and (4) the sanctioned property of everyday discourse. Each will be discussed in turn, with particular emphasis on their relevance to Freemasonry.

"Breaching," as explicated in Garfinkel's research, involves the radical disruption of a person's prior assumptions about the world, further compounded by attempts to prevent the subject from being given any background information, clues, or explanation to the meaning of the behaviour. This typically serves as the precursor to "accounting," that same person's attempts to "make sense of it all" and reconstitute a meaningful reality for the present encounter (Garfinkel 1967, 9).

Given Garfinkel's stress on situations where things radically depart from the ordinary or expected, clearly research might consider the "breach" of everyday, taken-for-granted reality that occurs when candidates go through their Masonic degrees. Being stripped of conventional points of reference—and one's clothing—and being given little guidance as to what to expect closely resemble the methodological criteria and practices set forth by Garfinkel. As they face the fear of the unknown and have various mysterious things done to them for no apparent reason, initiates may quickly search for "hidden meanings," later coming up with various (and invariably different) accounts of the meaning of the experience. The succession of degrees continues this process, and, just as one feels one understands, another breach of one's orienting understanding of Freemasonry occurs, calling for a fresh account. Beyond the degrees, breaching may occur each time a Mason is confronted with ritual imagery or practices that challenge, provoke, or stimulate an attempt to discern and articulate their meaning.

Further, given Freemasonry's traditional emphasis on ritual, etiquette, doing things properly, and propriety, breaching and accounting may be relevant when something is done wrong, mistakes are made, brethren's positions are challenged, or there are claims of impropriety. The party or parties involved may have to construct acceptable accounts or understandings to explain or counter the potential insinuations of deviance involved. Any study of contemporary Freemasons should be attentive to the implicit breaches and subsequent accounting involved.

But accounting does not take place in a vacuum. Individuals constructing accounts draw upon various interpretive resources in order to construct their accounts and maintain reality in various encounters. This is where the concept of indexicality comes in (Garfinkel 1967, 38). This involves assumptions, particularly the many items *not* openly stated in those matters that *are* explicitly verbalized. In this respect, much of the accounting that people make to each other about their behaviour is done in an abbreviated, shorthand form, because commonplace conversation assumes a "common understanding" of many things that are "left out." Terms that require mutual understanding that are not explicated verbally Garfinkel calls "indexical expressions" (1967, 38). Garfinkel refers to this practice of "filling in" the meanings to talk as the *"et cetera" principle*; it is a "shorthand" way of talking (Wallace and Wolf 1980, 273).

Needless to say, there is a lot of this going on in Freemasonry. Not only are many of the symbols and ritual practices intertwined in myriad, complex ways, but the argot used within the Craft frequently employs indexical expressions—so much so that, at times, outsiders may be unable to make much sense of conversations unless they are in possession of the context-bound, indexical aspects explicating these terms. Indeed, simply perusing the extensive commentaries on basic terms in Mackey's *Encyclopedia of Freemasonry* (1925), or the symbolic exposition of the rituals in Wilmshurst's *The Meaning of Masonry* (1922), corroborates that indexicality has long been a part of the Craft—and that Freemasonry as an ongoing accomplishment could not happen were it not for this indexical element of accounting. Nevertheless, a lot has changed in society since the above Masonic "classics" were written, and, even then, they probably reflected certain privileged interpretations of the terminology not necessarily shared by the rank and file. Thus, where possible, it will be interesting to consider the indexical resources—both internal to the Craft and externally from the brethren's social context—that contemporary members of the Craft draw upon when giving meaning to their verbalizations and actions.

But we must go beyond merely looking for the indexical resources that contemporary Masons use to provide accounts to emphasize the *constitutive* aspect of all this. That is where reflexivity comes in (Garfinkel 1967, 9). According to Garfinkel, reflexivity involves the synthesis of a practical meaning for the current activity. It is not merely the resources drawn upon, but the actual meanings enacted in accounts that are relevant to the study of contemporary Freemasonry. Since indexicality and reflexivity are two sides of the same coin in context-bound interpretive work (i.e., what is reflexively constructed at one moment becomes part of one's indexical resources the next), it is important to attend to the evolutionary interaction of these two elements as contemporary Freemasons attempt to struggle with—and create—meaning.

Finally, Freemasonry's reputation for "secrecy" suggests it will be interesting to consider the "sanctioned properties of common discourse" (Garfinkel 1967, 41). This refers to people's expectation that there will be no interference with the conduct of everyday affairs in the form of questions about what is "really said." It is expected and required that people will understand conventional talk and common practices so that affairs can be conducted without undue interference. Otherwise, one's presence may come into question. In

Freemasonry, given the strong moral overtones and successively tighter "inner circles" where "secrets" are only available to those inside, questions about "what is really being said," say, when ritual is being enacted, or behaviour in lodge that cannot be made sense of through brethren's indexical resources, may well result in testing, demands to account for one's actions, and so on. Such situations suggest attention be paid to the sanctioned nature of Masonic discourse.

Ultimately, then, ethnomethodology is highly relevant to the study of Freemasonry. Not only does it suggest a useful, micro-level, methodological orientation, many of its concepts suggest important areas to investigate further.

Implications for the Self and Identity of Freemasons

Uniting the diverse theoretical concepts reviewed thus far is the question of the impact of ritual practices, operating though the mechanisms above, on the selves and identities of contemporary Freemasons. There is little doubt, given the above, that there has historically been some effect on self and identity resulting from participation in Freemasonry. However, its nature likely varies by extent of involvement, by social background, and over time. In this section, I will lay out my preliminary thoughts on this matter, first reviewing the historical literature, then stating some tentative thoughts for the research that follows.

Many writers have commented on the historic impact of Masonic ritual on self and identity, and three prominent themes have emerged. First, some have portrayed involvement in Freemasonry, at least in part, as an opportunity for participants to engage in self-exploration and work toward moral self-improvement and general consciousness-raising (Hoffman 2001; Burke 1989; Carnes 1989; Jacob 1991). Such writers speak in terms of "civilizing the self" (Hoffman 2001) or simply "lived enlightenment" (Jacob 1991). While there is certainly recognition of social and historical context among these writers, this aspect places more emphasis on what the candidate *does* with the ritual experience, and their participation in the Craft, in social and moral life. The idea is that by giving the individual the tools to work on himself, he may become, in Masonic parlance, a "better man." Given that both interactionism and Freemasonry place a great deal of emphasis on individual interpretation and action, it will be interesting to examine how Masons both interpret and variously enact such themes in today's changing society.

The second theme stresses how ritual serves symbolically to both conceal and reveal broader structural tensions in society, along with its ability to provide solace and social support during stressful periods of social change (Summers 2003; Hoffman 2001; Hetherington 1997; Carnes 1989; Clawson 1989). The former aspect relates to "liminal rituals" that cathartically address members' anxieties (e.g., about gender and class) through symbolism without raising them explicitly. The latter refers not only to the camaraderie experienced in lodge meetings, rituals, and fellowship, but how this is fostered further by the process of inclusion/exclusion inherent in the metaphor of "brotherhood" (Summers 2003; Clawson 1989). Thus some critics of Freemasonry, while admitting that it built solidarity across traditional social boundaries by being highly tolerant of religious and class differences when these were the primary bases of social conflict, note that it historically did so, in practice, by excluding racial minorities from membership[5] and highlighting essentialist ideas about gender (Summers 2003; Clawson 1989).

I would suggest that while these were certainly major issues historically, they could remain, in a different sense, topics for investigation today. Given the vast social changes that have taken place since the 1960s—and ongoing social agitation for change—attending to such issues among contemporary Masons may reveal interesting avenues for investigation. For example, one might investigate *if* and *how* liminal rituals serve to symbolically defuse social conflicts in contemporary society (e.g., new configurations of gender, race, and class, along with newer divisions based upon the "virtual realities" inculcated by consumerism, the media, technology, etc.). It may be that some conflicts may be more readily defused by these rituals than others, and more so for Masons with certain backgrounds. There also might be potential for the Masonic concept of the "profane" (i.e., uninitiated outsiders) to take on a greater role in these respects, such that building solidarity through rituals of inclusion/exclusion may not only have new social referents, but working the old rituals may produce new identities as a result. The historic "gerrymandering," as it were, of boundaries of inclusion/exclusion through social change may be significant. This is true both politically and in relation to the emergent constructions of self and identity involved along the way.

The third, and final, approach to ritual and identity relates to Masonry as practised among marginalized, even stigmatized groups (Dunbar 2012; Marshall 2009; Walker 2008; Summers 2003; de Los Reyes and Lara 1999; Wallace 1995; Canepa 1990; Burke 1989). Freemasonry can play a role among marginalized subcultures much like that suggested for "deviant identity" (Rubington and Weinberg 1987), enabling them to manage their identities with the support and rationalizations of other members. Indeed, given that Freemasonry has shifted from being a broadly recognized, often elite organization of the past to the relatively *marginalized* group it is today, it may well be that interactionist ideas relating to deviant identity become *more* rather than less relevant to empirical investigation.

For example, it may be interesting to apply Lemert's (1951) concept of secondary deviance to Freemasons who continue to participate in the Craft despite opposition from others. It may be useful to look at the "vocabularies of motive," the "accounts," "disclaimers," "techniques of neutralization," self-deceit, and emotional countermoralism utilized by Freemasons when confronted by opponents (Mills 1940; Scott and Lyman 1968; Hewitt and Stokes 1975; Sykes and Matza 1957; Douglas 1977). It may be interesting to examine Freemasonry to see if anything useful may be revealed by applying the literature on deviant subcultures (Best and Luckenbill 1982; Rubington and Weinberg 1987). Time and empirical study will bear this out, but these certainly appear to be fruitful avenues for investigation.

Finally, in all of this, it will be important, again, to not attempt to apply past theoretical ideas in a "cookie-cutter" approach to the study of contemporary Freemasonry. Not only is Freemasonry a complex phenomenon, but ideas generated in the past may not be entirely applicable in the present. Moreover, the interactionist approach emphasizes creativity in innovation as well as in interaction. In changing times, this makes it imperative that researchers not only keep one eye on the past literature, but keep an eye out for new insights and new data-driven conceptualizations revealed through inductive study when investigating Freemasonry in the twenty-first century.

METHOD AND APPROACH

To empirically investigate these multi-faceted theoretical issues in the present day, I draw upon two primary sources of data: (1) interviews with contemporary Freemasons in two Canadian provinces; and (2) video footage shot for a feature film on contemporary Freemasonry.[6] I will briefly outline each before getting into the findings.

To first help shed light on the experiences of contemporary Freemasons, early in 2005 I negotiated unrestricted access to extensive video footage shot, with written consent, for the documentary film *Inside Freemasonry* (Arcadia Entertainment 2004), which primarily focuses on a group of men taking their degrees. These data consist of fifty-eight videotapes shot during the fall of 2003. They combine on-site observations, detailed interviews, and discussions with twenty-seven individuals (twenty-one Freemasons, three journalists, two spouses, and one academic). There are also forty-seven brief, random interviews with members of the public on their perceptions of Freemasonry. Furthermore, as an active participant in this film, I engaged in a lengthy roundtable discussion with three Freemasons and two journalists, in addition to providing one of the detailed interviews.

Next, between the fall of 2006 and December 2007, I followed up with comprehensive interviews of 121 Freemasons in two Canadian provinces. These include in-depth discussions probing the experiences and perspectives of seventy-two Masons in Nova Scotia and forty-nine in Newfoundland and Labrador.

I transcribed all of these data and analyzed them utilizing NVivo qualitative analysis software. Methodologically, I followed Glaser and Strauss's (1967) primarily inductive, "grounded theory" approach, where the relevance of theoretical concepts largely emerges out of the observations while the specifics of their operation in a given social context are data driven. This enabled me to be more open to matters to which I might not otherwise have paid attention, making for a more comprehensive analysis. Using a procedure of open coding, a systematic filing system was developed. Coding and analysis initially proceeded according to common topics (e.g., teasing before degrees). As the process of "minutely analyzing" the data progressed, these materials were recoded into theoretical categories emerging from the data as well (e.g., "manufactured curiosity" rooted in a dynamic interplay between dramaturgically induced anxiety and questioning). Throughout, emerging thematic categories and data were continually cross-checked and subjected to negative-case testing. If inconsistencies were located, emergent ideas were either discarded or reformulated until practical certainty was achieved.

CHARACTERISTICS OF THE RESEARCH SAMPLE

Very broadly, these data represent a relatively homogeneous group in terms of social background. They were largely White, middle-class, Christian men in their sixties or seventies with a wide variety of occupational backgrounds, but with more of an emphasis on white-collar than blue-collar. In this section I address these demographic characteristics in detail, including similarities and differences between the sources of data in terms of gender, age, ethnicity, religion, occupation, education, social class, lodge, and rank in the Masonic order.

First, with regard to gender, other than two spouses and one journalist in the video data and twenty-two individuals interviewed on the street, all individuals in this study were men. This should come as no surprise: the purpose of this study is to study the experiences of contemporary Freemasons, mainstream Freemasonry remains an exclusively men's order, and there are no female or co-Masonic lodges known to be operating in these jurisdictions. Nevertheless, the perspectives of these men on the changing role of gender— particularly in recruitment, involvement, and their interrelations with spouses and family—are represented throughout and, as will be seen, may be usefully contrasted with the views of spouses and women in the general public.

Next, as noted above, most individuals were older men in their sixties and seventies. However, table 1.1 illustrates some interesting variations among the various sources of data that must be kept in mind throughout this study.

By far, most of the Masons interviewed in both provinces were between 50 and 69 years of age, albeit with a slightly greater proportion in the 60–69 age cohort in Newfoundland and Labrador than in Nova Scotia. This is consistent

Table 1.1   Age of Respondents Compared by Source

	10–19	20–29	30–39	40–49	50–59	60–69	70+
Nova Scotia	0	1	2	13	23	18	15
Nfld. & Labrador	0	2	3	7	12	20	5
Videotapes	0	1	8	6	6	5	1
Interviews of Public	14	21	1	9	0	2	0
Total	14	25	14	35	41	45	21

with what is known about the aging membership of Freemasons noted earlier. Interestingly, there is a much more even age spread among the videotape data, which can be partially explained by the presence of several journalists and a young spouse, as well as by the emphasis in the film on looking at younger men joining the Masonic order today. Finally, the street interviews with members of the public show almost the opposite of the interview data, being predominantly young people in their teens and twenties.[7] Each of these varying demographics may be usefully contrasted with one another in order to look at the issue of contemporary Freemasonry from a variety of angles, ranging from the late-twentieth- and early-twenty-first-century experiences of older members to the recent experiences of newer and younger recruits.

Thirdly, in terms of ethnicity, respondents in all sources of data were predominantly White and of local origin. Thus there were only five immigrant Masons in the Nova Scotia data and six in Newfoundland and Labrador out of a total of 121 individuals. When considered in terms of ethnicity proper, the vast majority of interview respondents in both provinces had apparent European ancestry, with the exception of two individuals from the Caribbean and one from North Africa. There were only three visible minority members in these data (two Black men and one Arab). This undoubtedly reflects the relative ethnic homogeneity of these two provinces compared to larger provinces and more populous urban centres in Canada. Turning to the video data, a similar pattern emerges, but with a slightly greater representation of immigrants and visible minorities congruent with the intent of the filmmaker to illustrate the inclusive nature of contemporary Freemasonry. Of the twenty-seven individuals in question, all had apparent British or Northern European ancestry with the exception of four immigrants and two visible minority members. The former included one individual from the Caribbean and three from Southern Europe; the latter were two Black men. Finally, of the forty-three members of the general public interviewed, there were only two English immigrants and two African-Canadians that stood out from the crowd in terms of ethnicity.

Upon closer examination, however, one must not read too much into this. Over the course of my Masonic career, I have encountered greater ethnic diversity among particular urban lodges in both provinces. For example, while there are no Prince Hall (African-American) lodges in these jurisdictions as there are in the United States, there is one predominantly Black lodge in one of the major urban areas, another Masonic body reports approximately half its members are African-Canadian, and my first lodge had a sizable Christian membership from Lebanon. Thus, upon reflection, it would appear that the relatively low ethnic diversity of the sample reflects attempts to include Masons from all areas of each province, most of which are rural and less ethnically diverse. This, and the fact that ethnic diversity seems to concentrate in particular urban lodges, would largely explain the patterns above, which, in my experience, are not out of line with the Masonic population of these jurisdictions taken as a whole.

Turning next to the religious affiliation of respondents, one might consider this of interest as Freemasonry has historically built bridges across religious divides and allowed for interaction between people who would not otherwise meet (Jacob 1981). Indeed, aside from requiring a belief in a Supreme Being, the Craft does not get into doctrinal or theological differences and the discussion of religion is frowned upon in lodge. As such, one might expect considerable religious diversity in the sample. As table 1.2 illustrates, however, this is not the case.

Despite the large "unknown" component in these data, the information that is available indicates that the sample remains relatively weighted toward Protestant Christianity as the Craft has traditionally been in the past. True, there are a number of Roman Catholic brethren—something that likely would have been a rarity in the past given Protestant antipathy to Catholics in earlier generations and the long-standing opposition of the Catholic Church to Masonry. Yet there was no evidence of other religious backgrounds despite Masonry being open to them. This may have to do, in part, with cultural/

Table 1.2   Religion of Respondents Compared by Source

	Roman Catholic	Anglican Church	United Church	Other Protestant	Other Religion	Religion Unknown
Nova Scotia	3	6	1	7	0	55
Nfld. & Labrador	1	7	2	18	0	20
Videotapes	6	1	2	5	0	13
Interviews of Public	0	0	0	0	0	47
Total	10	14	5	30	0	135

Table 1.3   Occupation of Respondents Compared by Source

	Blue-Collar	White-Collar	Unknown
Nova Scotia	24	32	16
Newfoundland & Labrador	14	32	5
Videotapes	4	14	9
Interviews of Public	0	0	47
Total	42	78	77

religious opposition to Masonry. For example, while I have met four Muslim Masons in the past fifteen years, they remain relatively rare. Indeed, one respondent in the data spoke of a Muslim Mason he knew who left the Craft, giving religious/cultural reasons for having done so; the Islamic world remains one of the major areas where Freemasonry is widely frowned upon. The sample's lack of religious diversity may also have to do with the relatively homogeneous religious background of the two jurisdictions in question, which future research in a more multicultural social context could do more to address.

Fifth, in terms of occupation, I have divided these into "blue-collar," "white-collar," and "unknown" groupings.[8] Table 1.3 shows the results.

From this table it appears that respondents, in those cases where information is available, tend more to the white-collar than the blue-collar in terms of occupational background. As most respondents are Freemasons (aside from random members of the public and six individuals in the video data), this indicates that, despite a significant proportion of blue-collar occupations and an emphasis on making the Craft open to men of all backgrounds, these data continue to predominantly reflect the white-collar groupings traditionally associated with the order. This contrast is even more notable in Newfoundland and Labrador and in the video data. The extent to which this may reflect relatively prominent members of the order volunteering for interviews is, of course, a valid consideration that must be kept in mind, though this pattern is

Table 1.4   Education of Respondents Compared by Source

	Less than High School	High School	Community College	Some University	Degree	Post-graduate	Unknown
Nova Scotia	11	7	19	2	5	13	15
Nfld. & Labrador	4	5	8	3	9	19	1
Videotapes	1	0	3	2	8	4	9
Public	0	0	0	0	0	0	0
Total	16	12	30	7	22	36	25

Table 1.5   Social Class of Respondents Compared by Source

	Working	Middle	Upper	Unknown
Nova Scotia	19	46	7	0
Nfld. & Labrador	8	36	5	0
Videotapes	5	11	4	6
Interviews of Public	0	0	0	47
Total	32	93	16	53

certainly not out of line with my observation of the Craft in these jurisdictions over the past decade and a half.

Next, when considering the educational level of respondents, it would appear that, aside from the few instances where this information was unavailable, there was a good diversity of educational attainment shown among the data, with some emphasis on higher achievement (see table 1.4).

Particularly notable are the relatively high proportion of university graduates and respondents with postgraduate or professional degrees. Indeed, there are a number of current university students among the sample as well. Once again, this fits in with the traditional idea that, while not discriminating against other applicants of good character, the Masonic order tends to attract a disproportionate number of prominent or up-and-coming individuals. Those whose highest educational attainment was high school or less tended to be either much older individuals, those in rural areas, respondents with blue-collar occupations, or current/former members of the military.

Relatedly, I combined evident occupational, educational, and self-presentational impressions from the three sources of data to come up with a working estimate of respondents' social class background, as shown in table 1.5.

This reveals that, where information is available, the bulk of respondents in the interview and video data reflect a middle-class background.

Turning to respondents' lodges, it would appear that the sample includes representatives from most of the Masonic Districts in Nova Scotia and Newfoundland and Labrador, as well as a number of individuals from other jurisdictions. Thus, the interview respondents in Nova Scotia represent forty-eight of one hundred lodges in the province, and every district of the Grand Lodge of Nova Scotia save one, along with the only lodge left in the province under the District Grand Lodge of England (see table 1.6).

In addition, the video data contains interviews with members of two additional Nova Scotia lodges not noted above (one each in Kings and 2nd Halifax County districts). As well, there are three Nova Scotia Masons in the video data whose lodge and district are not mentioned, suggesting potentially greater geographic diversity again.

Table 1.6   Lodges and Districts Represented in the Nova Scotia Interview Data

District	Lodges Represented	Total Lodges in District
Annapolis-Digby	4	7
Antigonish-Guysborough	5	5
Cape Breton Centre	1	10
Cape Breton North-South	2	5
Colchester	2	7
Cumberland	5	9
District Grand Lodge of England	1	1
1st Halifax City	4	5
1st Halifax County	1	5
Hants	2	6
Kings	2	8
Lunenburg-Queens	8	9
Pictou	4	8
2nd Halifax City	4	5
2nd Halifax County	4	7
Yarmouth-Shelburne	0	4
Total	49	101

Turning to Newfoundland and Labrador, it must be pointed out that this is an unusual province in that there are two well-organized and well-represented grand jurisdictions operating in the same geographic area: the Grand Lodge of Newfoundland and Labrador and the District Grand Lodge of Scotland. Tables 1.7 and 1.8 illustrate the distribution of interviews for lodges in each of these jurisdictions.

As can be seen from these tables, the interview data contains respondents from fifteen of the twenty-nine lodges, and every district save one, of the Grand Lodge of Newfoundland and Labrador. It also includes representatives of seven of the eleven lodges in the District Grand Lodge of Scotland—including, fortuitously, a member of a Scottish Constitution lodge in Labrador.

Finally, both the interview and video data include a number of respondents from lodges in other jurisdictions beyond Nova Scotia and Newfoundland and Labrador. Thus the interview data includes members of three lodges in Ontario, along with single members from Quebec, New Brunswick, and Prince Edward Island. Similarly, as well as one Canadian Mason whose jurisdiction is unclear, the video data includes two senior Masons from New York and one from the United Kingdom. All of this adds to the diversity of the data in this study.

Table 1.7   Lodges and Districts Represented in the Grand Lodge of Newfoundland and Labrador Interview Data

District	Lodges Represented	Total Lodges in District
Avalon	8	10
Central	2	6
Labrador	0	1
Peninsulas	3	5
Western	2	7
Total	15	29

Table 1.8   Lodges Represented in the District Grand Lodge of Scotland Interview Data

Anik	•
Carbonear	
Conception	•
Harbour Grace	•
Heart's Content	•
Humber	
Kilwinning	•
Mackay	
Northcliffe	
St. Andrew	•
Tasker	•
Total	7

Table 1.9   Respondents by Highest Masonic Rank* Attained

	N.M.	E.A.	F.C.	M.M.	O.	W.M.	P.M.	G.L.	P.G.M.
Nova Scotia	0	0	1	10	10	6	23	21	1
Nfld. & Labrador	0	2	2	3	10	4	16	11	2
Videotapes	6	1	3	3	3	1	2	4	3
Interviews of Public	47	0	0	0	0	0	0	0	0
Total	53	3	6	16	23	11	41	36	6

* Non-Mason, Entered Apprentice, Fellowcraft, Master Mason, Officer, Worshipful Master, Past Master, Grand Lodge Rank, and Past Grand Master, respectively.

Of course, since this research is grounded in a very specific geographical context, the findings herein must be qualified by further research when considering other national and regional contexts.

The last dimension I outline involves respondents' highest rank attained in the Masonic order. Table 1.9 breaks this down based not only on possession of the three degrees (for new Masons) but also on whether respondents currently hold a lodge office, presently or previously served as Master, have been a Grand Lodge officer, or have been Past Grand Master of the order in their jurisdiction.[9]

From the above it is evident that, aside from members of the public and six video respondents, there is a wide range of Masonic experience represented in the data. While there are only nine newly minted respondents currently in the process of taking their degrees, there are sixteen Master Masons, twenty-three serving lodge officers, eleven Reigning Masters, forty-one Past Masters, thirty-six who have experience in the Grand Lodge, and six Past Grand Masters from six different jurisdictions. As such, while the interview sample is comparatively high on experience, one must consider that this may be what is important if one wants to get insight into the state of contemporary Freemasonry. Furthermore, this is offset somewhat by the emphasis placed by the filmmaker in the video data on closely following a group of young Masons as they go through their Masonic degrees.

Now that I have outlined the broad demographic characteristics of the various sources of data, I turn, lastly, to consider the organization of this book.

ORGANIZATION OF THIS BOOK

This book is organized into eight chapters as follows.

In chapter 2, entitled "Paths to Masonry," I bring contemporary data to bear on one key question: what brings candidates to the door of the lodge today? I detail six interactional elements that lead up to a contemporary person's decision to become a Freemason. These include (1) predisposing factors in one's social background, (2) the dramaturgical interplay between secrecy/mystery and curiosity, (3) organized/organizing encounters, (4) attractive/attracting aspects, (5) unattractive factors/hurdles to get over, and (6) strategies employed to overcome such hurdles. Variations within these elements are arranged in a series of Weberian ideal types, with most actual cases and the relative probability of joining arranged in the continuum in between. While one or another element may be emphasized to a greater or lesser extent in specific cases, they all occur with sufficient regularity to shed light on the significant question of attracting new members to the Craft in the opening decades of the twenty-first century.

In chapter 3, entitled "Taking the Degrees," I trace common themes in respondents' experiences of the three degrees in Freemasonry, during which they undergo a rite of passage meant to transform them from an outsider, a mere interested member of the public, to a full-fledged "brother" in the Craft. This is a ritually complex, interactive process in which respondents, inculcated with a tension between secrecy and curiosity beforehand and seasoned with strategic information leakages, find this dynamic further enhanced through a progressive series of rituals that alternate anxiety and reassurance, sensory deprivation and revelation, physicality and intellect, mystery and understanding in various measures as they are brought deeper into the trust and fellowship of the in-group.

I trace this process sequentially, from the period before candidates arrive at the lodge hall for initiation to the period after they have completed the third degree. Specifically, I discuss the making of a Mason under the following eight headings: (1) before first arriving at the lodge hall, (2) preparing for the degrees, (3) the first degree, (4) working toward understanding, (5) the second degree, (6) the third degree, (7) after the degrees are done, and (8) various logistical issues that affect the impact of these experiences.

It is my contention that the processes encapsulated in this rite of passage (Van Gennep 1960), when performed well, involve a tactical structuring of four primary theoretical elements: (1) dramaturgy (Goffmann 1959; Mangham and Overington 1987); (2) embodied emotion and its management (Denzin 1985; Hochschild 1990); (3) breaches or disruptions to prior paths, adjustments, and assumptions prompting the symbolic construction of meaning (Garfinkel 1967; Mead 1934); and (4) periodic zones of heightened liminality (Turner 1967, 1969), of being "betwixt and between," when the other elements coordinate to foster thought, emotional bonding, and an emergent sense of attachment, even identity. Yet I also point out ways that, in today's social context, these elements can be poorly coordinated, disjointed, interrupted, even short-circuited, leading to questions about the relative efficacy of initiation today.

In chapter 4, entitled "Social Atmosphere and Member Involvement," I begin answering one complex question. Once candidates have been attracted to Freemasonry and have gone through the ceremonies of initiation, passing, and raising, they may ask themselves, "What now?" New members are certainly free to participate in the ceremonies, business, and charity work of the lodge to the extent that they so desire and opportunities are available, but *why* would they do so? What encourages brethren to want to participate? What facilitates their ongoing involvement in the lodge and its activities? Conversely, what discourages them, fostering attrition in Masonic ranks? In the opening decades of the twenty-first century, one thing often heard in Masonic circles is that "it's not just getting them in, it's keeping them." This chapter seeks to empirically address this critical question facing Masonry today.

In this chapter I do three things. First, given the problem of accelerating membership attrition, including relatively shorter periods of involvement over the past half century as noted by Belton (1999) and Belton and Henderson (2000), I try to situate this in the broader social science literature on civic involvement, volunteerism, and social capital.

Next, I provide a brief overview of the factors that, in this and the next two chapters, emerged from the data as significant to respondents when they discussed ongoing involvement in the Craft. These included (1) the social atmosphere in the fraternity, (2) organizational factors, (3) educational issues, (4) the impact of other involvements and commitments, (5) moral and ethical matters, and (6) questions surrounding motivation.

Finally, as by far the most significant concerns were issues surrounding social atmosphere and organizational matters, I spend the bulk of the chapter discussing multiple sub-themes in relation to the first of these factors: the social atmosphere in the fraternity and how it relates to continued—or attenuating—involvement.

In chapter 5, entitled "Organizational Factors and Member Involvement," I move on to consider organizational matters that respondents noted were associated with greater or lesser involvement. The bulk of the chapter will discuss various organizational sub-themes that emerged in relation to involvement. These included (1) membership focus (i.e., getting new members versus retaining existing ones), (2) dues/fees structure, (3) the right to participate in lodge activities—and when, (4) issues surrounding Masonic offices and tasks in the lodge, (5) how lodge meetings are organized and run, (6) interactions with the wider community, (7) conflict and contentious dynamics, (8) relationship with the Grand Lodge; (9) relationship with the Shrine, and (10) demographic/generational issues. Respondents' comments about each will be discussed in turn.

In chapter 6, entitled "Further Factors in Member Involvement and an Overall Explanatory Framework," I first review the remaining factors that emerged in relation to involvement, including educational issues, the impact of other involvements and structural responsibilities in members' lives, moral and ethical concerns, and issues surrounding motivation.

Next, following classical sociologist Max Weber (1949), I construct a system of ideal types. I utilize the involvement factors above to outline an idealized series of polar opposites, one group illustrative of the ideal lodge and social context facilitating long-term involvement, the other one that ideally encourages the quick exit of its members. While these are extremes drawn for analytic purposes, and any real lodge will undoubtedly fit somewhere on the continuum between these two extremes, such an analytic exercise enables a clearer representation of elements critical to Masonic—and by extension—other kinds of volunteer involvement today.

Finally, I close the chapter with a few observations on how this may relate to rapidly changing social contexts, ideals, and social statuses today, arguing that it will be tricky for the Craft to maintain a fruitful tension between status and equality, facilitate productive engagement between generations, and carefully balance its ongoing involvement initiatives on these several dimensions.

In chapter 7, entitled "Claimed Life Changes since Becoming a Freemason," I outline in detail the typical thematic *claims* that emerged about the changes, if any, in the respondents' lives that they feel have resulted from their involvement in Masonic activities. First, I consider disclaimers that address the issue of whether there have been changes or not. Second, I consider the various thematic changes in their social lives claimed by respondents, most notably the dimensions of expanded social contacts and the multi-faceted experience of "brotherhood." Finally, I turn to outline the typical impacts on their character and abilities claimed by respondents, specifically those relating to (1) morality generally, (2) tolerance, (3) altruism, (4) confidence, (5) memory, and (6) inquisitiveness.

Since one of the basic tenets of sociological social psychology is that self is a social construct in continual development in mutual interaction with others (Hewitt 2003; Mead 1934), *to the extent* that respondents' comments herein reflect more than mere claims, but rather, actual life changes occurring in ritual social interaction, one may consider their involvement in Freemasonry a *transformative practice in relation to self.*

Finally, in chapter 8, entitled "Contemporary Freemasonry: The Direction Forward?," I try to pull together the findings above as follows. First, I elaborate the social and demographic composition of the Craft in relation to society and what this can tell us about where things may be heading. Next, I turn to issues of social stratification, noting that the makeup and organization of the Craft today in relation to the social structure suggests very different—and at times conflictual—dynamics in relation to social ideals than in the past. Third, given the concerns raised above, I turn to ritual, including the method or means of facilitating social bonding and integration of members across social boundaries, raising questions about its liminal flexibility, its ability to do so equally well for all groups, which may, along with the matters above, be ultimately reflected in form. Fourth, I illustrate each of these factors in an analytical model/series of figures representing the possible impact of each on the potential outcomes at each end of the continuum. Finally, I discuss the relevance of all of these matters for future research.

As this book is written for both academic and lay readers, it is humbly suggested that the former will find the literature review, sample, methodology, and conceptual analyses of most import, most particularly chapter 1, the analytic frames and theoretical aspects of chapters 2 and 3, the involvement literature in chapter 4, the involvement model presented in chapter 6, and the closing analyses in chapter 8. Lay readers, on the other hand, will likely be more drawn to the recounting of attractive factors in chapter 2, accounts of taking the degrees in chapter 3, respondents' comments about various factors facilitating or discouraging involvement in chapters 4 through 6, and the claimed life changes they recount in chapter 7. Nevertheless, all of this forms a complete whole and should be readily accessible to all.

CHAPTER 2

PATHS TO MASONRY

What brings candidates to the door of the lodge today?
I ask this question for two reasons. First, as noted in chapter 1, Freemasonry has had its historic ups and downs over the past three centuries, no doubt influenced by then-current social events, structures, and processes. Explicating Freemasonry's attraction—or lack thereof—in today's social context thus becomes an issue. Secondly, despite the considerable decline in membership since the 1960s noted earlier, there were also reports of a sporadic resurgence of interest in the Craft, and increases in initiations, in some areas. Given these developments, it is appropriate to delve more deeply into these matters, specifically to explicate contemporary Freemasons' understandings of what brought them to the Craft in today's society.

Data analysis revealed that people come to their involvement in Freemasonry in a variety of ways and for a variety of reasons. Their paths involve a multitude of predisposing factors, attracting conditions, countervailing concerns, social processes, organizational dynamics, key encounters, and personal investigative strategies—often occurring over a considerable period prior to joining. In what follows, drawing upon dramaturgical analysis (Goffman 1959; Mangham and Overington 1987; Fine and Holyfield 1996), I have attempted to make sense of these matters by inductively constructing an ideal-typical outline of the regularities in the ways that contemporary individuals come to the Craft. Specifically, while I argue that each applicant walks their own personal path to Masonry, I have been able to identify a series of commonly recurring factors and dramaturgically organized social processes that occur along the road for many. While not every applicant encounters each and every one of these prior to joining, or as deeply, all individuals in the data had experienced most to some extent. Indeed, the more attracting and fewer repelling factors that they encounter on their journey—the more of the good eggs that end up in their baskets—the more quickly they, in their active investigations, are able to overcome any concerns they may have had and join the Craft.

In what follows, I outline this ideal-typical model in detail. Specifically, I argue that it involves six elements that operate in concert leading up to a person's decision to become a Freemason. While, of course, individual cases may emphasize one or another of these elements to a greater or lesser extent, overall they include (1) predisposing factors in one's social background; (2) the social interplay between secrecy/mystery, strategic information leakage, and curiosity; (3) organized/organizing encounters; (4) attractive/attracting aspects; (5) unattractive factors/hurdles to get over; and (6) strategies to overcome these hurdles to joining. I discuss each element in turn.

PREDISPOSING FACTORS

Predisposing factors can generally be divided into four, often interrelated categories: (1) long-standing personal connections with Masons, (2) respondents' existing personal traits and interests, (3) unfulfilled social needs, and (4) experiencing a sense of anomie.

The first factor was by far the most prominent in the data. It is no understatement that the vast majority of respondents in this study had a long-standing family connection with the Craft. While it may be true, as a few respondents claimed, that more people are joining today with no family connection to the order—and for these, some of the other factors below are likely more significant—it remains clear that family history was key for many. Thus, fifty-seven respondents reported that their father was a Mason, followed by twenty-nine who pointed to their grandfather. Beyond these, there were a whole series of family connections, of both sexes,[1] mentioned by respondents in relation to their joining, such as (in descending order) uncles and aunts (sixteen), brothers (seven), wives (seven), in-laws (seven), cousins (five), mothers (four), and stepfathers (three). Many brought up more than one such relationship, sixteen adding that their family members belonged to the same lodge. Some also associated their Masonic relationships with significant family events, such as hosting a party to celebrate a relative's installation as Master, or, less happily, a father's Masonic funeral. Several even claimed that their interest in the Craft was a way to understand a grandfather (or some other relation or notable ancestor) "that I never knew." In contrast, I was only able to isolate five individuals in the sample who categorically denied any family connection with Masonry. Thus, it appears that one respondent may not have been exaggerating by much when he claimed that 90 percent of applicants have a family tradition in Freemasonry.

Parallel with such family connections, many respondents had prior personal links with Masons who were not members of the family. The three largest categories in this respect involve co-workers, friends, and neighbours. Thus twenty-six respondents indicated that they knew co-workers who were Masons prior to joining. Similarly, twenty-four respondents indicated that they had friends who were Masons, seven reported that family friends were in the same lodge, and three commented that, as children, many of their father's friends were Masons. Lastly, ten respondents indicated that they knew a neighbour who was involved in the order. Such examples, along with the family connections noted above, illustrate the significant predisposing role played by existing personal relationships in providing a foundation for membership, corroborating literature on the importance of interpersonal friendship networks and their integration into wider forms of collective solidarity (Kaplan 2014).

Second, it was evident that there was a combination of personal traits that could intersect to more readily facilitate becoming a Mason. This involved more than simply being a "joiner"; rather, it was something more akin to having developed prior interests in related matters like history, philosophy, religion, theatre, and the esoteric. For example, one considered how prior work experience as a theatrical stagehand, helping with various rituals, and a long-standing interest in history unwittingly laid a foundation congruent with his later involvement in Masonry. Indeed twenty-four respondents noted that such existing shared interests, being people "of like mind," served as predisposing factors that, when they later encountered Masonry, kicked in to encourage them to take the next step. One is reminded of Poulet (2010) who emphasizes the selection of members based on dispositions already possessed. In this respect one may see a grain of truth in the claim of one respondent that "a lot of men are Masons already who have never taken their degrees."

Third, a number of respondents claimed that, prior to joining, they had experienced unfulfilled social needs. Seventeen respondents asserted that one key reason behind joining was that they were seeking a way to make more diverse friends. Beyond this, an expressed need for "involvement" was related by a minority of respondents to factors such as retirement (five), boredom (five), experiencing a lack of "status" or "authority" in life (five), seeking to find "truer" friends (four), seeking "self-improvement" (three), feeling that "something was missing" in their lives (three), being a "loner" (three), severe illness (two), and seeking "a way to gain brothers I never had" (one).

Fourth, and relatedly, respondents claimed a distinct sense of anomie in relation to society today. Thus seventeen expressed disdain for what they saw as a "disorderly," "atomized," "relativized," "superficial" society, noting that they had been seeking an alternative to the "uncertainty," "stress," "social disintegration," and "meaninglessness" of today's world—whether they related this to the workplace and uncertainty of employment, the "age of absent fathers," needing a "space" away from men's greater involvement in the household today, "spiritual hunger," or just a sense of feeling "lost."

As such, there was a sense that these individuals were searching for something of their own, something with "order, structure, and propriety," to serve as "grounding in a world of uncertainties" or even as a traditional, structured form of "sanctuary" where they could "regenerate." This echoes, in a contemporary context, historic accounts of men seeking stability and support amid the chaos of life (Carnes 1989). Furthermore, in this context the Masonic concept of a universal, permanent brotherhood appears to have emotional appeal, suggesting a search for solace (Clawson 1989; Hoffman 2001), perhaps even a gendered way to manage feelings (Hochschild 1990) such as alienation in an era of social change. In effect, among this group we see individuals seeking a strong sense of authenticity, identity, and community that has become increasingly rare in today's "postemotional society" (Meštrović 1997).

Ultimately, one cannot make sense of respondents joining the Craft without considering the foundation laid by such predisposing factors in their social background and in society today.

THE SOCIAL INTERPLAY BETWEEN SECRECY AND CURIOSITY

Another highly significant factor in relation to recruitment is secrecy and its dramaturgical relationship, through strategic information leaks, to fostering curiosity among potential applicants. Despite denials by many Grand Lodges, and despite much supporting evidence—such as prominent lodge buildings, a history of public parades and cornerstone-laying ceremonies, the widespread availability of the ritual, and numerous books on the subject—the fact remains that Freemasonry is considered by many to be the quintessential "secret society."

In contrast to the stock claim that Masonry is "not a secret society, but a society with secrets," it is this *perception* of secrecy on the part of the public, combined with various secretive *practices* on the part of individual Masons, that plays a key role in fostering curiosity and interest in the Craft among others. In effect, subtle breaches (Garfinkel 1967) or inhibited social acts (Hewitt 2003) soon gave rise to emotion (Denzin 1984) and accounting (Garfinkel 1967). Hence, in the video footage used in this study, when members of the public were asked about the Masons, the term "secret society" came up repeatedly. The flavour of this perception comes out clearly in their comments, where they reflexively draw upon indexical resources in this relative interpretive vacuum to construct accounts:

> I know absolutely nothing. I've tried, I used to work in a store which is at the bottom of the Freemasons building and I would often see Masons going in and out, but it was a cone of silence in there. I never learned one thing about the Masons and I tried my best, but no one would tell me anything. Secretive. Very, very secretive. It seemed to be ... There was an iron curtain.

I don't know anything about them, and I think that's the point.

I want to think that they're okay, but because it's so secretive and everything, it's hard to know. I kind of think it's weird. Because if you're not going to tell people what's going on, it's hard to trust, just based on the fact that they're saying it's a good organization.

All you hear is sort of conjecture and myth mixed up with a lot of superstition and such. So what we know is secret society. Maybe they're the secret government. Maybe they're the ones that take care of the big picture, the very big picture. You know, those things that happen that just sort of coincidentally happen.

A friend told me, like, they're the Mafia.

Aren't they the Men in Black?

In line with this public perception of secrecy and mystery—seasoned liberally with rumours of conspiracy—consider that Masonry was once practised so secretly in some places that nine respondents claimed they were completely unaware that family members, friends, and co-workers were involved until after they joined: "At my initiation, I was surprised to learn that I knew almost everybody in the place."

But beyond such extreme examples, the dramaturgical operation of this secrecy was usually more subtly interactive. Thus, sixteen respondents indicated that members of their own family were Masons but they kept very quiet about it. Another thirteen respondents discussed the air of mystery surrounding Freemasonry among their friends, noting how "people wouldn't talk." Ten respondents stated that their fathers hid their Masonic stuff away from the rest of the family, and another seven that their father and other well-dressed Masons socialized in their home but wouldn't say much pertaining to it. Indeed, one noted how once, when visiting family, he walked in on a room full of male relatives, and "all conversation ceased." Beyond such "secret conversations" (such as one person who was observed sneaking down to the basement with a new initiate and whispering back and forth to teach lines in the ritual), several commented on the "mysterious lingo," the "mysterious membership certificates" that they "just knew should not be touched or even asked about," how their fathers virtually "ate" the lodge notice, which "quickly disappeared," and how there was a recurring image of their father or other Masons in the family "sneaking out once a month all dressed up with this little black case." All such dramatic actions or breaches of the practices of everyday life (Garfinkel 1967), supplemented at times by props and teamwork (Goffman 1959), revealed as well as concealed, and reportedly made respondents "wonder what was going on."

However much this secretive stance reflected a stricter policy against solicitation of members in the past, there nevertheless remained more proactive
methods of manipulating secrecy, and engaging in further selective, strategic
leakage, without running afoul of the presumed rule. The most common simply involved wearing a Masonic ring, which, at various times, people would
ask about. Thus, twenty respondents pointed to encounters with Masons
after they noticed the ring, asked about it, and interest was evoked (I have
experienced this as well). In addition, thirty-five friends, eighteen co-workers,
and fourteen fathers, among others, reportedly made cryptic, suggestive comments in this and other contexts falling short of openly inviting respondents
to join. Some examples:

> It's a secret symbol ... [response] *What do you mean secret?*

> [when doing house renovations] *Have you seen the square?*
> *That's a Mason thing, you know* ... [response] *So, what is it?*
> [silence]

> [after a prayer on a work site] *Oh, we do that in the lodge too* ...
> [response] *Tell me about this lodge.*

> [exchange between two friends walking together] *Wait here,*
> *I've got to go in there [the lodge hall] for a minute* ... [response]
> *Oh, you're one of those are you? What do you do in there*
> *anyway?*

> [upon greeting a friend as a Mason, then discovering he was
> not, feigning surprise] *Oh, you're not a Mason?* [response] *No,*
> *what do you mean?*

Beyond such "plays on words to whet the appetite," sometimes followed
by a dramatic pause, many Masons responded to the forthcoming questions
with statements such as "Oh, I can't tell you" and "You'll find out if you
join." Thus many Masons sought to foster interest in potential applicants by
revealing little snippets that dramaturgically left them hanging. Few Masons,
however, went as far as the father who had his son hold the ritual to help
him learn his part—nevertheless covering up key parts the son was forbidden
to read!

The response of respondents faced with such mysterious actions tended to
be heightened curiosity at the mystery of it all. In the words of one respondent,
"Wild curiosity, because nobody told me anything." Others claimed that "all
the mysteriousness kind of got me going," that the secrecy "makes it sexy," or
that they experienced "curiosity squared by family." As a result, some respondents, when young, wondered about their father's regalia, their grandfather's
mysterious membership certificates, "what these little books were"; some

even snuck a look at their stuff when they were out. Some claimed that the little that friends or co-workers revealed "was unsatisfying, I needed to learn more," and later took the time to investigate further. At least twenty claimed to have experienced great curiosity about what went on at lodge meetings, and ten claimed that they liked the idea of joining what is popularly considered a "secret society," driven by the excitement involved and the desire to find out the "secrets."

Interestingly, four other respondents also found their curiosity aroused after viewing membership certificates in a family tree, another upon discovering that he was the descendant of a very important figure in Masonic history, one after seeing the Masonic symbol on a relative's headstone, and another after being given an ancestor's Masonic ring.

Yet it must be pointed out that there has been an evolution over the years in both the official and unofficial social manipulation of mystery surrounding the Craft, a historical adjustment in what I term "confidentiality gerrymandering" in both the extent and contexts in which little bits of information are allowed to strategically leak out. At one time the boundary was tightly drawn and Masons reportedly took their obligation to secrecy far more seriously than they do today. Whether this was due to past persecutions or simply necessary to prevent the misuse of information, the fact is that many Masons didn't talk about it publicly, particularly between the late 1930s and the emergence of Masonic public relations beginning in the 1980s and 1990s. Many didn't know what they were at liberty to reveal, so they simply chose the safest course and said very little to outsiders, except perhaps through such cryptic examples as noted above. Thus, while meant figuratively, in the words of one Scottish Mason who was initiated in the early 1960s, "At that time, it really was quite a secret society."

This earlier stance seemed to work for a time; the relatively strict "no comment" policy of many Masons and most Grand Lodges through the middle part of the twentieth century did not seem to be hurting recruitment until the gradual decline in membership beginning in the early 1960s became apparent, and even that took time to sink in. However, beginning in the 1980s with the publication of a popular anti-Masonic tract in England (Knight 1984), with official questions being raised about Masonic membership in the British judiciary and police services, the subsequent proliferation of Masonic literature on the Internet, the growing fascination in popular culture with secret societies and conspiracy theories, and a generation more interested and willing to seek out information about such matters than the youth of the '60s and '70s did, there has been somewhat of a shift from the ostensible blanket secrecy of the past to a more open stance for a generation more willing to seek answers.

Thus more recently, while some Masons still dramaturgically engage in secretive actions such as those common in the past, in many areas there has reportedly been some shift in the boundary of the information preserve. Such an adjustment in confidentiality gerrymandering means that today there is much more of an emphasis—both officially and unofficially—on helping people to find out more and encouraging them to join. Thus, beyond relaxed rules about solicitation in some jurisdictions—and considerable debate about these—there has evolved a much more open public stance in the past several decades. Many Grand Lodges and their constituent lodges now host their own websites and produce pamphlets and videos meant to answer questions for potential applicants. Indeed, one respondent mentioned research by the Grand Lodge of New York that indicated that fathers telling sons about Freemasonry counts the most in recruitment. As well, there has been an enormous increase in the number of websites—both pro- and anti-Masonic—that disseminate materials once largely confined to dusty Masonic libraries, and many new popular books are being written about the Craft.[2] Hence twenty-one respondents noted that encountering information on the Internet fostered their curiosity about the Craft. Similarly, fourteen pointed to popular literature, seven their reading in the esoteric, four to newspapers or magazines, four to popular movies and video, two to the display of symbols such as on bumper stickers, one to a radio show, and one to a lecture.

Most interestingly, sixteen also claimed that anti-Masonic materials that they so encountered, such as the conspiracy theories that have become a wider cultural phenomenon in recent years,[3] helped to spark their curiosity. (In the words of one respondent, "We get blamed for everything. I think that drives curiosity. There's no such thing as bad advertising.") In one notable example witnessed by the author, upon reading about a presentation on "secret societies" in a student newspaper, one young respondent attended with classmates, several of whom were Masons:

> We went to actually see a guy who was supposedly doing a lecture on secret societies at [the local university]. It was advertised as a lecture, but, it turns out, it was a video lecture—he didn't want to be there to answer any tough questions. Like he was this right, like ... [sighs] I don't know how to put it, right-wing.... His theory was that we were basically the secret army of the Jesuits [laughs]. And we were ... there were about four or five people in the Craft that were there in the audience, and they were almost falling on the floor laughing. He was very anti-Masonic—and that's probably an understatement. But what was unique is that Masonry was, in fact, supposed to be a Catholic conspiracy. He was really messed up. And so, the thing ... the bottom line is, we walked out of the theatre and I said, "So, tell me guys, what's it all about?" And another fellow that was there with us said, "All that stuff you just heard,

that's all just bull." And I'm like, "Yeah, I know. I want to join now." [laughs]

Yet, in most cases, things were not so obvious, and the multitude of available exposés and inconsistent conspiracy theories, though often engaging, still revealed relatively little. As one respondent succinctly put it, "It's hard to separate the crap from the truth." Thus most in this subgroup sought to investigate further "by going to the source." The upshot is that, to some extent at least, curiosity fostered by *secrecy* is being supplemented by a curiosity fostered by *notoriety*.

Going hand in hand with this we also see a less reticent stance on the part of Masons in simply asking potential applicants to join. Thus, while more recent applicants also spoke of suggestive practices such as those related above, there are some who spoke of being directly asked to join: for example, nine were asked by friends, four by fathers/fathers-in-law, and three by neighbours. As well, three pointed to organized events such as "friend-to-friend" nights, and two to pamphlets they had been given by Masons.

Only time will tell if the direction of these ongoing social changes that maintain relative secrecy through a relative overabundance of uncertain information will, by themselves, foster wider growth in the order. What is certain, however, is that various social factors that foster and maintain a dynamic relationship between secrecy, organized forms of dramatic information leakage, and curiosity represent one key element on the path to Masonry for the respondents in this study.

ORGANIZED/ORGANIZING ENCOUNTERS

Neither of the above factors occur without an organized—and dynamically organizing—social context to both frame and facilitate their influence (Mangham and Overington 1987). In the case of family, friendship, and workplace relationships, this is rather obvious. Indeed, these frequently—though not exclusively—provide the interactional backdrop to the various actions noted that foster the productive interplay between secrecy, leakage, and curiosity, and to these we can add things like the historic shift in stance by Grand Lodges themselves from secrecy to various public relations practices, the growth of the Internet, and a renewed Masonic press in all its varieties.

Yet several aspects require further discussion in this respect. In what follows, discussion is divided in relation to (1) organized events, (2) the role of related organizations, and (3) the organized public relations stance of the Craft.

An obvious place to start this discussion is with the role of organized social events. The data reveal that these were part of the attraction of Masonry, especially in the past. Thus, eight older respondents indicated that they joined after attending a social or community event put on by the lodge, four referring to dances or "ladies' nights" and another four indicating that they or their spouses liked the "crowd" they had encountered. Similarly, it was pointed out by six respondents that lodges often held organized children's events in the past, such as father-and-son banquets, Christmas parties for kids in the community, and picnics. Both types of organized event tended to be looked back upon fondly by respondents. Inevitably the discussion turned to the fact that these had been either largely or completely dropped over time, whether due to the aging of the membership, lack of young people in the community, the cost of entertainment, competition from work or other types of recreation, liability issues, or the like. Three argued that there should be a return to holding dances, and another three stated that children's events should be reinstated, though, of course, the above factors would have to be taken into account in the process.

In more recent times, it was also clear that lodges have tried different organized events to attract members. Some, such as one rural lodge that sent an information/recruitment newsletter to households in the community, reportedly failed (later claimed to be because of a "lack of young people in the community"). Other events such as "open houses" and tours of Masonic halls in other areas were commented on favourably by five respondents in relation to joining, three further asserting that Masons should be open to holding—or renting out their buildings for—other community events. Other matters that were claimed to be of value include bingo fundraisers for a popular community cause (two), "friend-to-friend" nights (two), and Masonic church services (two). Similarly, the author is aware of a group of Masonic musicians who regularly get together to jam that has attracted members through such fellowship. Indeed, I, along with a small group of Masonic friends, inadvertently began to attract many new members to one lodge—and later went on to form our own—by simply getting together for drinks every Friday afternoon at the local campus pub, and we have decided to continue this social practice because it is both enjoyable and fruitful. Thus, one cannot consider paths to Masonry without considering the role played by the active organization of social events.

Second, we must consider the role of related organizations in fostering interest in the Masonic order. In this respect, the Shrine, the Order of the Eastern Star, and other fraternal organizations played a key role. Thus, given their far greater community visibility in parades, their well-known charitable role in funding children's hospitals and the like, fourteen respondents reported that they had been impressed by the Shriners and had asked to join but been told that it was necessary to become a Mason first. The Order of the Eastern Star—a coed Masonic organization composed of both men and women—also played a part. Seven respondents indicated that their spouse's involvement in the order encouraged their decision to become a Mason (one stating "now we can enjoy something together"). This was followed by those who mentioned their mother (three), grandmother (one), and aunt (one). One respondent whose grandmother belonged to the Eastern Star, upon asking her about an unsolicited gift she received, was told about the lodge and the family's Masonic history and was reportedly profoundly influenced by her comment that, contrary to what the baby boomers may think, "it's important to belong to something larger." He soon became insatiably curious about the order. Four more respondents indicated that their fathers were members of other fraternal organizations that adapted much of their ritual and structure from the Masons, whether officially associated or not. Lastly, one respondent had been a member of DeMolay (a youth organization associated with Freemasonry), while had another attended a school with its own associated lodge for alumni.[4] Related organizations cannot be dismissed in recruitment.

Third, there are evolving policies surrounding the organized public stance of the Craft vis-à-vis the public. To some extent this has been touched on above. However, there are specific matters that must be considered further in a widespread but uneven shift from secretive to active public relations. Broadly, these may be divided into matters surrounding solicitation of new members and public education about Masonry.

Solicitation policies, despite the trend toward greater openness, remained controversial among respondents. Indeed, among those who touched on this issue, twelve favoured open solicitation of new members and thirteen the more traditional stance that a potential applicant must first ask a Mason if he can join. In the first group, five claimed that "doing it the way that it's always been done will not attract members today," four claiming that many people today haven't heard about Masonry, another that it was "too secretive," and one that a slight increase in new applicants today may partly reflect relaxed rules on solicitation. Indeed, one respondent, who happened to have experience in writing commercials, enunciated an impromptu advertisement for Freemasonry during the course of the interview! Often such comments went hand in hand with the view that, despite resistance to change, Freemasonry had gone through numerous historical changes (e.g., from meeting in pubs to Victorian temperance), and today was "tied to an old vision" that needed to be brought into the modern world.

Of the thirteen opposing this stance, five claimed that "you can't push [potential applicants] or you will lose them" and that soliciting/chasing people "just drives them away." Another three expressed shock upon hearing of a television ad campaign elsewhere, and one was surprised and distressed that information is easily available for interested parties. Indeed, seven respondents decried the "numbers game," favoured quality over quantity, and expressed concern over how solicitation might "water down" the membership. Regardless of this ongoing debate, however, the fact remains that the Craft has—to

varying degrees in various jurisdictions—moved more in the direction of solicitation in recent years.

Broader public relations issues come into play as well. Most notable were
seventeen respondents who claimed that organized public education about
Freemasonry is important today. In some respects, this is seen by some as
counteracting the old "no comment" stance and diminishing public visibility
that largely held sway between the end of WWII and the late twentieth century, a means to offset simple ignorance of the existence of the order. Others
see it as a way to address various negative rumours and suspicions in light
of the growth in conspiracy theories in recent years. Given a felt need to
"humanize" the order, four respondents made positive comments in relation
to strategically promoting Masonic charity (as opposed to the old "Victorian"
stance of keeping one's good deeds to oneself and not seeking recognition).
Nevertheless, several indicated the need to publicly distinguish Masonry from
"service clubs" like the Lions and Kinsmen and suggested that there is more
to Masonry than can be found in these groups. Various promotional methods
were lauded, such as improved websites, the "Friend to Friend" video, "Freemasonry in the Community" initiatives, visible participation in other public
and community events, documentary films, revival of the historic "Masonic
press" (i.e., newspapers) that existed prior to WWII, the organization of social
activities, and the practice of Masons simply talking about the Craft to others,
essentially serving as a "liaison" in their social circles.

In addition, there was an expressed need to overcome challenges in promoting Masonic ideas in today's society, to effectively "rebrand" the Craft to
make it more relevant to the younger generation. It was argued that, among
other things, it is possible to "maintain the essential philosophy" but make
"adaptive surface changes" to distance the Craft from "old-fashioned views"
and "reflect contemporary society." Hence it was asserted that attempts
should be made to emphasize "diversity" and "inclusiveness" in contemporary Masonry (including emphasizing the existence of options for female
participation, such as the Eastern Star) and that efforts should be made to "tap
into the spiritual hunger today," to "merchandize" Masonry to a generation
more interested in "consuming" rather than "contributing," to emphasize
the "worldwide nature of the order," to promote the lodge to service clubs,
fraternities, and traditionally under-represented groups like Catholics, and to
market it as an "exclusive" or "elite" group—in part by lodges significantly
raising dues (the latter, according to one respondent, being extremely successful in recruitment efforts in certain US jurisdictions). While not all of these
ideas are consistent with one another—and there is some tension between
appealing to the wider society and a traditionalist, subcultural identity (Rubington and Weinberg 1987) that opposes modernization—these comments
give a good idea of the evolving, organized ferment of ideas in relation to the
public relations and recruitment efforts of the Craft today.

ATTRACTIVE/ATTRACTING ASPECTS OF THE CRAFT

By this point, individuals on the path to Masonry will have been exposed to varying amounts of information about the Craft from a variety of sources: family, friends, co-workers, various media, and contact with their potential sponsor, to name the most prominent. They may have been exposed to various other organized encounters and their curiosity aroused by the structured interplay between secrecy and curiosity and given an edge by cryptic, tension-inducing hints about what goes on behind the lodge door. Given these matters, this is a good point at which to outline the factors that respondents found attractive about Masonry.

First, applicants reported being attracted by the ethical and charitable aspects of Freemasonry. Thus, thirty-two respondents claimed that they were impressed by the character of Masons they knew. Sometimes this involved the charity of the Shriners (fourteen) and other Masons (thirteen), the kind gestures or favours of Masons to others (five, including three who pointed to Masons helping raise an orphaned child), observations of "how much" a sibling and his lodge brothers "trusted and respected each other" (one), and the dignified manner in which one Masonic co-worker withstood the abusive behaviour of a boss. Indeed, twelve respondents claimed that the principles of "commitment" to morality emphasized by the order were attractive, providing both an opportunity for shared moral and spiritual experiences and a disciplined "sense of purpose"—exemplified by one respondent who made comments about becoming a "knight of morality."

Second, the attractive, ethical aspect was seen by seventeen respondents to contrast significantly with what they saw as the unattractive features of society today. This is where an interaction between predisposing factors in this respect and the information they were able to obtain about Masonry becomes important. A lot of these comments revolved around the theme of "longing" for something due to the experience of anomie (Meštrović 1997). Thus these respondents decried today's "disordered," "atomized," "relativized," "disposable," and "superficial" world in favour of something that they could connect with that was principled, orderly, and structured (in this respect, one respondent even claimed, "I was born in the wrong century"). Whether the social problems they perceived were the "uncertainties" of the labour market, the need for "male bonding in the age of absent fathers," "men's greater involvement in the household today," observing others "wasting time partying and playing video games," "spiritual hunger," or simply a perceived "decay of society," rather than being another aspect of a "world that is going down the tubes" Masonry was seen, in the words of one respondent, as "the opposite of Jerry Springer." In their "searching" and desire "to feel attached to something," twelve respondents claimed to have found the Masonic concept of a universal, permanent brotherhood attractive. Seven claimed to be seeking "solace" from the "uncertainties" posed by society today, and five, from "meaninglessness." Another five claimed that they wanted a traditional, structured form back in their lives (one even added an appreciation of the dress code). Some added that they perceived that belonging to the order would alleviate this sense of being "lost" and would provide "grounding in a world of uncertainties," a place of "sanctuary" to "regenerate" for engagement with the world, even a way to help "fight against the decay of society." There were even five who claimed to find the various conspiracy theories surrounding Masonry not only fascinating, but "comforting!" (i.e., they felt reassured that "everything is under control"). Indeed, the comments of three respondents that Masonry is growing in countries with lots of social disintegration could bear further study.

Third, twenty-four respondents indicated that they considered Masonry a place where they could find people "of similar interests" or "like mind" with whom to socialize and enjoy fellowship (one respondent even spoke of searching for "a place of social and philosophical engagement"). Again this relates to their social background and the comment that "a lot of men are Masons already who have never taken their degrees."

However, this must be contrasted with younger respondents who tended to report seeking these commonalities of interest seasoned with social diversity. Thus, rather than simply "WASP" "squares" or "conservatives seeking a place to be," some spoke the contemporary language of integrating people from diverse social backgrounds. Thus, in addition to seventeen respondents claiming that one key reason behind joining was that they were seeking a way to make more diverse friends, seven claimed to see Masonry as a socially "integrating" factor, a way to "build bridges." While not necessarily extended to women (indeed five respondents reported being attracted by the male-only aspect of mainstream Craft Masonry, as opposed to the female auxiliary Order of the Eastern Star), seven, mostly urban respondents, among them several ethnic minority members, nevertheless lauded the willingness of lodges to accept a plurality of applicants today, whether in terms of race, culture, ethnicity, or even sexual orientation. Thus one respondent from the Caribbean happily reported how "excited" the brothers were when he sought to join; another proudly exclaimed, "there's more multiculturalism in my lodge than on the street today." Thus, Masonry may be attractive to some because it can be seen as providing a principled core around which men with shared interests, from diverse backgrounds, can socialize and engage around a shared core of activities vis-à-vis the disarray of contemporary society. In effect, unlike in the Victorian era, when race and gender served as the foils against which brotherhood was measured (Carnes 1989; Clawson 1989; Hoffman 2001), today gender appears to be more prominent—in effect if not intent.

Fourth, forty-four respondents were reportedly attracted to the Craft by popular images associated with it. For example, twenty-one encountered information on the Internet, fourteen in popular books, four in magazine and newspaper stories, and five in television or radio programs. Indeed, while not all of the images were positive, the encounters nevertheless seem to have fostered an interest in investigating further.

Fifth, nineteen respondents pointed to how they were attracted by the rich and varied history of the Craft. In this respect, ten pointed to famous Masons in history, seven to historic architecture, six to historical mythologies surrounding the Craft, and six to an interest in religious history. Three claimed that it was impossible to understand history without a knowledge of Freemasonry. One reported being attracted to the "oldest fraternity in the world," and another to something with "roots" and "tradition" that is "unchanging." Interestingly, a non-Mason who happens to be a professional historian mentioned how Freemasonry provides "virgin academic territory" for the study of social history, adding that many lodges contain amateur Masonic historians that pursue historic research. Thus, the connection with history as an attracting factor appears solid.

Sixth, and relatedly, an existing interest in spirituality, broadly defined, made Masonry attractive to respondents. Sixteen expressed curiosity about Masonic symbolism, eight reportedly having come across references to Masonry in their reading in the esoteric. As well, fifteen claimed to have come to view Masonry as an "alternative to formal religion," with which at least a few were disillusioned. Ten saw their interest as a by-product of a wider "growth in spirituality today," six noted that they felt Masonry would provide them "with a path for exploring the big questions," and four claimed to be inspired by Masonry's "search for truth."

Seventh, respondents claimed an attraction to Masonry due to its image—rightly or wrongly—of being associated with the successful, the prominent, and the powerful. Eighteen respondents claimed that this was an attractive feature. When coupled with predisposing factors such as the unfulfilled social needs outlined above, it is not surprising that an anticipated increase in status by association with such a group would seem appealing to some. While ten respondents similarly admitted that they were attracted to Masonry as a means to network and further their career or business (despite this being frowned upon in the order) and another five saw it as a path to "self-improvement," in one way or another the predominant theme here involves the attractions of status—even potentially an alternate status hierarchy. Perhaps this also explains the dismissive comment made by one respondent about people who join "as a way to boost their name in the obituaries."

Eighth, and partly related to the charitable aspect of the Craft noted above, nine respondents, in one way or another, found information about the "social service" function of Masonry attractive. Beyond claims to further "social integration" discussed above, five pointed to how the lodge could provide a valuable source of social and financial support in hard times—and, indeed, such "insurance" was one of the main historic attractions of the Craft and other fraternal organizations before the rise of the welfare state (Beito 2000).

Finally, while not a common attraction, there were three respondents who mentioned that they were attracted to the lodge as a means of maintaining existing social ties that had been put at risk by changes in their lives. Thus, while much has been written about the large group of former military who joined the Craft after WWII to maintain the camaraderie found in the ranks, two respondents who were former military claimed the same. As well, there was one respondent who had moved away from a rural community who claimed to see joining the local lodge as a regular, organized means to stay connected with hometown friends and family.

UNATTRACTIVE FACTORS/HURDLES TO GET OVER

To the extent that potential applicants were able to glean information from their interactions with family, friends, co-workers, reading, and potential sponsors, it was clear from the data that not all aspects were positive. Thus, it is important to consider the various unattractive matters that serve as hurdles to get over prior to initiation into the Craft.

The first logical hurdle is, of course, lack of information, indeed lack of knowledge—even of the existence of Freemasonry as an organization. While this was only mentioned by four respondents, in the words of one of them, "Ignorance is the big killer." Of course, such a small number might be expected among the many respondents who have had social connections with the Craft. However, among the members of the public interviewed on the street, a higher proportion—thirteen of forty-seven—had either not heard of the Masons or had but could tell the interviewer nothing. This partially substantiates the claim of one well-placed Mason that "Masonry is unknown to many today." Indeed another bemoaned the "challenges in promoting Masonry today." Thus, while the extent of this ignorance is admittedly unclear, to the extent that it remains it serves as a logical hurdle to members of the public becoming involved.

The next hurdle for potential applicants involves membership requirements, presumed or otherwise. Thus, four respondents initially believed that Masonry was *only* comprised of members of the upper class—the successful, prominent, and powerful of society—and that they would therefore be barred from joining. Another two initially thought that Roman Catholics couldn't join, one who lived in a largely Catholic community adding that "99 percent of Roman Catholic people think this." Beyond these presumed requirements, there were two respondents who had admittedly struggled over the male-only aspect of mainstream Craft Masonry. As one put it, "You have to do it in spite of all kinds of problems. You know, the issue that it's only men, joining a club with 'no girls allowed.' That was really on my mind when I was going into it—because that's usually 'not on' under normal circumstances in this day and age." Another admitted to taking some time to grapple personally with the actual Masonic requirement of a belief in a supreme being (something that may be a problem in a society where traditional religious beliefs are no longer part of the mainstream). Finally, there was one African-Canadian respondent who had obtained a copy of the ritual and was initially put off by the archaic language that one must be "freeborn" to become a Mason (upon later investigation, the respondent discovered that this was actually a historical reference to the existence of prior medieval feudal obligations rather than race). One way or another, perceptions surrounding membership requirements clearly hold the potential to dissuade applicants.

Third, respondents reportedly faced various negative stereotypes of Freemasons in both their social milieu and encounters with media materials. The most prominent of these was the stereotype of Masonic nepotism in high circles. Thus, despite the respondents mentioned above who were admittedly attracted by the prospect of advancing through networking, there were also fifteen respondents who claimed to have been initially concerned by stereotypes about nepotism in the Craft. Further, some mentioned controversies in this respect, such as unsubstantiated rumours surrounding the awarding of public contracts, stories about individuals not being hired or not advancing in their careers, allegations about Masons in the police and judiciary, and the difficult public relations image at times faced by the Craft in the United Kingdom, along with a British proposal to officially question public servants about membership. Indeed, after they later joined, respondents were at great pains to counteract such stereotypes by pointing out that anyone asserting motives like these will not be recommended for joining, that such behaviour is "wrong," and that those "mercenary types" who somehow slip through find the Craft ineffective for this goal anyway and "don't stay long." In the words of one, "No one sticks through for potential business contracting. There's no insurance salesman in the world who would think it was a good investment of his time to join Masonry for that."

Beyond this, there were a series of other negative stereotypes faced by prospective Masons prior to joining. First there was a series of more lurid negative images, such as rumours that Freemasonry was a "pagan cult" (five), that its members engaged in dark "conspiracies" (three) or were "devil worshippers" (two) and/or "White supremacists" (one). These claims raised the tension level surrounding the Craft, and, although they did not scare these respondents away, they certainly prompted further investigation. One wonders in how many other cases they are successful. Conversely, one also wonders about, in the words of one respondent, "who might be joining as a result."

Finally in this respect, there was the stereotype, expressed by six respondents, that Freemasonry was an "old man's club" and was what "old farts did." This went hand in hand with the assumption that it was a group of "old boys" that was "closed in on itself" and identified with "social conservatives." The upshot of this type of negative view was "why bother?"

Turning to the fourth factor, some respondents faced social opposition to joining. There were those who encountered opposition to their interest in joining from their family and friends. Four respondents reportedly faced family opposition or concern at first, and three reported the same from friends. One young respondent spoke of a fervently religious mother's opposition to Masons' presumed "pagan practices" and another reported a spouse's initial concern over how much time his involvement in Freemasonry would take away from their home life. Still another spoke of a concerned friend repeatedly trying to turn him away from becoming a Mason and bombarding him with anti-Masonic materials over several months. While these matters concerned a small minority among respondents who later joined the Craft, and those asked generally indicated their partner's initial assent to their joining the order, nevertheless, as women were historically not always happy with their partner's involvement (Clawson 1989), one cannot dismiss the potential significance of this factor. Again, while these data cannot answer the question, one wonders how often today, given vast changes in social attitudes, religiosity, and gender politics, opposition from spouses, family, and friends is effective in preventing potential Masons from joining.

Fifth, respondents often faced hurdles to joining in their own personal situations. In this respect, the most common response, given by nineteen respondents, was that they had to wait for the right time in their lives to join. Thus, there were respondents who pointed to demanding jobs, "hard times," lack of work, interlocking family commitments, and the emergence of changing interests as they matured. To some extent this hurdle also related to a perception that Masonry would take up a great deal of their time (two) and that they would have to "be selling tickets all the time" as did members of some other groups (two). Undoubtedly these perceptions were fed by observations of other, more heavily involved Masons and of the extensive involvement of the Shriners and other community organizations that spend much time raising money for causes.

Sixth, and relatedly, respondents pointed to societal and cultural factors that often served as hurdles to joining in today's society. Thus eight respondents pointed out that, compared to the past when involvement in the lodge was one among relatively few social and recreational outlets available—indeed, sometimes "the only game in town"—today there are far more

competing activities and distractions available in a "fast-paced era of mass leisure and consumption" where "people are much more interesting in consuming and getting something out of organized group activities than in contributing to them." Five respondents claimed that baby boomers are much more
into "being their own people" and "doing their own thing" than becoming
involved in something so "old school." Some added that it was often necessary
for both spouses to work today; others, that today's lifestyle is more family-
and couple-oriented than in the past. The upshot, claimed nine respondents,
is that Masonry "missed a generation," four adding that there now exists a
problematic "generation gap" in Masonry. Indeed, given such a social milieu,
one can understand the comment of one respondent: "Why someone would
find Freemasonry to be of value is not necessarily evident today."[5]

Finally, there were a series of organizational factors that prospective
Masons may have heard about from one source or another that may have
discouraged them from involvement. For example, some had previously been
aware of an unattractive intersection between internal bureaucracy and the
generation gap noted above. Nine respondents commented on how older
members used bureaucratic means to maintain the status quo: by preventing
younger members from gaining positions of authority (six respondents); by
stifling initiatives by younger members (two respondents); and by using the
length of time that it takes to progress to discourage younger members (one
respondent). Beyond this, some were aware of Masonic politics through their
connections; this included seven respondents who were aware of controversy
in some areas about people joining the lodge as a mere stepping stone to
becoming a Shriner, and indeed controversy over the relationship between the
Shrine and Craft lodges generally. Seven respondents expressed aversion to
the image of an organization that let its historic buildings crumble into disre-
pair or unceremoniously disposed of them in favour of unattractive, modern
structures. Finally, one individual dropped his first application due to lack of
contact or support from the sponsor (i.e., no follow-up), only deciding later
to apply a second time and join. To the extent that such negative information passes into the broader community, it may serve to dissuade prospective
members from progressing into the Craft.

OVERCOMING THE HURDLES

Up to this point, I have largely discussed various factors that might be seen
as impinging upon potential applicants in one way or another. These frame
a dramatic tension around and within the individual between curiosity and
various concerns. Yet beyond the various factors that may be said to push
or pull, attract or dissuade individuals from ultimately becoming Masons, I
would be remiss if I did not, in the end, attempt to reframe some of these,
and to discuss others as key prompting encounters where potential applicants

actively use various methods or strategies to overcome questions or concerns and come to the ultimate decision to move forward. In this, I emphasize the dynamic interplay between secrecy and trust in "dangerous leisure" (Fine and Holyfield 1996), particularly those encounters enabling potential candidates to actively neutralize anti-Masonic imagery and innuendo, overcome indifference, or learn enough credible information to enable trust to proceed.

Of course, in one respect, prompting encounters initially involve things like mysterious behaviours by Masons; suggestive, secretive comments; or, more often today, a request to join by a family member, friend, or co-worker as discussed earlier. Beyond those which get the ball rolling, as it were, there are numerous other interactions that may occur—both informally and in a more organized fashion—throughout the period a potential applicant moves along their path to Masonry. In this respect, prompting encounters may also be seen as conduits for key bits of information being passed to the potential applicant—both pro and con—that may influence their ultimate decision. But the decision to join or not cannot be simply reduced to the balance of positive and negative information without more strongly emphasizing the more active, reflective role of the subject. It is thus to the potential Mason's role in all of this to which I now turn.

First and foremost, potential applicants made their own initial assessment of the individuals that they knew in the Craft—particularly, of the individuals' character. Thus, again, I call attention to the thirty-two respondents who claim to have been impressed by the character of the Masons that they knew. For those with close family members and personal friends involved in Freemasonry, this was usually pretty straightforward and positive. Thus, eight respondents specifically commented how already knowing family and friends in the Craft helped address their concerns. In the words of one respondent, "I knew that these were good people and that nothing bad was going to happen to me." Of course, it is possible that those with family problems or issues with their Masonic friends may not join, but the nature of the data does not allow further elaboration on this issue. As for those not initially on as close personal terms, as with, say, co-workers, a little more thought might go into the assessment, but the idea remains the same.

Second, and relatedly, potential applicants engaged in ongoing personal observations of Masons they knew in order to assess both their character and the Craft more generally. Thus the data contain examples such as the respondent whose family was going through some difficulties, and who also had a brother who had joined the Craft, who commented on how the brother's life was "changing," particularly his "ability to handle adversity." Beyond this, there were respondents who were favourably impressed by the dignified ways that Masons held up in the face of ridicule—ranging from one who withstood an abusive boss with dignity to a Masonic friend who stood up to teasing about involvement. Finally, there were respondents who observed a Mason's kind gestures or favours—toward another or toward themselves—and made a positive evaluation of membership on that basis. In this latter respect, for example, there was even one respondent who decided to join after revealing his adoption to a Masonic friend, who then, upon making discreet and tactful enquiries in the community, introduced the applicant to his birth family. In these first two respects, we see the extension of friendship and intimacy to a broader organizational context, the partial blurring of personal and collective ties (Kaplan 2014), but this time more in terms of strategies by potential applicants.

Third, potential applicants often did personal research and investigation on their own before moving forward. Thus, fourteen respondents commented on how they took time to investigate further before making the decision to join, eight adding that doing their own research on the organization helped them make up their minds. Many sought information on Masonry in the various sources available, whether this involved books, websites, materials available through the Grand Lodge, other media sources, or word of mouth among non-Masons. While four did specifically mention that anti-Masonic materials and comments that they encountered along the way slowed them down somewhat, they simply took the time to investigate further and address various concerns before moving forward. While the nature of the data do not permit conclusions on potential Masons dissuaded from joining through such investigations, as noted earlier, they do point out that some report being even more interested in joining as a result of anti-Masonic material. Ultimately, where so much information is now available, it is hard not to agree with two respondents who claimed that people are much better informed about Masonry than those coming in years ago, and that "those coming in today have really thought about it."

Fourth, and relatedly, sixteen potential applicants spoke to Masons that they knew and asked questions to address any concerns that they had before moving ahead. In many cases this involved discussions with family, friends, and co-workers. Eight specifically mentioned seeking social support from their potential sponsor (who could come from any of these groups). These respondents claimed that the anxieties and concerns that they had—such as about what might happen to them during initiation related to the secrecy, cryptic comments, anti-Masonic materials, and even teasing encountered at the hands of other Masons—were alleviated by the support received from sponsors (the "good cop/bad cop routine"). Indeed, some had helpful reading materials given or suggested to them.

Fifth, and related to the earlier hurdle of not having enough time for involvement, it was the case that nineteen respondents who were interested in Masonry but whose other responsibilities got in the way waited until a time in their lives where they had the available free time to participate. Thus, some waited until their children were grown up or until they retired, others until they had a less demanding job, and so on, before petitioning to join.

Sixth, there were four respondents who chose the collaborative strategy of sharing the experience. Rather than join the lodge separately, they submitted their petitions to join the same lodge at the same time, at least in part as a means to offer mutual support to each other along the way. Another respondent noted he had witnessed Masonry "snowball among groups of friends." When these actions involved close friends or family members, they were claimed to be particularly meaningful strategies of overcoming concerns and of reaching the destination on one's path to Masonry.[6]

Finally, there is an active, interactive process—both dramaturgical and bureaucratic—that serves as the culmination of the above tentative engagements facilitated by one's various contact(s) with the Craft: the investigation process. This occurs at two levels. First, there is the ongoing dance of secrecy, strategic leakage, and curiosity, noted earlier, between a potential applicant, their contact(s)/sponsor (a.k.a. proposer), and other information sources. Secondly, there is a formal investigation process by a committee appointed by the lodge itself (which does not include the sponsor). Ideally, these operate in tandem, in what Goffman (1959) calls "teamwork." Both dramaturgically manipulate the boundary between front and backstage, between what they know and the applicant doesn't, to foster greater curiosity in the applicant.

Generally, if the interactive strategies to overcome the hurdles above have been successful, a potential applicant asks their closest contact in the Craft (whether a family member, co-worker, friend, or acquaintance) to get them an application. This contact then takes on the role of sponsor and obtains an application, which the applicant fills out and submits through him. Information is exchanged at this time between these trusted individuals, but it is largely about what the sponsor enjoys about the order and the various formal steps to follow. Details about the initiation ritual itself are generally kept out of things throughout, except for some teasing to simultaneously raise both tension and curiosity (specifically commented on by six respondents).

Next, once the application to join is submitted, a formal investigation committee is appointed by the lodge to meet with the applicant and his spouse and family. This takes place between the time that the individual has petitioned to join and the actual initiation. This is a formal, organized encounter in which additional information is provided to the applicant by members of the lodge, where the requirement of a belief in a supreme being is discussed, all present have the opportunity to ask questions, and each ultimately will come to a decision as to whether to proceed further. Both the applicant and the committee must be in favour to proceed.[7]

The sponsoring and, particularly, the investigation processes that follow are clearly organized events structured by the constitution and bylaws of the Craft in a given jurisdiction. Nevertheless, as noted, they also have a dramaturgical order. Thus while much of the initial stages of sponsoring have been detailed above, particularly in relation to curiosity-raising encounters, respondents commented on the role played, and the information provided, by the investigating committee in their ultimate decision to continue on and be initiated. Nineteen respondents found the opportunity to meet, discuss, and ask questions of the members of the investigating committee a useful, two-way exercise in information gathering, one that often helped them—and their families—to frame a decision to move forward. In particular, four commented that the request by the committee to speak to their spouse separately was helpful, as the spouses were able to privately ask questions and express any concerns without interference. Beyond this, some were reassured that this—and their general discussion with the committee about social events, charitable activities, and Masonic values—provided evidence that the lodge valued their family and that "family came first."

Also at this stage applicants may be given information regarding when and how they will likely be initiated, but little more. There may also be further, discreet hints, even a bit of teasing, about the upcoming initiation, essentially more mysterious leakage serving to highlight tension and curiosity as they await the first degree.

In all of this, respondents were not passive; they actively involved themselves in pushing and pulling, in mutually manipulating the boundary between secrecy and curiosity in deciding to move forward and join the Craft. All in all, this elaborates, in a new empirical context, how the "seemingly oppositional forces" of trust and secrecy can combine to foster social integration, stabilize organization, and provide a foundation for communal allegiance (Fine and Holyfield 1996).

DISCUSSION AND CONCLUSION

Theoretically, for individuals to complete the initial path to Masonry, they must actively progress through a social process involving a dramaturgically organized interplay between available resources, those of family and friends, and the "institutional talk" of the order (Holstein and Gubrium 2000). Applying the dramaturgical frame of "organizations as theatre" (Mangham and Overington 1987), members of the Craft help to theatrically transform potential applicants' realities by affectively staging social action and experiences in conventional ways for particular audiences, but in specific ways to metaphorically emphasize *mystery*. Most who join the Craft are gradually drawn in by structured breaches or disruptions in everyday life and the Craft's mysterious nature, while popular stereotypes, cultural ignorance, and manageable opposition are handled in tandem with trusted others. This dramaturgical tension, this optimal balance between secrecy, evolving strategic leakage, and trust, is interactionally facilitated by *organized* hints, cues, and utterances, both formal and informal, supportive and tension-inducing, enabling, indeed embodying curiosity while emotionally managing concerns. Valued personal narratives of onstage friends or family, teamed with formal encounters and the institutional talk of the order, gradually heighten—indeed, *manufacture*—curiosity. In the process, relationships weave an emotional "cocoon," deepen attachments, and immunize candidates from potential risks of upcoming activity, enabling them to see dangers as manageable (Fine and Holyfield 1996, 25–26).

On the basis of the above, I would assert that, in an ideal-typical sense, these processes are most effective today when potential applicants to the Masonic lodge are individuals who (1) have predisposing factors in their social background; (2) are sufficiently engaged in the interplay between secrecy/mystery, information leakage, and curiosity in their social context; (3) are exposed to organized/organizing encounters surrounding the Craft; (4) have been made well aware of attractive/attracting aspects; (5) have limited exposure to unattractive factors and/or fewer hurdles to get over; and (6) engage in the above-noted strategies to overcome hurdles they have encountered. Such are the individuals who have walked their path to Masonry and are about to knock on the door of the lodge.

Conversely, as summarized in table 2.1, it can be logically surmised that those who (1) have no predisposing factors in their social background; (2) are insufficiently exposed to the interplay between secrecy/mystery, information leakage, and curiosity in their social context; (3) are not exposed to organized/organizing encounters surrounding the Craft; (4) have not been made aware of its attractive/attracting aspects; (5) have much exposure to unattractive factors and/or more hurdles to get over; and (6) do not engage in the above strategies to overcome any hurdles they have encountered are unlikely to walk the path to Masonry and comparatively unlikely to ever knock on the door

Table 2.1   Ideal-Typical Distinction between Individuals Likely/Unlikely to Become Masons

Likely to Join	Unlikely to Join
Predisposing social background	Unrelated social background
Engaged curiosity construction	No curiosity construction
Organized/organizing encounters	No such encounters
Awareness of attractive aspects	No such awareness
Few hurdles to get over	Obstacles to overcome
Strategies to overcome hurdles	No or ineffective strategies

of the lodge. Most cases fall somewhere in the continuum between these two ideal-typical polarities.

While, of course, the nature of these data do not permit firm conclusions regarding those exposed to some of these factors who did not join, logic alone suggests that lack of exposure to the first four combined would largely short-circuit the above path (with a hypothesized descending probability of joining upon exposure to fewer of the four). Moreover, discussion throughout, particularly in relation to the latter two, certainly suggests a series of ways in which those exposed to information could fail to pursue membership. Undoubtedly these preliminary results call for more research, particularly for a research design that somehow is able to incorporate interviews with potential applicants who have been exposed to varying components discussed above who have not joined the Craft. All the same, the above model provides us with a great deal of information on the principal features of a successful path to Masonry, which was the research goal at the outset.

Finally, future research should delve more deeply into the strategic role played by "confidentiality gerrymandering" in all of this—both historically and in relation to official, cultural, and technological developments in recent decades. Where and to what extent does the traditionally more closed approach by brethren still work to attract members today? Among what groups? In which areas? Which demographic is better engaged by the contemporary, overabundant style of dramaturgical "leakage?" Can both work at the same time for different groups, or are they of necessity inconsistent, perhaps even impossible to reconcile in such a manner today? Follow-up research on these matters in different geographic and cultural locales, and on attracting members today using a variety of methodologies, could provide further information of great benefit to not only academics studying membership in other community-based organizations, but to the very future of the Craft itself.

CHAPTER 3

TAKING THE DEGREES

O nce a candidate has walked the initial path to Masonry, submitted a petition, and been investigated and voted on by the lodge, the next major step is initiation into the Craft.[1] This involves a series of three ceremonies or "degrees," usually separated over a series of months, during which the candidate navigates a rite of passage (Van Gennep 1960), moving from being a member of the general public toward the status of Master Mason. In passing through these dramatic, disorienting, and variously meaningful and confusing rituals, candidates are welcomed into the order, socialized in its practices and principles, and educated in its lore, and they variously attempt to come to an understanding of what they have gone through as "Mason" is gradually constructed as a core identity category (Mahmud-Abdelwahib 2008).

In what follows, I trace this process sequentially from the period before a candidate arrives at the lodge hall for initiation to the period after having completed the third degree. Specifically, I discuss the making of a Mason under the following eight headings: (1) before first arriving at the lodge hall; (2) preparing for the degrees; (3) the first degree; (4) working toward understanding; (5) the second degree; (6) the third degree; (7) after the degrees are done; and (8) various logistical issues that affect the impact of these experiences. I then elaborate a theoretical model of the sociological processes at work.

BEFORE THE CANDIDATE ARRIVES AT THE LODGE HALL

The time between a respondent submitting a petition for initiation and the day of their initiation—a period that can vary depending on the lodge's schedule and the time needed to prepare for each ceremony—involved a range of anticipatory feelings including curiosity, excitement, and apprehension, which respondents attempted to manage in various ways (Hochschild 1983, 1990).[2] As the time approached, reflexive accounts in face of the impending breach

(Garfinkel 1967) conveyed a building sense of anticipation characterized by both excitement and curiosity. While some respondents recounted how they uncharacteristically lay awake at night thinking about it beforehand, others put more emphasis on "stepping into the unknown," most notably one man who exclaimed, "It's thrilling to know that there's something you don't know." On the other hand, there were those who claimed to be more apprehensive. One man pointed out that the discussion that led up to his initiation took about six months due to his level of apprehension. Indeed, as another put it, "the first degree is the most nerve-racking, as it's the first time." Such were the initial, emotional foreshadowings, indeed the "feelings about feelings" of the impending ritual separation, then liminality to come (Denzin 1984; Van Gennep 1960; Turner 1967, 1969).

The social context behind such feelings, however, always bears keeping in mind. Up to this point, candidates have already experienced a series of social encounters with Masons—family, friends, proposers, the investigating committee, and so on. Considering Mangham and Overington's "organizations as theatre" approach, where organizational activity is studied in a manner similar to what theatre-goers bring to a drama (1987, 25–26), respondents' earlier encounters were generally characterized by a dramaturgical interplay between secrecy and curiosity, between the strategic leakage of positive and negative information, between supportive and apprehension-inducing encounters (e.g., teasing versus reassurance) that served to heighten or even manufacture curiosity in the process leading up to submitting their applications. Candidates' experiences at this stage were undoubtedly influenced by the predominant colour of these expressions.

In response to the anticipatory breach, separation, or liminality that has been socially engendered up to this point (Garfinkel 1967; Van Gennep 1960; Turner 1967, 1969), respondents attempted to manage these feelings in four basic ways: (1) engaging in research (or choosing not to); (2) drawing parallels with other social contexts; (3) limiting expectations; and (4) attending to advice. Interestingly, three of these were largely individualistic, an aspect of masculine coping strategy noted in other contexts (Cook 1988).

The first strategy, advance research to help build indexical, interpretive resources (Garfinkel 1967), was by far the one commented on most frequently by respondents—both pro and con. As noted in the previous chapter, there were a great many respondents who sought to access at least some reading on Masonry beforehand, and at least some of this had to do with the degrees themselves (indeed in one extreme case, a respondent reported how a candidate in his lodge showed that he had downloaded the rituals of the three Craft degrees, as well as all thirty-two in the Scottish Rite). Undoubtedly, whether minor or major, such actions involved attempts both to satisfy the curiosity that had been engendered and to reduce the attendant anxiety. Thus, aside from two respondents who claimed, "There was no Internet in my day, so I could find out very little beforehand" (which is only half true, given the many books and exposés published over the past 200 years), many spoke about the value of a candidate reading about the initiation ceremony beforehand. Nevertheless, the predominant view, variously expressed by thirty-four respondents, was that "it's one thing to read beforehand, but another to experience it yourself." Indeed, five of these claimed that reading about it "lets you expect some, but not all of it," two more adding that they did not feel that their reading spoiled the experience.

Various reasons for this position were given, including the difficulty of ascertaining whether a source was reputable, the fact that more senses are in play in the degree ceremonies than one uses when reading a book, the "sacredness" of experiencing the ceremony and learning within the temple itself, variations in the rituals, idiosyncrasies in the degree work of particular lodges, and the differing quality of their work. Hence, while such individuals may "come in a little better prepared today," this research strategy seems to largely function in terms of reducing "lived feelings" of anxiety and curiosity beforehand (Denzin 1984). Respondents still claimed that "you can't get the sacredness of it from reading in a book," and what appeared "almost meaningless before" may still become significant (e.g., "It's a whole new ball game." "Oh, that's what that meant. Now it makes sense"). Ultimately, many respondents who had engaged in such strategies later claimed, "The secrets of Masonry are in your heart, not on the Internet."

On the other hand, twelve respondents claimed that they strategically avoided reading about the initiation ceremony beforehand, ostensibly to heighten the experience of initiation. Ten of these said that this was because they did not want to "spoil the experience." One put this succinctly when he stated, "I don't want to know all that's coming and ruin it for myself." Four added that they were personally advised not to read about it for this reason. Individuals engaging in this dramaturgical, excitement-building strategy, one that effectively left them solely to their previous indexical, interpretive resources, typically anticipated that the experience of initiation had the potential to leave them, in the words of one man, "like a deer in the headlights."

Yet, beyond the decision to research or not, it was noted that respondents engaged in three further emotion-management strategies to deal with the curiosity, excitement, and anxiety they felt before taking their degrees. First, they dealt with this impending "breach" or "disruption" of their previous adjustment, this anticipated ritual separation (Van Gennep 1960), by, pragmatically, constructing meaning (Mead 1934), often drawing upon indexical resources in a reflexive exercise in accounting (Garfinkel 1967). Hence five respondents sought to draw parallels with what they saw as related experiences in an attempt to colour in the rough outlines of what was to come. Two of these claimed that they had some idea beforehand of "what fraternities do" and "didn't mind." One mentioned that he had gone through other initiations in various branches of the military and thus was quite "comfortable" with the concept of a "rite of passage" and the "bonding" that went along with it. Yet another had already been initiated in another fraternal organization and felt that he, as a result, had some idea of what to expect. Finally, one man tried to draw upon his youth and young adult experience in cubs and military cadets to inform his expectations.

Next, three respondents dealt with the curiosity, excitement, and anxiety leading up to their first degree by variously attempting to manage their emotions (Hochschild 1983, 1990), often through trying to limit their expectations about the initiation ceremony. Thus, as they "knew it would be different," they variously commented how they "tried to prepare" themselves "emotionally and intellectually," and "tried to temper" their "expectations [and] to wait and see."

Finally, there were a few who dealt with their feelings before initiation by attending to the advice, support, and indexical resources provided by mentors and other Masons that they knew. Thus, aside from relying (or not relying) on the advice about reading noted above, candidates attended to various instructions regarding what were seen as appropriate standards of comportment for the night of their initiation. (For example, two were essentially told to "shower, shave, and dress up in a suit and tie like you're preparing for church," while another had been warned that the brethren had been "unimpressed," and candidates "embarrassed," when previous candidates showed up in "street clothes.") Relying on advice, of course, could leave candidates wide open for teasing by others (a subject that will be dealt with at length in the next section), but, when successfully employed with a trusted mentor, this strategy often resulted in vaguely reassuring statements of support (e.g., "Just go in there with an open mind and you'll be fine").

Such details initially suggest not only the significance of dramaturgical analysis (Goffman 1959), but the relevance of predominantly solitary, highly masculinized forms of emotion management (Hochschild 1990; Cook 1988) utilized in a preparatory fashion to either heighten excitement or dampen anxiety.

PREPARING CANDIDATES FOR THE DEGREES

Upon arrival at the lodge hall on the day of their initiation, candidates suddenly walk onto a new stage (Goffman 1959), one that, whatever their advance preparation may have been, still retains the ability to throw them off balance. Most had "never seen the inside of a lodge room before," nor were they prepared for the visual impact of seeing "all of these guys dressed up in suits wearing aprons with gold braid looking like the Lord Mayor." On this first stage a transformative, dramaturgically organized experience awaits them, one which involves the manipulation of props, costumes, lighting, script (implicit and explicit), and teamwork among actors, all of the components of a dramaturgically organized social institution (Mangham and Overington 1987; Goffman 1959).

Most generally, respondents spoke of this unsettling time of preparation in terms of four broad, interrelated dramaturgical elements: (1) being ritually prepared, (2) teasing and tension-building practices by others, (3) their resultant nervousness, and (4) advice and tension-reducing support offered before they enter the lodge. I will deal with each in turn.

Soon after their arrival at the lodge hall, candidates are taken to the "preparation room," adjacent to the (then-"backstage") lodge room, where they are ritually prepared for their initiation. On this initial stage there are a series of dramatic surprises: they are told to undress, stripped of their valuables, instructed to dress up in an unusual ritual garment that leaves parts of their bodies exposed, and "hoodwinked" (blindfolded) before it is time for them to enter the lodge for initiation.

The first surprise, after having been previously told to dress up in a suit and tie, usually occurs when they are suddenly told that they must take their clothes off. In one dramatic instance,

> *The Tyler barked, "Get it off!" and I stripped buck-naked.*

While not all candidates took things quite so literally (both men in the exchange above were embarrassed, but later laughed about it), twenty-five respondents did comment that they experienced feelings of shock and anxiety upon discovering that they had to undress in front of others. Responses included the following:

> *What the Jesus is going on here?*
>
> *It was a shock to the system.*
>
> *I kind of thought the boys were nuts.*
>
> *I had no idea what I was in for. I was super nervous.*
>
> *I was never so scared in my life.*

Going hand in hand with this were anxiety-provoking comments by the officers and brethren, the most common being "I hope that you're wearing clean underwear." All of this dramaturgically heightened anxiety among candidates, many of whom fed off the verbal and non-verbal body language of others, often sharing telling glances while undressing in the small room as they tried to account for what was going on. Indeed, it was noted that this was even more unsettling for lone candidates, faced with no one but the officers to share their experience. At least one respondent admitted that "I almost bolted" at this point, while another was reportedly so "spooked" that he did, in fact, leave, but did more research and came back for initiation a few months later—rationalizing that he was asked the question about clean underwear "because I would be changing in a communal changing room."

Part of this stripping process also involved the removal of candidates' valuables (watches, rings, wallets, jewellery, etc.) before the degree. While this relates to a specific part of the initiation ceremony (as discussed later), candidates at the time do not know this, and having their distinctive, identifying property taken for "safekeeping" provides but another source of anxiety. Again, it was only much later that respondents came to rationalize the above matters, to construct meaning out of this breach (Garfinkel 1967), this disruption in their prior adjustment (Mead 1934), as with one candidate who came to see this as "an equalizer, that you're no better than anyone else."

Candidates were told that the point of undressing is that they must put on the initiation outfit that they will wear during their initiation. This consists of what one respondent referred to as "loose-fitting pyjamas" (which have buttoned flaps where a breast may be bared), along with a pair of slippers. Fifteen respondents commented how they were "thrown back a bit" upon viewing the "uniform" that they had to wear:

> You've got to be joking.
>
> You can't be serious.

Yet serious they are, and having to dress up in this costume did nothing to assuage the free-floating anxiety, the multiple "sensible feelings" (localized sensations) and "feelings of the lived body" (fully embodied emotions) that respondents were experiencing (Denzin 1984, 1985) as they struggled to account for it all. Many nervously joked about "the partial nudity," the funny costume "with half of it open," and "the rolled-up pant leg." Indeed, several amusing anecdotes were related by respondents about factors that affected their feelings during this whole process. Some spoke of the temperature of the room, ranging from the man who found it an uncomfortably cold place to change ("where I could see my breath in the air") to another who sat on a hot radiator as he changed into his outfit, later exclaiming, "They do brand Masons!" One man, who had been nagged repeatedly beforehand to wear socks, had some choice words when he had to remove them, much to the amusement of others. Another claimed that he was "too big for the PJs," and took some ribbing, though he later expressed surprise at his lack of embarrassment. Whether for amusement or as an emotion management strategy, however, such joking around only partially dealt with the unsettling nature of the situation respondents suddenly found themselves in.

Then, shortly before the initiation begins, yet another surprise awaits. Candidates are given blindfolds, "hoodwinked," and a rope known as a "cable tow" is tied around their neck. Exchanges like the following often occur:

> Tyler: *Can you see?*
>
> Respondent: *No.*
>
> Tyler: *Good.*

Thirteen respondents commented on the impact of this sudden "exercise in sensory deprivation," three pointedly adding that they were "scared to death" as a result:

> *They say, "Trust us, nothing bad will happen." I was scared to death and then they blindfolded me.... Uh-oh!*

While usually done just prior to entering the lodge, this could reportedly make anxiety worse if a candidate was left blindfolded for some time prior to the degree. Again, only later did respondents come to re-evaluate this experience and symbolically construct meaning out of this "breach" or disruption in their prior adjustment (Garfinkel 1967; Mead 1934). For example, one man commented that "it teaches you to trust your brothers"; another interpreted it as putting one in the position of "playing a poor blind person."

Up to this point, I have largely discussed the ritual preparation of the candidates, particularly the embodied, interactional aspects of ritualized stripping and preparing respondents into a common form, facilitated by standard dramaturgical elements such as props, costumes, and so on. In many respects, these served to "breach" candidates' prior, taken-for-granted realities (Garfinkel 1967), their existing pragmatic adjustments to the world (Mead 1934). They most dramatically underscored the "separation" stage of the rite of passage (Van Gennep 1960) and clearly leach into the first aspects of liminality (Turner 1967, 1969). However, implicit in much of the above was the second aspect of preparing candidates for initiation: dramaturgically organized teasing and tension-building practices to heighten candidates' senses, and their attention to phenomenological "feelings of the lived body" (Denzin 1984, 1985) before the degree.[3] There is no doubt that teasing often went on even before candidates' arrival at the lodge hall, and respondents reported as much. Yet it was after arriving at the lodge hall that this went into high gear. Fully thirty-five respondents stated that they were teased in some way by officers and brethren of the lodge, only six claiming that it "wasn't too bad," and just a single respondent stating that he was not teased before initiation.

While there were many ways in which this occurred, such as the comments above about clean underwear, by far the most common, indeed the oldest Masonic jibe in the book, occurred when candidates were told, "You'll have to ride the goat." Fully twenty respondents reported being told this at some point after arriving at the lodge hall, and several others beforehand. This theme of the goat (or, in some cases, sheep) got played out in various ways. Phrases such as the following were simply said to most (or to others) in passing:

> *Did you bring the sheep?*
>
> *If you hear a goat, don't worry about it.*

Others were given more oblique references:

> *Oh, we got something for you ...*
>
> *We'll see how good you are.*
>
> *No matter what happens, let it happen.*

In still other cases, further props were used, such as two respondents who were shown a picture of "the goat" before their degree. Indeed, in one lodge located in a rural area, a member actually borrowed a goat from a local farmer and tied it up outside the lodge in plain view of candidates arriving for their initiation!

Many respondents would also agree that "there are some good stories that could be told" about teasing before initiation beyond the dominant theme of the goat. For example, one candidate was told by the Tyler, a gruff local police officer, "that if I tried to run, he'd shoot." Other respondents overheard disturbing comments, such as when one officer attending the preparation room was pulled aside by another who stated "the senior steward is erect." Other teasing ranged from an officer's comment that "my scars are all healed now," to a picture on the wall of the preparation room showing candidates being beaten with brooms in a barrel, to being advised to make "no sudden movements" upon entering the lodge room. Such dramaturgical, tension-building practices, together with the ritual preparation itself, generally evoked unsettling indexical resources for the interpretations flashing through candidates' minds (Garfinkel 1967; Denzin 1984) and served to heighten candidates' anxiety, their phenomenological "feelings of the lived body," even further.

This brings us to the third aspect of ritual preparation: anxiety. Thirty respondents admitted to being very nervous before their initiation, largely due to the fact, mentioned by twenty-eight, of the "fear of the unknown," coupled with the above.

I didn't know what they would do to me.

My old jokes about the Masons came back to scare me.

Indeed, when some ventured to ask questions about all of this to those preparing them, they were often met with further comments such as the following:

Oh, you'll find out.

There's more surprises. Wait for it.

Beyond the obvious tension-inducing practices, respondents pointed to other matters indexed (Garfinkel 1967) to their concerns, such as "stories" that they had heard (six), not knowing anyone else there besides their sponsor (four), and the other brethren being much older (one) or of a different ethnicity (one). These, and the other matters above, were often flashing through their inner thoughts and feelings in the "phenomenological stream" (Denzin 1982, 1984) as preparation unfolded.

Yet there were others who at least expressed a different view, indexing mitigating elements. Thus there were eight respondents who claimed that their nervousness was attenuated by the fact that they "knew," "trusted," or "respected" the men in the lodge, three more adding that they "knew" that the above was "just teasing," "not true," or "not going to happen." This was followed by nine respondents who were careful to assert that they felt "apprehension, not fear"—tipping their hat, as it were, to male gender norms of emotional expression, two even adding that they were not so nervous because "I could take care of myself if necessary."

Regardless of such rationalizations or self-presentational bravado, however, it was clear that the ritualized stripping, uniform outfits, and organized teasing practices above translated, on balance, into heightened nerves accompanied by "feelings of the lived body" (Denzin 1984, 1985), both of which play a key role in preparing candidates for initiation (indeed, five respondents later explicitly highlighted this fact). Perhaps the most telling comment in this regard is from a candidate who stated, "It sure makes you pay attention to what's going on."

This nervousness cannot be allowed to get too extreme, however, or the candidate may either be tempted to bolt (as above) or be too anxious and miss the key points of the degree (as discussed later). This brings us to the final aspect of preparing the candidate: advice and support given by one's sponsor or Masonic friends prior to entering the lodge. Particularly helpful for respondents who did not rationalize as above, sponsors or Masonic friends often came to visit candidates in the preparation room before initiation, eighteen respondents noting how they were told that "nothing bad would happen" and that "we've all been through it." Thus one candidate remarked that he was told,

> You see those old men? Some went through it recently and they're fine. Don't worry, we're just having a little fun with you. You'll have your chance with someone else later on.

Such social support had a slight muting effect on some candidates' anxiety—of those commenting on their response, six claimed to be less nervous afterwards; however, another six were still as nervous, due to the unknown. In the words of one respondent,

> On one hand you hear about the goat; on the other, stuff to make you feel a bit better.

Yet this "good cop/bad cop" strategy, this alternation between dramaturgical tension-building and supportive cooling out, did appear to enable some to focus better on key pieces of advice that were also offered at this stage:

> Listen, picture it in your mind—where you were and what you did—and then try to remember it.

> Listen, think about it, sleep on it, and it will make sense tomorrow.

Those respondents who not only felt supported, as above, but were given such advice, later looked back on it as helpful to their later understanding of the initiation experience.

In sum, such use of setting, props, costume, stripping identifiers, sensory deprivation, and teasing served as dramatic buildup for the experiences to follow (Goffman 1959). In effect, a slowly building, dramaturgically organized set of interpersonal actions in the "interactional stream" set in motion heightened intrapersonal effects in the "phenomenological stream" of candidates' thoughts and emotions (Denzin 1982, 1984). This building cascade breaches, disrupts prior pragmatic adjustments (Garfinkel 1967; Mead 1934), and puts stress on candidates' emotion management (Hochschild 1983, 1990), setting up a combination of "sensible feelings" (localized physical sensations) and "feelings of the lived body" (Denzin 1985, 228–30) that, taken together, emotionally soften candidates up, separating and preparing them for the liminality of initiation (Van Gennep 1960; Turner 1967, 1969). The presence of other candidates—and mutualized anxiety in the preparation room—often further heightened such feelings vicariously (Denzin 1985). Hence, trusted mentors are often nearby, even sometimes serving as candidates' physical "conductors" to ease potentially overheated nerves.

INITIATION: THE FIRST DEGREE

At this point candidates have been ritually prepared for their initiation and are ready to enter the lodge. Separation is dramaturgically moving increasingly into liminality (Van Gennep 1960; Turner 1967, 1969). Generally, as the time approaches, candidates are lined up outside the inner door of the lodge and wait to be admitted. There is usually some nervous conversation, coupled with a bit of teasing and some supportive comments, while candidates' "conductors" (i.e., those who lead them in and around the lodge while they remain blindfolded) get in place to take them into the lodge when signalled. It goes without saying that those men who initially knew their conductor, or who were conducted through the first part of their degree by a family member or friend, claimed to both literally and figuratively feel supported in that fact.

Very few other comments were made by respondents about this stage, other than with regard to unhappiness about how long the wait had been (especially if a key officer was late, or the lodge was conducting business before the initiation). As well, one man commented that, just prior to entering, he had been impressed upon hearing "about 150 people singing the initiation ode while I was waiting outside."

Then the initiation begins. There are loud knocks from the inside of the inner door which are answered in turn by the Tyler (a guard with a sword). A series of questions and answers are then exchanged, after which the Deacon leads the ritually prepared and blindfolded candidates, supported by their conductors, into the unfamiliar terrain of the lodge room itself.

Twenty-eight respondents remarked on their state of mind—the activity in their phenomenological stream—as they entered, most notable their anxiety about "entering a room blind, not knowing what's there," "not knowing what's going on," or "where I'm being led" or "pushed." Indeed, aside from one man who claimed to feel relatively calm "as I'm used to working in the dark," five respondents highlighted "feelings of the lived body," speaking of how they were "shaking" or "entered the lodge with knees knocking," and two others claimed that they "heard their heart beating," one at "twice its normal beat." Beyond this, three said that having "no idea how many people were in the room" added to their anxiety as well.

Candidates' first surprise occurs almost immediately. They are "received" on the point of a sharp instrument (a dagger) applied to their exposed breast. Some, particularly those who were very nervous by this point, got a bit of a "jolt" where the "sensible feelings" involved provoked "feelings of the lived body" (Denzin 1984, 1985); others at least appeared to take this more calmly and thoughtfully, using this breach or disruption as a clue when attempting to construct meaning in the "phenomenological stream" (Garfinkel 1967; Mead 1934; Denzin 1984, 1985) to "account" for what was happening (Garfinkel 1967):

Then they make you jump. It's a rush.

This has to be symbolic.

But the overall, liminally revealing response upon first entering the lodge, stated by thirteen respondents, is

What the hell have I got myself into here?

While a great many candidates remained confused and puzzled about their initiation both during and for some time after (which will be discussed later), it was also the case that some at this point were already engaged in trying to "process" these breaching disruptions (Garfinkel 1967; Mead 1934), in concert with the ritually induced "sensible feelings" and "feelings of the lived body" (Denzin 1984), to phenomenologically construct symbolic meanings about what they were doing and why they were doing it. Thus there were accounts like the following:

I'm being kept disoriented for a reason. In order to learn, you've got to be shifted out of your comfortable self.

It sparked my interest. I wondered about the meaning behind it all.

I said to myself, "Try to drink in as much of it as you can."

There is also a dramatic shift in mood that is impressed upon candidates once inside; in contrast to the teasing that occurred outside, there is now a sense of seriousness and solemnity. This was noted by fourteen respondents. Here are two examples of their reactions:

I picked up on the solemnity of the ritual, the reverential way that it was being done.

I knew it was best to be quiet.

At this point, after being asked if the initiation is a matter of their own free choice, and then being instructed to briefly kneel for a prayer, blindfolded candidates are conducted around the lodge room in a series of "perambulations," stopping in front of the three principal officers seated at the symbolic East, South, and West. At these stations, after the loud knock of a gavel, questions about the candidates' qualifications are demanded and answers given by the Deacon on their behalf.

As all of this is going on, there is often whispering between candidates and the conductors who physically (and emotionally) support them, typically combining instructions, resources, and supportive statements. Some respondents' germane comments:

> *Going through it with others helped.*
>
> *Leaning on a brother when you're blindfolded helps.*
>
> *My conductor was always talking in my ear as I went. He answered my questions and I never felt unsafe.*
>
> *I knew my conductor—my family doctor. That was reassuring.*
>
> *From his mannerisms, I realized that my father was my conductor. It was a proud moment.*

Of course, there were some interesting variations—both amusing and meaningful. There was one respondent who got a bit of a surprise when his "conductor banged me into a heating duct," to the great amusement of those present. Conversely, there were four respondents with some form of disability, such as needing to use a cane, and they found it very meaningful that the lodge accommodated them and ensured that conductors gave them extra support throughout. In the words of one man, this "revealed I was in with a good group."

As candidates were led around, obscure passages from scripture were read, unfamiliar songs sung, and candidates were generally exposed to elaborate ritual language utilizing archaic English forms, many spoke of how they listened and struggled to understand. Beyond the one respondent who spoke of "heightened hearing" and another who "recognized a voice," many simply claimed that they tried to "listen and pay attention as best I could." However, this was often difficult for various reasons. Beyond the many whose nerves interfered with comprehension, five complained about the "archaic language," seven more about the amount of new material amounting to "sensory overload," and two couldn't understand a speaker's accent. Indeed, one respondent joked about how the Deacon had a very thick accent and no front teeth, which "got me into a laughing fit"—an awkward moment to say the least. Thus there were comments such as

> *I couldn't understand a word.*
>
> *I didn't know what they were talking about.*
>
> *About 2 percent of it registered.*
>
> *I still can't identify the songs.*

Yet candidates soon face another challenge: after being briefly instructed in the ritual manner in which to walk, they are conducted to an altar in the centre of the lodge and told that, to proceed, they must make a sworn obligation to secrecy on the Bible (or another set of scriptures, as appropriate to the candidate) in front of all the brethren present. They are advised that there is nothing immoral about what is to follow, nor is there anything that will interfere with their other social or civic obligations (which one candidate pointedly claimed "calmed me down"). They are then asked if they wish to proceed. If they do (and I have never seen a candidate refuse), the Master of the lodge comes to the altar, the Deacon and conductors help candidates kneel in a ritually appropriate, awkward, and physically uncomfortable position, and they then repeat the Master's words with their hands on the book and key symbols of the lodge (the square and compasses). Respondents commented on what they saw as the positive and negative aspects of this:

> There's nothing more uncomfortable than being at the altar, especially in that yoga position.

> At my initiation, the Master asked my father to deliver the obligation on our family's Masonic Bible. That was quite something for me.

> It was very moving. These guys want me to make a promise to them and not break it all of my life. That's very special.

During the swearing of this obligation, they also dramatically hear, for the first time, the blood-curdling (yet symbolic) penalty for divulging the secrets of this degree. Simultaneously, those attending the candidates physically mimic the movements described on the blindfolded candidates, at times with dramaturgically staged sensible feelings translating into feelings of the lived body as a result (Denzin 1984, 1985). Respondents' comments included

> Hearing the penalty sure made me sit up and take notice!

> It [the penalty] was powerful. My father gave the penal sign ... [with] cold steel ...

> My father was a coal miner and his hands were rough. He gave the penal sign with his thumbnail and almost drew blood![4]

After candidates have finished swearing the obligation and seal it with their lips on the scriptures, a key dramatic moment of their initiation occurs. They are asked what their greatest desire is at that point, the Deacon whispers "light," the candidates so answer, the blindfold is suddenly and dramatically removed, and they are "brought to light"—often accompanied by a loud collective bang made by the brethren present.

While this is usually a very serious moment for all concerned, sometimes things go awry in amusing ways. Most notably, one respondent, when asked his greatest desire, said, "a beer" before the Deacon whispered "light." As the room began to erupt, the Deacon frantically whispered "light" into his ear, and the respondent said, "Okay, a light beer!"

All humour aside, however, after the sensory deprivation, physical discomforts, and the lived feelings that go along with them, a dramaturgically significant moment follows: suddenly, for the first time, candidates are able to, in the words of one man, "get a visual impression of the inside of the lodge" room that they have been led around, including the people, props costumes, and furnishings therein. The most prominent statements made by respondents, after they "finally get to see where I've been walking around," concerned the "rest of the crowd," many of whom surrounded them, lined up around the altar. Six respondents commented about being struck by the membership present, particularly in terms of occupational status, when known. Indeed, recognizing others was often the most meaningful result:

> *I was impressed by the Master. I knew him to be a prominent man.*

> *Okay, this isn't so bad. I recognize a few faces.*

> *I was surprised by the number of guys that I knew.*

> *The lodge was full of guys I had sailed with. It was like a submarine reunion.*

> *My co-workers showed up to welcome me in. It was a well-kept secret.*

Of course, there were other instances where recognizing others was more of a shock. One respondent recounted a story where a boss in his workplace had treated another employee very badly for some time. When this boss was initiated into the lodge, and he was brought to light, he was suddenly faced with this very same employee, who was the Master of the lodge. According to the respondent who witnessed all of this ("You should have seen the look on his face"), this revelation, and the fact that the mistreated employee "showed great character" by not blackballing his boss, had quite an impact on the boss's subsequent behaviour and character.

Beyond witnessing who was present, upon being brought to light, five respondents reported being impressed by the various Masonic dignitaries sitting facing them wearing elaborate regalia; five religious candidates reported being impressed by seeing the scriptures on the altar in front of them; and two respondents commented on the impressive architecture of the lodge room itself:

It looked like the House of Commons.

Masons try to decorate the lodge as a spiritual place.

The combined effect of this sudden sensory burst varied. Some respondents were overwhelmed, while others started to come to an initial understanding of what had happened thus far:

It was a very impressive moment. I was overwhelmed.

Suddenly all of the Master's words rushed into me and it all made sense.

The next step is for the candidates to be given the principal secrets of the degree that they have sworn to keep, along with comments on the penalty for divulging them. Generally the Master physically demonstrates the various steps and signs while candidates are at the altar, then asks the candidates to rise. After the rope is symbolically removed from around the candidates, the Master may then delegate another officer to demonstrate the secrets of the degree. In so doing, it is dramatically revealed to candidates the injuries that they have just avoided on entering the lodge. After this, the handshake and password are revealed, along with the specific procedure as to how these are to be discreetly given.

Being well versed in these secrets is important, because they involve how one Mason can ritually recognize and prove himself to another, especially when visiting a lodge where he may not know anyone. Thus, after the initial demonstration at the altar, candidates are again led around the room to the principal officers and made to demonstrate the signs, grips, and password to each. As one respondent stated,

I realized that the same questions were being asked and repeated many times, that they were trying to nail this into me.

Of course, as before, there are cases where things go awry, whether due to a candidate's incomplete initial understanding, poor hearing, or even difficulty understanding what was being said. Thus there are cases, such as that recounted by one respondent, where he could not understand the Deacon—who had "a thick accent." As he was being led around and tested, he simply "repeated the same gibberish to the Wardens," much to the amusement of all concerned until the wording was clarified.

Next, candidates are presented with a plain, white apron by the Senior Warden in the West, and its symbolic significance—both for stonemasons and historically in the construction of Solomon's Temple in the Old Testament—is briefly explained. They are told that this is the attire of a newly initiated Mason.[5]

From there, candidates are led to the northeast corner of the lodge, where a brief lecture is presented. The lecture makes a series of symbolic analogies between them and the cornerstone of a building, linking a well-ordered self to a well-constructed building, and all of this to social morality. Suddenly, the talk turns to charity and another dramatic twist occurs: candidates are "put on the spot" and asked to donate something to charity—yet, as noted earlier, they now have no valuables on their person, "not even a penny." Then, after a pregnant pause, it is explained to them that this was not done to play with their feelings but to impress upon them the moral importance of looking out for the less fortunate. Fourteen respondents commented on this, and on the feelings of the lived body involved:

> You feel like shit. It's like a real slap in the face, but the lesson hits home.

> I was scared to death.

> The way it was said, the Master's tone of voice, really hit home.

> It was humbling. I realized that you could have nothing and still have friendships.

Again, however, there were interesting exceptions, such as the man who claimed to be so "disoriented" by this point that he bluntly answered "No" when asked to give ("You should have seen the look on the Deacons' faces!"). All the same, there was another man who did get it who stated how he "now makes a point of putting a penny in," along with whatever else he gives, after every meeting: "It's personal to me."

After this moral lesson is driven home, two lectures are presented. The first is a lecture on the "working tools" of a Mason, in which the principal moral symbolism of Masonry is explained in relation to various hand tools used in stonemasonry; a series of analogies are drawn between the individual Mason and dressing a stone for building and fitting harmoniously into society and the spiritual universe. The second is the lecture ("tracing board") of the first degree. Each is presented by officers who have been delegated to do so. The officer presenting the former illustrates his points with props (physical tools) for emphasis, while the officer presenting the latter often works with an easel, chart, and pointer. Both deliver detailed presentations on the history, symbolism, morality, and significance of Freemasonry to help the newly initiated brethren at least begin to grasp what all of this ceremony has been about.[6]

Looking back on these presentations, thirteen respondents claimed to have been "impressed" by the lessons in the lectures, while the rest, who often remained nervous and disoriented by the experience, found the whole thing "confusing," claiming that it "went over my head." Yet one thing clearly stood out about these lectures: twenty-six respondents reported being deeply impressed that these presentations were recited entirely from memory. Indeed, when this was combined with a personal touch, such as when an old friend is brought in as a surprise to deliver a lecture, one respondent reported being "touched" and then wondering, "What's this I'm into here?"

It must be noted that this practice of memorization is something usually expected of everyone involved in putting on the ceremony of initiation. While there are variations both between and within lodges in their ability to adhere strictly to this standard, it is the usual ideal. When done particularly well, many would certainly agree with the words of one man who said:

> I'm impressed the degree team put on all of this work for me.

At this point, after receiving a few parting words from the Master, signing the lodge register, being led to the altar, and saluting (usually with assistance of the Deacon), candidates retire from the lodge room and get changed back into their clothes, and the lodge is closed prior to a social get-together afterwards.[7] As they do so, they often joke around, discuss what happened, and try to process what they have just gone through. At this point, impressions range from the experience having been either "terrifying" or "exciting" to "lengthy" and "ridiculous." Thus eight respondents, notably ones who had been particularly nervous beforehand, indicated that they found it "terrifying" and were "relieved" that it was over (indeed one claimed that he was "shaking" afterwards). Another five claimed that it had been "exciting" and an "adventure," followed by four who claimed both terror and excitement ("I was frightened, but not in the way I'd thought"). Conversely, three found that the ceremony stretched on for too long (one claimed to have thought, "Come on, get this over with"), while another two thought it was silly ("Some stuff seems kind of ridiculous at the time").

Once candidates get dressed, however, they meet up with the rest of the brethren to share food and drink, and there is usually a great deal of handshaking and congratulating, not only by those friends and family in the Craft, but by the many men who are present. There are often touching and meaningful aspects to this organized social support that respondents recall fondly even years later.

> My father presented me with my grandfather's Masonic pin after my initiation. He had taken it off [my grandfather's] lapel before they closed his coffin. I was stunned.

> My old boss came up to me after my initiation, shook my hand, and called me "Brother." That meant a lot.

Here we see the continuation of processes whereby interpersonal ties are translated into wider forms of solidarity, along with the ritual erosion of distinctions between personal and collective ties (Kaplan 2014). However, once the conviviality and the celebration are over and all have gone home (and some of these celebrations do go late), newly made Masons embark on a long process of coming to understand what has just happened. It is to that process that I now turn.

WORKING TOWARD UNDERSTANDING

While throughout the degree candidates' feelings of the lived body communicate "an emotional definition of the situation" (Denzin 1985, 230), in the liminal period following, new Masons often try to process this unusual experience, to construct meaning out of this disruptive breach (Garfinkel 1967; Mead 1934) and come to some sort of initial symbolic understanding. Overall, some do so more successfully than others. Indeed respondents' predominant "accounts" (Garfinkel 1967) fell into two large groupings: (1) those who claimed to form at least some sort of broad initial impression,[8] and (2) those who claimed to have found the experience largely incomprehensible.

The first grouping shows a sixfold variation, ranging from impressions that were more common and broad to those less frequent and specific. The first variation includes forty-nine respondents who felt a profound sense of being "welcomed" into the group, echoing both contemporary and historical works in this respect (Kaplan 2014; Hoffman 2001; Clawson 1989). Often because of the many friends, dignitaries, and brethren that came up to congratulate them in the social following their degree, such respondents recounted feeling a meaningful sense of "brotherly acceptance," even "belonging":

> I was amazed at the warmness of my reception for just passing through the ceremony, of the many brethren coming over to welcome me.

> I felt I was let into something wonderful.

> I felt like I had been embraced by a larger community.

> I felt like part of the crowd right from day one.

> It was touching. I got a strong sense that here were people that cared. I feel like part of the family now.

While there was still some degree of confusion in some ("I knew I had found something; I just didn't know what"), others found such "bonding" very meaningful. One even compared it to a marriage ceremony. Perhaps most dramatically in this respect, one respondent recounts how his brother, who had long resisted joining a lodge that included many members of his family in a small, rural community, suddenly called home late one night from another province in tears. He had been initiated there, then called his brother, claiming "I get it now"—and expressing profound regret and sorrow that he had not done so at his family's lodge back home.

The next aspect of this first grouping involved broad assessments of the initiation ceremony that contrasted prior nervousness with subsequent relief, even enjoyment. There were twenty-three respondents who made statements such as

> Once I learned to relax and enjoy the moment, it was quite enjoyable, educational, and fun.
>
> It wasn't as bad as I thought it was going to be. Why was I so worried?
>
> I enjoyed it, but I was glad to get through it.
>
> It was like a feeling of deliverance. My apprehensions disappeared that very night.

Thirdly in this respect, there were eighteen respondents who found themselves enamoured with the venerable tradition and history of the Craft as displayed in the initiation ceremony and its lecture. Given the prior historical interests of some who come to join the Craft, this was hardly surprising:

> I realized that this was a serious group with a rich history, high expectations, and serious obligations.
>
> I admired the beauty of the tradition, that the ritual has been the same for centuries.
>
> When I realized that I was reciting the same words as my grandfathers did, the sense of connection to my past was overwhelming.

The fourth variation involved fourteen respondents who initially saw their initiation as some sort of transforming "rite of passage" (Van Gennep 1960). One young university student explicitly interpreted the ceremony as "a rite of passage into my manhood." Other respondents spoke of passing through a "barrier," of experiencing a "renaissance" or "rebirth"; two added,

> I felt I came out a different person—for the better.
>
> I feel like I have a whole new reality, a whole new perception.

The potential identity-construction aspects here cannot be ignored.

Fifth, there were fifteen respondents who claimed that their initiation provoked an even deeper interest as to what Freemasonry was all about. Responses included

> *My initiation fostered a greater interest in me, a deeper curiosity about the meaning.*

> *The initiation made me want to learn more.*

In other words, for some, the dramaturgical interplay between induced anxiety, strategic information leakage, and social support resulting in increased curiosity continued to build after initiation.

The final—and closely related—variation in this respect involves fifteen respondents who claimed to have already experienced some degree of "intellectual stimulation" resulting from their initiation as they engaged in attempts to symbolically understand its significance (Mead 1934):

> *I didn't sleep a wink the night after the initiation. I kept replaying the significance, the impact, the strangeness of it all.*

> *I started to realize that I was being taken on a philosophical journey through life.*

> *I started a lifelong learning process. I realized that I needed to settle in for the long haul. It's an internal journey for me, and I suspect that's how it's supposed to work.*

In the second broad grouping, on the other hand, forty respondents claimed that they "didn't pick up too much from the ceremony," often describing it as a "blur." Thirteen of these described the ceremony as "confusing," another twelve asserting that they were "oblivious" to what was going on during their degrees. Indeed, twenty-five more respondents claimed that they "still didn't really know what happened" afterwards, eleven of these adding that "if asked what happened afterwards, I'd probably have drawn a blank." Finally, nine respondents spoke of how the "mystery" or "secrecy" of the experience held on for them throughout. Clearly, a substantial proportion of respondents initially found their initiation experience largely incomprehensible, lacking the indexical resources or typifications to understand (Garfinkel 1967; Schutz 1962).

Taken together, these various initial impressions of the initiation experience, among men who later went on to become active Masons, show diversity mainly in whether some predominant understanding has emerged or not and the degree of specificity within the impressions that do. While, of course, it is tempting to speculate that a greater number of men who do not go on to complete their degrees come from those confused by the initiation ceremony, these data cannot speak to that question. What is possible, however, is to note how some of the initial understandings proffered by respondents relate to themes noted in the previous chapter, such as, for example, (1) the contrast between the sense of anomie expressed by some prior to joining and the profound sense of "welcoming," "brotherhood," even "bonding" expressed afterward (Kaplan 2014; Hoffman 2001; Carnes 1989; Clawson 1989), which can serve as an example of how rituals building on trust and secrecy can result in aroused emotionality and a sense of authenticity sharply contrasting with today's "postemotional society" (Meštrović 1997); and (2) the interest in history and tradition later echoed in candidates' impressions of the first degree.

Yet this is not the whole story. Another reason that we may see variations in respondents' initial understanding of their initiation undoubtedly involves the quality of the degree work itself.

Respondents made many comments in this respect. On the one hand, fourteen respondents used complimentary terms in relation to how well their lodge did the degree work, including "professionalism," "knowledge," "power," and "respect." Indeed, there were another thirteen respondents who specifically noted the "solemnity" and the "reverential" way that their ceremony was conducted, nine adding that they "couldn't wait" to see what the next degree holds. On the other hand, five respondents were less than impressed by officers "walking around with the book" as they did their parts rather than memorizing them. That the dramatic quality of the work is significant was variously stated by fifteen respondents:

> When it sounds important, what we're doing is important.
>
> When it looks important, what we're doing seems so and vice versa.
>
> Doing ritual well gets candidates grounded in what Masonry is all about.
>
> Doing ritual poorly sends the wrong signal do both the candidate and observers.

Such comments appear to be particularly germane to those officers giving lectures. Of course, this raises the issue of delivery, and respondents had no shortage of opinions in this respect. On the positive side, ten respondents praised their lecturer's "eloquence"; six, his use of "proper inflection, dramatic pauses, and emphasis"; five, his "passion"; three, his "knowledge" of its meaning; and one, his "humour." Faced with a lecturer of this calibre, respondents stated,

> He had an impact on me I've never forgotten. When I talk about it I get a chill down my back.

*His delivery was so calm and easy, it was like he was having a
conversation with me.*

He fostered an intense interest in me.

Conversely, respondents gave various reasons as to how lectures—indeed
the degree itself—could be less than profound. Five claimed that it could "dis-
appoint" when done poorly and a lack of effort was evident ("take the time
to do it right"). Six did not like what they saw as "machine-gun delivery"
("knowing the words is only part of it"; "it means nothing to the candidate").
Then there was the issue of not speaking clearly, which irked five respondents.
Some were willing to make allowances, such as the man who stated, "It's okay
if the delivery is not perfect so long as the emotion is there," and another who
thought that "reading is okay if done with the proper tones and sincerity."
Nevertheless, the predominant view remained that quality in both memory
work and delivery made a big difference in candidates' understanding—and
assessment—of their initiation experience. Whether it has an impact upon
candidates failing to go further in Masonry is, of course, beyond these data—
though certainly a worthy topic for future research.

The above comments relate largely to respondents' initial impressions of
their initiation. However, the data evince a clear evolution in their understanding of the initiation experience over time. This was particularly the case for
those respondents above who found the ceremony confusing. Fully twenty-
seven respondents claimed that it was not until they shifted from candidate to
observer and witnessed others going through the ceremony that they began
to understand it. More broadly, twenty-one indicated that they "picked it
up" or "understood it better over time," followed by eleven asserting that
"each time you watch you see something new" or something "different."
As a result, nine noted how they gradually began to see "interconnections"
between various things such that the "puzzle pieces started to come together,"
six adding that they had gained an emerging appreciation of the "allegory"
involved in the ritual. While there were variations in how soon this "watch
and learn" process began—depending on how often lodges did degree work,
varying opportunities to visit and watch ceremonies elsewhere, the candidates'
schedules, interest, indexical resources, and intellectual abilities—even relatively new candidates spoke of the importance of watching others' initiations
to their understanding of what they had gone through:

I could sit back. I wasn't under pressure as a candidate.

*I watch and listen actively—and the first time I saw it, I did
particularly intently.*

Watching the ritual stirs memories of what it was like for you.

Substantive meanings that respondents took from the ceremony also evolved in this process. Some came to a "basic" understanding of how the ceremony was a "morality play" or "story" based in the Bible that provided the "symbolic basis" or "foundation for the Masonic lifestyle." Others put more work into it and spoke of how they came to construct a symbolic understanding of the "life lessons" in the degree later on (Mead 1934):

> It wasn't just that a whole bunch of stuff happened. In fact, even though I was robbed of at least one of my senses and all my worldly possessions, there was a rhyme and reason to it. There was a pattern. And in fact, once revealed, the whole thing was interconnected. And I went away from that night thinking, "Wow, that's very interesting. That's a good lesson on life."

Indeed, some respondents over time spoke of how the ritual provided one of the few ways to get into the "deeper aspects," even the "essence" of Freemasonry by providing a "starting point" or putting a "structure" in place enabling members to "research the deeper meanings" and interpret them from where they stand:

> I've come to the realization that what you see there often obscures what you don't see, and that where you are in your life, even what's on your mind that day, has an impact on the philosophical lessons you perceive as important.

Nevertheless, respondents noted that "you have to work at it—otherwise you only get the really basic stuff."

In time, such work might involve participating in portraying the ceremonies themselves. However, between their first and second degrees, two further interrelated factors reportedly impacted respondents' evolving understanding of what they had gone through: the first was mentoring, and the second was the memorization of a series of specific ritual lines in order to "prove up" before their next degree.

Mentoring involves a range of supportive, educational activities whereby the lodge provides opportunities for newly initiated brethren to learn more about Masonry. Where present, these range from informal practices such as brethren expressing willingness to go through what happened with new Masons and visit other lodges, through the lodge assigning a particular brother or brothers to assist them, to, at the most formal, having new brethren participate in a structured "mentoring program" to educate them about the Craft. Indeed, both Grand Lodges in this study have put in place formal mentoring programs, in which lodges participate to varying degrees; as well, particular lodges in each jurisdiction often institute varying programs of their own to help educate new candidates. Respondents generally spoke favourably about these, forty-two noting that having people "walk you through what happened" and "explain" things (i.e., provide indexical, interpretive resources/typifications) helped them to "understand" the experience better:

> It's one thing to go through the ritual, but if it's never explained you don't necessarily get the meaning.

In particular, twelve respondents stressed the importance of "one-on-one personal contact" in this respect, particularly that mentors and other brethren stay in contact to "ensure we're not left on our own." Six emphasized "regular get-togethers" in "a non-threatening environment," five more adding how "elders" in the lodge were very helpful. Indeed one respondent strongly emphasized how being offered brethren's personal phone numbers was meaningful to him. Respondents who had such support were more likely to relate comments such as the following in the context of mentoring:

> All of a sudden the mist cleared and I could see how things were connected.

Conversely, poor or non-existent mentoring was commented upon negatively by respondents:

> The mentoring program existed on paper, but I had a mentor who did not ment. Offering to get together the night before my next degree was not enough.

> I had no mentoring. It was just like "show up for your next degree and have fun."

> When are we going to learn something?

Indeed, nine respondents decried the lack of mentoring in their lodges, another eleven adding that there should be more time for education and the development of candidates' understanding before moving on to the next degree. Furthermore, one respondent expressed a fear that his lodge was losing candidates before they moved on to the next degree as a result.

Mentoring was particularly important for another reason. New brethren are always assigned a specific educational task upon the completion of their initiation ceremony: they are given a little booklet containing a series of lines that they must memorize, relating to the degree that they have just completed. They are told that before they can proceed further, they will have to present these verbatim in open lodge, "proving up" to render them eligible to take the next degree. This is an unexpected dramatic twist for most. Needless to say, rote memorization is an unfamiliar task for most people today, and many respondents were somewhat taken aback by this dramaturgical project.

> *The catechism made me nervous. My memory is not that good.*

> *The next morning, I stared at the little blue book, then looked at the trash can real hard.*

> *There's no way that I can do this before the next meeting.*

Indeed, twenty-three respondents spoke of how having to memorize their lines provoked a new sense of anxiety in them. Moreover, such memorization anxiety often came swift on the heels of relief over completing their initiation ceremony. Yet there were also variations in the lived expression of such anxiety, and reasons were given in this regard. On one hand, respondents claimed that this was a more daunting task for candidates with poor memories, little time due to other commitments, or poor English skills in the face of archaic ritual language, as well as for those facing lengthier texts in different jurisdictions,[9] those working alone, those who procrastinated, and those who lacked effective mentoring, communication, or support. On the other hand, those who claimed "I can remember stuff fairly easily" or who felt they had sufficient time to study, had shorter "catechisms" to learn, had good English skills, were able to spread the task over time, and had strong mentoring from members of the lodge claimed less difficulty.

Beyond these factors, one strategy loomed particularly large in helping a candidate successfully prove up: teamwork (Goffman 1959). Seven respondents spoke of how they "split stuff up" to memorize it; another three of "working with my fellow candidates." Beyond those respondents who studied alone or with the support of their sponsor or mentors, such co-operative practices had two key benefits: (1) they "made it easier" (per nine respondents), and (2) they facilitated "bonding" among candidates:

> *We became tight through the process and remained friends for years.*

> [Working together] *was a good start to the idea of brotherhood.*

Candidates who go through alone, however, do not have either of these strategies available, and thus working together with their sponsor or a mentor becomes more critical for support.

Over time, respondents noted that, whether they largely studied together or studied alone in places like the car or the bathroom, they found two things: (1) that "you get the flow of it" (e.g., "It's almost like a mantra"), and (2) that the process of memorization enables the ideas to "sink in more," eventually fostering reflection in the "phenomenological stream" (Denzin 1982) and the reflexive construction of symbolic understandings (Garfinkel 1967; Mead 1934).

> Quite frankly, I got the little book to study, looked at it and thought, "This is silly." But once you start going through it for a while, you start seeing things. Stuff starts jumping out at you from something that—on the surface at least—just looks like a silly text. I could see in doing this, in repeating, going through the material like I did, that there's a lot more written between the lines than there's written in the lines. There's an awful lot of symbolism there, a lot of stuff that you may not see unless you do repeat it over and over. That kept my curiosity high throughout the process.
>
> It may not have meaning now, but it will be there for you to access and will stick out at the right time.

Yet, when it was time to perform, "performance anxiety" quickly became an issue (e.g., "I'm the kind of guy that aces everything until the exam"). Six respondents spoke of lived feelings, such as increasing "stage fright," as the day of their examination approached—well aware that it would be more difficult to recite their lines "onstage" in front of the brethren in lodge:

> Once you do the initial thing, they ask you to memorize some material. You've got to speak it in front of everybody. That was hard; my memory is not the greatest. It took about two months to memorize the passages they gave me. Once I read it and had it going good I felt really great. But then, I had to do it. That's when it hit me, when I was about to walk on and I knew they were going to call me up to recite my memorization. The butterflies hit big time, my knees got a little weak there. But I had a friend, my guide. He was the one asking me the questions, and it was nice to have a friend there with me. It made it easier, and I pulled it off really well, so I was glad.

Here another dramatic twist takes place. Respondents usually discovered—to their surprise—that they were capable of much more extensive memory work than they had previously thought. As well, several respondents who did this as a group spoke of how they continued to support each other by whispering hints during the exam; others commented on how they have witnessed a line of candidates on the floor where one is speaking his lines and the rest are mouthing them quietly to themselves. Thus a sense of further bonding can go hand in hand with this exercise in memorization and performance; in the words of one respondent, "Aye, we were there together on that night."[10]

Of course, the men who complete this ordeal are usually given a round of applause for their hard work, as well as formal and informal congratulations by the brethren afterwards. Thus relief is often accompanied by much social support and feelings of elation at having accomplished such a feat. Indeed, the upshot of having completed this process, among the ten respondents who commented, was "a great sense of accomplishment afterwards" (i.e., a positive sense of self and identity):

> *I felt alive in so many ways I hadn't felt.*
>
> *I was proud of myself, especially since I did it alone.*
>
> *You surprise yourself. Once you do it, the words stick with you and you could do it again.*
>
> *Now I'm getting more confident when I speak.*

Thus, all of the above dramaturgical activity combines to stage—indeed, to organizationally enable—personal and emotional results (Zurcher 1982, 1985).

At this point, once respondents have taken the time to do the work and have proven up in open lodge, they are eligible to move on to take the second degree.

THE SECOND DEGREE

It is commonly said that the first degree symbolizes birth, the movement from darkness to light, while the second degree exemplifies education and work, the movement from ignorance to knowledge. In many respects, the second degree builds upon the basic moral and symbolic teachings of the first, but the ritual emphasizes that candidates work to educate themselves in both the "liberal arts and sciences" and the "hidden mysteries of nature and science" exemplified in Masonry. In the process, it significantly elaborates the central story of Masonry—the building of Solomon's Temple—and elaborates the significance of its symbolism for the Masonic Craftsman.

The second, or "Fellowcraft" degree, is relatively short, contains many phases that are similar to the first, and is frequently overlooked by Masons— often seen as a "stepping stone" to the ultimate goal of completing the third degree and becoming a full-fledged Master Mason (e.g., "I was anxious to get it over with"). If taken in that sense, it may effectively serve as a ritualized form of liminality that occurs within a broader liminal frame (Turner 1967, 1969). While I have heard Masons claim that this outlook is unfortunate given the intricate symbolism and lessons contained therein, the plain fact is that respondents themselves made significantly fewer comments about the second degree compared to those made about the first and the third. Indeed, there were contrasting comments such as the following:

The second degree holds a great deal of meaning that many times is glossed over.

I don't remember much about it.

Thus, before moving on to the third degree, I will provide a brief overview of the second degree ceremony, interspersed with respondents' relevant comments as appropriate.

At the outset, candidates again arrive at the lodge and are taken to the preparation room. Things are much less unfamiliar to them this time around, as they have already seen the inside of a lodge room, have met the brethren, and have a baseline against which to compare their experience—notably that their original fears were not realized. Respondents' comments prior to the degree include the following:

I'm starting to relax by this point. I'm not as nervous, but still excited.

There wasn't so much teasing this time around.

I've heard it's supposed to be a bit harder.

Briefly, the second degree proceeds as follows. Candidates again change clothes, with but slight variations in the ritual costume, and are conducted to the door of the lodge. Upon the appropriate knocks, there is an exchange with the Deacon, and soon after candidates are conducted into the lodge room. They are again immediately challenged, and they are received on the point of a square applied to their naked breast. Following this, they kneel for a prayer and are then conducted around the lodge to show that they are both properly prepared and proficient in giving the appropriate ritual responses and gestures of the first degree. The Deacon, meanwhile, prompts the candidates when necessary, particularly in giving a password leading from the first to the second degree (which they would have been given by the Master in open lodge prior to getting changed). Upon being taught by the Senior Warden to approach the East in due form, candidates are again conducted to the altar to take the obligation of the second degree. They are again told by the Master that there is nothing immoral about this, and that there is nothing that will conflict with their other obligations. After expressing willingness to proceed, the Master descends from the East to give the obligation, which the candidates repeat on the scriptures and key symbols at the altar. After the obligation and penalty are sworn, the candidate witnesses the brethren standing around him giving the appropriate ritual gestures of this degree. The Master demonstrates these signs and their significance in relation to the obligation and penalty, then proceeds to demonstrate the handshakes and secrets of the second degree with the assistance of the Deacon. Following this, candidates are conducted to the two Wardens and tested, with the assistance of the Deacon, in the things they have just been shown. They are then presented with the appropriate apron and the working tools of this degree, and the moral significance of these is explained.

Ultimately, much of the above is not that dissimilar to what candidates experienced in the first degree, hence respondents' comments, such as

> *There's a certain amount of repetition.*
>
> *It builds on the first [degree].*
>
> *You feel like you're really getting it now.*

It is at this point that the real centrepiece of this degree occurs: the lecture (known alternately as the "second degree tracing board" or the "Middle Chamber lecture," depending on the jurisdiction). While varying somewhat in both detail and length between the two jurisdictions studied, this highly intricate and symbolic lecture, at its most basic, tells the story of the construction of Solomon's Temple, its description and symbolism, the various craftsmen involved, the derivation of the Fellowcraft password, and its use when Masons proceeded up a winding staircase to collect their wages in the middle chamber of the temple. The striking symbolism—and considerable length—of this allegorical lecture was commented on by respondents:

> *I was mesmerized by the Senior Deacon's delivery of the Middle Chamber lecture. Not only was his memory phenomenal, he was so animated and passionate about how he told the story that I just stood there stunned.*
>
> *I really like the imagery of working your way up the stairs and through the doorways, along with the historical aspect.*
>
> *Learning the principles of "brotherly love, relief, and truth" were key for me.*

Of course, as in the first degree, the impact of this central lecture varies depending on the quality of its presentation. Hence, again there were respondents who complained about "too much information" being "delivered with no breath or stop," calling attention to the importance of preparation and delivery for candidates' experiences.

After the lecture, salutes, and so on, candidates again leave the lodge, get changed back into their clothes, and retire for a social with the rest of the brethren, where they are congratulated by all and sundry. Afterwards, respondents reflected upon the experience, some constructing understandings as they went:

The second degree I like to call "being shown the ropes," because that describes what happens in the degree. It's a further explanation of what you've seen, and it builds on the first and brings you into some of the principles or tenets of Freemasonry. You sort of feel, after the second degree and you're Fellowcraft, you really feel like you've got it now.

Some of this degree was more logical, really a bit clearer. I got a little more out of it.

Yet, before leaving, candidates are again given a little book to study to enable them to prove up before taking the third degree. Respondents were thus faced with "more memory work" and somewhat split on whether it would be harder (due to length) or easier (due to similar phrasing overlapping with what they studied the first time). Beyond being "anxious to get it over with," many of respondents' earlier comments about (1) understanding more by watching the ceremony again; (2) the role of mentoring in education; and (3) the intersection of nerves, studying, and co-operation to prove up apply equally to the period between the second and the third degree and need not be repeated here. Thus I now turn to the culminating ceremony in candidates' experience: the third, or Master Mason, degree.

THE THIRD DEGREE

After "proving up" again, and experiencing the combined sense of accomplishment and relief that goes along with it, candidates move on to take their third and final Craft degree—in the words of one respondent, an "epic test of faith, hope, and charity" that lives up to its name.[11] Respondents typically claimed that this was the "main event" or "the most important of them all" and that becoming a Master Mason was "the goal that all want to get to."

Upon entering the hall and again getting prepared for the ceremony, eleven respondents reported feelings of "excitement"(e.g., "Part of me wants to see some magic stuff happen"; "I'm expecting a little bit of enlightenment"), while another ten reported "nervousness" or worse (e.g., "I was terrified despite having gone through the others"). Conversely, there were nine respondents at this liminal threshold who claimed to have been relatively nonchalant, who seemed to have been lulled into a false sense of security, thinking what was to come simply involved "more of the same" (e.g., "I feel like I'm already a Master Mason, that this is just one more thing where I'm going through the motions"). Similarly, there were another eight who were satisfied with their progress to date and not really concerned about their ability to get through another level (e.g., "I've done the studying to this point and seem to have passed this far").

Various reasons were given for respondents' feelings prior to the degree. Some said that excitement had "rub[bed] off" from interactions with excited brethren while preparing for the degree, or was due to the fact that Masonic friends and family were coming in specially for the ceremony. Nervousness, in turn, was related to the increased teasing that often goes hand in hand with the third degree (e.g., "Oh, you're going to see the lights tonight!"). Nonchalance, finally, was related to past experience, as above, as well as a number of management approaches, including conversations with others (e.g., "Dad went through this. He wouldn't let anything happen to me that's bad"); "getting to know the guys' sense of humour"; having "too much other stuff on my plate"; and even, in one case, to medication (e.g., "I was on medication for an injury and cool as a cucumber for the third degree. The old fellows were upset because I was so calm despite their teasing").

After candidates change in the preparation room, are ritually prepared, and the lodge is ready, a knock is made at the inner door, a challenge is made, and various lines exchanged before the candidates are admitted to the lodge. Again, they are conducted into the lodge room and received on the point of a sharp instrument, this time the points of a compass applied to both naked breasts. They kneel for prayer and, when done, are conducted around the lodge, saluting the Master and being examined by the two Wardens on their proficiency in the ritual signs and gestures of the two previous degrees. This also serves to show the brethren present that they are ritually prepared for the upcoming degree. Following a stop at the Master's station, where they are instructed in the grip and password leading from the second to the third degree, they are conducted to the Senior Warden, who instructs the Senior Deacon to teach them how to approach the East by the appropriate ritual steps. Once at the altar, they are then dramatically informed:

> A most serious trial of your fortitude and fidelity, and a more solemn obligation await you. Are you prepared to meet them as you ought?

Once the candidate assents, they are again made to kneel at the altar with their hands on the scriptures and principal symbols of Masonry to take the obligation. The Master descends from the East and the brethren surround the altar as before, while candidates swear the obligation and hear the penalty they are to face upon its transgression.[12] They are then again "brought to light," and the Master calls attention to the position of the symbols and assists the newly obligated candidate to his feet.

Up to this point, there is much similarity with what candidates have been through before, and they could be forgiven for thinking as much. Yet, this is where things change—both for candidates and between the differing rituals of the two jurisdictions.

In the Grand Lodge of Nova Scotia, the candidate is again taught the various signs, grips, and words of the degree by the Master (with the assistance of the Deacon), conducted to the two Wardens to be tested in their proficiency, and presented with their Master Mason's apron before retiring back to the preparation room. Up to this point, respondents often think that they have simply gone through more of the same and that they are now finished the degree. Yet they are soon informed that they are not, and that they will be returned to the lodge room individually to complete the rest of the ceremony.

This sudden, dramatic twist often provokes nervousness and, often, when there are several candidates, there is discussion among them as to who will go first or last. As each candidate goes in, those that remain often get more and more nervous. Thus there is one story of a group of candidates playing pool in another room while awaiting their turn, knocking more and more balls off the table as their numbers dwindled and their anxiety increased. Similarly, there is the story of one man waiting behind in the preparation room whose fellow candidate had been particularly nervous. After this nervous colleague had been inside for a while, the various surprises he encountered caused the man to let out "blood-curdling screams." As a result, after each scream, the respondent noted that "the Tyler was almost bursting at the look on my face."

Upon re-entering the lodge, each candidate is dramatically informed by the Master,

> You are not yet a Master Mason … nor do I know that you will ever become a Master Mason. You have a way to travel that is extremely perilous. You will be beset by dangers of many kinds and may perhaps meet with death, as did once befall an eminent brother of this degree.

Respondents reported being "shocked" by this sudden dramatic change, and this was added to when they were told that they must again be blindfolded, return to the altar, kneel, and, rather than have someone else pray for them as before, "now you must pray for yourself." Reactions included the following:

> *I lost it a bit there. I could see the smirks on the faces.*

> *Then the blindfold goes back on. I'm like, "O My God, I thought I was there!"*

They are then informed that, in the drama that follows, they will be playing the part of the principal architect of King Solomon's temple, Hiram Abiff. This drama (which is largely described in lectures rather than acted out under the Grand Lodge of Newfoundland and Labrador), in Nova Scotia often involves many members of the lodge and, in some places, is even done in full costume.

As each blindfolded candidate is conducted around the room, the story of Hiram is recounted: a group of workmen had conspired to violently extort from him the principal secrets of a Master Mason, and they had sealed off the various entrances of the temple while he was engaged in noontime prayers. As the candidate moves around the room, he is suddenly accosted physically by brethren playing each of these renegade workmen at the various gates. The Deacon answers for the candidate that he "would rather die" than give up the secrets, and each "ruffian" individually threatens the candidate violently. One candidate remarked on his feelings:

> My conductor said I'd rather die; meanwhile I'm thinking, "Shut up!"

In fact, it is at this point in the drama where much of the "horseplay" traditionally begins (much more common in the past; "roughness" in the portrayal is frowned on by Grand Lodges today). Brethren portraying each of the ruffians physically accost and threaten the blindfolded candidate in succession, provoking "feelings of the lived body" and reflexive accounts (Denzin 1985; Garfinkel 1967). Respondents commented,

> The ruffians put the fear of God into me.
>
> One ruffian grabbed me, then moved me around to further confuse me.
>
> Bang! I thought, "You just wait until …"
>
> They surprised me. I was ready to fight.
>
> The ruffians were rough in my day. They left marks on my shoulder.
>
> Suddenly I heard my godfather's voice as the ruffian; then he belted me.
>
> Oh, dear God, they're going to dump my body in the harbour.

Indeed, this part of the drama provides some of the more memorable anecdotes reported by respondents. In addition to the "blood-curdling screams" of another candidate that so frightened the respondent in the preparation room, another respondent, when challenged by one of the ruffians, simply said—to the amusement of those present—"It's late, and I'd like to go home now." Other respondents had a more robust response: "He shook me and I shook him back." Nevertheless, things could still progress assertively:

> My cousin got a police sergeant to be one of the ruffians. The guy literally picked me up and shook me, and my feet weren't touching the floor!

> *My third ruffian was really cranky. He grabbed me, dragged me to the steps, and growled "We ain't got time for this foolishness."*

In the story of the drama, the first two ruffians encountering Hiram are said to injure him, then, each time, he stumbles forward to the next exit trying to escape. However, the last time, the candidate is led up several short steps to meet the third ruffian. Simultaneously, brethren quietly form up behind the candidate firmly holding a canvas. At the culmination of this last ritual confrontation, the third ruffian suddenly strikes him with a padded "setting maul," then pushes him backwards into the canvas as the brethren below catch him. Respondents commented on the lived feelings they experienced:

> *I heard a smack, then suddenly found myself lying in a canvas.*
>
> *I was completely blindsided. It was really cool.*
>
> *In those days, the knock-down was quite something.*
>
> *It was fun for the others, but terrifying for the candidate.*

Yet, the data reveal that a number of things must be said about this dramatic part of the degree. Beyond amusing anecdotes given by respondents claiming that "the guys barely had time to put the canvas behind me," or that "the guys were having trouble holding the canvas tight," the fact is that there are variations in both ritual practices and respondents' experiences. Thus there was widespread agreement that this part of the degree was much "rougher in the past," with Grand Lodges prohibiting the more vigorous horseplay today, and most lodges going along. Indeed, I have noted three historical variations on this in the data, ranging from both the roughest to the gentlest, the past to the present: (1) being pushed into the canvas, then tossed in the air before being laid down on the floor; (2) being pushed into the canvas, then laid down; and (3) being laid down gently by brethren onto the floor. Respondents' relevant comments on these variations include

> *It was rough in those days, but care was taken that you weren't hurt.*
>
> *It's still rough in some rural places, but you have to search to find it.*
>
> *We gauge the level of roughness to the candidate.*
>
> *I went along with it. I knew and trusted these guys.*
>
> *It was all done in good taste.*

They were gentle with me, and someone said, "Just lay back and relax."

Up to this point, I have discussed the drama of the third degree as portrayed in the Grand Lodge of Nova Scotia. However, this ritual murder, where the candidate plays the victim, is not as often acted out in such an elaborate fashion in the two Newfoundland and Labrador jurisdictions.[13] Instead, more often following contemporary Emulation working, following the obligation there is a speech where the candidate is instructed that the point of this degree is to "instruct you how to die." Then, after being conducted to the centre of the lodge, the Master essentially describes the story above to the blindfolded candidate, while the Wardens on either side gently mimic the ruffians' blows with the appropriate symbolic tools. The Master gives the final tap to the candidate with the padded setting maul, who is then gently laid down either in a canvas or on a cloth resembling a grave. As above, there have been variations historically in how roughly things were done. In some older rituals, the canvas was used and candidates were "bounced off the ceiling"; even today, in some rural areas, there are lodges where, in the words of one respondent, "I'd pay to go and see their degree work." Yet, for the most part, given legal and insurance concerns and the position of Grand Lodges, vigorous horseplay is getting rarer all the time in favour of the practices found in the newer ritual described above.

At this point, the candidate in either jurisdiction represents the murdered master architect Hiram, lying in a grave due to his fidelity in not betraying the secrets of a Master Mason under threat of violence from those undeserving of them. Candidates spoke of the profound, sometimes vicariously amplified feelings of the lived body (Denzin 1985) engendered during this "grave scene" where, in a darkened room, they were "actually put in a symbolic grave," sometimes alongside other candidates who had gone in before them.

Things really slowed down and I could sense the tension in the room.

I felt the other candidate's hand in the darkness. I was afraid.

It made me think of the end when it comes. It was life-changing.

This is what it's like to die.

All the while, in between hymns, the story of Hiram continues. Whether it is acted out, as in Nova Scotia, or simply further described, as in much of Newfoundland and Labrador, candidates are told that, after Hiram's death, King Solomon was informed of the murder conspiracy by other workmen, who had backed away from participating in the crime. These workmen were told that their fate would depend on their ability to bring the others to justice, and they were sent out in a search party to find the killers. In time, they found both Hiram's body and the killers, who had been unable to flee the country due to a travel edict issued by the king. The murderers were subsequently brought to justice and executed according to the penalties of the three degrees—which they had each been overheard saying by the search party in their guilt and remorse immediately prior to capture. The king, meanwhile, in his sorrow, travelled to Hiram's gravesite, and with the assistance of others, attempted to remove the body from the grave using the various grips of the Masonic degrees. The first two failed, but the king then raised the body using a new grip, that of the third degree.

It is during this story that candidates in both jurisdictions are built up to the dramatic culmination of the third degree. While lying in the symbolic grave in the darkened room, their hands are grasped symbolically in the first two grips, but to no avail. However, when given the grip of the third degree by the Master, they suddenly find themselves "raised" to their feet and embraced in a ritually significant position. The secret Master Mason's word is whispered in their ear, the blindfold is removed, and they suddenly see the Master, with the charter of the lodge above him, in the presence of all the brethren. Being "raised" is probably the most dramatic part of the degree. Respondents' comments included the following:

> I'm still in awe of the moment the blindfold was removed.

> When [the Master] slapped his hand on my back and whispered the words in my ear, [it] hit home.

> He was a big guy, a real ritualist, and he meant what he was doing. They're something you'd expect in a real friend.

> The symbolic death and resurrection was profound.[14]

The degree is almost over at this point, with the exception of the candidates being instructed in further signs, the position and manner in which the Master's word is given, the word itself, and the sign of distress. They also hear a lecture further explaining the symbolic and historical significance of the ceremony. After this, they are formally welcomed as full-fledged Master Masons, the lodge is closed, and all proceed to another bout of congratulations and refreshments.[15]

AFTER THE DEGREES ARE DONE

After completing the third degree, and at least formally moving from the formal liminal phase into incorporation (Van Gennep 1960), newly minted Master Masons over time continue to work toward understanding the experience, to more practically exit a lingering realm of the "betwixt and between"—much as they have in relation to the other degrees. Respondents had a series of broad initial impressions in this respect. Thus, eight commented that this degree was a "powerful experience," three that it's "something that you won't forget," three that "the whole thing had meaning to me," and two that "there's no other experience like it."

Another broad theme, indeed, one brought forward from earlier degrees, revolves around the ideas of belonging, bonding, and support (Kaplan 2014; Hoffman 2001; Clawson 1989), reflecting the further claims of intimacy afforded by the ritual collapse of personal and collective ties (Kaplan 2014). Thus, after completing their third degree, fourteen respondents claimed that they felt the brethren would be there for them if needed:

> I got the sense that they were with me, behind me, even ahead of me to aid me.

> If you make a mistake, they will support you. If you have problems, it's not held against you.

Twelve spoke of the brethren in terms of their goodness and potential friendship:

> I've never met so many wonderful men in my life.

> A lot of good men have gone through this.

> There's a tightness in the group; we're deeper and closer friends.

> I stayed close to the people who were there that night.

> I consider every one of the brothers a friend and warm up to them easily.

There were also two more involved symbolic interpretations that emerged out of the succession of breaches (Garfinkel 1967), the rolling series of dramatic disruptions involved (Mead 1934). One man stated,

> My revelation at the end of the third degree was "Hey, all those explanations that I got in the first and second degree that I thought revealed Masonry, they had explanatory power, but didn't reveal anything at all." During the third degree a whole other layer is revealed. I think it's a very interesting philosophy that I took right back out of the lodge into life: just because someone explains anything to you with a given set of facts, doesn't mean the explanation is correct.

Indeed, there was even one man who went so far as to claim to have experienced "déjà vu" during the third degree, prompting him to speculate on such mystical and metaphysical ideas as karma.

Overall, respondents' impressions of the third degree were overwhelmingly positive. There were, however, two whose initial impressions were less favourable:

> *Initially I was disappointed: where's the magic bullet?*

> *I had little or no experience from the degree. It was weird.*

Many would agree with the respondent who claimed that "not everyone takes away the same things," and, as before, the significance of what they have gone through did dawn upon some respondents over time:

> *I didn't get the meaning until I saw it a few times.*

> *I had to work toward a deeper understanding over time.*

> *I'm still discussing, reading, and figuring out the degree and its meaning.*

> *There's always new things to see and learn.*

Ultimately, completing the third degree and becoming a Master Mason served as both an end and a beginning. Finishing their Craft degrees rendered respondents eligible to take an office and to begin their Masonic careers. Indeed, five respondents indicated that completing their degrees fostered greater curiosity and interest in the Craft, one adding that the responsibilities he later assumed as a result enabled him to learn more:

> *I learned more about Freemasonry by teaching candidates from the new Grand Lodge book than I did in the previous five years of meetings, minutes, and bills combined.*

This, of course, leads to another side of the period following the completion of respondents' degrees: ongoing involvement. While factors impacting this will be discussed at length in another chapter, suffice it to say that four respondents, in the context of completing their degrees, said something akin to the following:

> *My interest continued, even grew, but the others I went in with did not [feel the same way].*

This raises the difficult question of attrition following the degrees— one which the present data can only partially answer. Nevertheless, in the following chapters, factors and observations that long-standing Masons claim relate to involvement will be discussed at length, shedding some light on this issue. At this point, however, it is appropriate to elaborate the final issue that relates to respondents' experiences thus far: how the degrees were done.

HOW DEGREES WERE DONE

Respondents discussed a series of factors, building on those discussed earlier, that contributed to the overall quality of the candidates' degree experiences. These may be grouped as (1) family participation, (2) the presence of other key figures, (3) the composition of the candidate group, (4) the quality of the work, (5) logistics, and (6) the ongoing controversy surrounding accelerated degree programs in some jurisdictions. Each will be dealt with in turn.

First, respondents spoke of how their degree experience was greatly enhanced by the presence or involvement of family, which, given the relatively large number of respondents with family connections, goes hand in hand with their original reasons for joining noted in the previous chapter. There were four respondents who spoke of how meaningful it was to have their father present; four, of participation in the degree by family members; and, most notably, two whose fathers delivered their obligation and two whose fathers raised them. Indeed, one man recounted how his obligation was taken on the family Bible; another, what a special surprise it was to be presented with his late grandfather's apron, and still another, how the lodge secretly arranged for his stepfather to fly in for his degree, commenting that he "almost cried" when he saw him. It is not unusual for such family involvement, when it occurs, to significantly enhance the degree experience. Not only does one often "get the full treatment" for that reason, I have personally witnessed degrees, such as one where a young man was put through the third degree by his father and two grandfathers serving in the principal offices, in which proud tears were quietly shed by otherwise taciturn, stoic older men. Such examples speak volumes—not only about gender, but also about the merging of personal and collective solidarity (Kaplan 2014).

Second, and relatedly, respondents spoke of their degree experience being enhanced by individuals other than family who were present. Some were impressed by "all the brass there that night." Others recount seeing men who had played a significant role in their lives. Thus there were stories, such as that recounted by a long-standing member of the military who was "awestruck" when his former sergeant major from basic training, "who was just short of God," came to the floor and spoke to him warmly after the degree.

Third, the size and composition of the group going through played a role in respondents' degree experience. I have already noted the sense of camaraderie experienced by candidates who go through together, and, of the thirty-one respondents who provided information in this regard, twenty-four emphasized how they appreciated having someone else to commiserate with in this respect—several even claiming that "I would never want to do this alone." Indeed, while one respondent countered that "when you go through with a group, you miss something, as not all get the full treatment," the seven who did go through alone nevertheless claimed that this fact alone made the degree more "stressful" as a result. Apart from the size of the group, the three respondents who went through the degree with friends and one who went through with his brother reported a positive experience, while the four who went through with "strangers" regretted not having had any time to "bond" with their fellow candidates beforehand.

Fourth, as stated earlier, the quality of respondents' degree work plays a major role in their appreciation of the lessons taught therein, and respondents' above comments in that respect apply *mutatis mutandis* here in relation to all three degrees. A lodge that did the work necessary to present degrees with professionalism, solemnity, respect, and obvious effort tended to garner better impressions from respondents. Indeed, in such cases, certain snafus did not seem to dampen the impression. Thus, one prominent Mason laughingly recounted how his canvas in the third degree "smelled of furnace oil," but still spoke highly of his degree experience. Even those who had been through a bit of a rough ride spoke favourably:

> *It was rough at times, but they were compassionate. They gave a good impression in their work, unlike some.*

> *Despite the roughness, I was treated very well, and the guys were right there to shake my hand afterwards.*

Indeed, one man recounted that a candidate in his lodge was accidentally injured, went to the hospital, got stitched up, and then promptly returned to the lodge to finish his degree! The candidate remains active and supportive of his lodge to this day.

Nevertheless, as in relation to the first degree, respondents were less forgiving of lacklustre degree work, where officers "didn't know their parts," were "walking around with the book," or "seemed confused about where to be and when." When combined with things like "tedious, monotone reading" or "machine-gun delivery" of the lectures, the meaningfulness of respondents' degree experience suffered.

> *If people invest what they're doing with enthusiasm, people get a lot more out of it. In some respects, the way things are done, it just does not come out. They don't derive the emotional impact that they could. We have to find a way to bring this to the enactment of ritual to keep people there rather than just do it by rote in a dry and unappealing fashion.*

Fifth, a series of logistical considerations played a part in respondents' degree experiences. These involved the ordering of candidates, where the degrees were done, whether respondents were left waiting beforehand, whether respondents were eligible to attend lodge meetings in between their degrees, the length of time it took to become a Master Mason, and special accommodations made for candidates. Four respondents pointed to the importance of their lodge arranging for multiple candidates to be "raised one at a time so that we could watch the others being raised"; one, of the "advantage of going first so you can watch the others"; and another, of how he was left for last and "got the full treatment" because he had family visiting. Nine respondents noted that they did their third degree in another lodge and would have preferred to have done so "at home." Indeed, four of these said that having their degree thus done "by strangers" added to their "nervousness." Two respondents were less than happy with the fact that, after advising them to arrive at a set time, their lodge conducted a lengthy business meeting before their degree, leaving them, in the words of one, "cooling my heels" outside for a considerable time beforehand.

Relatedly, there was the issue of respondents' ability to attend and participate in lodge meetings in between degrees. At one time, particularly in Nova Scotia, most lodges conducted their business on the third degree, effectively meaning that candidates were barred from attending and participating in lodge affairs until they had completed all of their degrees. Four respondents reported being unhappy with this state of affairs when they went through, though three quickly added that things have changed and lodges are now able to open and work on the lowest degree of anyone present, enabling candidates to participate immediately after initiation and feel "part of things." Newfoundland and Labrador respondents, on the other hand, rarely faced this problem, as the predominant Emulation working and close variations enable new initiates to be involved, to vote, and even to "act" as a minor officer temporarily when needed immediately.

There was also the logistical issue of time to completion. Four respondents noted that the earlier Nova Scotia practice of doing business on the third degree "pressured lodges to ram candidates through the three degrees quickly." Conversely, a Newfoundland and Labrador respondent stated that, in Emulation working, "there's no need to rush you through." This issue of speed through the degrees received much comment:

> My lodge saw the third degree as the objective, not the lessons along the way.

> Most in my lodge prefer to get them through quick, then promptly put in an office within about three to six months.

That may be fine for those in a hurry to finish, but eleven respondents said that the degrees should be spread out more so that candidates have more of an opportunity to grasp the lessons therein:

> *It took me about five years to get my three degrees, so people shouldn't complain about a few months.*

> *I'm glad the Master spread my degrees out so that I could take the time to visit other lodges, observe degrees, and study more along the way.*

There were also special accommodations that respondents found meaningful in relation to their degree experiences, ranging from a respondent who claimed "it meant a lot" that his lodge did his degrees when he was home over the summer to another who commented how the lodge "accommodated my disability, showing that they were there for me."

All of the above logistical considerations bore an impact on the overall impression that the degrees had on respondents. Yet there is one, final logistical consideration that must be discussed in more detail: experiments in some jurisdictions (e.g., the Grand Lodge of New York) where putting candidates through the three degrees happens in an expedited fashion. Despite not being practised in either of the two jurisdictions in this study, respondents nevertheless had a great deal to say about these new and controversial "one-day, three-degree" programs introduced elsewhere in order to increase membership in an increasingly fast-paced society.

Overall, respondents were not in favour of this approach. Fully fifty-six respondents made negative comments in relation to these programs, in which a large group of men watch as a "representative candidate" is put through all three degrees over the course of a weekend, even sometimes in a single day. The primary theme, put forth by thirty-four respondents, was that conducting candidates through all of the degrees in this accelerated fashion renders it virtually impossible for them to come to a comparable understanding of what Masonry is all about:

> *I can't see how candidates can get the same understanding or appreciation in one day. It's like trying to instantaneously mass-produce a developmental process of moral and spiritual development and growth. Rushing people is not the way.*

> *It's like giving someone a crash course in discipline and dedication.*

> *Nothing worth having comes without taking the time and doing the studying to understand.*

Certain things are worth waiting for.

Everybody should have to do just as much memory work as I did. There's a certain level of education that you have to go through in order to understand.

Indeed, five respondents claimed that these programs are nothing more than a "quick fix" put forth by Grand Lodges facing declining membership; four saw it as reflective of a society that regularly seeks "instantaneous results"; and three regarded it simply as lodges "changing for convenience." Ultimately, such respondents took the position that "if people want to become Masons, they can do it the traditional way." For the above reasons, they did not want to see such programs instituted in their own Grand Lodges, considering them neither valuable nor "dignified." As one respondent rhetorically asked about candidates put through such programs, "Will they still be here in ten years?"

On the other hand, there were thirteen respondents who spoke in favour of such programs. Claiming that "you've had an opportunity for the past forty years to prove the old way works, and you haven't," such respondents asserted that "we need to change the old ways of doing things." The various claims made by this group of respondents included the following:

These programs help get people involved that have scheduling [and] time constraints.

The one-day programs help us deal with higher demand today.

People today are not willing to spend as long as an Entered Apprentice.

The prevailing view among supporters was that "these candidates can be just as good Masons as those [who] do it the old way." One respondent claimed that "the retention rate is dead even" with those initiated the traditional way; another, that there is "more participation" among candidates initiated in the accelerated fashion. To counter the argument above regarding education, three respondents added that candidates put through these accelerated programs still have to learn their ritual by rote regardless. Whatever the truth of these claims, it appears that the rationale for these accelerated programs, so controversial among respondents in this study, is that, in the words of one man, "some will be like-minded, get it, and stay; others will be shown the ropes and leave." That is to say, bringing in larger numbers quickly, even if there is significant attrition, will still result in larger numbers of men active in the Craft over time compared to the traditional approach. Time and future research will determine if such claims surrounding significant changes in the logistics of the three degrees are accurate or not.

In the end, all of the above factors relating to how the three degrees are done were commented on by respondents as having an impact on candidates' experience of their Masonic degrees.

CONCLUSION

This chapter has traced respondents' experiences of the three degrees in Freemasonry, during which they underwent a rite of passage meant to transform them from outsiders, mere interested members of the public, to full-fledged brothers in the Craft. This is a ritually complex, interactive process in which candidates, inculcated with a tension between secrecy and curiosity beforehand and seasoned with strategic information leakages, find this dynamic further enhanced through a progressive series of rituals that alternate anxiety and reassurance, sensory deprivation and revelation, physicality and intellect, and mystery and understanding in various measures as they are brought deeper into the trust and fellowship of the in-group.

It is my contention that the processes encapsulated in this rite of passage (Van Gennep 1960), when performed well, involve a tactical structuring of four primary theoretical elements: (1) dramaturgy (Goffmann 1959; Mangham and Overington 1987); (2) embodied emotion and its management (Denzin 1984; Hochschild 1983); (3) breaches or disruptions to prior paths, adjustments, and assumptions prompting the symbolic construction of meaning (Garfinkel 1967; Mead 1934); and (4) periodic zones of heightened liminality (Turner 1967, 1969), of being "betwixt and between," when the other elements coordinate to foster thought, emotion bonding, and an emergent sense of attachment, even identity. These processes echo, but empirically elaborate earlier formulations on the ritual collapse of personal and collective ties (Kaplan 2014) and the construction of "Mason" as a core identity category (Mahmud-Abdelwahib 2008).

I would argue that when the dramatic interplay between, for example, teasing and support, manufactures deeper curiosity—both in lodge and in other social settings—this puts candidates into a bodily state of anticipation. While they engage in masculine emotion management practices to temper this embodied preparatory liminality, they are nevertheless simultaneously rendered susceptible to the dramatic, ritual practices that occur in initiation, punctuated by "sensible feelings" and "feelings of the lived body" (Denzin 1984) at key moments. Just as these heighten the sense of being "betwixt and between," they also serve to facilitate, underscore, even ratify, the construction of symbolic meanings and indexically informed accounts (Mead 1934; Garfinkel 1967), along with the new Masonic identity being mutually constructed by themselves and the brethren in the evolving phenomenological process of reflexively coming to working understandings.

To some extent this description fits respondents' lived experiences of each of the degrees, just as it covers, in a broader sense, the process from initiation to that elusive time, following their third degree, that they come to their own working understanding of what Masonry is about and how they see themselves in relation to it. In other words, there is a rite of passage writ large punctuated by a series of smaller, strategic passages. Each of these—within and without the lodge—serve as stepping stones whereby an individual, in concert with others, dramaturgically moves, with the prods to understanding provided by ritual practices, embodied emotion, and moral imagery, to a new, highly symbolic social identity as part of the Craft. When successful, and repeated through observation and practice, these processes can, over time, layer, sedimentize, even laminate a new sense of self, a new valued identity, underscored by "feelings of the self and moral person" (Denzin 1984, 1985), where the individual is no longer a mere a member of the public, but a Mason. Taken together, as one man put it, "it separates us from everybody else."

However, it is obvious that the level of coordination between these elements is relatively complex and is susceptible to breaking down at various points and in various ways. Hence, for example, when dramaturgical coordination is lacking for various reasons (e.g., lack of interest shown in the candidate beforehand, poor ritual work, and so on), key elements framing these interconnections break down, short-circuiting the emotional meaningfulness, deflating liminality to a sense of inconsequence, and turning ritual into mere "ritualism" (Merton 1968). If ritualism as a deviant mode of adaptation is, as Merton feels, a state of pure anomie, and, if, as noted in the last chapter, some are joining the Craft out of a sense of anomie in the wider society, then what difference does the Craft provide to them under such circumstances? Without effective dramaturgical coordination between these elements, the lodge is just more of the same. New, meaningful identities are not born from such ingredients.

The theoretical model emerging from this preliminary study may be usefully fleshed out by future researchers in a number of ways. Thus, there is a need to dig more deeply into how these experiences today compare to the past, to brethren in different jurisdictions and cultures, to those of different age groups, social statuses, and so on. Indeed the interplay with the wider culture is of particular significance, seeing as we have evolved from a culture of widely shared traditions, status, and deeper social capital to one of greater diversity, an emphasis on equality, and low social capital. I have already hinted that coordinating the construction of Masonic identities with the wider culture may be just as important as successfully coordinating the various interactional elements above.[16] Indeed, the identity being constructed through these rituals must hold social value to new brethren or they may not consider staying—and, given that the problem of attrition has been accelerating in recent years (Hodapp 2013; Belton 1999), this fear is not unfounded.

Whatever direction future research in this area takes, the results of this preliminary study, and the theoretical model that emerged, should provide a foundation to build upon.

CHAPTER 4

SOCIAL ATMOSPHERE
AND MEMBER INVOLVEMENT

O nce candidates have been attracted to Freemasonry and have gone through the ceremonies of initiation, passing, and raising, the question arises: what now? New members are certainly free to participate in the ceremonies, business, and charity work of the lodge to the extent that they so desire and opportunities are available, but why would they do so? What encourages brethren to want to participate? What facilitates their ongoing involvement in the lodge and its activities? Conversely, what discourages them, fostering attrition in Masonic ranks? In the opening decades of the twenty-first century, one thing often heard in Masonic circles is that "it's not just getting them in, it's keeping them." Respondents had much more to say on this matter than expected—indeed, they spoke about it more than any other issue. Thus, this chapter begins the process of unpacking what they had to say about this critical question facing Masonry today.

In this chapter—the first of three on this complex and important issue—I start by reviewing the literature on involvement from both Masonic researchers and social scientists, seeking to situate the Craft among volunteer/community groups more generally. Next, after a brief introduction to the six key issues that emerged from the research data in these respects, I spend the rest of this chapter discussing multiple factors related to the social atmosphere of the lodge. In chapter 5, I continue looking at involvement by focusing on the significant and complex web of organizational factors that that emerged in this respect. Then, in chapter 6, I wrap up the discussion by outlining what the data reveal about the significance of Masonic education; the impact of brethren's other involvements and commitments; moral and ethical concerns; and questions surrounding member motivation. I then conclude by constructing an overall theoretical framework for understanding Masonic involvement today.

MASONIC LITERATURE

Research on the issue of involvement has been far from encouraging. Belton (1999), in a quantitative study of a sample of lodges throughout the English-speaking world, noted rapidly decreasing periods of involvement from initiation to resignation/exclusion (deaths excluded) during the latter half of the twentieth century. Average duration of membership went from twenty-plus years up until the 1950s to approximately ten years by the mid-1970s, then fell to a range of between four and six years by the early 1990s. Other statistical analyses of Masonic membership trends highlight the significance of this issue, suggesting that the Craft currently faces a serious crisis in retention of members (Belton and Henderson 2000). Thus, even if there has been an increase in initiations over the past decade, when the shortening duration of member involvement and ongoing deaths of older members are considered, this does not bode well for the future of an organization that, despite massive population growth in society, is already at its lowest membership in eighty years (Masonic Service Association 2014). Getting a handle on the issue of member involvement is thus important to the very survival of the Craft.

The Masonic leadership is keenly aware of this issue. Thus, the Masonic Service Association, beginning in 2004, put together a program called "It's About Time," detailing many significant matters related to the decline in involvement and articulating specific issues to be considered in improving member retention. Similarly, many Grand Lodges have put together membership development programs such as the widely distributed "10 Steps to Lodge Renewal" developed by the Grand Lodge of Iowa (Masonic Trowel 2012). Included in these broader programs is one widely adopted strategy whereby Grand Lodges put together "mentorship programs" in which individual lodges assign "mentors" to new members to maintain social contact, answer questions, encourage participation, and so on. Indeed, the two Grand Lodges in this study have officially adopted this approach.

Yet, despite the uneven implementation of such organizational strategies, the retention problem remains an organizational priority. Thus, it is imperative at this point to move beyond the membership numbers that we have and consider qualitative data from contemporary Freemasons themselves to see what their experiences can tell us about this important issue.

However, before moving on, it may be helpful to briefly move beyond specifically Masonic materials to consider the broader sociological literature on community organizations to see what light can be shed on the question of involvement from that perspective.

SOCIAL SCIENCE LITERATURE

The social science literature on involvement in volunteer/community associations revolves around six broad themes, each of which will be briefly discussed in relation to the problem at hand.

Perhaps most significant to the present issue, it would appear that the decline in civic participation posited by Putnam (2000), and frequently discussed in relation to Freemasonry, has been far from uniform. Indeed, a fairer characterization might be that the nature of volunteer participation has *changed* rather than declined in a number of Western countries. Thus, while religious involvement was historically the most important predictor of volunteer participation,[1] its massive decline has not led to a decline in volunteerism. Instead, since the 1960s, secular associations have compensated (Bekkers and de Graaf 2002). Since about 1980, there has been a shift in the pattern of participation, with higher involvement not only in expressive associations, but also in those oriented toward social participation and solidarity (Bickel and Lalive d'Epinay 2001). Thus, for example, between 1992 and 2002 in the Netherlands, there were increases in all forms of participation except religious organizations (Broese van Groenou 2010). In Australia, decreased membership in traditional service clubs has been offset by increased involvement in other kinds of community activities (Cox 2002). Indeed, closest to home, results for both Quebec and English Canada disprove the thesis that voluntary-association activity has been on the decline in North America since the 1960s. The only exception is religious group involvement (Curtis et al. 2003). All of this suggests that the above situation facing the Masonic order needs to be considered in this broader social context.

Secondly, one must look at the social context from broad as well as narrow standpoints. From a broad, international perspective, volunteerism has been statistically higher in nations that have certain characteristics, most notably, (1) multi-dimensional Christian or predominantly Protestant religious compositions, (2) prolonged and continuous experience with democratic institutions, (3) social democratic or liberal political systems, and (4) high levels of economic development (Curtis, Baer, and Grabb 2001). It might be surmised that recent developments in relation to some of these factors may have an impact on levels of volunteer activity, perhaps more so in some areas than others. Thus, beyond the potentially greater impacts of religious decline in some areas of volunteerism,[2] developments in political economy may play a role. Hence, on the one hand, it may be important to consider the relative historical density of civic associations, as this slows decline in social capital (P. Hall 2002). Similarly, extensive welfare state expenditures reduce participatory inequalities between social groups, with some variation depending on type of organization (van Ingen and van der Meer 2011). These must be contrasted with the historic role of neo-liberal modernization over the past few decades, with its commodification of volunteer activities, undermining of the welfare state, and potential to destroy the character of organizations and disrupt the moral basis of local community (Simpson 1994).

Of course, this leads to the related issue of employment. Neo-liberalism has resulted in policies favouring more worker flexibility, fewer full-time jobs, and more labour mobility. Moreover, unlike in the past, today it is often necessary that both partners work to maintain even a modest standard of living. Thus, research has pointed to the significance of employment issues in relation to volunteer involvement (Ryle 2002). Studies have noted the importance of both spouses' working hours, life stage, and social class (Becker and Hofmeister 2000); moving and mobility and their relationship to community resources and involvement (Ortiz 2010); and work histories, notably whether one has a stable job or a disorderly series of jobs (Rotolo and Wilson 2003). Overall, job instability has a negative effect on community involvement—at least in the traditional, sustained, long-term sense—with one exception: layoffs themselves have a positive effect (Ryle 2000).

This calls attention to the fourth, broad category of issues: the relative convergence or divergence (the "fit") between one's social background and one's ability to engage in volunteer activity. In some respects these factors are structural/demographic in nature; in others more dispositional. Structural factors—and their variation over time—undoubtedly play a part in either facilitating or restricting possibilities for volunteer engagement. In this sense, studies have pointed to the relevance of variations in social class, marital status, health, income, education level, gender, age, access to transport, and Internet connectivity in relation to the issue of volunteer involvement (van Ingen and van der Meer 2011; Mesch and Talmud 2010; Osborne, Ziersch, and Baum 2008; Perren, Arber, and Davidson 2003; Marcello and Perrucci 2000; Lammers 1991). In the latter, more dispositional respect, there needs to be a good fit between member predispositions and organizational rewards (Poulet 2010), as these are related to membership satisfaction and plans to remain in the organization (Bonjean, Markham, and Macken 1994). Thus, studies have shown differences in motivation between younger and older volunteers (Omoto, Snyder, and Martino 2000), suggesting differences in successful strategies to increase volunteer involvement in different age cohorts (Tang 2006). Similarly, while it has been asserted that those able to participate tend to be those who already enjoy levels of social and economic privilege (Osborne, Ziersch, and Baum 2008), studies have shown that starting volunteer activities gives the greatest boost to social resources among those with fewer possibilities of acquiring them in other contexts (e.g., the elderly, people without partners, and ethnic minorities) (van Ingen and Kalmijn 2010). Thus, fit—and ways of articulating it to those who may most benefit—remains key to volunteer involvement today.

Relatedly, volunteers need to be motivated. Studies have shown that there are four major types of motivation for community involvement (egoism, altruism, collectivism, and principlism) and that strategies need to be put in place to diversify/maximize their satisfactory engagement (Batson, Ahmad, and Tsang 2002). To some extent this involves playing to, and remaining relevant to, prominent societal values. As well, it must be kept in mind that motivations for organizational involvement evolve. Studies have shown that motivations for involvement change over an involvement career. Initiation and continuation motivations vary, with continuation emphasizing actual organizational accomplishments/improvements in collective goods (Renauer 2001). Novice volunteers do not have the same motivations as experienced ones; in other words, the factors that motivate volunteers to join are not the same as those that motivate them to stay (Ilsley 1990, 15–32). It is important for researchers studying involvement to remain cognizant of these facts.

Fifth, there is the issue of identity. Organizations that foster a strong identity among volunteers are likely to encourage greater involvement. It has been asserted that the role identity model best explains sustained volunteerism (Chacon, Vecina, and Davila 2007) and that this common identity/bond is related to relative organizational emphases on (1) recruitment versus retention, (2) focusing on issues versus going off topic, and (3) limiting group size versus allowing uncontrolled growth (Ren, Kraut, and Kiesler 2007). Even more significant is the relationship between the external social identities of volunteers and those acquired by virtue of participation in the group. As Scott (1987, 175–76) writes:

> The strategic question facing all organizations is how to recruit participants and harness their roles and resources in the service of organizational goals (whether goal attainment or survival), while avoiding or minimizing the danger of becoming captive to participants' external interests or personal agendas. Once pipelines are established, resources may flow in either direction.... Problems can occur from either of two types of imbalance—when an organization imposes too many or too few restrictions on the type (and imputed relevance) of other roles held by its participants. When nonorganizational roles impinge on organization roles inappropriately, then we have the problem of de-bureaucratization. The simplest examples are those of nepotism or corruption. The reverse problem occurs when organizational roles improperly assume priority over nonorganizational roles, leading to overbureaucratization [such as found in] the unreasonable requirements placed by some corporations on the personal lives of upwardly mobile managers and their wives. It is by no means always a simple or noncontroversial matter to determine when external roles are or are not properly impinging on organizational roles, and vice versa. Clearly, value judgments are involved, and depending on which normative system provides the standard, different judgments are likely to be made.

Hence, while it is important for organizations to foster a strong sense of group identity among volunteers, they must strike a careful balance whereby members can draw strength from their external social roles and abilities without their social lives becoming completely engulfed.

Finally, organizational dynamics play a key role in volunteer involvement and retention. A number of factors have appeared in the literature, including the possibility of volunteer status attainment (Poulet 2010; Welser 2006); the need to attend to the emotional dynamics of groups (Summers-Effler 2004); being committed in other programs, feeling supported, having few problems with program administration, and receiving a stipend (Tang, Morrow-Howell, and Choi 2010); the dangers of moves toward volunteer professionalization and the workplace model (Ilsley 1990); and how all of this relates to successful organizational ritual performance, or in failure concentrated in a perceived breach between appearance and reality (Mangham and Overington 1987). All such organizational factors can impact on commitment reflective of participant's values—whether volunteer, organization, client, or social-vision centred (Ilsley 1990, 33–56). As Ilsley states in relation to commitment:

> Reflective of both participants' value structures and the meaning derived from involvement, these can vary in intensity, from casual to all consuming. Commitment cannot be measured by hours spent or duration of service alone. It is quite variable in terms of the amount of effort exerted, risks taken, and sacrifices made. Dedication to a cause is a matter of personal choice, although the ways in which that dedication is expressed are influenced by such things as organizational setting and the attitudes of staff and managers.... Through questioning and observation they can learn that commitment's objects. They can gauge the intensity of each volunteer's commitment so that they expect neither too much nor too little of that individual. Finally, they can respect the values that lie behind commitment and recognize that those values, along with the commitment that springs from them, may change during the course of volunteers' work. By doing these things they can design programs that draw on volunteers' commitment and deepen it at the same time. (1990, 33–56)

Thus, perhaps most important for those managing volunteer organizations is the ability to observe the waxing and waning of volunteer commitment in relation to such dimensions of organizational dynamics and to adaptively make adjustments when necessary. Administrators who simply stay the course and do things the way they have always been done without attending to such organizational factors do so at the organization's peril.

Ultimately, when examining the involvement issues articulated by respondents in the present study of contemporary Freemasons, it will be vital not only to place their responses in the specific Masonic context, but to consider them in relation to the additional matters raised by this broader sociological literature on volunteerism. Put bluntly, if Freemasonry is losing members relative to the population and if the length of involvement is declining yet volunteerism is not declining in the broader society, then we have to look at what it is about Freemasonry—both in its external social and its internal organizational aspects—that puts it on the wrong side of this trend in volunteerism. As Richard Hall (1987, 205) states:

> Organizational death is the final and ultimate outcome of organizational decline.... There are four sources of organizational decline. Organizational atrophy occurs as the organization becomes unresponsive to the pressures it is facing. Vulnerability is ... seen among small, new organizations with their liability of newness. Loss of legitimacy is particularly evident ... as once popular programs become targets of criticism and budget cuts. Environmental entrophy refers to the reduced capacity of the environment to support an organization. These sources of decline occur during the transformation process. Death is but one outcome—as ... organizations can be revitalized.

Certainly the scenario facing Freemasonry outlined above is suggestive of several of these sources of decline, particularly atrophy, loss of legitimacy, and environmental entropy. Whether these contribute to its death or the Craft is able to adapt and revitalize itself for the twenty-first century remains an empirical question. However, if it is to do the latter, reliable information will be needed. Thus, it is to the data that I now turn.

FINDINGS

The data contained more commentary than expected about the current state of Freemasonry, and much of this revolved, in one way or another, around this issue of maintaining involvement—whether by new, recently minted Master Masons, or in relation to re-engaging brethren who had not been heard from in some time.[3] In some respects, comments related to what Masons liked and didn't like about the Craft in general—or their own lodge in particular. But respondents went much deeper than that. From the tenor and detail of their comments it was clear that many had spent some time thinking about matters related to continued involvement in the Masonic order—or their lodge—in the future.

Respondents' comments fell into six broad categories: (1) the social atmosphere in the fraternity, (2) organizational factors, (3) educational issues, (4) the impact of other involvements and commitments, (5) moral and ethical matters, and (6) questions surrounding motivation. By far the most significant concerns were issues surrounding social atmosphere and organizational matters, which together accounted for 65 percent of the comments on involvement (31 and 34 percent, respectively). Indeed, these broad themes served as umbrellas that sheltered a diversity of sub-themes apiece, testifying to both their relative complexity and their significance to this issue. These were followed in significance by a series of issues related to specific dimensions of Masonic education (20 percent), the question of brethren's other involvements and commitments getting in the way of their Masonic activities (10 percent), and finally, questions of surrounding morality (3 percent) and the motivation of brethren (2 percent). Beyond this general ranking in terms of frequency, overall responses between each of these broad categories tended to be more or less favourable than others, ranging from highest in relation to social atmosphere to lowest in relation to motivation (and there were great variations within each category as well). In this and the next two chapters, each of these broad themes will be unpacked in greater detail, concluding with an overall theoretical framework for understanding Masonic involvement at the end of chapter 6. This chapter begins the process by dissecting the key issue of social atmosphere.

Respondents spent a great deal of time discussing the social atmosphere of their lodge in particular—and of the Craft in general—as a key factor influencing ongoing involvement in Freemasonry. This was expressed in relation to a series of interrelated but distinct dimensions, as outlined below.

"Fit" between Member Predispositions and Social Rewards: Meeting Needs and Interests

As noted, it is important for there to be a good fit between member predispositions and an organization's social rewards, as these are related to membership satisfaction and plans to remain in the organization over time (Poulet 2010; Bonjean, Markham, and Macken 1994). This theme of "fit" was most notably expressed by forty-five respondents who claimed that the "continuity" and "familiarity" of the lodge experience and ritual provided a "break" from what was otherwise going on in their lives while harmonizing with their broader needs and interests. There were several aspects to this.

First, respondents pointed to the "comfort" that they derived from their membership in the order compared to the difficulties and stresses of their job and other difficulties in their lives. They referred to how, for them, the Craft was "a centre of calm in a crazy world," a "safety valve," a place of "sanctuary," a "haven," a "living space," "a real solace," even "an escape from the real world." For some, this "balanced out" or served as a "haven" of peace away from the trials, tribulations, stresses, and "uncertainties" of work, which, as noted, has been made more difficult for many due to the neo-liberal policies in vogue today.

> *The Masonic order, it's a place you can actually go and spend an evening and totally forget everything else about the outside world and just enjoy yourself. I think that's the thing, it's just*

that comfort away from it all. It's an unusual environment, and I think that's it. I've heard other Masons with the same feeling. Some of their wives have expressed that. Two or three say that their husbands, in their jobs, are so distressed. But when they come home from a night at lodge, they're a different person. And I've had it.

It's a place I go to get my charge every month. I can go out any night. I can go out tonight if I want. I can recharge when necessary.

This suggests that, at least in part, Freemasonry may be best served by involving those facing stresses resulting from the political economy of the early twenty-first century.

Yet there are other types of stresses fostered by the vagaries of contemporary social structure and normative standards. In this respect, Freemasonry was seen as a "balance" for "negative social forces" such as anomie. Such matters were noted by respondents as related to involvement:

How do you take yourself out of this fragmented social world? There is a sort of isolation, whether it's a spiritual ... I don't mean that you cut yourselves off from other people, but that it gives you this sort of space—it all sounds very insular—that you have sort of a walled area where you can regenerate. And I don't think that's a bad thing. It's sort of a place of regeneration. For a lot of Masons, it's actually a driving force.

I grew up without a father and I was looking to the Masons as maybe some sort of supportive family-type thing that was missing before. Yes, I think I was. Once you're a Mason, you can go pretty well anywhere in the world, find another Mason, and they're sort of obligated, if you're in need, to help you. Just to have that family unit all over the world as well is a big benefit I think. It's definitely an attraction for me.

Freemasonry taps into the spiritual hunger today that research shows exists despite decline in mainline denominations. It's the opposite of our disposable society. Men are searching for something, not knowing what that is. The Masonic tradition continues to intrigue men because there's a lack in our society, especially presently, of an institution. The church no longer has the kind of power. There isn't really anyone addressing some of the larger spiritual questions that everyone considers—but especially younger people. When you get to a certain age, you start to ask some of the bigger questions and want to explore larger ideas, and Masonry has the potential to present a path. And I think that it is not any type of stricture. It is literally what

*you bring to it, you will get out of it. It is simply a guidance
and an infrastructure from which to explore—and there really
isn't anything in our culture that has that kind of weight and
the kind of power to do that any more.*

*Why we have a few more younger members today is because
there is a standard that they don't have in their world, and I
know what their world looks like. I think the young people,
or the new Masons that we're getting now, are people who,
because of all the different things that are happening in their
lives, are much more looking for this sanctuary, this grounding
peace, and the peace of mind that the lessons of Freemasonry
bring.*

Indeed, some respondents pointed to the importance of the stability provided by a structured order in a society undergoing rapid social change, a
place offering "a kind of permanence and security" where "you know what
to expect." Thus, they often pointed to the value of ritual:

*You feel comfort in the sameness, like putting on a favourite
piece of clothing, or eating comfort food.*

*The universality of the ritual brings people together. I went to
Japan and felt comforted by the familiarity of what was going
on, even though I couldn't speak the language.*

*Some people come to Masonry because they want structure, or
they want ritual, they want things done in the proper way, the
proper manner. There's comfort in that. As I look around the
world today there are very few places that ritual is maintained ...
according to the way that things have always been done. In
today's world, there is no such thing as the proper way of doing
things.*

*There's a serious lack of ritual, rites of passage, or story today,
so you're left very unsure, right? What develops the change in
your life? I see the lodge as a kind of replacement in face of
secular distrust of traditional churches and politics. Ritual is
important. I think people want ritual, and if I can find a way
to have ritual in the sort of secular world, then I kind of grav-
itate to it.... I can see the appeal of ritual, and I think as the
world becomes increasingly secularized, I think rituals actually
become more and more important to people—in the same way
that storytelling is still important in our age, as well as metaphor. Ritual is a way of feeling part of something special.*

Finally in this respect, and implicit in much of the above, respondents noted that it was a particular type of person, or one with a particular set of dispositions (Poulet 2010), in the above social contexts that was a particularly good fit for Freemasonry:

> *I think that one of the most attractive parts of Freemasonry is a long history and a sense of ceremony, ritual, and tradition, and I think that as some of the other things that have offered that in life fall away, I think people who are interested in history, ceremony, ritual, and tradition are attracted to Freemasonry.*

> *As a Master, I get the impression, when I talk to these younger men nowadays, that they want to belong to something that has continuity, something with roots, something that doesn't change very much over time. I guess they're basically squares. They're conservatives, and they wanna find a place to be.*

Indeed, nineteen respondents took this further and noted that their involvement in Freemasonry was accentuated due to their own prior personal interest in history. Two of these even admitted to being "Masonic pack rats" who owned various historical items related to the Craft. Another four added religion to the list of prior interests accentuated by their involvement in Freemasonry.

> *I've always had an interest in history and Freemasonry has fed that along way. I've read some really interesting stuff about what we've supposedly done. When I can't sleep, my wife finds me on the computer in middle of night digging through this stuff.*

> *Freemasonry is an organization with a profound sense of engagement with history. There's a great range and extent of amateur historical research going on among Freemasons, and historic legends like the Knights Templar fascinate people and encourage further exploration.*

> *My involvement in Freemasonry was fuelled—to some extent at least—by the fact that I had always been interested in various religions.*

What this all suggests is that involvement in Freemasonry—at least as it is currently constituted—may be bolstered by appealing to a particular demographic: those undergoing the stresses of employment in a neo-liberal environment, those alienated by social fragmentation, and—because there are many of the above—perhaps most importantly, those interested in structure, order, history, and religion and who exhibit conservative viewpoints generally.

These are individuals with a traditional world view who are concerned about the "disappearance of the sacred" (Meštrović 1997, 101–22), the relative absence of emotionally meaningful rites in the Durkheimian sense, and are searching for authenticity, for "collective effervescence" in today's mass-mediated cultural terrain, where, for example, hazing rituals and rites of passage have been making a comeback as ways to set groups apart and make members feel special (1997, 113). Unfortunately, given the trends in volunteerism noted earlier, such individuals appear to be in increasingly short supply today.[4]

A second—and contrasting—way that contemporary respondents articulated the question of "fit" related to how its ritual and imagery provided them an appropriate pathway to comfortably explore spiritual questions without the dogmatic restrictions and negative connotations that they associated with organized religion today. While, of course, there were many respondents involved in traditional, organized religion, for twenty-seven respondents, Freemasonry served as a much "freer" alternative:

> *Freemasonry provides an alternate type of spirituality for folks who aren't involved in church and organized religion, especially in today's world, where many are disgusted with organized religion but interested in spirituality. It's an alternate living space.*

> *What does a real Mason do? You give him the tools and knowledge, but yet, at the end of the day, you're the one who builds the thing, right? So, you could look at Masonry not as a build-your-own-religion kit, but there are certain aspects that you can build and customize in a way that you can get that fulfillment that you need. Maybe that's one of the real secrets of Freemasonry.*

> *Freemasonry is not a religion, but yet there's something religious about it. For me it's the closest thing to—it mimics religion to large degree. It's the basis of my living. I like the freedom of thought and interpretation, the non-dogmatic nature of the Craft, yet with a similar sort of ritualistic, ceremonial commitment. I think it replaces religion. I wouldn't have had an easy time fifty years ago.*

While this attitude does not necessarily conflict with that of the more traditional members above, it does indicate the importance of the inclusive ritual in providing space for both traditional and contemporary perspectives on spirituality. Indeed, given the decline in religious civic participation noted earlier, yet the often-noted fact that many today still define themselves as "spiritual," the ability of the Craft to effectively tap into this may be one aspect of fostering involvement.

A third—and related—way that respondents articulated the issue of "fit" related to "being a curious person," one who "likes to dig into things," "to challenge myself intellectually," who is "intrigued about taking the higher degrees," the "mysterious, formal language in the ritual," and so on. Twenty-three respondents took up this theme in one way or another.

> Plain and simple curiosity—about life and other people and the lodge and history. That is the common denominator that I see amongst the folks who are there. Folks who are just curious about everything, and interested in everything. That would explain 99 percent of the folks who are there long term. So if you come in because you're curious, then I'd say you have the best chance of all of sticking.

> Some have just got to have the mysteries, to seek the higher degrees. Not everyone is going to dig into it like me. The people who don't grab it, who don't go looking for what's between the lines, they'll not be members long. Membership in this organization is not free.

Fourthly, twenty-six respondents articulated the issue of "fit" by rather vaguely referring to "the type of person that it clicks with," those who "get it," who are "already Masons in their heart," and so on (i.e., compared with those who do not stick around over the long term). In some respects this may reflect a resonance of compatible values and identities between individuals and the Craft (Poulet 2010).

> It doesn't matter why you come in. What matters is, once you're there, does the light come on and you go "Hey, yeah, this is who I am. This is what I'm all about. These are the other people who are like me." If they are, then you stay. If it's not, you don't.

> There are a lot of Masons who have never taken their degrees. One of the first questions you're asked [is] "Where were you first prepared to be a Mason?" [The answer:] "In your heart." I think that's ... I think if Freemasonry never existed, I think the majority of us here would have been part of something that was probably just as good. We're already Freemasons. The organization is just there to ratify it, organize it, or channel it. Maybe we shouldn't expect everyone to have that click.

> There are brethren who jump in feet first and there's brethren who join and Freemasonry is not for them. For every Mason, there are probably twenty persons who are at heart Masons but

just don't know it. If it's right for you … if you like the Masons that you know and the kind of things that they do, then fine. If there is a right reason to join, it's something you're going to find in your own heart.

I think Masons are more or less born. I've only really come to that conclusion recently. But I don't think we can make a Mason. Either you believe … It's in your heart at some level— whether you know it or not—or it's not. And there's a lot of examples of people that try to be Masons but don't really understand what it is.

Finally in this respect, thirty-two respondents articulated the idea of "fit" in terms of Freemasonry remaining relevant to its members today, to—in effect—maintaining that resonance between members' lives and involvement in the order. A number of interrelated issues were mentioned by members in this regard, generally revolving around the idea that the Craft needed to redouble efforts to retain its "historic adaptability in relation to changes in society" to appeal to a diversity of members.

People are involved for different reasons: social, status, administrative, spirituality, etc. You're always going to have a cross-section of people. I think that the reasons for joining Masonry are as varied as the folks who join Masonry. We have to ensure that the different groups [and] the different reasons for being a Mason are all satisfied. We've got to help people find their niche in the lodge.

We've got to remain relevant today. We have to recognize that the social needs and wants of new brothers are not the same as they were a hundred, even thirty years ago. We're not dealing with the pre-boomers nor necessarily with the baby boomers. Today's youth, unlike the boomers, are more interested, but we've got to consider the economy of their paths, that their lives are more uncertain.

We've got to ensure that what we are doing is relevant to people's lives today, not by changing the ritual but by incarnating it or making the fellowship around it relevant. The culture of Freemasonry must evolve in tension with tradition in order to make it more understandable, more readily interpretable in relation to today's world. Thus we could look at the music, new takes on the imagery, emphasize the crossovers and connections between Freemasonry and popular culture, whether it's in relation to common phrases, TV, and movies like The Simpsons *or* Lara Croft, *and so on. The lodge should sponsor subgroups or activities for members interested in specific matters. We're too shy about drawing attention to these things.*

In respondents' comments throughout this section, there seems to be an overall tension between these latter comments about "fit" and many of the rest. Most of the earlier comments point, in one way or another, to a specific group or groups in society today—be they traditionalists, those affected by anomie, those interested in—or curious about—history or religion, or those who simply feel in one way or another that the organization "clicks" with who they are (and there is considerable crossover between this latter item and the rest). Such characteristics would imply that the Craft could facilitate involvement and retention of members by targeting such "well-fitting" groups for involvement. To some extent this is what has in effect been going on, as such traditional—and often older—individuals seem to be the most deeply involved. Nevertheless, as noted above, this is but a small, and, to some extent, shrinking subgroup in contemporary society, so such a strategy would not bode well for the long-term survival of the Craft—hence these latter, contrasting comments about broadening the appeal of Freemasonry by "covering all the bases," remaining relevant to a broader cultural demographic and ensuring that everyone is able to find their niche. It remains to be seen whether a group with a large involvement of traditionalists—one that "missed a generation," so to speak—will be able to make the latter kind of changes quickly and effectively enough to become relevant to and involve the diverse membership that it needs to survive.

Before closing this section, it will be helpful to consider some of the comments by brethren who, in one way or another, were struggling with whether they really were a good "fit" for Freemasonry. Two major themes emerged: not having their original expectations met and the irrelevance of much of the terminology for people today.

The former theme was articulated by fifteen respondents who did not find that their original reasons for joining the Craft were borne out. In some cases this may have been because—despite representations to the contrary—they had joined for the wrong reasons, such as to "network," facilitate business contacts, and get ahead. Similarly, there were those who were originally interested due to the many literary allusions to "Masonic conspiracies," the "new world order," and all of the "cloak-and-dagger stuff." In the words of one disillusioned respondent in this respect, "The big secret is that there is no secret." Yet there were other respondents that went beyond these superficial reasons who noted dissonance between their original conception and what they were experiencing. One brother who had done a lot of research found that "there is a disconnect with the reading." Similarly, a relatively new Mason, having attended a number of meetings after being raised to the third degree, appeared confused about what were, in effect, business meetings. Indeed, he got up and pointedly asked, "Can anyone here tell me, what do Masons do?" For such individuals, the Craft needs to formulate a meaningful answer or there is a risk that it will lose them.

As for the second theme, the relevance of many lodge practices today came into question. Twenty-three respondents articulated this theme in various ways, pointing to things like the "arcane English," the "God-language," the "irrelevance of the music," and even the use of "historic construction terms in the ritual for people today."

> *Symbolism based on historic construction tools like "the twenty-four-inch gauge, level, plumb," and so on are out of touch with a society that uses metric and laser tools. We need to keep up with the times and make our imagery relevant. Our ritual language needs to be updated in a way that the young can hear it. Just try to explain to someone how a computer works if they've never heard computer language.*

In this latter respect, such respondents are suggesting that, again, Masonry as it is currently practised is not relevant today—or at least not relevant except to a small and diminishing group. In the words of one man, "What was once a radical, youthful, and enlightened organization is now largely old and conservative."

Ultimately, this question of "fit" between members' prior needs and interests is a crucial one. It is also one in which respondents' comments illustrate an ongoing tension between, on the one hand, playing to a specific—and shrinking—subgroup in contemporary society that is more likely to become and remain involved, and, on the other hand, making the activities of the lodge more relevant to a wider spectrum of people in society today. Unless the Craft finds a way to strike a more fruitful balance and resolves this tension to its advantage, it will find it difficult to find a productive long-term "fit" with members of the broader society. Indeed if that is the case, it will likely continue to face issues with retention into the foreseeable future.

Close Friendships

Perhaps the most positive social aspect noted by respondents in relation to their involvement in Freemasonry had to do with the close relationships that they had either developed or deepened during their time in the Craft (Kaplan 2014). Fifty-three respondents articulated the importance of close friendships in the order. They stressed how their Masonic activities, such as travelling together regularly to meetings (seven respondents), enabled them to meet up with old friends or acquaintances (six) or to engage in "friendship networking" (three)—even to meet new friends after moving to a new area (two). In the words of one man, "I always seem to have a friend somewhere." Significantly, several credited the efforts of brethren to maintain a personal connection with their decision to remain in the organization rather than be excluded.

Conversely, two pointed to how the poor attendance—even disappearance—of their friends from the lodge was discouraging, noting that it "feeds on itself."

Family Ties

Closely related to the issue of friendships was the existence of even closer ties: those to family. Thirty-six respondents emphasized that the involvement of other family members in the lodge encouraged them to be and remain involved as well. Indeed, thirteen indicated that their father–son relationship encouraged, and was in turn deepened, as a result of mutual involvement in the Craft, particularly when sons were encouraged to follow in their father's footsteps or when serving as officers together. Some of these also stressed their long family history in the Craft (e.g., fourth or fifth generation), a tradition that they would find hard to let down by ceasing involvement in the order.

Good Fellowship

These last two dimensions, in a relatively straightforward fashion, point to the importance of having close relationships in the lodge to maintaining involvement in the order. Yet not every new member already has family members in the Craft, nor are many—even most—of their outside friends necessarily involved. In such cases—which are likely more common today as the relative proportion of Freemasons in the population declines—what is necessary for new Masons to make the close connections that will help insulate them from leaving? The most prominent answer was "fellowship," the facilitation of sociability noted historically (Morrison 2012). Fifty-five respondents spoke of the importance of having "good fellowship" to foster involvement in the lodge, whether expressed in terms of members being made "comfortable" with the membership or in developing a "sense of belonging" or "camaraderie" with the brethren.

To achieve this, several approaches emerged as significant. First, forty-one respondents stressed the need for the lodge to be "welcoming" to new members. Seventeen of these stressed the importance of other members' efforts at making a personal connection and thereafter maintaining communication and human contact. Fifteen noted the significance of their being made to feel that they were welcomed into the group, especially when others of status welcomed them or brethren showed an interest in their personal background. Nine more of these noted the importance of having a "down-to-earth, welcoming membership," brethren that are "happy to see you, not critical—even if you've been away for a while." Two further indicated the importance of being called by name; one, of being introduced to others. All of these things helped brethren feel comfortable about their involvement, to "like the crowd" and, in the words of one man, "to make the lodge to feel right." The significance of this cannot be understated, particularly in today's society where relationships and social supports are often fragmented, jobs are demanding and uncertain, and so on. To give just one example, eight respondents stated that the sense of welcome that they experienced in the lodge contrasted sharply with their experiences at work, which were more difficult. This shows the significance of groups attending to the emotional dynamics of their members (Summers-Effler 2004).

Next, thirty-seven respondents stressed the need for lodges to organize activities in such a way that their spouse and whole family could be involved (i.e., to offset the individual and "men-only" aspect of the order). Yet, differences appeared as to how this spousal and family integration might be achieved. Older, committed members and their partners more often spoke of providing related opportunities for women through organizations like the Order of the Eastern Star; of having "ladies' nights," widows' suppers, and New Year's levees; and even of reviving dances and kids' Christmas parties. In this respect, older men stressed mutuality while women stressed the opportunities for travel and female companionship:

> *The Eastern Star is an opportunity for her to get out, too. You wouldn't believe the togetherness that we have with all our wives when we put on a function.*
>
> *I really enjoyed the year that the lodge officers and other wives travelled and hung out during their terms in office.*

However, younger members were not necessarily of the same mindset, both in terms of the nature of women's and family involvement and the type of activities employed. Some noted how the Eastern Star was originally formed in "self-defence," given women's historic opposition to the male-only aspect of the Craft. Moreover, given "different gender roles now," younger members more often expressed the need to "find ways for Freemasonry to work with changes in lifestyle that are increasingly family- and couple-oriented" and to "involve different leisure activities."

Third, and relatedly, twenty-seven respondents pointed to the need for the lodge to plan and organize more social and recreational events for the brethren themselves. Various examples were given—fishing and hunting trips, golf tournaments, barbecues, opportunities for brethren to meet at the hall to play pool or hold study groups, and so on—but the emphasis nevertheless tended to be on two aspects: (1) to make sure that these events were relevant to the membership of a given lodge, and (2) insofar as was possible, to make the lodge a hub for regular social activities, not just occasional events.

Fourth, fourteen respondents pointed to the good fellowship that they experienced when visiting other lodges or attending other Masonic events (e.g., "I was welcomed into that lodge and accepted as if I was a life member"). While it is not always possible to get members to participate in visiting, respondents suggested a number of ways good fellowship could be increased by making connections with other lodges. These included holding joint meetings (suggested by three respondents), joint degrees (three), or joint social events (three); twinning or making connections with far away lodges with annual road trips (three); and creating reciprocity arrangements (two).

Finally, nine respondents emphasized the need to show that they were enjoying themselves, to exude good humour and the sense that they were having fun with what they were doing. In this respect, in the words of one respondent, "You pick up that sense of well-being, your environment will change, and it feeds on itself." Moreover, if brethren are having fun, if "word gets out that it is a fun lodge, word of mouth brings people out." Thus, even when this was more apparent than real, it suggests that a combination of self-presentation (Goffman 1959) and, where necessary, gendered emotion management (Hochschild 1983) may nevertheless be, in part, a useful involvement strategy.

Before closing this section, however, it is important to consider the downside of fellowship. Respondents pointedly noted a series of related, negative practices that discouraged good fellowship, practices that did little to foster a sense of bonding and discouraged member involvement in the lodge. In contrast to the comments above about the lodge being a "welcoming" place for new members, eleven respondents stated that it was discouraging when no efforts were made to make new members feel welcome. Some pointed to "cliques" that made them feel that they were "not feeling that personal connection," or that "the lodge crowd doesn't feel right," as if they were being "marginalized" or "left alone," or even being "ignored" when they had problems. Apparently this kind of thing can start quite early, with two respondents complaining about lodges that do not keep their candidates up-to-date on lodge activities or events. It can also relate to the poor treatment of visitors ("you [should] never let a visitor stand alone"). A bigger problem, however, pointed to by nine respondents, is when new members are ignored after they receive their third degrees. In the dismissive words of one man, "Here's your apron, show up and have fun." Another stated,

> You go to the next meeting, you just sit on the sidelines, you don't know what's going on, what you went through, and nobody tells you nothing. People are standing up and sitting down and they're saying these words. Well, what are they saying? And nobody ... So you're lost for a long time.

Such discouraging practices were exacerbated when, as above, members are "left out of the loop" and not informed of events and activities.

Beyond these major themes, respondents reported discouragement about two other matters: ritualism (Merton 1968) and problems surrounding social events. In relation to the former, four respondents mentioned the following:

> *Always doing the same thing in the same way without any kind of fellowship.*

> *People standing up and mouthing off. All that hot air at the end of the night is wasting my time.*

> *People giving insincere, obligatory compliments or congratulations. It's such bullshit.*

In relation to the latter, two respondents complained about there not being enough social events, particularly those that members of the community could enjoy, yet they also bemoaned the increased costs and liabilities involved in holding social events today.

The above highlights the importance of good fellowship for maintaining member involvement in the Craft. Rather than doing things the same old way, efforts must be redoubled to make lodges feel welcoming to new and long-time members—particularly those who do not have other family or friendship ties to the Craft. Newly raised brethren need to be given attention and information. Social events must be regular, advertised to the brethren, enjoyable, more frequently inclusive, and relevant to the membership. More innovative ways to foster social intercourse between lodges need to be encouraged. Finally, efforts must be taken to keep ritualized formality from turning into insincere ritualism. All of these fellowship issues are important, since, in the observations of several prominent, long-standing members,

> *Most become Master Masons, go no further, accept the basic moral teaching, and just seek to enjoy the fellowship.*

> *The majority of people in the Masonic fraternity find it as being a night out. It provides a social avenue for them and that's probably about it. They go with a basic meaning that allows them to function in the Craft and do the things right. An interested Mason, a student Mason, I say they are certainly the minority, about 7 to 12 percent.*

If fellowship is as important to member involvement as the above comments suggest, and if it is what most brethren ultimately seek in the Craft, in the final analysis it is crucial that efforts be directed at improving the social experiences of member to retain members over time.

Receiving Attention and Recognition

A facet of fellowship implicit in the above involves members getting attention from others (Derber 1979, 2000). To some extent this aspect of the symbolic and emotional economy has been addressed by comments about new members being either made to feel welcome or left alone on the sidelines, and there is no need to repeat these here. Rather, in this short section I briefly outline respondents' comments in relation to what I term earned, quasi-altruistic, extraordinary, and negative attention in relation to the issue of involvement,[5] all of which further illustrate the need to attend to the emotional dynamics of groups (Summers-Effler 2004).

First, twenty-two respondents felt it was important for brethren to receive recognition when it was due (e.g., receiving meritorious service medals for extensive contributions to or work for the order, Past Master's medals following a term in office, pins for long periods of membership, Lewis jewels presented by proud fathers to their sons in the Craft, and so on). Eight more respondents pointed to the opportunities for achievement and personal satisfaction involved in becoming a Grand Lodge officer. In a very straightforward sense, such attention is earned and ritualistically confers a symbolic and emotional reward of status for involvement (Collins 1990).

Next, there were thirty-one respondents—including both brethren and family members—who noted being the recipients of quasi-altruistic attention in appropriate circumstances, most notably receiving "support when I have problems." This is not to say that such brethren—and those around them—did not necessarily take the view that they had done anything beforehand that merited such attention. There was often an element of Candace Clark's (1987) sympathy biography involved, whereby respondents' prior involvement in the Craft and working with the members of their lodge were factors in the extent of such support. Indeed, eight referred to "networking and helping each other out." Nevertheless, this was balanced with an element of genuine concern shown to respondents that went beyond mere reciprocity—partaking of the Masonic motto "brotherly love, relief, and truth." Thus, several brethren pointed to meaningful attention by brethren in the lodge when they were struggling with alcohol. Others pointed to support when they were dealing with family problems or divorce, or when they or members of their family were ill, injured, or in hospital undergoing treatment. Still others pointed to the presence and support offered by numerous unknown brethren who showed up at family funerals. Such attention, along with what one man called "ritual therapy," facilitated positive assessments of membership. Some related comments, the first from a long-time lodge officer:

> *I've been in here* [a nursing home] *now almost two years and the stream of people coming in and out of here is remarkable.*

I'm the most [visited person.] *I would say probably 90 percent of them are Masons.*

I had a pacemaker put in, and members of my lodge came to see me before church people came to see me!

My oldest brother had been a Freemason for about five years before I joined. I really took notice of how his life was changing, how he was dealing with different things especially within the family core. Also with some really serious family issues. My father had just passed away, and the way my brother took on the role willingly ... that's what I like about Freemasonry, to be able to face adversity no matter how much it hurts, and having the ability to do that with the confidence of knowing that I have brothers with me to do that without question.

Freemasonry sometimes carries people through difficult points in their lives. For seventeen years after I was divorced, Freemasonry was my life. Having to do stuff with the boys forced me to go out. It's helping now that I'm having problems with my daughter. It gets me out of the house, gives me focus and direction and keeps me active. Never underestimate that aspect of the fraternity.

The daughter of one Mason stated:

My father is a Mason, and the organization has really helped him and our family. We always used to have the security blanket that, if something happened, where the one of us was ill, they would look after us if something happened.

Indeed, in perhaps the best example, a long-time lodge secretary who kept up his administrative work despite a progressive disability that quickly moved him from walking with a cane to using a wheelchair was touched to discover that most lodges in his district quickly installed wheelchair ramps so that he could attend. Not only did he feel that his focus on the work "certainly" helped him "cope with this situation," indeed "probably saved my sanity," he was immensely gratified by such a show of support from the brethren. In his words, "It was, and it is, very meaningful."

But sometimes positive attention is not seen as something that has been earned—at least in the eyes of the recipient. Rather, it is perceived largely as a gift to those who do not necessarily see themselves as deserving: it is *extraordinary.* Fourteen instances of extraordinary recognition occurred in the data, all of which were noted positively in relation to involvement. One newly raised Master Mason reported being "dumbstruck" when asked by the Grand Master to join him and sit with the dignitaries in the East. But most common among such respondents were thirteen who reported strong encouragement and support for taking an office despite facing great difficulties, even a prior disability, that would normally preclude them from doing so. There were two cases where functionally illiterate members, including one manual labourer, were encouraged to become Master of the lodge. Indeed, that same man stated it made him "feel better about myself." Beyond this example, there were others meaningfully encouraged either to become Master or take another responsible office in the lodge ("You can do it, and we'll support you"). There were respondents with speech impediments or with mobility issues, those dealing with progressive, debilitating diseases, even elderly members whom the brethren "didn't want to die [without becoming] Master." Such respondents often thought they didn't have it in them, or struggled against great difficulties, but they were encouraged and supported by all while difficult matters were taken over by others, their mistakes along the way were forgiven, and so on. All found that such faith in their abilities under trying circumstances was a powerful spur to involvement. In one particularly touching instance, one disabled man who got enthusiastic applause after giving a speech broke down in tears. All such examples of extraordinary recognition served to reinforced member involvement.

Such extraordinary recognition did not go unnoticed by other respondents, who took the idea further and suggested an even more comprehensive approach. As noted, members are involved in the lodge for various reasons (i.e., social, ritual, spiritual, administrative, and so on). Since there are members who do not want to take an office in the lodge, it was stated by twelve respondents that there should be a way for them to be recognized, "made to feel useful and appreciated as well."

Finally in this respect, there is the issue of negative attention. Going beyond the disintegrative impact of merely being ignored, respondents articulated two forms of negative attention that did not facilitate involvement in the Craft over time.

First, respondents again pointed to the issue of ritualism. While ritual performed well and with spirit can be a unifying factor—and academics from Durkheim up to the modern day have taken up this theme—it is not an end in itself. Indeed, if taken that far it may approximate, more than anything else, the form of deviance articulated by Merton (1968). Thus, twenty-two respondents decried what they referred to as "anal retentiveness" and "perfectionism" in relation to the lodge ritual as something that discouraged them:

Some lodges are very straitlaced, and that's painful. [mimicking] "This is the way that we do it ..."

No matter how you do it, you will be hearing from someone. That turns off the less-educated brethren and fosters disunity rather than support.

This was related by seven respondents to lack of attention and support for officers and leaders doing their jobs, who then had to "learn on the job" in the face of such criticism—in effect, a form of emotional micropolitics (C. Clark 1990) employed by critics in corrosive power rituals (Collins 1990). Active Masons who needed support but were instead criticized by others were, needless to say, less inclined to have as positive a perspective on involvement.

Secondly in this respect there was negative attention garnered by members who took "the "networking thing" too far. Fourteen respondents made critical comments about those who engaged in "nepotism." The view expressed was that "one does not become a Mason for selfish reasons." Such men "don't join Freemasonry, they join their own greed," and "if they persist in self-seeking, they will not be looked upon favourably." Members who draw attention to themselves in such a manner run up against the normative structure of the Craft—and this is hardly conducive to long-term involvement. Moreover, five respondents noted that times have changed externally: "Unlike the old days, career advancement is not really an issue, though this was an important driver of membership historically." Nor, another five added, is joining the Craft something expected, "something that you just do, like in the past." Neither are there as extensive insurance, burial, or benevolence benefits as those offered before the rise of the welfare state, so it is much less likely that people will join simply to carry a dues card in their wallet and get ahead. In sum, the career advancement opportunities have historically declined but the normative structure has remained. Thus, the few who slip through and get involved in the Craft for such reasons are likely to face negative attention that is less than conducive to their long-term involvement in Freemasonry.

Ultimately, the issue of members receiving attention occurs in several iterations. Beyond the need for lodges to provide good fellowship and a welcoming social environment as discussed above, to truly foster involvement they also need to encourage avenues for earned recognition, to facilitate quasi-altruistic attention, and to find more ways to meaningfully incorporate extraordinary recognition into their activities, all the while reducing negative attention that may turn members off from continued involvement. Moreover, insofar as it is necessary in Masonry, the lodge needs to focus on the unifying and integrative aspects of ritual, not the corrosive, disintegrative elements that sometimes attend ritualism and are nurtured by emotional micropolitics.

The Composition of Fellowship: Equality, Status, and Sources of Attention/Recognition

While respondents stressed the importance of having a "welcoming" lodge and receiving attention from the brethren, it is also the case that they spent a great deal of time discussing the social composition of the lodge in relation to these matters and their involvement. Much was made of the "diversity" of brethren on various dimensions, though these claims were often overblown except for in relation to social class and age.[6] Nevertheless, two broad—and interrelated—themes emerged in tension with one another: (1) meaningful inclusiveness, the egalitarian levelling of social distinctions in the Craft; and (2) the significance of receiving brotherly recognition, attention, or acceptance from high-status members. Obviously, one cannot exist without the other, and it is this tension that can be differentially meaningful and problematic in relation to involvement. Each will be dealt with in turn.

First, sixty-one respondents commented on the opportunities that they had in the Craft to meet diverse people as equals, particularly how involvement in the order enabled them to cross social boundaries, to integrate into a "melting pot" of "brotherhood." Whether speaking in terms of class, ethnicity, religion, sexual orientation, education level, income, age, or other ordinary bases for social distinction, but more broadly than the blurring of class noted by Clawson (1989) in the nineteenth century, such respondents heralded the "inclusiveness" of the fellowship they encountered in Freemasonry today as significant to their involvement:

> *I like the fellowship you have with people you'd never [otherwise] rub shoulders with. It's not the same old crowd like at work. Otherwise, what's the point? I've met some fantastic men in Freemasonry in a variety of different fields—anything from fishermen and farmers to brain surgeons, anywhere from lawyers through to great intellectual professors at universities. I've met young people who are willing to explore. I've met old people who have thought things through, who can offer the calmness of age. I've met a variety of people. One thing I haven't met is anybody I thought was a bad person.*

> *What I think is unique about Freemasonry, what I really love about it, is in the fact that it allows me to come together with people of any race or creed, but we have one thing in common—a belief in God—but we have no dogma. It allows men of many religious persuasions to come together and do things for the betterment of mankind and not let politics and religion get in the way. Everybody can contribute in some way regardless of their background.*

> *Freemasonry crosses social boundaries, even more than in past given our increasingly multicultural society. It's an integrating factor. What I like is that new Canadians make up more than 50 percent of the new members of our lodge. I can say with absolute certainty that I see more multiculturalism in my lodge than I do on the street today. For example, Black men are very enthusiastic Masons. They're accepted.*

By rubbing shoulders with such a diversity of others, it enables
me to see their viewpoints and to understand my own situation
better.

Indeed, fourteen of these brethren explicitly drew upon the Masonic symbolism of "meeting on the level" to underscore the egalitarian ground, the meaningful levelling of social distinctions found in the Craft. Men of different ranks in the military simply referred to each other as "brother" in the lodge, as did managers and employees from the same workplace.

My father was a Mason. What impressed me as a child—and
what still appeals to me today—is that I would be sitting in a
room with the treasurer for the province, the premier, and an
electrician, a plumber, and a mechanic. It was a huge mix! And
they were all on the square, on the level! [bangs table] They
were the same when they were in that room!

I like that I can go to a meeting and talk to brethren at length
and not even ask what they do. I could be talking to a street
sweeper or the president.

Finally in this respect, six of these respondents commented on how, "unlike the old days" where Freemasonry was "only for the rich," there has been a welcome democratization of the membership in recent decades where there is a greater diversity of individuals involved:

These days, you don't have to be wealthy, prominent, or a
merchant to join. There's a whole different membership now.

Yet, as noted above, it is often the inclusion of external status distinctions in various ways that render such egalitarian claims as meaningful as they are. Thirty-four respondents showed awareness of this in one way or another. Indeed, one respondent stated it succinctly:

On the level? Some people aren't so much interested in bring
ing higher status people down onto their level as they are in
elevating themselves to the status of these others. It's the sort of
idea that one can gain status by association—or equality with
someone of higher status.

Such insights bring us to the second aspect above: the significance of being able to gain a sense of status through involvement. What this effectively involves is an alternate status hierarchy (or "aristocracy," to use Simmel's (1908) term), the opportunity for some to become a big fish in a small pond.

Indeed, status attainment has been found important to involvement in both Masonry and volunteer associations (Bullock 2007; Welser 2006). Thus, there were respondents from marginal backgrounds who found it very meaningful that they were able to succeed in the Craft. For example, one man who was functionally illiterate rose through the ranks to become the highest-ranking English Mason in Canada. Another stated:

> I was a grease monkey, but I had the opportunity to get to the top of my lodge. It's taken me from down in the depths to feeling respected. It doesn't matter whether you're unemployed or whether you're a millionaire—your lodge, you can go through. It's the way it should be anyway. You should be able to start at the bottom and go right to the top and be the head man, be the boss.

Although some respondents qualified their comments by noting the difficulty of rising in rank when someone is too eager for status, or by identifying particular individuals with little outside status who rose in rank more because they wanted to make a contribution than to achieve status, there nevertheless remained many comments backing up the existence of such an alternate status hierarchy as being significant to the involvement of some brethren, particularly in relation to their position in society:

> I think where you come from in life is a factor in how you view the lodge. I believe I get status in my work. Some people get it, you've got it in your work. You know, people who have managerial titles get it in their work, but some people don't— and so they need that. Some people come in with a great sense of the historical importance of Masonry, and being the head Mason, and they're still living in that era. That's important to them. Others, it's not important to. You know, it's like I don't need it. I didn't join for status, I joined for comradeship and to learn more about this organization that's been around for hundreds of years.

> Some people are compensating for something. In a broad sense that's right. I can think of a few individuals who have gone up through the highest ranks of the fraternity who were there literally because they want to serve. I see some who go there because [bangs fist twice] "I want to wear those jewels. I want to be a big cheese." But I find that those guys, they are coming out of—I think that they feel that they've underachieved on the outside, and that they should do that.

> If you have a challenging, demanding job, you're not looking for challenging, you know, stuff at the Masonic lodge. What's

the point? You're looking for a different experience. Somebody
who doesn't have much authority or responsibility in their life,
then it's important to them.

This status hierarchy had several referents that contributed to its meaningfulness. In addition to the social background of the individual, as noted above, these included the external status associations of fellow brethren, the internal system of rank within the Masonic order, and various ritualistic practices that signified the exclusivity of membership.

In relation to external associations, thirty-two respondents commented on both the historical exclusivity of the order and the opportunities that they have to associate with "important people" today:

> *I knew as a young person that Freemasonry was very exclusive.*
> *There's the historical connection with royalty, many famous*
> *individuals have been members, and how in the old days the*
> *leaders of the lodge were often merchants or the leaders of the*
> *colony. Masons were seen as influential, and they didn't let just*
> *anybody in the group. Consequently, most people wanted to*
> *join. My father was a Freemason, and you had to be of some*
> *social standing, some economic standing. Only certain people*
> *outstanding in the community were Freemasons. What the hell*
> *are you guys doing that you won't let just anybody in?*

> *Since I joined the Masons, I've had the chance to meet doctors,*
> *lawyers, politicians, movers and shakers, a whole bunch of peo-*
> *ple who impressed me, people I look up to and respect. If I'd*
> *never joined Masonic, I wouldn't have the opportunity to do it.*

> *I enjoy the people that I'm getting to know as brothers. They're*
> *a lot of fun, and it so happens that some of them are important*
> *people. I wouldn't consider myself one yet, but hopefully some*
> *day. I want a piece of that action.*

The internal status hierarchy was also noted as significant by twenty-nine respondents. They spoke of "opportunities for achievement," to "have influence," and thereby to "gain personal satisfaction." Thus, sixteen of these commented on becoming Master of the lodge; five, on the existence of additional orders with "higher degrees"; five, of becoming a Grand Lodge officer; two, of being awarded honors, awards, or medals; and one, of being on lodge committee and thus "part of the inner circle." Indeed, one new Mason summed up this aspect of hierarchy well:

> *I would like my name in our lodge history with the great names.*
> *I aspire to be much more than just a third-degree Mason. I've*

an interest in taking one of the office chairs. I'd like to have my name written down in history books as "in the lodge with" and "part of" and Worshipful Master or Grand Master alongside my name.

Finally, seven respondents pointed to ritualistic practices that fostered an in-group/out-group sense of exclusivity. These ranged from strictly testing visitors before admitting them, the secret handshakes, requiring all but Past Masters to leave during the "inner work" during lodge installations, and so on. Such ritualistic practices served to further reinforce the alternate status hierarchy and draw brethren closer to involvement in the Craft. Indeed, it is interesting that some respondents suggested increasing exclusivity today to facilitate better retention of members:

We need to have more associated accoutrements suggesting an elite organization. It would be good to have an exclusive restaurant or bar or members area, etc. We could have people knocking on our door saying, "Please let me join," instead of members going around asking "Wanna join? Wanna join?"

To improve membership involvement we need to attract more elite members that others will want to associate with, from politicians to business leaders to the arts, not the salesman or wannabe politician.

Despite the above, however, there was a downside to all of this. While in some instances there was a productive tension between the levelling and status dimensions that facilitated member involvement, in others the balance was pushed too far in the latter direction such that status became a problem respondents felt was not conducive to member involvement and retention. Twenty-two respondents, in various ways, complained that certain members were "not really on the level," that members of the lodge were too concerned about "building another level of hierarchy," and particularly that the resultant "excessively bureaucratic features of this organization" were a problem.

If administration starts to take up more than 25 or 30 percent of the time, then we're in trouble. That's the sign of a dying organization.

A similar flavour came out in many respondents' related comments about the Grand Lodge—discussed in a later section—that there seemed to be too much concern about, and attention given to, Grand Lodge issues compared to those of the rank-and-file members of the local lodge.

The gist of all of this is that status can only be a driver of involvement if it is carefully balanced with equality, where opportunities and attention are spread around sufficiently to maintain a sense of commonality among diverse brethren and where bureaucracy and its connected growth outside of the local lodge do not usurp the importance of rank-and-file members. Such comments speak to the dangers of moving toward volunteer professionalization and the workplace model (Ilsley 1990), and to the ways in which such trends relate to successful organizational ritual performance, or, in failure, are concentrated in a perceived breach between appearance and reality (Mangham and Overington 1987). They also add considerable complications to work suggesting a relatively straightforward replacement of social hierarchies with Masonic ones (Poulet 2010).

Social Bonding and Trust

Much of the discussion thus far has had to do with factors that bring members closer together. Whether this involves "fit," a welcoming group accepting of diverse members, good fellowship, or sufficient attention from people of status both inside and outside the lodge, such factors can serve to facilitate integration and involvement. In this section, I build upon such matters to consider those things that respondents specifically highlighted as facilitating bonding and trust between members—and often greater involvement in the order.

First—and closely interrelated with the discussion of "fit" above—sixty-four respondents spoke of the importance of discovering meaningful commonalities with other brethren in the lodge after they became involved (Poulet 2010). There were many variations. Some spoke of identifying with brethren of similar occupational, military, ethnic, cultural, school, community, or geographic backgrounds:

> After joining the lodge, I realized that several of the boys I already knew from my days in the submarine service. The brotherhood we have here parallels—and builds upon—what we had in the military.

> I met a lot more local guys from my country once I joined. In fact, some of the others joke that we should hang the Lebanese flag on the door of our lodge. It's true we stick together and have been really involved in working to make our lodge as successful as it is.

> Our lodge is a big part of a small, tightly knit rural community, my home town. In fact, even though I don't live there any more, it acts as a key tie to the town and my family. Driving back for meetings, having family in the lodge, it helps me stay connected.

Furthermore, beyond discovering or identifying with commonalities in background, respondents discovered that they shared interests *and* dislikes with others, or groups of others, in the lodge:

> *I found a place to talk about important issues with like-minded men. I'm not into sports. I'm not into wasting my time in pubs. It's kind of reassuring to know that there's this network and circle out there of people who are on the same path and on the same road.*

Indeed, to the extent that these commonalities were discovered after becoming involved in the Craft, this is one way of backing up the literature stating that people stay involved in organizations for different reasons than they join them (Ilsley 1990).

Secondly, thirty-nine respondents reported that working together for a common goal served to foster connections between members. Whether this involved preparing for and performing a degree on a candidate or working together for a worthy charitable cause, co-operative, common activity with purpose seemed to facilitate what Durkheim ([1912] 1965) called "collective effervescence" between members. Respondents spoke of a "bond forged in common activities and shared tasks," of how "despite different groupings in the lodge, we come together to do the work," of how doing charity work ranging from "bagging horse manure for charity" or having a "fundraiser/benefit to recognize the troops" to "everyone pulling out $20 bills so the son of a single mother could buy hockey equipment" "made everyone feel great." One man commented that "when a group is organized, active, and engaged in working toward a planned goal in a small town, people take notice. That's pretty special." Another pointed to the new bonds formed when lodges jointly practise and put on degrees. Indeed, another recounted a meaningful incident where the members present were touched when a brother walked into a lodge practice, stood at the altar, and spontaneously quoted a biblical line from the ritual: ""How good and pleasant it is for brethren to toil together in unity." All such examples speak to the value of collective, co-operative action in forming bonds between members.

Thirdly, forty-two respondents reported that such common activities went hand in hand with a normative tendency "to see what we have in common rather than our differences." To some extent this involved how "we have gone through the same things" (i.e., the ritual initiatory experience), how respondents swore the same moral obligation, or how having access to common things "gives us something to talk about." Indeed, these served as the foundation—the building blocks, as it were—of a "Masonic identity" (Mahmud-Abdelwahib 2008), which is significant given the literature suggesting that organizations fostering a strong identity among its volunteers are likely to encourage greater involvement and sustained volunteerism (Chacon, Vecina, and Davila 2007).

Fourth, eighteen respondents pointed to how anti-Masonic encounters or materials fostered a deepening of their bond to the Craft and its ideals. Thus, one man said that his awareness of "persecution of Freemasons in my home country makes my involvement a lot more meaningful here." Another commented on how a negative encounter with a religious critic of the Craft "opened my eyes to how some people are not free and remain chained to dogma." Others, now that they were involved, went further, even joking about the anti-Masonic materials that they had encountered:

> *Thanks for the fun conspiracy theories! You know, there's no such thing as bad advertising. All that stuff just makes Freemasonry more sexy and mysterious. In fact it just makes some of us more curious and want to dig into it more.*

> *All of this stuff you hear about what we've supposedly done— well it's at least reassuring that somebody is in charge! It's comforting in a weird way. [teasing another] but it's not a cult until we start killing! [laughter]*

Regardless of whether anti-Masonic encounters were personal or merely literary, an in-group/out-group dynamic was fostered, with subcultural bonds evidenced either through serious commentary or levity.

Finally, there were again comments that veered away from linking traditional commonalities—whether in background, experience, or collective action—to those that emphasized attempts by lodges to remain relevant to today's changing society. Of the fourteen respondents that sounded this theme, one man commented,

> *We don't need to change the ritual, but to incarnate it in relation to current issues and make the fellowship around it relevant.*

Similarly, there were eight among this group that emphasized drawing attention to the many parallels between Freemasonry and popular culture. There were even two who suggested having different lodges to cater to people with different backgrounds and interests, ranging from traditional to contemporary:

> *I don't think every lodge should be identical.... I think that maybe there should be different lodges with different flavours for different people. If we did that, we could find a way to channel like-minded people to the same lodges.*

Thus, taken together, respondents indicated that having—or discovering—commonalities with other members, sharing in mutual activity toward a common goal, sharing the common experience of initiation into a subculture that provides something common and normative to talk about, experiencing or encountering individuals or materials that oppose or sensationalize one's involvement, and a context where the organization remains nimble enough to remain relevant to contemporary society—all these tend to foster bonding to, and involvement in, the order.

Indeed, the ultimate product of the bonds that have been formed as a result of these and many of the other factors discussed thus far in the chapter is a willingness to share and a strong sense of trust between brethren. Twenty-seven respondents articulated this theme, and two main dimensions to this rescaling of the social distance between individuals (Kaplan 2014) were noted by the respondents. First, ten commented on how, in today's risky society, knowing that someone is a Mason "reverses the onus of trust."

> *I would more readily offer the hospitality of my home to a brother Mason. They're not like other strangers. I can more readily make positive assumptions about them.*

> *Out of two people, I would buy a car from a Mason over someone else because I would trust him.*

> *I value each and every Mason I've had friendship/brothership with more so than anybody I've met in my workaday life. I would leave my wallet on the table and walk out of the room with any of the guys here.*

Similarly, twelve respondents in the group spoke of how it was easier to form connections with fellow brothers:

> *When I'm travelling and meet a brother, I feel an automatic contact, an instant rapport much more often than with others. Really, the worldwide fraternity is an asset. Having that ritual similarity across languages, cultures, and religions is extremely comforting. I've got friends all over.*

Indeed, the strength of the bonds and associated trust that can be built up between brethren in the ways discussed above becomes apparent when they are tested. This is profoundly illustrated by one man who, as an adult, discovered that his father—once a prominent Mason—had been abusing his sister. Enraged by this news, he spoke to fellow brethren, told them how upset he was that his father had done this, and angrily indicated that he planned to quit as a result. Yet another Mason—"a guy who's not usually very profound"—quietly suggested that the now-disgraced father's actions were his own, not those of the other brethren whom the son had come to know and trust. He then said something that "struck" the respondent: "Your father may be the reason that you joined, but he doesn't have to be the reason you stay." In the end, following the father's disgrace and expulsion, the respondent indicated that this encounter, and the bonds he had formed with the rest of the brethren, facilitated his decision to remain involved.

What all of this suggests is that brethren who have gone through the above bonding process can gradually take to heart the people and ideas that they are exposed to over time, and from internalizing these in various activities can eventually develop intimately what respondents called a "Masonic identity." In perhaps the most notable words to this effect,

> I've been a Mason all of my life and I'll be a Mason until I die. I mean I'm a Mason. I don't mean I'll just be saying it. I'm a Mason, and there's a lot of things to Masons besides a ring and a meeting.

Of course, it is also the case that the bonding process above may be short-circuited along the way by poor "fit," lack of meaningful common activities, too many differences that divided members, indifference by others in society, or a particular lodge's inability to remain socially relevant. Untrustworthy behaviour is certainly not helpful, nor are many of the other negative factors discussed thus far in the chapter (e.g., neglecting members and not keeping them up to date on activities, an excessive emphasis on status, etc.). The factors respondents related to bonding, to the formation of trust, and to the development of a Masonic identity do not exist in a vacuum; they must be seen in the broader context of other factors discussed herein. If the balance between the various positive factors and processes outweighs the negative, bonding and ongoing involvement appear to be favoured. If, however, the balance is negative, then the bonds will fail to form or will be relatively weak, such that continued involvement is either less probable or more easily disrupted.

CONCLUSION

As is by now apparent, the social atmosphere of the lodge is clearly one of the major factors underlying Masonic involvement. Given that many brethren are largely "social Masons," in a broad sense lodges with a good social atmosphere are likely to do better at involving and retaining members—and the converse would also likely be true. As well, implicit in this chapter are undoubtedly a number of suggestions for hypothetically improving social atmosphere and, by extension, improving member involvement in lodges.

Nevertheless, given the complexity of the factors detailed here, variations in the membership and social context of a lodge must always carefully considered when seeking to apply these in any given case.

Yet social atmosphere is not the whole story. The next chapter moves on to consider the important and complex organizational factors that have emerged in relation to Masonic involvement today.

CHAPTER 5

ORGANIZATIONAL FACTORS
AND MEMBER INVOLVEMENT

T he two most prominent areas discussed by respondents regarding involvement were related to social atmosphere and organizational factors.
Now that I have looked at the former, it is time to turn to the diverse—yet
frequently interrelated—series of matters related to organizational structures,
processes, strategies, goals, practices, and dynamics that respondents claimed
were highly significant to member retention. These include membership focus,
dues structure, right to participation, the distribution of offices and tasks,
organization and running of meetings, community interaction, contentious
dynamics, relationship with the Grand Lodge and the Shrine, and demo-
graphic/generational issues. Each will be discussed in turn.

MEMBERSHIP FOCUS: GETTING NEW MEMBERS OR RETAINING
EXISTING ONES

There was a tension in the data between respondents who emphasized the need
to bring in new members and those who felt it was important to focus on,
invigorate, and retain the involvement of those members already on the rolls.
Given the shortening periods of involvement noted in the Masonic literature
(Belton and Henderson 2000; Belton 1999), the former is one practical way
that lodges can—and have—maintained enough members to continue their
activities and sustain their programs. While many respondents recognized the
need for both types of organizational policies for a robust, involved membership, for analytical purposes it will be useful to separate these comments to
bring out their interrelated components.

First, respondents stressed the need to get new members to maintain
involvement in the face of inevitable attrition. In the words of one man,
"Every once in a while you have to add membership to have membership."

Several prominent themes appeared in this respect, largely involving the issue of relative openness and the utility of being either more or less secretive to recruit "new blood." The ideal-typical themes on each side of this debate on organizational recruitment policy are contrasted below.

On the one hand, there were respondents who favoured less openness in recruitment. Seventeen respondents favoured the traditional secrecy—and its attendant aura of "mystery" and "sexiness"—as a means of building the membership through attraction. Comments favouring this approach often referred to how the secrecy and mysterious language enhanced the respondents' own experiences:

> It really was quite a secret society back then [1963–64 in Scotland]. I loved the mystery of it, how men hid away their aprons and medals, the strict "no comment" policy, how you'd see men filing in and out with black suits and briefcases like the Men in Black. It was part of the draw. "Man, I get to join a secret society!"

> It's thrilling to know that there's something you don't know, like there's a secret behind there and you actually want to get at that secret, and when you actually get there, it's like an achievement and it's pretty exciting.

> I like the fact that it's a so-called secret society. I think it might be appealing to the kid in me.... It makes it special, and I have fun with it.

Similarly, many such respondents tended to be very much in favour of the traditional organizational policy against soliciting new members (i.e., potential candidates must ask a member if they may join). Thirteen of these respondents opposed "soliciting":

> Chasing them just drives them away. If you've got to push, it's not going to work.

> I know lodges that recruit and they don't retain. Not everybody fits into Freemasonry, and those who stay more likely were not solicited.

> Public availability of information kills the mystery. Advertising can backfire, like it did in Prince Edward Island.

Not surprisingly, many such respondents were of the view that open-lodge recruitment policies were problematic in that they "favoured quantity over quality of candidates." Twenty-three respondents took this stance, another eight adding that they were opposed to the "one-day classes" organized in some jurisdictions (e.g., New York), where large groups of solicited candidates get their three degrees quickly. Some comments:

> *A lot of places, lodges have reached the point where, if you have a heartbeat and can sign your name we will consider, we will even accept you. If we keep doing that, our fraternity will cease to have any real meaning. More may come in, but many also won't stick with it.*

> *The one-day classes bastardize Freemasonry. They're linked to our instantaneous society. Some things are worth waiting for. They take time and work for understanding and development. People who go through these won't get the full benefit.*

Finally in this first respect, twenty-one such respondents stressed the need to more carefully screen candidates by ensuring that they had an appropriate background enabling them to fit well into the order. This view often went hand in hand with the opinion that current investigation practices were far from sufficient:

> *We need to consider whether people are likely to be active. Not everybody fits into Freemasonry, so we should try to see if they are like-minded people. Regardless of their background otherwise, we must be more selective to ensure that they will stick around, not vanish after their first or third degree.*

> *These checks we do, I mean, bluntly, they're a joke. When they came out to meet me, they had a cup of tea and a cookie, asked me if I believed in God, and said "Yeah, you'd make a good Mason." The whole time I've been in the lodge, I've only seen one potential member voted down, not let into the lodge. Oftentimes the proposer only knows the guy for short time and the seconder doesn't know him from Adam.*

Thus, there is a body of opinion that a recruitment policy directed at maintaining involvement should revolve around creating an aura of secrecy and mystery, attracting rather than soliciting candidates, and putting strategies into place that ensure quality rather than quantity of candidates in order to improve the odds that those who enter become involved, take the time to understand, and stay.

Nevertheless, this approach to recruitment, to keeping the numbers up, was opposed by another group of respondents who took contrary views on many of these same issues. Twenty-three respondents argued that Freemasonry needed to be "less secretive." One reported that there was a study showing that one of the biggest problems behind lagging recruitment numbers in New

York was "fathers not telling sons," while another recounted an anecdote about one Grand Master who never told his son. Others claimed that "this whole idea of it being a secret society has been taken too far over the years" and that this is "out of sync with the advertising rhythm of today's society."

Secondly, twelve of these respondents favoured soliciting new members:

> Most Masons don't publicize the fact that they're Masons. Because of the secrecy, nobody seems to know that the organization even exists. If I had been gently nudged, I would have been in it, been involved when I was in my twenties.

> Too many men that would have been good Masons have been denied the chance because of this stigma of being invited. If I hadn't been asked, I would have missed out otherwise, and asking saved our lodge—one that would have gone into darkness otherwise.

> There has been an influx. I think some of it has occurred since the regulations have been relaxed a little bit on approaching people. You're allowed to gently nudge someone to and drop suggestions and that sort of thing, and I think that has helped.

Indeed, twenty-one such respondents emphasized various practices that enabled them to better attract members today. These ranged from "being accessible to those seeking information," "dropping hints" to entice men to ask (something also done by the first group above), and making connections with members of other organizations such as service clubs, churches, and fraternities, all the way to outright solicitation/advertising.[1] Whatever the degree of this emphasis on openness, however, such respondents stressed the need to "remain relevant to today's society" and spoke of drawing connections to the crossover between Freemasonry and popular culture, focusing on contemporary demographics, and so on. In perhaps the farthest extension of the dual themes of promotion and relevance, one man who favoured advertising—and whose job involved writing commercials—commented on the busy pace of modern life and ongoing social changes, then spontaneously launched into a "commercial" for the Craft:

> You need to take one night a month for yourself and go somewhere where you can put your feet up, relax. Here is something for you that's not stressful, but for you to put all your other worries aside. One night a month, and we can offer that to you—something interesting, something with decorum, something that means something—something you'll want to come back to.

Interestingly, this latter group of respondents who favoured greater openness also frequently favoured bringing larger numbers of candidates in so that, even with attrition, the lodge would still retain a larger number of committed members. This standpoint came out most strongly in relation to the controversial practice of running "one-day classes" for large groups of candidates:

> *I think their feeling is that, out of that bunch, there'll be some people who will get it and who are really there because they are like-minded folks in the first place, and then there are other folks who will realize "Oh, this is not for me" and they'll just go off. Like, show them the ropes and if they stay, they were the good guys, and if they don't stay, well, they weren't with you anyway—and it doesn't matter so much. It's better to have 2 to 5 percent of 1,000 men than not get any new. Besides, the retention rate is dead even and they still have to do the work in the end.*

Thus, there is a tension in the data over organizational recruitment policy—a matter that is increasingly important if the order is to maintain membership numbers in the face of shortening retention periods in recent decades. On the one hand, there are those who favour a traditional, restrictive approach emphasizing mystery, attraction, and building membership through attention to quality, socially congruent candidates who will likely stay involved; on the other hand, there are those who favour a more open approach to recruitment, a greater quantity of candidates, and retaining more members by drawing from a larger pool in the first place. While these remain ideal types, and most respondents would likely find themselves somewhere in the middle of this analytical continuum rather than at either extreme, this exercise has laid bare a tension in one key policy issue that the Craft is struggling with today in efforts to maintain the involvement of sufficient numbers to survive. Resolving such issues will be essential to the future of the Craft.

But, as noted in the last chapter, Freemasonry must also have appropriate organizational strategies in place to involve and retain brethren that are already members of the order, to curb declining lengths of involvement by addressing the oft-noted theme that "it's one thing to bring people in, but then you have to do something to keep them."

Respondents were well aware of the ongoing problem of attrition. Thirty-one commented on this issue, nine of whom noted that they themselves remained involved but that most of the others with whom they went through their degrees did not.

> *The average length of involvement is dropping—just like marriage!*

> *I kept involved—others in my group didn't. Of the nine guys I went through with, I think there's four who are still active.*

> *Out of seven of us going through, I think I'm the only one left!*

Indeed, such respondents often questioned how many new initiates would stay:

> *It will be interesting to come back in five or six years and see how many of today's candidates have stayed. I've observed many youth coming in [who] stayed two years, then trailed off. But you can't predict who will stay. One guy I wouldn't have predicted became very active.*

> *Our lodge had quite a number of young Masons in their late twenties and early thirties. Most of them we've seen once or twice after their third degree. How many Masons do we see who join the organization, go through the three degrees, put on their ring, and just walk away? Maybe one out of twenty will stay and be a good Mason.*

> *I was taught that, no matter what, I'm only going to retain 50 to 60 percent at best, if it's important to me. If it's not, I might keep 20 percent ... and then when they pass on their percentage of the original 100 percent, down it goes. Soon there's nobody to teach and nothing is being taught to them.*

As a result of such concerns, twenty respondents articulated the importance of having retention policies:

> *Don't put so much emphasis on new members and ignore the rest.*

> *There's younger members that are coming into this that are an opportunity, and they're coming for a reason! [bangs fist] We have to give them a reason to stay! [bangs fist]*

> *We have lots of members, but we don't have enough Masons. I think it's just about time maybe we stopped looking for people to put on the membership list and started looking at the list itself and getting at those people.*

Respondents who articulated such themes went further, suggesting various organizational policies that they felt would be helpful in re-involving existing members. Nine respondents stressed that the lodge should be "welcoming" to members who have not attended for a while. There were men who noted the value of being "encouraged to come out when you meet," of other brethren being "helpful for those who forget the signs" (e.g., by coming to their house to demonstrate), of Masonic acquaintances "vouching for them before meetings," and of generally being offering a friendly and inviting environment. One such man who had been invited back noted the positive impact of such an approach:

> I was welcomed with open arms. I found it like putting on a comfortable dressing gown in the morning. It was just like I'd been there every month, and I've been there ever since.

Another man reported witnessing a brother who, returning to the lodge after a long absence, received a rousing welcome, noting that "he had tears in his eyes after coming out." Thus, providing a welcoming social environment for returning members can be one way to reinvigorate involvement by lapsed members.

Similarly, eight respondents suggested that the lodge make better efforts to stay in contact with its members, inform them of ongoing events and activities, and show concern for their concerns and events in their lives: "I think we leave people alone too much. You keep them by making them feel a part, that they are important to you." Two of these even suggested that the lodge produce and send its own newsletter to the brethren as a means of doing so. This latter suggestion could also highlight to members when something notable or interesting will be going on at upcoming meetings of either their own or other nearby lodges, better enabling them to plan to "avoid the boring business meetings" when attending or visiting.[2]

Five respondents also mentioned accessibility issues, recognizing that some members would be involved if they could better afford the dues or had a way to get to the lodge. Two of these mentioned finding better ways to offer discreet help to brethren on fixed incomes. Two others mentioned the lodge putting in place "carpools" or, more informally, encouraging members to offer to pick up a brother and drive him home. One man also mentioned making lodge buildings (especially the older ones) wheelchair accessible for those who cannot attend otherwise.

Finally in this respect, four respondents suggested addressing poor attendance by putting in place policies to deal with what might be called "problem cases." Two of these suggestions were more conciliatory, two were not. Of the first two, one suggestion involved contacting a lapsed member to "find out if anything has upset them"; the other involved putting in place "an amnesty for excluded members" (i.e., those who had been dropped from membership for failure to pay their annual dues). The second group took a harder line, suggesting that the lodge make attending one or several meetings a year "mandatory" or the member would be dropped from the rolls: "Otherwise, it's just your money. It's not that important."

Several related policy matters were articulated by those who indicated why they thought brethren lessened their involvement over time or even left the order altogether. Four respondents complained about being left alone and not being informed about lodge activities and events. Another two complained about their lodges "ignoring" inactive members "except when you go after them for dues." When a lodge does not adopt, or when it lets slip, policies such as those above, the involvement of existing members and the potential re-involvement of others falters. Soon, in the words of one man, "After making one excuse, it becomes easier to make the other ones."

From the above, it is clear that lodges, to maintain involvement, need not only a recruitment policy to keep adding to the ranks but also a practical set of retention and renewal policies directed at revitalizing existing and dormant members. The most fruitful balance between these approaches may vary from lodge to lodge, from jurisdiction to jurisdiction, but going too far in either direction is unlikely to be as effective in the long run as paying careful attention to each.[3]

DUES/FEES STRUCTURE

Another factor affecting the involvement of brethren, although it was noted by relatively few respondents, is the ongoing cost of being a member. Beyond initiation fees at the front end, Masons pay annual dues to their lodge, which, in some cases, became an issue for discussion.

Interestingly, however, the debate was not merely about affordability—though some respondents did mention this. Instead, the dominant expression—articulated by fifteen respondents, revolved around the theme that "we sell Masonry too cheap." To some extent, this is informed by the fact that attempts to keep membership fees low and easily affordable since the mid-twentieth century have neither prevented declining membership nor improved retention (Tabbert, 2007). In the words of one man:

> We sell ourselves too cheap. We are nickel-and-diming our
> Masonic system to death. The dues we pay in most of our
> Masonic organizations are ridiculously small compared to the
> value most of us get out of it. Meanwhile, our lodges are facing
> financial difficulties, building and repair costs, and we're not
> able to do some of the things we should be [doing] to make the
> organization more effective.

Several of these brethren went further, claiming that, like one of the French Grand Lodges and certain Prince Hall lodges in the United States, it would be best to set high initiation and membership fees, along with "targeting certain groups," to make the order more exclusive (e.g., holding lunchtime meetings/degrees for professionals, such as is done in Ontario and Washington state). Indeed, it was pointed out that such lodges have a "huge waiting list," that people are "clamouring to join" and "won't just join on a whim. Otherwise, it's a lot of money."

Nevertheless, three respondents did point out that even modest dues could sometimes be a burden for some members, particularly older brethren living on fixed incomes. Indeed, this could be worse for those involved in several Masonic organizations; these relatively small amounts began to add up. In order to deal with such difficulties, one advocate of higher dues and exclusivity suggested that it would be best to follow the example of the Prince Hall district he described, where there were some lodges with high dues and others with the traditional fee structure. He asserted that this gave potential members the option, but that they "were all brothers" and "anyone can visit."

Running through these comments we again see the tension between the attracting—and presumably retaining—power of status versus the need for equality. As noted earlier, this tension can at times be productive, but things cannot be taken too far in either direction or it may backfire in relation to member involvement. Finding the right balance is a difficult task—and may vary somewhat given the different characteristics of each lodge and jurisdiction.

THE RIGHT TO PARTICIPATE IN LODGE ACTIVITIES—AND WHEN

Another issue that shares this theme of status versus equality involves the right of members of different rank to participate in certain activities of the lodge. Generally, a new member is able to vote on business matters once they have been initiated into the lodge. However, they will still not be allowed to attend when the lodge is operating on the second or third degrees until they go through those ceremonies as well.[4]

This participation issue is usually not a problem for those lodges that utilize English Emulation ritual—that is, ones that both open and do all of their business on the first degree. However, there are lodges in some jurisdictions that traditionally open and do all of their business on the third degree. In effect, this excludes Entered Apprentice (first-degree) and Fellowcraft (second-degree) Masons from participating or attending until they have completed their degrees. In between—especially if there are lengthy gaps—they may lose interest in the order.

As a result, respondents noted that an increasing number of lodges have been opening and doing their business on "the lowest degree of those in attendance." Seventeen respondents spoke in favour of this more egalitarian organizational policy, and none spoke against it. Indeed, six more noted that new brethren not being able to attend lodge until they get their third degree was problematic, four adding that taking too much time in between presented difficulties for the long-term involvement and retention of new members.

Beyond this dominant theme, there were only three other issues raised by respondents in relation to the right to participate. One noted that his Grand Lodge had recently lowered the minimum age for initiation from twenty-one to eighteen (and my own Grand Lodge has for some time done so for the sons of existing Masons), thus enabling younger individuals to participate in the order should they so desire. A second respondent again pointed to accessibility issues for those brethren with physical disabilities, in effect asserting their equality and the need for the order to take measures to ensure their right to participate in lodge activities. Finally, there was one respondent who complained about those of Masonic rank who stand up at the end of a meeting and "mouth off about nothing," "spewing hot air and wasting everyone's time." This speaks to the privilege of the highest ranking Grand Lodge officers, particularly the Grand Master, speaking last—which irritates some in the rank and file after a long night.

Nevertheless, the predominant issue raised in this section was the need for lodges and Grand Lodges to ensure the right of brethren to participate as often and as equally as possible from the outset to head off the possibility of dissociation at the front end.

ISSUES SURROUNDING MASONIC OFFICES AND TASKS IN THE LODGE

The next matter interacting with involvement—both as cause and effect—relates to the distribution of both formal positions and informal tasks in the operation of the lodge. While it is trite to say that having a position or task to perform means that one is by definition involved, it is also the case that requests concerning—and exposure to—various tasks, along with recognition of one's participation in a given position, may foster more and greater interaction with the brethren, enable the realization that there is more meaning to the order than one might find sitting on the sidelines, and ultimately encourage one to remain involved over time. In other ways, such encounters may have quite the opposite impact. It is to such matters that I now turn, considering respondents' interactions surrounding offices and tasks to see what they have to say about their role in encouraging or discouraging involvement.

Taking the positive side first, twenty-three respondents pointed to the ability of the Master and officers to tactfully, in one man's words, "encourage benchers to take a part rather than the usual suspects." Two stated that "some people need a boost"; two others offered that it was "important to start with small things." In this, it was seen as "important to let people take their time to learn something," but such encouragement would both "give them an opportunity to succeed, to know and love the organization" and foster a sense of inclusion by "making them feel a part of it." Nevertheless, five qualified their comments on the basis that there must be "brethren willing to take parts, do the work, and pitch in," a reminder that tact is only part of the complex story of involvement.

Next, nineteen respondents commented that it was important that there was "fairness in allotting offices and responsibilities." This related not just to individuals but, as three noted, also to the dynamic between groups and member interests and abilities; it also involved "a fair distribution of the workload" among the officers and brethren, the Master "having the ability to delegate and involve others" and not allow people "to hog certain parts." The Master can also "give people the benefit of the doubt" when they decline a role, thus "supporting people who want to advance only so far." In effect, this means that members feel that they have some "input" on what role they play, on the "direction of the lodge and its activities."

Closely related to this was the third factor, noted by thirteen respondents: the existence of "opportunities for advancement," the ability to "achieve" and gain "personal satisfaction" by taking certain parts in the ritual or filling a series of offices on their way to the status inherent in the Master's chair. Several organizational aspects were noted that might facilitate this, such as the need for Masters to be "selective" in choosing "quality officers" or "dynamic individuals" on "merit or proficiency" rather than just having an "automatic line" of progression (noted by six respondents). Two respondents also mentioned the importance of "good mentoring practices." Finally, and implicit in all of this, two men stated that the lodge needs to "encourage healthy competition over offices and parts," which can foster greater involvement and "an active and engaged membership."

> The only reason why I learned the Middle Chamber lecture was because someone said I couldn't, and someone said I couldn't present it. "Okay, screw you, watch this." But then, the ego kicks in because someone says "Oh my God, this is the best thing ever." Oh yeah, so I mean, that's why I do it.... There's a couple of guys that are super competitive; well, we're all competitive—not in a bad way, but in a good way. Like someone says, all right, what are you going to do? Well, who's going to be Master first? It's like, "I'll be Master first." Okay, well, who is going to learn this first? Who's going to learn that first? And when three, four, five of us get together, it's a mini-competition—but I think our lodge feeds from it.

Indeed, the importance of opportunities for advancement is shown in situations where they are absent or blocked, where competition has no outlet or is stifled by existing elites. Four of these respondents complained of situations where "the old guys hog everything and keep you down," of "people getting in the Chair that don't want to leave, who are on a power trip," and of "the dangers of relying on an unofficial degree team where 'I've always done that part'—that excludes others." Healthy competition cannot exist when there is nothing to compete for.

Fourth, forty-five respondents commented that "feeling supported" in the office or task that they are doing was important to their involvement. In the words of one man, "It's a supportive environment, not like at the office where people just wait for you to stumble." Eight of these individuals commented on compliments from others for doing a good job, four mentioned how others provided advice and answered questions, four reported receiving encouragement and positive reinforcement at practices, and three talked about the importance of being reassured that others had made mistakes along the way. One man pointed to how meaningful it was to have one of his friends follow him throughout his time moving "up the line" of offices, "supporting me throughout my Masonic career."

Finally in this respect, twenty-four respondents spoke about the importance of "good administrative leadership by the Master." This had essentially two components. On the one hand, eleven respondents noted that this involved the Master—in tandem with an efficient secretary, good organizational skills, and a well-oiled business plan—"running good meetings." On the other hand, thirteen respondents noted the importance of spreading out degree work at intervals throughout the year so that positions and parts could be arranged and practised well ahead of time.

In all of these ways, respondents noted that the brethren's participation in various Masonic offices and tasks can be encouraged—and their involvement facilitated—over time. Yet, as already hinted above, there are a variety of negative encounters in these areas that can turn brethren off, discouraging their involvement in a number of ways. Four interrelated areas were of concern in this respect.

First, forty-seven respondents noted that involvement was hampered when key officers felt a lack of support from others when doing their jobs. For example, some key officers complained that "I'd been elected, but felt upset not knowing what the job entailed. I had to learn on the job." Others commented about Immediate Past Masters, Past Masters, and other brethren "not supporting the Master during his time in office." This did not create an atmosphere conducive to long-term involvement, given comments "criticizing those who need support" (e.g., about someone "being moved up too quickly," about another "wanting to be Master, but not being willing to do the work to get there," or "members putting someone incompetent in office then leaving him on his own"). One respondent even made a point of noting brethren's common lack of support for a Master-elect when he visits other lodges to invite others to his installation ceremony.

But it was in relation to the ongoing operation of the lodge, especially regarding ritual work, that this lack of support was most often noted. On the one hand, fifteen such respondents complained about how "poor ritual work by the Worshipful Master and officers is unimpressive." In this vein there were complaints about how they "couldn't even open and close," exhibited "poor floorwork, wobbling around the altar," were "reading out of the book, just going through the motions," and often "missed the dramatic part" as a result. The general feeling among such brethren was that the whole thing was "undignified." In the words of one man, "Some lodges are really very slack. It hurts." Yet, respondents on the receiving end of this ritualism had their own complaints, typically centred around the idea of "perfectionism" and "nitpicking" in relation to the ritual. Twenty-three of the above respondents commented that, in the words of one man, "this anal-retentiveness about ritual turns people off, fostering disunity rather than support."

In a similar vein, such lack of support was noted in relation to administrative tasks. On the one hand, seven respondents complained of, as one man put it, "poor administrative leadership by the Worshipful Master." There were various complaints that, on the one hand, the Master "couldn't run a meeting," or exhibited a "lack of good organizational skills"; yet on the other hand, that he "unfairly shuts down discussion," and "is a control freak who does everything himself, totally unable or unwilling to delegate." Such administrative complaints surrounding leadership were often coupled with criticism over the "excessively bureaucratic" nature of the organization, a point raised by nine respondents. These kinds of views reveal the emotional micropolitics that can occur in Masonry, and they hardly encourage a feeling of support among those who take an office.

Secondly, and undoubtedly related to some extent to the above, twenty-one respondents complained about a "lack of people willing to come forward to take offices and share responsibilities, even when they are not busy otherwise."[5] While respondents noted that their lodge was "short of people to do the jobs" and spoke of having to "recycle Past Masters for offices" and "scramble at the last minute to find someone" and of "aging talent not being replaced" and "people leaving partway through their office term," how these problems were often dealt with was also problematic. Nine respondents complained about others "pushing" or "pressuring me to take an office." One man commented that "I'm always under huge pressure to move on, and I just don't want to at this point in my life." Others, who said they "just want to sit on the sidelines, watch, and listen," complained about how officers "implicitly look down on us benchers. I'm just as good a Mason as they are."

Third, when criticism, lack of support, unwillingness to come forward, and "arm-twisting" were combined, such anti-involvement micropolitical dynamics often resulted in a small group of seasoned brethren carrying most of the load, with the rest either on the sidelines or sitting at home. Twenty respondents complained that "10 percent of us do 90 percent of the work," that it is often necessary to engage in "subbing offices," and that "it's always the same people." Indeed, eleven of these respondents used such phrases as "too hectic," "stressful," "overextended," and "wearing too many hats," and "burnout from too many offices and responsibilities." This results in some, such as Past Masters and Secretaries, "stepping back," seeking "downtime after a busy year," even "disappearing" after their term is up. In the words of one such man: "I've done my part." When a lodge reaches the kind of scenario drawn above, it becomes much like "rearranging the deck chairs on the *Titanic*: death is not far off."

Finally, and related to all of the above, was the controversial issue, noted by twenty-three respondents, of why they see people quit in relation to the issue of offices and tasks. Yet there was a split here. Keeping in mind that many of the respondents were themselves involved in Masonic offices, it is perhaps not surprising that eleven suggested the best thing to do is to encourage people to get involved "so they can maximize the benefits." This viewpoint was expressed in various ways but tended to revolve around the idea that "there is nothing duller than sitting on the sidelines," that "you get out of it what you put into it," and that "people quit because the level of involvement is entirely left up to them." Indeed, there were two respondents who had never taken an office who said that they "waited for someone to ask," one adding he "was not given a fair chance." Comments suggesting that a more proactive approach was needed were opposed by twelve respondents who disagreed with "pressure" to take an office. Several such respondents noted that "most people just want to come, sit, and listen," one claiming that a Grand Lodge survey showed this figure to be 90 percent. Several such respondents added that they were reluctant to take an office for reasons such as "fear of public speaking" or being "easily embarrassed." At the very least, these opposing responses call for discretion, selectivity, and tact whenever approaches are implemented to encourage brethren other than "the usual suspects" to take an office.

In the end, how a lodge allots and encourages brethren to take Masonic offices and tasks remains a key issue. Respondents noted a series of factors, interactions, and approaches that can either foster brethren to take an office and deepen their involvement or undermine the level of involvement that they have. Meaningful encouragement coupled with fairness, opportunities for advancement, healthy competition, and a feeling of being supported in a well-administered organization must be contrasted with negativity and criticism that undermines feelings of support and minimizes the number of brethren willing to come forward, leading to arm-twisting, burnout, and withdrawal. The trick is that any actual lodge will contain a different mix of both these positive and negative dynamics, and the ability of leaders to attend to and manage the emotional micropolitics of groups is key (Summers-Effler 2004; C. Clark 1990). When present, this can foster effective leadership and consultation to find a meaningful way to diplomatically maximize the former while minimizing the micropolitical fallout.

HOW LODGE MEETINGS ARE ORGANIZED AND RUN

> *Travelling around to various lodges, some are fantastic: the meetings are conducted well, things are snappy, the floorwork is good, the ritual is done perfectly, it's an exciting place to be if you like that thing. Other lodges, you walk in and think, "Why am I here?" It's very monotone, very unexciting, they never make eye contact, they never change things, and you think, "Why have I come here? This does not make sense. Where's the door?" You look over at the person beside you and think that person could be stone dead and nobody would catch on. There's no movement, no life. If you've got that situation it's quite deadly.*

As this respondent makes clear, a critical matter related to involvement is the question of what, exactly, goes on at lodge meetings that might make members want to attend. Conversely, is there anything about the way regular meetings are organized and run that may discourage members from spending their time there? The monthly lodge meeting serves as the organizational vehicle that frames many of the issues we are dealing with in this chapter, and respondents had a great deal to say on such issues—positive, negative, and in terms of advice to improve the meeting experience. Thus it is to such significant matters that I now turn.

Respondents emphasized three broad elements that they claimed made for a good lodge meeting: maintaining a focus on the lodge experience, having good meeting content, and various accoutrements of exclusivity. Similarly, when things went wrong in these respects, they were seen as less than helpful. Each will be dealt with in turn.

First and foremost, fourteen respondents claimed that it was "important to maintain a focus on the lodge experience" to facilitate involvement. Thus, rather than getting caught up in business or focusing on Grand Lodge issues, meetings themselves needed to be satisfying in a number of ways and for a broad group of members:

> *I think there needs to be more of a focus on the lodge, the lodge as the heart and soul of Masonry and your Masonic experience, and that is manifested in the monthly meetings. That, to me,*

should be the essence of your experience, spiritually, socially, educationally, and from a fun point of view. That should be in the lodge, and the lodge should be really where it's at—and it's not. And senior Masons just don't get it, in my view.

At meetings we should ensure that the different groups, the different reasons for being a Mason are all satisfied, because you're always going to have a cross-section of people.

Lodges should ask themselves, "Why are we here?"—and then give people reasons to be in practice.

A quality experience will bring people there. The meat should be in the meeting itself, not downstairs. People should leave at the end of the night feeling that it was rewarding to be there.

Yet, as intimated, such a focus can at times be lost—for example, through a focus on business or on the Grand Lodge hierarchy.

I find that senior Masons focus all of their time and attention on Grand Lodge. They seek each other out and talk about that business while little attention gets focused on the actual lodge and your average member. It affects the lodge experience itself.

Secondly, respondents extensively discussed the content of lodge meetings. There was a strong preference shown for providing more interesting content for those attending. Fully fifty-seven of the respondents suggested that it would be a good idea to "provide content," "educational talks," or other "learning activities" during lodge meetings, particularly when there was no degree work being performed. It was suggested that this would "make the meetings more interesting." Similarly, two suggested "having actual discussions in lodge on a set question or topic." Indeed, one man even suggested that it would be helpful if members "could find a way to know what other lodges were doing before visiting to avoid boring business meetings." In one way or another, respondents were seeking better, "more interesting" content in their lodge meetings—"more beef in the bun," as it were. That such an approach can be successful is exemplified by the words of one respondent:

Lodges have to make things interesting or exciting to keep people. We were a very small lodge in terms of people who were actually living [with]in, say, 60 km of the lodge. We used to have an over 85 percent attendance rate of people within 60 km [bangs table] every meeting. Why? Because we were about Masonic knowledge, we were about making the lodge interesting every night that you were there. It wasn't necessarily about rushing the candidates through or anything like that. It was about what made it. What made the lodge good? What made it a place you wanted to come?

As hinted above, this desire for more interesting content had a great deal to do with the extent to which the handling of the lodge's regular "business" dominated the meeting as opposed to "interesting" matters. Sixty-two respondents, echoing Hodapp (2013), claimed that too much time and emphasis was placed on "boring" business matters such as meeting minutes, accounts, and so on to the exclusion of other interesting content—and that this was highly discouraging to ongoing involvement. Some notable comments emerged where emotion management evidently broke down:

> *I've had my doubts. What am I doing sitting here? It's boring! And I think something has to be done. I think that's part of our membership problem, why people aren't coming. [mimicking] "Well, I'm not going to sit there and listen to them read minutes and pay bills every night." And that's right. Look, why should I get dressed up in a tux [and] drive to a meeting to hear somebody read the minutes, ask whether there are any applications, do the balance sheet, then go around the lodge to go over it, and ask if there's anything further? You're not going to get anywhere just running meetings, 'cause those days are gone. Our lodges are stuck in just going through the motions. Think about it. If you're just going through the motions, and your plan is to bring in members, you've already defeated yourself!*

> *We get all dressed up, go down there and have a business meeting for thirty minutes, then turn around and go back home. What for? Why come out? Hell, I can pay my own bills at home!*

> *The business bores me. We just go to the meeting, do the same thing in the same way without any kind of fellowship, then go home. Nothing more.*

> *Lodges with few candidates fill the evening with business. They think there's nothing else to do and it becomes a vicious cycle. They're hiding behind the basics, the mechanics of it.*

One of the most notable aspects of this was a perceived shift from the traditional emphasis on Masonic content to a "business model"—and the volunteerism literature suggests that adopting a workplace model poses dangers for involvement (Ilsley 1990). Respondents noted that this had the effect of undermining, in at least some cases, respondents' original reasons for interest in the Craft:

Unlike Europe, we've moved over time from an education/ mentoring model to a business model with self-directed study. There's nothing in lodge other than the regular business. There's nothing before or after the meeting, you are not talking about your ritual, or principles, or anything else. There's no venue within my own lodge whereby brethren come together to discuss their ritual or the philosophy of Freemasonry. It's this, then this … and so, when I think about the old structure, there's no way. I can see why people leave…. They get disinterested because, within the lodge, the lodge is not structured for that.

People are coming to us in part because they're feeling a deeper need, a fraternal sense. There's a spirituality to it, and they want to understand what that is. They don't want to come into bureaucracy, and they don't want to come into a bunch of people who say, "Okay, you stay there and we're going to keep it like this." They want to come in and understand what the real meaning of that was. They've read books, they've seen movies, and they're really curious! And so, you've got to answer their curiosity.

All of this business stuff is a real disconnect *with the reading [emphasis added]. Some of us are coming in interested in the esoteric aspects but don't find it. We find business, and other lodges' meetings are even more boring than ours. We can't stay at this because we're doing the same thing over and over. We're not learning anything new. There needs to be more to be there for.*

Most of the meeting is business. It really drags on, and there's little time to get into deeper aspects. You go there and there's just the secretary and the treasurer, and all the widows, and all the dead and sick guys, and all that thing. You burp three times from the pork roast, and you go home. [laughter] You know, if that's it, how are you going to stay? There's nothing else. You can't work discussion with no words.

As a result, respondents made suggestions about content. In addition to the many respondents above suggesting the need for interesting Masonic education, eight suggested that it would be best to "be careful about the length" of the minutes, to "streamline" them, or just "hit the high points." Indeed, another six respondents suggested that it would be best if the minutes were simply distributed to members and later approved in open lodge if there were no errors or omissions. In a similar vein, seven respondents felt that it would be best to "limit the accounts" at regular meetings. The general feeling among such respondents was that business took up too much time during meetings, that it would be best to "avoid the cookie-cutter trestle board found in many places," and instead to exhibit a "willingness to innovate, to explore new ways of doing things."

Beyond the numerous comments about routine business taking up too much of the meeting, four other discouraging aspects of meeting content were highlighted: critical comments about ritual work, the perception that "most of the meeting was spent on minutiae," the tendency toward bureaucratization, and poor attempts at providing educational content. In the case of the first, insofar as the business of a lodge meeting involves ritual work (always during the opening and closing, and more on nights when a degree is being conferred), not only was the quality of ritual work important, "commentary from the peanut gallery" was an issue, seventeen respondents complaining that "anal-retentiveness" and "nitpicking" in relation to ritual performance was a "turnoff."

Nine respondents took issue with what they saw as wasteful arguments over such menial things as spending small amounts, whether to wear aprons at a scholarship presentation, or what meal to have at a social event:

> People do not want to come to lodge to hear them argue over $45 or $50 or $60, or about going out to pay the Sears or the extra flowers. This is what a lot of it is, 'cause they'll say, "I'm not going to listen to this guy arguing whether we should pay this up there. How much did we spend on that fruitcake for the widows?" That shouldn't be done in lodge. That should be done by the committee. You know, there's a lot of stuff that shouldn't be in lodge.

> I get the greatest charge out of people who say we're trying to take over the world. Come to our lodge and see the trouble we have with minor issues. You think this group could take over the world? Take a good look at this crowd—for heaven's sake, we couldn't referee a dogfight, most of us!

> All I see is just business meetings, some amateur theatrics, and a lot of arguing over silly stuff.

Nine respondents decried the growth of bureaucracy:

> Bureaucracy is a problem. Right now we're building another level of hierarchy. It gives people something to do, but also creates bureaucratic inertia.

Finally in this respect, six respondents also complained about the nature of education when it was offered. Two simply complained about "boring, monotone educational presentations," while four noted that, rather than focusing on meaning, there was an emphasis on the "how-to" aspect, or what one man derisively called "the sergeant major's lecture on dress and deportment."

All of this suggests that lodges have a great deal of work to do in relation to the content of their meetings. Management and vision are key. Rather than leaders "hiding behind the business," the "cookie-cutter trestle board," and doing things the way they have always been done, leadership in better organizing meetings and filling them with interesting content is vital to fostering involvement. Indeed, considering that many of the above problems have a management component, it is little surprise that seven respondents pointed to "poor administrative leadership" as playing a part in poor meeting experiences and the discouragement that results.

The third, and final, major aspect noted by respondents in relation to meetings related to their dramatic setting, costumes, practices, and accompaniment. In this respect, respondents spoke of how various accoutrements of exclusivity could add to the meeting experience. Seven spoke of the significance of holding their meetings in "historic, architecturally significant buildings" (versus a modern "block of steel" that left brethren "uninspired"). Eight others spoke of how "dressing up adds dignity, pride, and a sense of importance to meetings" (indeed, one provided an example of a lodge that "went downhill after dropping its dress code"). Four more noted the importance of "strictly enforcing" a "failing custom" where visitors are supposed to be "tested" (i.e., on their knowledge of the Masonic signs) before being allowed to enter a meeting: "Having standards sometimes brings people in rather than keeping them out." Lastly, two recommended having musical accompaniment during various lodge activities, and one stated that holding a "festive board" (Masonic dinner) before or after meetings would be helpful.

Of course, not all respondents agreed with this emphasis on accoutrements of exclusivity. Four didn't like "having to get dressed up," and three sought instead a "happy medium" between strictness and making things more "accommodating." One man stated that "we have to know what should be rigid and what should be relaxed." While again evidence of the ongoing tension between status and equality, it is perhaps best to conclude that some such accoutrements are beneficial to member involvement.

In the end, insofar as the regular lodge meeting serves as the arena—the organizational frame—for many of the issues discussed in this chapter, it is imperative to membership involvement and retention that the above issues be addressed. There should be an ongoing effort to focus on providing a quality lodge experience for members, to provide interesting educational content rather than fill up meetings with business, and to choreograph a delicate balance between accoutrements of exclusivity and hallmarks of equality. Meanwhile, there is a need to re-examine the business model, review the tendency toward bureaucratization, and reign in the related focuses on minutiae and nitpicking. Effective leadership is necessary to do all of this, in order to create and manage lodge meetings that members will want to attend—rather than avoid—over time.

INTERACTIONS WITH THE WIDER COMMUNITY

When the focus was shifted from internal interactions within the lodge to the impact of its external encounters with the wider community, it was clear from respondents' comments that these matters were a key component to both building and sustaining member involvement. Two interrelated factors came to light: the various charitable activities and goals that the lodge pursued and other ways that the lodge engaged in community outreach.

First and foremost, thirty-four respondents pointed to the positive impact of working together for a common, worthy goal. Similar to the comments earlier in relation to building social bonding and trust through common activity, respondents found that charity was a "unifying factor" that fostered positive feelings both among brethren and toward the organization. There was only one negative comment in this section, that of a man who felt that the Masons were "no longer doing enough for the community." Otherwise, respondents found that "getting out there" gave them a "purpose" over and above their regular lodge meetings.

Fifteen respondents went further and claimed that lodges, rather than continuing the "old-school view" that those engaging in charity should not seek recognition, should instead be both more open and thoughtful about how they go about the charity work that they do.

> We need to show what we're doing for the community, that it's not just the Shriners doing these things. We've been too inward-looking for too long. We've got to get out of our holes, get out from behind these walls, think, reflect, and plan.

> We need to move away from the old idea of fundraising and taking money out of the community to cover our expenses. Instead, if we set higher dues to deal with those and use the Masonic Foundation to match our charitable givings, we can put money and resources back into the community.

This leads to the issue of the lodge's broader approach to the community—how they engage in forms of community engagement beyond charity itself. There was strong support among respondents for the lodge being "less inward" and "more integrated" into the wider community at large. In one way or another, forty-one respondents articulated this theme. Ten of these spoke generally of the need for "community outreach"; eight supported having a website; six spoke of "visiting" and "providing support" for widows, shut-ins, or sick children; seven recommend engaging in "public relations" or speaking/acting on Masonic ideals in public "to help address negative stereotypes," and four suggested exhibiting a willingness to "respond to curious questions from others." Regarding this last idea, one man said, "I like to keep my tux on when I go out for coffee after a meeting to prompt curious questions from others." Other, individual respondents spoke of other strategies such as "holding community social events," "selling tickets," "merchandizing," operating a community newsletter," and holding "co-operative ventures with other organizations" as ways of better engaging with the community. Overall, there was strong support for being "less insular" than in the past, one man noting that this would be "impossible if you're only hanging with other Masons."

Nevertheless, eighteen respondents noted various problems in achieving this goal of greater community engagement. Seven claimed that, despite the numerous books, websites, and other media attention in recent years, compared to the past, there is a relative lack of public awareness of Freemasonry as an institution today. In the words of one man, "If people don't know, they can't act upon it." Another added, "Unlike the old days, it's no longer expected, something that you just do." Relatedly, six mentioned that "the Shrine has a prominent public profile; the Craft lodge doesn't." Finally, four noted the "perception that Freemasonry is just an old man's social club, nothing more."

These factors may be problems in some areas more than others, but they may just as well be reasons for lodges to engage in some of the engagement strategies suggested by respondents. If lodges are to foster that sense of greater meaning and purpose found beyond the lodge meetings themselves, these should be seen as opportunities for—rather than impediments to—involvement.

CONFLICT AND CONTENTIOUS DYNAMICS

I now turn to a series of relatively unpleasant matters that were noted by respondents, matters which, by their very nature, serve to discourage long-term involvement and retention of members. Some of these involve interpersonal micropolitics, others involve relationships between institutions, and still others relate to demographic concerns. In one way or another, however, the inability to address such emotional dynamics in groups (Summers-Effler 2004) can raise bones of contention that may, in one way or another, irritate or upset members and have a negative impact on their long-term involvement in the Craft. In this section, I will introduce these matters in a general sense; I will then move on in subsequent sections to deal with more specific problems.

First and foremost, respondents spoke generally of "internal politics"—and the attendant "infighting"—as a factor that discouraged their involvement.

(Indeed, one man went further, noting how his father witnessed this among family members and "never joined as a result.") Various hot-button issues were noted: some already familiar, such as "perfectionism" about ritual (mentioned by seventeen respondents) and "excessive bureaucracy" (seven); others less so, such as perceptions of unethical behaviour—nepotism, hypocrisy, two-facedness, backstabbing, insincerity—on the part of others (twenty-two); brethren seen as taking sides in contentious politics between the Craft and the Shrine (twenty-two); struggles over whether or not to sell a historic lodge building and move elsewhere (twelve); conflict or resentment over who was in a particular position (eleven); "insensitivity" to minority (e.g., Black, gay) candidates or brethren (seven); disagreement over candidates (three); "cliques running everything" (two); and "notorious characters" driving people away (two). Twelve simply mentioned "internal politics" and "infighting" in general. To get the flavour of such comments, consider the following:

> I can't handle hypocrisy. This is not an old boys' network. It's not about getting jobs or promotions. I've had run-ins with brothers who don't practise it, who don't walk the talk like they should. There are Masons, and there are Masons in name only—and I'd say at least half the members of my lodge don't get it.

> Don't be nice to me in lodge, and tomorrow, when you're amongst your other friends, pretend that you don't recognize me. Don't be positive to my face and then trash me behind my back. Are you my brother, or do I just call you brother? You know, in a lot of cases, we're just calling another brother.

> Some people only see us as a stepping stone to the Shrine. Do they really belong to Freemasonry, or are they just pursuing a goal?

> They let our beautiful old building run down, rented storefronts to low-end tenants, and built a case for us to move to a block of steel across town. Nobody will listen. They're tired of hearing it. Oh boy, I'm inspired.

> I was passed over for a position despite having done a lot of work for them. It turned me off, and I resigned from a lot of things.

> We had a gay candidate last year. Let's just say eyebrows get raised among some groups whenever some new element, for lack of a better word, is introduced.

> There's a small group that has everything all sewn up. This clique runs everything.

> *There's a guy in our lodge that has pissed off a number of people. They won't attend if he's around.*

While such matters were obviously problematic in relation to ongoing involvement, there were five brethren who pointed to various coping skills that enabled them to emotionally manage problematic encounters. Two spoke of choosing to limit involvement to their local lodge to avoid getting involved in the "swampy politics" of the Grand Lodge; as one man stated, "I don't need to willingly submit to it." Three others commented that they had developed an "ability to shrug off" difficulties with others in the Craft, one of these adding that he chose to see such encounters as "constructive criticism, especially when done politely and discreetly."

While such issues are hardly limited to Freemasonry, where prevalent they do pose problems for long-term member involvement. Indeed, given that so few respondents commented on how they successfully counteracted such difficulties, it is possible that some, in the words of one respondent, simply "voted with their feet" over time rather than continuing to operate in such contexts. Thus, facilitating methods of minimizing and handling both interpersonal and organizational conflicts would be a good idea to help ameliorate problems that have great bearing on long-term involvement and retention of members.

RELATIONSHIP WITH THE GRAND LODGE

A specific matter that prompted much discussion among respondents was the amount of time that the lodge and its brethren spent on concerns related to the Grand Lodge. In some respects this echoes the earlier comments about putting emphasis on the lodge experience to the exclusion of other matters, as well as the disdain for bureaucracy. Similarly, though Welser (2006) has highlighted the importance of status attainment for involvement, the comments below reflect the tension between status versus equality that has already come up on a number of occasions—which can involve either an attractive, productive tension or a corrosive elitism, depending on both the degree and the position of the respondent. In this section, I briefly address these matters, pointing to where respondents saw value in the association with the Grand Lodge and where they saw it as problematic in relation to involvement and retention.

The first thing to note is that there were relatively few positive comments. Two respondents pointed to how the Grand Lodge, particularly its district associations, provided support for their lodge and helped with organizing community events. One noted that it provided "an effective and efficient organization," while another wryly noted that, by its very nature, the "strength of the organization is its independent, cell-like structure of Grand Lodges, where recognition flows like capital in international capitalism."

Despite these few comments, however, the vast majority of respondents had negative things to say about the Grand Lodge. There were essentially two areas of contention noted by respondents: (1) elitism, and (2) contentious policies and practices.

First, thirty-two respondents, in one way or another, complained about the elitism that they perceived to be inherent in the Grand Lodge. This dramaturgical breach between appearance and reality (Mangham and Overington 1987) was particularly noted in relation to how respondents thought that some members seek to identify with its structure and titles to the detriment of brotherly equality:

> *Some people only identify themselves as part of Grand Lodge. The whole Masonic movement, as I've seen it, is very status conscious. Extremely. Absolutely. It's very important to people to be seen—who I am, what I do—and to be on the important forums dealing with important issues. How is that on the level?*

> *Senior Masons focus their time and attention [on] Grand Lodge and seek each other out, while little attention gets focused on the actual lodge, the average member, and the lodge experience itself.*

> *There's Grand Lodge, and then there's us—though we all pay dues to them each year. Watch them drape the Charter when someone from Grand Lodge passes away.... How are you on the level [with] that? They're more important than we are.... It's the same in concordant bodies. That's where you get on the level with the bankers.*

> *There's this belief that Masonic rank really means something in the world.... I know several men who have gone through successive grand bodies not because they thought they could really contribute something but because they thought it would make them look good. It's a general consensus that some go up for the glory. They fit right with that group that really didn't get it, the few for whom I do not hold much respect.*

> *As far as I'm concerned, emphasizing to new candidates that they could someday move up into Grand Lodge insults the average member. Grand Lodge shouldn't be seen as the only way to Masonic redemption, so to speak.*

Indeed, the practices leading to this perception of elitism served as both a source of resentment by those trying to climb the ladder and a source of derision by those observing it. Consider the following comments, the first by a respondent who did not obtain the position he wanted, the second by an observer who thought that the titles and ranks were hollow in respect to Masonic knowledge:

I've done a lot of work for this organization, but I got passed over for a Grand Lodge position. Within the lodge itself, there is no problem. It's when you get into the governing bodies, it's less than altruistic. I took it personally. It really turned me off and I resigned from lots of things.

[Referring to Grand Lodge officers sitting in the East] *I've come to the conclusion that they know fuck all.* [laughter] *They just hide behind a bunch of gold braid. 'Cause if I ask them a pointed question in open lodge … there's just silence.*

It would seem that such perceptions of elitism in a context where "the emperor has no clothes" are problematic for retention in today's society. Unlike some writers, such as Poulet (2010), who stress existing dispositions, selection, and apprenticeship in replacing social hierarchies with Masonic ones, these data reveal that this is by no means simple or straightforward. At one time in the past, when society was more structured in terms of formal hierarchies, classes, and rank, and when deference to authority was more normative, it may have been possible to place greater emphasis on such a formal hierarchy. Today, however, the societal norm is more egalitarian and the external statuses of members less notable, so while certain people are still hunting for status, the relative incongruity of internal and external position leaves them more open to criticism. Yes, a tension between status and equality remains important, but, in light of the above, it is necessary to find a way to recast this into a more productive form than that which currently exists institutionally in the order.

Turning now to contentious Grand Lodge policies and practices, thirty-six respondents weighed in with regard to issues of concern. Of the comments in this respect, the largest group (nine respondents) claimed that the Grand Lodge was "excessively bureaucratic"—complaining both about how this involved "building another level of hierarchy" and about the "bureaucratic inertia" that was the result. Several other issues were noted. First the administrative structure was questioned. Three respondents complained that the Board of General Purposes "runs everything"; four, that "it's overloaded with incompetent old fossils who like the way it's always been"; one, that "observers can't speak or vote"; another, that "they are unlikely to vote to change themselves"; and one, that, as a result, "brethren don't attend, even when the issues are important." Much the same was said about the fact—at that time—that Master Masons couldn't vote at the Grand Lodge and did not bother attending as a result.

Secondly, eight respondents complained that the structure of the jurisdiction was unfair in relation to their lodge. There were complaints about how the Grand Lodge rules penalize lodges financially, how "little lodges are outvoted," how Grand Lodge officers do not make as many visits to rural lodges or stay and socialize as they did in the past, and how lodges in rural areas are given little information about key decisions.

Finally, five respondents reported contentious issues such as lodges taking different positions over the formation of a new Grand Lodge from a district Grand Lodge, "tunnel vision" over the sale of old buildings in favour of new facilities, the treatment of minority shareholders, lack of information being provided to key parties, and the Grand Lodge allegedly "demonizing lodges and individuals who question or criticize its direction." In one way or another, whether in matters of bureaucracy, the structures and procedures of power, relations with lodges in the jurisdiction, or the handling of contentious issues, problematic actions of the Grand Lodge were key matters of concern in relation to respondents' ongoing involvement, matters that merit some reflection.

RELATIONSHIP WITH THE SHRINE

Another matter that garnered considerable discussion was the past and present relationship between Freemasonry and the Shriners. The Shrine is an appendant fraternal organization associated with Freemasonry. It is commonly referred to as the "playground of Masonry," where members engage in a great deal of conviviality while selling tickets and raising money for children's charities; they are often seen dressed as clowns in parades and at public events. Its formal rules currently require that one be a Freemason to be eligible to join. Not every Mason goes on to join the Shrine, but a good proportion of them do. Thus, all Shriners are Masons, but not all Masons are Shriners.

From its inception in 1870 until the late twentieth century, a Freemason had not only to get the third degree but to pass through the degrees in one of the concordant bodies—either the York Rite or the Scottish Rite—before becoming eligible to join the Shrine. However, this rule was changed such that, currently, Freemasons having their third degree are now permitted to join the Shrine directly. The effect of this change in Shrine policy was to significantly curtail the number of Freemasons joining—and remaining involved in—either branch of the concordant bodies, resulting in a certain degree of controversy among Freemasons.

Thirty-seven respondents weighed in on these matters, with thirty-three making negative comments about these developments. Eight complained about how applicants joined their lodge simply as "a stepping stone to the Shrine," and five asserted that some members "put the Shrine first." Similarly, six complained about how "the Shrine has a prominent public profile and good PR; Freemasonry doesn't," five more noting that "many people can't separate Freemasonry, our Craft lodges, from Shrinedom." On top of these matters, three expressed concern over long-standing (and persistent) rumours that the Shrine may eventually drop the requirement to be a Mason altogether (with a potential parallel negative impact on Craft lodge membership), while another complained about how Shriners who never attend drop out of their Mother lodge in favour of maintaining nominal membership in lodges with the cheapest dues. Finally, four respondents complained about how internal politics in the Shrine has spilled over and caused problems within their own lodges.

To be fair, however, not all respondents had negative views:

> *While my interest in the Shrine brought me to Masonry, I opened myself to it and learned to appreciate it on its own terms. It hit me when I got here. I wouldn't have known about it otherwise.*
>
> *Nowadays people are joining Freemasonry more for its own sake.*

One man claimed that he "puts the Craft lodge first" as it "is the foundation, it's where I came from." Indeed, there may be other attractions: "I like being in something where you're not always pushing tickets, bingo, and so on."

All the same, these matters surrounding the relationship between Craft lodge membership and the Shrine constitute an important issue, if for no other reason than that more time spent on one can leave less time for involvement in the other.[6] Thus, it will be important to consider the possibility of any changes in Shrine policy, or in ongoing issues affecting joint members, as they can have an impact on the lodge experience. To paraphrase an old saying, when the Shrine coughs, Craft lodges may catch a cold.

DEMOGRAPHIC/GENERATIONAL ISSUES

The final organizational factor noted by respondents is one that tends to cut across a number of the involvement issues discussed in this chapter thus far: demographics. In particular, many respondents asserted that there was a notable "generation gap" in Freemasonry, largely due to most men of the baby boomer generation "taking a pass" on something they saw as old and (ironically) "square." As a result, when a modestly larger crop of new initiates began entering the Craft around the turn of the millennium, they encountered a large number of older men, many of whom had entered the Craft in the boom years between the end of WWII and 1959. Such widely differing generations—even granted the fact that there remains a sizable number of traditionalists in both—result in social dynamics that may have an impact on involvement and retention of members.[7] Thus, it is to such issues that I now turn.

First, twenty-four respondents, mostly from urban areas, claimed that there was, indeed, a generation gap in their lodge involving "two groups with little in common":

There's definitely two groups within the lodge, and they don't understand each other. We have few people between forty-five and sixty-five. There's a whole generation missing.

There is a perception out there today that Freemasonry is an "old man's club." It doesn't help when a brother says to a new member that "it's nice to see candidates with full heads of hair."

We're not into the kinds of things the older guys are. Things need to be sort of updated, younger ideas have to be injected into the role of Junior Warden—"ladies' nights" and this idea of a ladies' auxiliary, my wife would laugh every time she'd get the notice paper, you know? I think part of it is the stigmatism associated with Masonry that it's an old boys' club. I mean, there's one notice paper where there was the announcement about the birth of my daughter, and then the next thing was somebody celebrating their fiftieth wedding anniversary, right? It was in the same notice paper. So my wife sees the notice paper, and says, jokingly, "Well, who broke their hip this month?" Things like that, you know?

While respondents noted that older members possessed a wealth of experience, Masonic knowledge, and wisdom that they could draw upon, the overwhelming bulk of comments referenced negative aspects of this demographic situation.

There was first the problem, noted by thirteen respondents, that over time many of the older members would simply get "too old or sick." They were seen as "less interested in going out at night," as having difficulty climbing stairs or going to lodges without wheelchair access, as members who felt "too old to take an office," or, unlike their younger counterparts, as tending to "go home early so there is little social discourse after the meeting." All of these things, taken together, were seen as having an impact on their own—and others'—involvement.

Coupled with this was the claim, more often articulated by older members themselves, that they were doing the "heavy lifting" and had been for some time. Eight respondents, in one way or another, claimed that, in the words of one man, they "were doing the job of the missing generation." However, there was also grumbling that "aging talent is not being replaced" and that the older members were getting "tired" of the situation. These comments were more notable among respondents from rural lodges with fewer young members, yet they played a part in urban lodges with younger members as well.

In these latter situations, twenty-five younger, largely urban respondents articulated the other side of this dynamic, claiming that it was the "old guys resisting change."

*What I see is just a bunch of old men that sit around think-
ing "the guys at the beginning had it right." You've heard the
joke about how many Masons it takes to change a lightbulb?
"Change?"*

*The older group don't want to let the younger generation into
power. They want to keep things just the way they are: work
and effort to change things is seen as not worth the trouble
rather than an investment.*

*There's nothing more depressing than sitting in a room full
of Past Masters who aren't going to let go and they know
it. They're just meeting every so often, going through the
motions, doing everything by the book, stifling discussion and
innovation.*

*Things are too controlled. The meaning hasn't changed in fifty
years, reflecting a very old-fashioned view of British society.
Nobody seems to want to do too much, do they? They're not
adapting to society any more. How do we move on?*

*It is important that, as a member, you have input about those
nights, and if you have an opinion, and you can suggest something, go and do it.... These old guys are not the future of this
lodge.*

In lodges where this demographic divide was most notable, several factors were seen as exacerbating the emotional dynamics: perfectionism and
negative comments surrounding ritual work from veteran members (reported
by eighteen respondents); a tendency to ignore new, younger members and
relegate them to the sidelines after their third degree (nine); outdated cultural
attitudes that may be seen as "insensitive" (e.g., the term "ladies") (seven);
differing attitudes toward internal political controversies (e.g., the disposal of
historic properties) (four); either dropping social events or hosting activities
irrelevant to the younger generation (two); and a general attitude that "youth
are not likely to stay as long as the older generation"—which runs the risk of
become a self-fulfilling prophecy.

Two factors loom large here: (1) the need for youthful input and
(2) finding ways to involve younger members and better integrate them into
the activities of the lodge. In line with the comment above, greater efforts
need to be made to encourage input and develop programming suggested by
the cohort of relatively young brethren who have joined the Craft in the last
decade and a half. Similarly, greater efforts must be made to let younger members take more responsible positions and make more active contributions than
has been the case. While some may object that lodges are constantly striving
to get "new blood" into offices and give the older generation a break, the

data here suggest that this is not uniform across lodges or with respect to the more powerful offices. In certain lodges, the influence of the older generation reflects less the positive influence of experience, knowledge, and wisdom than a tendency to hold on and to keep things the way they have always been. The results can be discouraging to involvement and retention. In such instances, in the words of one man:

> *Youth are not being given jobs or made to feel included. Let the young guys go ahead, because if you keep on getting Past Masters to do something, you could do it forever. That becomes a stagnant lodge, and then you end up going to these lodges and you see twelve to thirty guys sitting up there that are dead and just don't know it yet—and the young brothers see that as a barrier. That's an issue that comes from the demographics.*

CONCLUSION

The above factors underscore the importance of organizational issues in relation to Masonic involvement in the twenty-first century. These matters are obviously complex and interrelated in many ways, with some comments variously hinting at the dangers of loss of legitimacy and organizational and environmental atrophy highlighted by Richard Hall (1987). Nevertheless, attending to the issues and concerns raised by brethren in these respects, with another eye on the specific social context of a given lodge, would likely go a long way to improving Masonic involvement.

Now that I have reviewed the two most frequently noted and internally complex involvement factors in the data, in the next chapter I will move on to consider a collection of other matters before developing an overall conceptual scheme to explain Masonic involvement today.

CHAPTER 6

FURTHER FACTORS IN MEMBER INVOLVEMENT AND AN OVERALL EXPLANATORY FRAMEWORK

A s explored in chapters 4 and 5, the two Masonic involvement factors mentioned most often and in the greatest complexity were social atmosphere and organizational concerns. Nevertheless, four other factors relating to involvement emerged from the data and remain to be fully discussed. Without them, a comprehensive understanding of Masonic involvement would be far from complete. Hence this chapter begins by discussing what contemporary Masons had to say about (1) educational issues; (2) the impact of brethren's other commitments and activities, and thoughts on gender; (3) moral and ethical benefits; and (4) motivation in relation to their involvement in the Craft. Following this, the chapter concludes with the explication of a detailed theoretical model to explain Masonic involvement in the early twenty-first century.

EDUCATIONAL ISSUES

Several researchers have pointed to the role of pedagogy—tacit or otherwise—in the process of integration into the Masonic order (Poulet 2010; Mahmud-Abdelwahib 2008). Respondents, too, saw the educational potential inherent in Freemasonry and commented extensively in this respect—both positively and negatively—in relation to involvement in the Craft. There were basically three dimensions to their comments, which included statements related to (1) mentoring candidates, (2) the value of learning by doing, and (3) suggestions for improving Masonic education and deepening interest for the otherwise uninvolved.

Mentoring Candidates

In many respects, Masonic education and its potentially attractive impact on involvement begins at the outset—when a new Mason is progressing through the degrees. As a result, respondents commented on the issue of "mentoring" new candidates, both in terms of formal programs that may be available and informal interactions with the brethren of the lodge. Several themes emerged.

First and foremost, because the degree work they are passing through is front and centre for new brethren, twenty-six respondents commented on the fact that the rituals had to be performed well, with "dignity," "professionalism," "high standards," "vigour," "good floorwork," and "dramatic effect" for people to "get the message."

> *Your lodge work has got to be impressive. You've got to say "Jeez, that was something," not "What the hell was it?"*

> *I don't think that anything attracts people to meetings like degree work, but it has to be done well. If it sounds important, it is important. Say it like you mean it.*

> *Ritual can be a very profound experience. It can also be very dry and meaningless. It depends what you bring to it—and if people invest what they're doing with meaning and enthusiasm, they get a lot more out of it. In some respects, the way that things are done, it just does not come out. People don't focus on those common symbolic objects. They don't derive the emotional energy from it they could. And we have to find a way, not only to tap into the spiritual, but people also have to find a way that people can bring this to the enactment of ritual that will keep the people there—once they are there—rather than just sort of do it by rote in a dry and unappealing fashion. These are important aspects that need to be re-emphasized.*

Next, to supplement the messages contained in the degrees, forty-four respondents pointed to the need to informally mentor candidates as they were progressing.

> *When I propose somebody, I see it as my duty to in fact be their mentor, and it's a responsibility that I don't take lightly. I make myself available, regularly meeting for coffee, providing papers and reading material, and so on.*

> *During a meeting, it's too formal. You need more of an informal situation where the candidate feels free and he can ask you what, you know, he thinks are silly questions maybe, but they may mean a lot. We have to teach the basics. Explain the ritual to them, regularly meet and say, "This is what happened,*

*what you did, and why you did it." Explain the history behind
the ritual, explain the underlying story, themes, and what to
do—and then they'll feel more confident about moving on to
another degree.*

*Don't just give them information, give human contact and
friendship. I'll defy a new Master Mason to walk out if you
grab him and put your arm around him, show him some brotherly love, and say, "You went through what I went through.
Now, let's really talk about it."*

*One of my friends sat for hours with me in my office going
word for word over everything, because there's no way any
uninstructed person can look at the ritual and get any ... make
any sense of it. You need someone that can help you. It did keep
me interested in wanting to go back.*

Third, beyond such informal practices, some lodges have adopted more
formal mentoring programs for their new candidates. In some lodges these
are developed internally; in others, they have been adopted after being prepared by the Grand Lodge. Thirty respondents spoke in favour of having
such programs, particularly those that require some kind of task together
with "testing" or "assessment" throughout (e.g., a "project," an "essay," or
"group work," before moving on to the next degree). It was felt that giving
candidates a standardized task would both be educational and invest involvement with deeper value:

*We should give them something to do and expect it to be done
well. Falling standards should be arrested. We've been settling
for something less than a good performance. Many of the guys
I see would never have been let through in the old days.*

*Keep the bar set high. If something is too easily come by, you
don't value it nearly as much as if you really have to work for it.*

Finally in this respect, respondents felt that it was important to ensure
that mentoring—whether formal or informal—remained relevant to candidates for them to reap the most educational and personal benefits. Thus,
eight commented that it was important throughout to note the crossovers
and connections between Freemasonry and popular culture. Two added that
it would be important to find a way to "identify and engage those who want
deeper study for those in Freemasonry for other reasons." By both targeting
what is common and tailoring what is specific to a candidate's personal interests, the idea, expressed by three, was to utilize Masonic education to foster
a "Masonic identity" and thereby a deeper connection to the Craft. Indeed,

organizations that foster a strong identity among its volunteers are said to encourage greater involvement (Chacon, Vecina, and Davila 2007).

Yet respondents' comments were not all positive in nature. Thirty respondents complained about the lack of proper mentoring in their lodge. Fourteen of these specifically pointed to the fact that proposers were not supporting or mentoring their candidates as they should:

> *To me, if you propose or second an initiate, you have a responsibility to mentor them. And I think, in some cases, too many people are willing just to sign the application just to get the individual in, and then they leave them. I know of one lodge where there was so little contact or support that two candidates never showed up for their Entered Apprentice degree.*

> *I know of one proposer (a high-ranking Freemason), supposedly a mentor, who never showed up to assist a man with his lectures. The candidate left before getting his second degree, [saying], "This is it. I don't want anything more to do with that lodge."*

> *It's not right when a candidate doesn't hear from anybody for months between degrees. They shouldn't have to be coached through when proving up.*

Moreover, in some lodges education seemed to take a back seat to simply getting new candidates through all of their degrees. Nineteen respondents felt that this did the candidates a disservice, undermining the education that they were supposed to be receiving at this point (e.g., "not exposing them to the depth of the ritual, why we do things, and so on").

> *In some lodges, the third degree seems to be the objective as opposed to the lessons along the way, and then you have to pick those lessons up after you go through. I've heard candidates say, "We're not learning anything. When are we going to start?" Lodges are losing members before they get to their third because they're hitting a disappointment of "Where's the education that we thought we'd receive?"*

Finally, five respondents complained about the formal mentoring program. While one noted that not all lodges participate (i.e., that it is "spotty throughout the jurisdiction"), four others asserted that lodges or those responsible were not conducting the program properly:

> *Every lodge I went to did it wrong. Lots of stuff got lost in translation. Grand lodge must be more hands on and give better*

guidance with this. It's a good program, but it needs to be run. It needs to be managed.

Despite the formal program on paper, I don't consider a mentor being someone who meets with me one night before my degree work as a mentor, nor [hands me] a booklet, saying "Go read this."

The results of such practices were problematic in several respects. Twenty-eight respondents complained that they had to "learn along the way," to "pick up the deeper aspects by studying on my own." Twenty-three respondents felt that they did not learn much from the meetings themselves, where they found there to be a "lack of Masonic education" (or at least "quality" education). Indeed, nine complained about simply "being left on the sidelines once you have your third degree," which was problematic when, as seven noted, they were faced with a lot of "business" coupled with "arcane," "irrelevant," "complicated language that goes over people's heads and turns them off."

On the other hand, respondents could also get an unwelcome education via a "baptism of fire." This related to the unfortunate practice in some lodges of "rushing people through their degrees and ramming them into office without taking enough time to observe, reflect, and learn." Eight commented negatively on this practice—which is apparently becoming more common as lodges age and the need to replace aging talent becomes more acute.

What we need to do sometimes is actually slow down. Stop and smell the roses. Today we're in such a hurry to put anybody through to get them to go into an office. In my day, to get to each station was to achieve a goal, and so it was seven years to become Master, and that's what we did. I went through the blue lodge properly and I took my time.... That's where I find these days it hurts.... Candidates, once they're raised, are into an office and, before you know it, he's a Master with very little experience. That can be rough.

And, of course, being thrust into such a "steep learning curve" can be even more problematic when, as twenty-two respondents noted, one is faced with "perfectionism" and critical comments about how one does things along the way.

Lodges that wish to provide their candidates with education as one meaningful benefit of involvement in the Craft would do well to consider respondents' comments in this section. Education requires committed, meaningful interaction, not neglecting or using candidates as a means to an end. Bringing in members is not an end in itself. These new members must be meaningfully engaged by the things they learn from the outset, not turned off by them.

Attention must be paid to such "emotional dynamics" in mentoring (Summers-Effler 2004), in particular whether new members feel "supported" (Tang, Morrow-Howell, and Choi 2010). Otherwise, the attachment of a nascent Masonic identity may be unsuccessful.

Learning by Doing: Claimed Educational Benefits of Active Participation

In partial contrast to the situations above where respondents expressed concern about being pushed ahead before they were ready, many nevertheless spoke of the educational payoffs that can come from increasing their active participation in the lodge and its activities—indeed, how their interest in Freemasonry had been deepened as a result. This idea that "involvement begets involvement" took a number of forms in relation to such educational rewards. Fifty respondents spoke of "the benefits of taking an office rather than sitting on the sidelines."

> For me, personally, I wouldn't have gotten what I needed to get out of this organization if I was to sit on the benches. My office means I have to learn about this part. I have the responsibility to study and prepare for the job. I'm learning more and it keeps giving me a reason to come back.

> It's only through getting involved and doing things that you learn, and in the end you become a better person for it. Really, it's important to be given something to do. It helps you feel involved, part of something. If you're involved, you've got a reason for coming. There's not much in those meetings for people that are not involved in their offices.

> A man should do as many [offices] as possible before going to the chair, reading and learning more along the way. That will engage him. You should be doing this right after being raised [to the third degree]. Getting them involved will keep them involved.

Indeed, beyond whatever meaningful content that they acquired, twenty-six respondents spoke of the "useful"—often "transferable"—skills that they picked up as a result of taking Masonic office. Nine of these spoke of either "learning" or "honing" administrative skills such as running a meeting, nine spoke of the opportunity to develop or enhance their confidence through public speaking, and eight spoke of how taking an office "exercises the brain" by providing an "opportunity to train the memory." Given such benefits, it is hardly surprising that sixteen additional respondents went further, suggesting that "going all the way" (i.e., to the Master's Chair) was a useful educational experience. In one man's words:

You know, I was curious. I kept getting kicked out at installations! Finally I took the plunge. It was both exhilarating and terrifying at the same time. But, after I became Master, the flower blossomed. It was an amazing transformation for me. The whole world opens up. It pulled everything together. Everybody should do it.

A second aspect of the Masonic maxim that "You get out of it what you put in to it" involves preparing and presenting various educational lectures. Thirty-nine respondents, in one way or another, asserted that this had a positive educational by-product: "You learn when you teach."

Preparing and doing the Middle Chamber lecture, I got interested in learning more and progressing further. Now you'll see me before a meeting talking to myself, practising my lines, and only see me sitting on the sidelines listening about once a year. Really, if you don't study it and try to pick it apart, it's like, "So what?" I guess it's the old teacher in me.

By studying and preparing a talk, you are more likely to become curious about something and investigate further. It sinks down to the heart as opposed to mere reading, where the depth doesn't penetrate. It's more of an intellectual challenge. Now, it's become almost an obsession with me, and I take pride in the job I do.

Thirdly, thirty-six respondents pointed to the other side of this dynamic, asserting that their involvement was facilitated when the lodge put on interesting talks or other types of educational activities (e.g., moderated discussions, educational games, short talks on Masonic history, the social impact of prominent Masons, interpretations of ritual, and even presentations on broader community issues relevant to member concerns, such as specific charities, managing finances, and avoiding common frauds). In some respects related to the organization and running of meetings discussed in a earlier section, such practices, as one man put simply, "make the meeting more stimulating."

Fourth, twenty-seven respondents claimed that their involvement had been deepened as a result of participating in degree work—the initiation, passing, and raising of other, new Masons:

To me, that is the best part of Freemasonry, doing the ritual work. When you get on the floor and do the thing, and do it right, then it makes you feel good ... that I got something across to someone. It's a great educational experience.

When you talk about degree work, the key word is work. *You learn by doing. It's the only way I've learned what Masonry is all about. I find that you learn a lot more by getting up and making mistakes than by just sitting on the sidelines. We all know nobody's perfect. I have difficulty understanding how I can be part of this by sitting and watching. You know, to be ... proficient as a carpenter, I'd need to be in there doing carpenter's work.*

For me, Masonry is the method. Doing the work fosters curiosity. You're suddenly like, "Oh, this is starting to make sense now." It's not all just doing the memorization; it's feeling it.

Fifth, twenty respondents reported that their appreciation of and involvement in Masonry had been deepened as a result of their own reading and research. As one stated:

I've read some really interesting stuff. It's fascinating the more you dig into it. If you stick with it, your ability to discriminate is going to kick in and you'll begin to see where fluff is fluff, just some guy's wild idea, and where something has some meat to it. Your own intelligence will help you weave your way through.

Relatedly, twenty-six respondents claimed that Masonic activities can feed prior personal interests, particularly in the areas of history and religion.

The ritual didn't just emerge full-blown in the 1700s. Previously people just couldn't do it openly before that because of religion. There are lots of clues to follow, lots I'm curious to dig into.

Historic legends like those of the Knights Templar have a present purpose. They fascinate people and encourage exploration.

Finally, respondents claimed that going further in the Craft—getting more involved—deepened their interest. In one way or another, eighteen spoke of how joining one or more of the concordant bodies was "educational." They variously claimed that these bodies and their ceremonies "pull it all together," "help with interpretation," and "fill in holes" and that "you don't get the full picture without [them]."

Thus far, all of the comments point to the fact that involvement has educational payoffs, which in turn encourage deeper involvement. Yet, despite these comments, things were not always positive in these respects. In lodges where there were few educational activities or presentations to engage members in the first place, sixteen respondents complained about the "lack of Masonic education in meetings."

> *There's almost a sustained effort to make it Masonic-content-free. That is the underlying thing today, in my mind, why men do not stay in Masonry.*

> *Without something more, the meetings themselves won't hold you. They're too controlled, even meaningless.*

Moreover, twenty-eight respondents felt that their Masonic experience was lessened by "having to pick up the deeper aspects by studying on my own." As one man stated,

> *I had too many questions and not enough answers. I almost demitted.*

Such a lack of educational engagement is related to a variety of underlying factors in particular lodges. Some respondents related it to the extensive "secrecy" surrounding the Craft in the "old days," some to the "traditional male role where you don't talk about things, just chew it through on your own," some to their lodges "having few candidates" and "filling meetings with business" to compensate, and still others to the "lack" or "poor implementation" of "mentoring programs" for new candidates. All such factors can come together in one way or another in particular lodges to have the same result: candidates who feel, "We can't stay at this because we're doing the same thing over and over. We're not learning anything new."

Where educational opportunities were present, while there were six respondents who complained that they were "not interested in Masonry for that reason," more were concerned about other things, such as the content, format, execution, and so on. Five complained that the focus was more on the "how-to" aspect or on "proprieties of dress and things like that" rather than on "meaning." Four expressed concern about the "irrelevance" of the terminology or music being presented to younger people in society today, one spoke of the "arcane" ritual language, and one stated that "Masonry has too much internal referencing." Two more complained about "boring, monotone educational presentations." Thus, while not all members may have an interest in Masonry because of its educational potential, it is clear that any education provided must be both relevant and meaningful to the broadest possible group of members if it is not to risk backfiring in terms of future involvement.

It is notable that twenty-two respondents who did make the effort to get actively involved and take a ritual part spoke of the discouragement they encountered as a result of the "comments from the peanut gallery"—those members who were "perfectionistic" about how the ritual had to be memorized and performed a certain way and were not shy about letting participants know it. In the words of one man "some lodges are very straitlaced, and that's painful." Such "self-righteous" "nitpicking" was said to "turn off less-educated brethren" and to "foster disunity rather than support." Of course, if members are turned off before they take part, or even early in the process of taking part, they are less likely to ultimately have their interest deepened through the process of actively working through and picking apart the ritual as noted above. It is in this way that criticism may actually serve to undermine the kind of hands-on "learning by doing" education that helps foster greater involvement of members over time.

Suggestions for Improving Masonic Education and Deepening Interest

Respondents' comments in the previous two sections on education can easily be read in terms of what to do—and not to do—to foster Masonic involvement through education. However, these remain somewhat narrowly focused. In the former, there were few comments about education after one has finished one's degrees, and, in the latter, it is clear that not everyone makes the effort to take an office, participate in degree work, give a lecture, or educate themselves about Masonry on their own time. However, respondents also extensively commented on ways that lodges could foster Masonic education and deepen interest for others—particularly through innovative strategies that often went beyond the traditional style of Masonic education offered in the lodge. It is to these that we now turn.

First, twenty respondents were quick to point out that "more information is available today," pointing to the proliferation of websites (both pro- and anti-Masonry), books such as *The DaVinci Code* and *Freemasons for Dummies*, spoofs like the "Homer the Great" episode of *The Simpsons*, and a whole host of documentaries. As a result, "People come in better informed, but will they take the extra step and learn?" Yet, even though we have more resources than were available in the past, these are not necessarily the answer. Given the earlier comments about self-directed learning, some will avail themselves of these, and some won't. What about the latter?

Next, and in line with the comments above about "boring" educational presentations or the near exclusive focus on the "how-to" aspects, there was an expressed need to provide educational opportunities after formal mentoring ends to reach those not amenable to traditional forms of Masonic education, such as taking office and listening to lectures. Respondents' comments in this regard revolved around two themes to improve education and, thereby, interest: individually targeting brethren's prior interests and engaging in innovative educational practices.

Regarding the former, thirty-one respondents commented that there needed to be "organized opportunities" available "after formal mentoring ends," yet that "we need to find a way to identify and engage those who want deeper study from others." Evidently such screening involves targeting of "education that fits with prior interests," which would better, in the words of one man "provide stuff you can dig into." This could be done either informally "through mentors" or through some more formal method, such as a brief questionnaire. Regardless of how screened, however, the idea was to provide education "in interesting, bite-size pieces that people can get the taste from and go further." This could be of benefit to the thirty-three respondents who expressed interest in "exploring the deeper aspects" of Masonry, the ten interested in learning the "how-to aspects" and "terminology," the three who wanted to learn about non-Masonic matters, and the two who wanted to learn about "issues members themselves select." Implementing screening and selectively targeting education to member interests—in effect, "leading them to it"—could go a long way to "sparking an interest, lighting that seed," and fostering deeper interest in the order for those at the end of mentoring and not yet involved in traditional methods of "learning by doing."

Nevertheless it was not just targeting that respondents considered important. They also expressed the need to move away from the traditional lecture or reading formats to a more engaging, participatory model in comfortable, informal environments. Various ideas emerged, but one stood out above the rest: thirty-eight respondents noted the need for more informal discussions, but only five of these suggested that these occur in the lodge itself.[1] Finding a way to encourage more relaxed, informal discussions was seen as the way to go, and such respondents gave examples. Seven musicians met weekly to practise their instruments, have a drink, and vigorously discuss Masonic matters in a way that they felt "balances out the boring, unbalanced lodge meetings." Having visited this group, I can personally vouch for the bond evident between the members. Similarly, two respondents suggested having monthly dinner group discussions before lodge, while three pointed to how their regular Masonic discussions at a pub on Friday afternoons were so successful that a new lodge was formed by the group and incorporated some of their ideas. Various other ideas were put forth, from having a "Masonic reading group" to the promotion of Internet chat sites. One man's comment summed up the general feeling:

> There's no better way to help you understand than to have a back-and-forth discussion as opposed to hearing a lecture or reading a pamphlet, and then, when you call someone, they don't even know the answer—and that sort of thing. This way you rub shoulders with people from different backgrounds, with different opinions. If you're thick-skinned enough, it's challenging, informative, even rewarding. It draws you out of yourself and encourages open-mindedness.

Indeed, one thing struck me in the process of conducting this research: six respondents that I interviewed in separate, interactive group settings strongly emphasized that there needed to be "more things like today's interview" where one can "brainstorm an issue." One man commented, "I've talked about this more today than I have in the past ten-plus years. Talk about Masonic education!" Another simply added, "It's the first Masonic discussion I have had, period." Thus, finding a way to provide informal, Masonic intercourse among interested parties, perhaps as a targeted extension of ordinary fellowship, would likely go a long way to engage those brethren not otherwise engaged after mentoring ends.

Of course, knowing the direction is not as easy as getting there. Four respondents pointed to examples of more formal Masonic discussion groups that "fizzled despite best-laid plans." One lodge, for example, had planned a "school" that went nowhere, there were educational "conferences" planned by another that "had bugger all turnout despite the ads," and a lunchtime discussion group ceased to operate due, it was claimed, to a "bad schedule" and "poor attendance."

Such notable failures serve as a caution. In some respects, successful, informal groups such as those described above cannot be formally planned; they are organic entities that typically develop on their own around shared activities or common interests. They cannot be created by fiat or from the top down in a formal, bureaucratic sense. Yet, they can still be encouraged: brethren can be prompted to share their interests, and those sharing common issues can be introduced if they have not already found each other. If lodges can find ways to discover the prior and ongoing interests of brethren and to match these to both formal educational programming and informal friendship groups, and if informal friendship activities can be fostered around common matters to balance out the more formal activities in the lodge itself, these will likely go a long way to further both education and involvement by those brethren in the critical post-mentoring, non-office-holding group at greatest risk of demitting.

Summing up this section, education is one tangible benefit of involvement in Masonry, one that can, when meaningful, be a reward that fosters greater involvement in the Craft, while meaningless strategies, or lack of education altogether, serve to undermine involvement. Masonic education must begin early—and be accompanied by good degree work, regular social contact, quality mentoring, and relevant material. For those who take an office, the educational benefits of "learning by doing" must be made more explicit, with a minimum of being left to their own devices and others' disillusioning criticism. Finally, effective methods must be found to provide meaningful education to that critical group of Master Masons who do not take an office and are not necessarily amenable to traditional, formal forms of Masonic education.

Targeted, meaningful education that links their prior interests and social inclinations may be the greatest service that can be simultaneously provided to them and to the Craft in terms of involvement.

THE IMPACT OF MEMBERS' OTHER COMMITMENTS AND ACTIVITIES; THOUGHTS ON GENDER

The next area that respondents commented on as having a significant impact on their involvement in the Craft is an obvious one in today's complex, busy society: the amount of both time and commitment that they already have invested in other social involvements. In a very general sense, the fewer additional involvements individuals have, the more free time they will have available for involvement in Masonry; the more additional involvements, the less room they will have for Masonic activities. Nevertheless, available time is not the only factor, as existing commitments to various institutions or significant others may contain ideological elements that are either relatively favourable or opposed to the Craft (e.g., ideas surrounding gender). In this section, I outline the interrelated impact of both involvements and commitments to social ideals in the changing social landscape of the twenty-first century. I begin by considering factors that respondents articulated favouring involvement in the Craft and then move on to those that, in one way or another, may serve to dissuade it.

First in this respect, fifty respondents, in one way or another, emphasized that their involvement was predicated on "having the time to do it, to be involved." Beyond the most general comments in this respect, when broken down further, the single biggest subgroup involved twenty-five who claimed that it was a "good outlet," "focus," or form of "mental exercise" for them now that they were retired:

> Once I retired, I said, "The time for excuses is gone!" I started getting back into it then. I never had time when I was working.

Beyond the relative free time enjoyed by the retired, four respondents claimed that, now that their kids were grown up and out on their own, it "frees up time." Three more said that it was easier for them to be involved as they were currently single, while other comments included respondents who had jobs with "flexible hours," even one whose company was on strike during his entire term in one office! Having convenient meeting nights and fewer competing fraternal organizations than in the past also fit in here. One way or another such comments illustrate the basic point that involvement is related to one's available free time in various social contexts.

Thirteen additional respondents pointed to the responsibility of Masons to their other social involvements. They commented on the importance of "knowing your limits," "having a balance," and "taking on only so much as you can" in terms of involvement. They cautioned that it is important to "be careful about volunteering," pointing out that one "can easily get caught up into doing too much," suggested "don't make it like work," and claimed that ultimately it was good to "have your priorities straight as we're taught: family, work, then Masonry."

However, as indicated above, other social commitments involve not merely time but also support (or opposition) from other people—in particular, members of one's family. Forty-two respondents spoke of the importance of spousal support for their involvement in Masonry.

> I could not do it without my wife's support. If she were different, I might have to stay home to please her. If you don't have a happy woman, you don't have a happy life.

> When I joined my wife was okay with it. She just said for me to ask before involving her in anything. Now she wants me to go to justify the dues that I pay—maybe she just likes having me out that much! Now, I come in the door and she says, "The buffalo is home," and jokes around trying to figure out the handshake. Still, she knows I'm out with a good bunch with certain morals. She knows where I am. She has no worries and all that.

> My wife and I have actually discussed the gender thing. Surprisingly enough, she sees nothing the matter with having a men's organization. It's like she understands the importance of men being in an environment together, just like there's an importance for women to be in a women's environment together.

Moreover, several respondents' wives commented positively as well:

> My husband enjoys it and I don't mind him being involved—and he does a lot of good things. I made a lot of very good friends through it. I've met a lot of people from different places and have enjoyed it all.

> My husband takes pride in what he does as Master; he really does a very good job. I've met so many of the gentlemen that are Masons, and most are very kind, considerate, and treat each other as brothers. It's just a wonderful way to live your life, and I really think it's a good thing. We've met people we wouldn't have met otherwise from across Canada and the States. Our circle of friends has grown. They're a bunch of good people.

Beyond the above, there were several specific reasons mentioned for spousal support. First, thirty-six respondents noted the significance of lodge activities, events, and opportunities—both joint and separate—for their spouse and family to participate in. These included regular socials, dances, dinners, tours, kids' activities, picnics, and holiday events. As one respondent enthused, "You wouldn't believe the togetherness that we have with all our wives when we put on a function." One member's wife commented, "I'm the one that gets to go on tours with the girls while you're sitting in a room all night."

It was also noted that some lodges were attempting to move beyond more traditional activities such as "ladies' nights," dinners, and dances to find (unspecified) "ways to make Freemasonry work with changes in leisure lifestyle that make leisure activities increasingly family- and couple-oriented."

Nevertheless, a second reason noted for spousal support involved the spouses' own family histories in Freemasonry. Twelve respondents noted such a family history on their spouse's side of the family: Seven of respondents' spouses had family members who were Masons, while five had women in the family who were, or had been, members of the Eastern Star (a related order for women). Apparent positive familiarity with the Craft seems to have fostered a positive attitude by spouses toward respondents' involvement.

Beyond spousal support for Masonic involvement, eight other respondents added that their spouse was, in effect, indifferent to their lodge activities, as they each had their own interests. In one man's words, "She does her thing and I do mine." Whatever this may say about their relationship, it is at least not active opposition.

In addition to the stance of their spouse, respondents commented on other avenues of support for their Masonic activities. Twenty indicated support from the rest of their family (e.g., one man, an Italian immigrant, commented on how his mother bought him his apron and Masonic ring, relating that his brother presented them to him touchingly in the lodge, speaking entirely in Italian). Another five respondents reported relative family indifference. Six reported support from religious leaders, and two reported positive feedback from friends. In all instances, such social backing—or at least acquiescence—from significant or respected others was said to facilitate involvement in the order.

But what about the role of negative effects related to other involvements and commitments? The data were rife with such comments. Forty-six respondents pointed in a general sense to conflicting responsibilities or schedules that made it difficult for them to be deeply involved. The general feeling was that "life is so fast-paced today" and "there are so many other demands on young people." When asked to be more specific, all forty-six pointed to conflicting work schedules—either their own or that of their spouse (the latter, of course, is more relevant than in the past, given the necessity in most cases today for both partners to have paid employment). Many felt "too busy just trying to make ends meet." Indeed, one man stated that he found it "hectic rushing to go to a meeting, then having to get home because I'm working in the morning."

Beyond the formal workplace, nineteen respondents also pointed to the fact that they had children at home—ones who, more often these days, have "their own activity schedules." One man plainly stated, "That's why I missed twenty years." Several respondents commented on the difficulty of balancing lodge activities with family and work:

> We have difficulty maintaining active, participating members from their early twenties up to forty because of career and family obligations that they have.

> There are times when you're younger that the Masonic order has to take a back burner in line with the times. Masonic activities must balance with, and be within, reason.

> It's hard to juggle family if you don't have the home support network.

In light of such comments, one man simply said, "I'll be more involved when I can, probably when I'm retired."

Third, nineteen respondents pointed out that, unlike in the past, when there were fewer competing entertainment or recreational activities, today the lodge faces stiff competition.

> The TV keeps people home. Young people are into doing their own thing today. The pubs keep them busy. There are other things. Like many other fraternal or civic organizations, Freemasonry is not terribly appealing in an era of mass leisure and consumption. The idea that you join an organization and pay a subscription, and you don't necessarily get anything much back from it other than the enjoyment of going to meetings, is one that seems increasingly alien in the sorts of leisure that we're used to today. You can no longer expect someone to dedicate a whole evening to one thing if they're not getting anything out of it. It's the same problems facing other groups.[2]

Finally in this respect, ten respondents pointed to circumstantial factors that made involvement difficult, including distance from the lodge (three), dying rural communities (two), accessibility issues (two), meeting times, (two), even weather (one). All were seen, in one way or another, as external factors impeding involvement.

However, given the earlier discussion of social support, I must now turn to consider respondents' comments surrounding social opposition to involvement in the Craft. Respondents commented extensively on various sources of opposition to Masonry. In order of descending frequency, these included the many negative stereotypes that have been circulated by conspiracy theorists in popular culture (cited by fifty-three respondents); religious opposition (twenty); spousal opposition (twenty); family opposition (twelve); and a variety of other matters such as regulatory constraints (three), friends' opposition (two), secular ideals (one), and comments from disillusioned former members (one). Each will be dealt with in turn.

First, fifty-three respondents noted the negative stereotypes that surround Masonry, in particular the idea that it is some form of "conspiratorial cult." Respondents commented on how the Craft has been lumped in with devil worship, the Ku Klux Klan, "secret societies," and a host of other nefarious groups in a wide variety of profitable books, films, and on the Internet. Much has been made of the "Morgan affair," a murder in the early 1800s allegedly committed by Masons in New York State to prevent the disclosure of their secrets. Others noted acquaintances' claims about the "black-hearted Masons" that "run this town." Respondents were aware of the shaky foundations of such claims and saw them as "exaggerated," "sensationalized," and "taken out of context."

> I keep thinking—join the lodge, or ask a Mason about these things.

Nevertheless, they were aware that "ignorance promotes speculation" and many respondents saw such negative stereotypes as "hurdles to get over" in relation to maintaining involvement. Such materials, at the very least, could serve as resources to crystallize opposition to one's Masonic activities in the social context at hand.

Next, twenty respondents commented on the presence of religious opposition to involvement in the Craft. There were comments about the "historic opposition of the Catholic Church" to Freemasonry; about ongoing problems with "fundamentalists" who make claims about "pagan" influences and "no mention of Jesus in the ritual"; about the opposite perception—that is, that the lodge is a "Protestant, Christian organization"; and about perceptions that Freemasonry is "anti-Islamic." Indeed, one respondent noted that a Muslim member left the lodge shortly after 9/11, claiming, "I can't serve two masters." To the extent that members are religious or susceptible to such opposing religious claims, these can serve as brakes on involvement in the Craft.

Third, twenty respondents spoke of the importance of emergent spousal opposition to involvement in the Craft, a sentiment that Clawson (1989) notes was also apparent in the nineteenth century.

> *Even supportive wives don't like it taking up too much time and keeping their husbands away. They can be iffy if you go out to "too many meetings."[3]*

> *You cannot be a Mason and not have support at home. I'm hoping to get through my year in the Chair without a divorce.*

> *There's nothing like having a wife that's not for it. You need an understanding wife.*

> *If you don't get your wife behind it, you might as well give up.*

> *For me, my least favourite thing about Freemasonry is that my wife doesn't share my interest.*

> *My wife doesn't like the male-only aspect—and things like ladies' nights and ladies' auxiliaries don't appeal to women today. They're laughable.*

Fourth, and relatedly, twelve respondents spoke of family opposition to the Craft, which supplemented several of the other bases above, whether religious (e.g., one man's mother, a staunch Catholic, seeing Masons as "devil worshippers"), or secular (e.g., a man with a family tradition in the Craft being told he was "too involved," such that he was "hardly home").

Finally, there were seven comments noting other avenues of opposition. Three respondents had lived in jurisdictions where Masonry was either persecuted or faced legal regulation (e.g., they had once lived in a fascist or communist state, or had been required to state their membership when employed by the UK civil service). Two had friends who had drawn upon anti-Masonic literature to question their choices. One secular man struggled with the requirement of belief in a supreme being. Another man had encountered a disillusioned former Mason who had disparaged the Craft. All such opposing circumstances served to dampen involvement.

Some of the above forms of opposition are relatively straightforward. The increased access to information, and thus anti-Masonic materials, in recent decades has generated numerous resources for opponents in one's social milieu—religious or secular—to draw upon when opposing one's involvement in the Craft for various reasons. The Internet alone is a technological treasure trove of such narratives that opponents can draw upon as needed, facilitating active opposition in ways that critics could only dream of a few decades ago.

Yet there are other matters that relate to social structural changes in the past few decades that are more complex. The role of gender is key here. Respondents who commented in this regard were nearly evenly split about the traditional "men-only" policy found in regular Freemasonry. Thus, twenty-three respondents supported this approach, claiming that this provided men with a supportive "place to have their own thing, like women do," which echoes Clawson's (1989) claim that nineteenth-century men built solidarity against the backdrop of gender.

> *Can there not be some things that are guy things? Cause I just ... I don't have anything else in my life that is a guy thing. And that seems fair.*

> *Women have their segregated groups and events, so we should be able to as well.*

> *I just think it's good to be able to have a thing that's yours, among other men.... Maybe there's some things we can do that the guys would do together and some things that the girls would do together. It doesn't make anything less or more equal. It's just that there's a conviviality among men or women that can be recognized. You know, fair's fair.*

When pressed further, respondents gave various reasons beyond the above for keeping things the way they are. Some simply saw Masons as men by definition, others adding that any attempt to change things would result in withdrawal of recognition, their ceasing to be involved, or both:

> *A Mason is a man by definition, just like a bachelor is an unmarried man.*

> *Freemasonry is a fraternity, simple as that. Women can join Eastern Star.*

> *That's when I take a demit, when I see a skirt coming through the door.*

> *We cannot admit women without ceasing to be Masons. There would be immediate withdrawal of recognition by other Grand Lodges, like what happened to Minnesota when they tried it.*

This last respondent raises an interesting point. In 2001, the Grand Lodge of Minnesota granted fraternal recognition to one of the three main Grand Lodges in France (La Grande Loge de France). Controversy erupted in 2002 over a number of matters, one of which was the allegation that the Grande Loge de France maintained relations and dual membership with the atheist Grand Orient de France, mixed lodges such as Le Droit Humain, and women-only Grand Lodges. Within weeks, four US Grand Lodges suspended fraternal relations with Minnesota, which soon grew to eleven US and four international jurisdictions. As a result of Minnesota brethren not being able to visit lodges in these other jurisdictions (and vice versa), along with the practical problems this would pose for hosting a conference in 2003, the Grand Lodge of Minnesota soon revoked its recognition. The implication is that formally admitting women likely poses serious issues for any "regular" Grand Lodge that considers it—despite this clearly being an issue percolating in the social background.

Others respondents gave more thoughtful views. Some spoke of how Freemasonry was particularly geared toward the male gender, a means to male bonding in shared activity and emotion and identity management:

> *Freemasonry, in some respects, is a very male institution—men, traditionally at least, not being very open about their feelings and things like that. I think it's uniquely suited to men in some respects because what they get out of it, they often keep to themselves. They read into the rituals and that sort of thing— and they take it with them—but it's not often commented on. They sort of chew it through themselves, so it's suited to the traditional male gender the way it operates.*

> *Part of the reason that I did join was because it was a men-only organization, once I knew what it was all about. Especially today, I think males still need a bonding thing of some sort. Not like women, who can just hug and cry together, they actually have to have something organized that they can do together. A lot of other organizations I'm in have gone coed, so I think it's important that it remain men-only because times are changing and men lose a lot of identity in these different groups.*

Others were more open to the idea of finding support from other men, often noting the value of fellowship among men similar to that experienced by others of like background:

> *In today's world, men need a place to bond. Although it's not PC to say so, I think it is important for men to have a place where they can ... I think where they can feel some sense of comfort insofar as there are other people who are like-minded, living similar lives, doing similar things, who can trust each other for advice, who can offer support to one another. I think that's important for anyone. I think it's important for women to have women's groups. It's important for children to be involved in children's groups. And, likewise for men, I think it's import- ant for men to come together and say, "Okay, this is our venue, and we can talk about the things that matter to us, and we can decide how we want to impact society and, in a more specific sense, our families."*

> *Like ethnic groups and teens, for example, I think what is important to Freemasons is for men to stay together in a group, to have that level of freedom of conversation, of fellowship that*

comes from men who are not sportsmen, men who are not a bunch of drinkers, men who are not of this ilk or that ilk, but men who form [around] a common group of intellectual ideas.

I hope Freemasonry stays a men's group for the sake that there's a kind of fellowship that is needed by getting together with people of like mind or a like gender, or a like approach or a like philosophy—and that doesn't offer itself in today's society very often.

I only came to support the traditional position in retrospect. It's like in bereavement groups. It's important for it to be for men only because when you're talking with the guys, you can open up a little easier, a little quicker. There is something to be said about a fraternity, plus the history behind it where a lot of the ideas, a lot of the moral codes and understanding are military. So, with that, a lot of that has to fall right back on the male gender.

I grew up without my father, so maybe that's part of the attraction for me, the male bond kind of thing.

Yet there were twenty-five respondents who felt that the traditional men-only policy was anything but encouraging: for them it was problematic. Pointing to how today there are "different gender roles than in the past," comments included the following:

I don't see a particularly compelling reason for it to remain men-only. Sooner or later this is going to blow up in our face with a lawsuit.

Okay, the family unit has changed. When you think about the old days, my father's day when he joined Freemasonry, typically you had the stay-at-home mother who looked after the family, the husband went off to work, came home, and then decided what he was going to do for relaxation for the night, right? Over the past decades we've seen the family unit evolve such that the male is much more a participant in the family in terms of helping to bring up the kids, doing the dishes, etc. There's a much more equitable split in what the family unit chores are, okay? It's not like the old days when the man could go out and the wife would stay home with the kids, and the kids could play outside, and you weren't running them here, there, and everywhere. You can't do it the way you could then.

Thus there was a split among respondents on this issue, largely reflecting both changing gender roles and the generation gap between older and younger respondents. One man summed it up nicely: "The gender issue is probably drawing some members in and repelling others." In effect, using gender as a foil can no longer work as well as it did in the nineteenth century (Clawson 1989). The old strategy of providing a bounded sanctuary from feminine cultural ideals is experiencing slippage as new gender norms enter the lodge along with new members. The trick for the Craft today is to find a way to encourage involvement from both traditional men and those more open to women's involvement beyond traditional institutions like the Eastern Star (where it exists), all the while avoiding the international recognition problems encountered by Grand Lodges that made "innovations" elsewhere (e.g., Minnesota). Accommodating all of these issues is a tall order, but one that is crucial in maximizing involvement and minimizing opposition to involvement in the Craft in today's rapidly changing society.

Summing up this section, then, today's evolving society, undergirded by neo-liberal economic policies and rapidly changing gender roles, among other things, has resulted in a social landscape that often differs from that of the past, resulting in a faster-paced life, different competing involvements, and different ideas about the legitimacy of involvement in the Craft. Not only do members need time in their schedules to be involved, they also need the interest to separate it from other draws on their free time. They also need to see what they are doing as valid and have the support, or at least not the opposition, of others in their social environment. Scott (1987) cautions about the potential for internal and external social identities to become problematic for organizations, and the social world today is affecting all of these matters, making involvement in Freemasonry more difficult than it was in the simpler world of the past.

MORAL AND ETHICAL BENEFITS

Beyond the factors outlined thus far, respondents were vocal about the moral and ethical benefits that they felt facilitated ongoing involvement in the Craft. Such comments were couched in the language of, on the one hand, "self-improvement" and "becoming a better man," and on the other, "standards" that stand out in relation to the state of society today.

In the first sense, thirty-six respondents claimed benefits to their involvement in Freemasonry in that the moral obligations they swore to uphold helped to improve their "character," "outlook," or "moral actions" over time. Respondents spoke variously of "learning a lot about myself" and becoming "more tolerant," "less volatile," "less materialistic," and "more selfless," some reporting that, as "historically lodges were about fair dealing," "now my word is my bond." There were also a few dramatic stories, such as those of brethren who claimed to have ceased engaging in previous "immoral" behaviours, or situations where former adversaries had been able to make peace with one another, even to become friends, due to their mutual involvement in Masonry. One man summed up the various moral benefits of involvement as being "like multiplication—it just keeps on growing." Another pointed out how "the symbols can jump up like flags or prompters in day-to-day life." Overall, however, the idea was that, in the words of one man,

> *Freemasonry provides a system, a subtext, and an infrastructure in which to practise moral imperatives within a community.*

Such comments were often linked to the latter aspect noted above. Eighteen respondents contrasted the morality taught in Masonry with the state of contemporary society, seeing it as beneficial in that it "provides a firm foundation to live by in today's crazy world."

> *The lodge is a place where I get guidance on how to live a good and productive life that contributes not only to my personal life, but to the world and the community at large.*

> *There are a lot of things going wrong in our world right now, and I think if the world had a close look at how Masons behave when they're together, the world might be a better place if they would take some lessons from it.*

> *Somebody has to stand up and really keep certain ideals alive. The moral codes today are being watered down. Really, the social fabric is starting to decay. What I see in the lodge contrasts with the Jerry Springer morality I see today. It's solid—not superficial—ground in a world going down the tubes. Freemasonry is about fighting that decay.*

The tenor of these comments fits in well with the idea that building a strong role identity is a good way to explain sustained volunteerism (Chacon, Vecina, and Davila 2007).

Nevertheless, where there are moral claims there are usually negative judgments as well—and in this context they served, in the eyes of eighteen respondents, as "turnoffs" to involvement. Eight of these respondents perceived "nepotism" in Masons "helping each other" like an "old boys' network," while, for example, others did not get jobs, promotions, or contracts. Another three spoke of what they saw as "unethical," "improper," even "abusive" actions by brethren that had come to light: "We're human beings first, and there are bad Masons." Six commented more specifically on having had "run-ins" with "hypocritical" brethren "who don't practise it" or "walk the talk like they should." Finally, one spoke of "inappropriate behaviour" in open lodge on the part of a certain "notorious" individual that "kept others away." In one or another of these ways, perceptions of immoral or inappropriate behaviour by other brethren undermine building the kind of strong Masonic role-identity helpful to facilitating involvement.

MOTIVATIONAL ISSUES

Finally, there were also a few respondents who sought to explain long- or short-term involvement of brethren in the Craft in terms of motivation. Thus, nine respondents suggested that "being a curious type" or "a person that likes to dig into things" fostered long-term involvement:

> *Plain and simple curiosity—about life and other people and the lodge and history—that is the common denominator that I see amongst the folks who are there. Folks who are just curious about everything, and interested in everything. That would explain 99 percent of the folks who are there long-term. So if you come in because you're curious, then I'd say you have the best chance of all of sticking.*

> *You've got to have the mystery. The people who don't grab it, and don't go looking for what's between the lines, they'll not be members long.*

Second, nine respondents spoke of how it was important to have the right "attitude" in the first place for "commitment" to develop:

> *You get out of it what you put into it. If people have some expectation of what Masonry is going to do for them, they've got it backwards. Unless you do something for Masonry, Masonry does absolutely nothing for you. If you pay your dues and never darken the door, don't expect anything other than a bill for dues once a year. If you associate, if you take part in the fraternity itself, there's a million things to get out of it.*

> *There's all kinds of other things that you can belong to, but Freemasonry is the one that requires commitment. I think if you just come in this lodge and sit on the sides, don't do the offices or don't take part in degree work, you get very little out of it. I mean, if I did it that way, I probably wouldn't be here now. I would probably have lost interest long ago.*

> *I'm not the type that believes in stopping something once I've started. I'm going to get as much out of it as I can.*

Conversely, nine respondents pointed to what they perceived—in one way or another—as motivational failures lying behind lagging involvement:

> Some people just don't have the motivation. They fear com-
> mitment or think that it's too hard. After making one excuse it
> becomes easier to make the other ones.

> There's no immediate payoff. You spend your time doing this,
> and, by definition, you cannot know the end towards which you
> are working. You're working, literally and figuratively, in the
> dark, towards a light that you don't understand. People don't
> allow themselves to see the importance of it, because they don't
> become involved long enough to realize.

As a result of such characterizations, three respondents claimed that "we need
to be more demanding of members in terms of commitment and behaviour,"
another adding that candidates should be more carefully "screened" in terms
of their motivation to take an active part. In fact, one respondent, when faced
with complaints from others, turned the question around and asked, "How
has Freemasonry gotten better since you joined?" Such claims highlight the
role of personal motivation—in concert with other factors—in maintaining
or mitigating member involvement over time.

Finally, respondents commented on the need to address differential motivations for involvement. In the words of one man,

> People are involved for different reasons: social, status,
> administrative, spirituality, etc. You're always going to have
> a cross-section of people. I think that the reasons for joining
> Masonry are as varied as the folks who join Masonry. We have
> to ensure that the different groups, the different reasons for
> being a Mason, are all satisfied. We've got to help people find
> their niche in the lodge.

While the above comments reflect the views of those respondents who
made specific remarks about motivation, they also unduly individualize and
oversimplify this issue. Indeed, these claims might be characterized as vocabularies of motive (Mills 1940), examples of actors in a particular social context
that impute and avow typical interpretations of conduct in others. They are
representative of an individualistic grammar that formulates a type of person (Blum and McHugh 1971), one without the motivation or the personal
"commitment" to continue. Indeed, they may be seen as examples of motivational rhetoric—specific, organized attempts, characterized by manipulative
strategies and tactics, to persuade oneself or others to act in a particular manner—which both propels them and legitimates their activity (Taylor 1979).

Yet, as noted in chapter 2, motivations such as curiosity occur in a social
context, and, by extension, it is the ongoing social construction of differential
motivations that, in many respects, has been implicit throughout this section

of the book. At this point I would submit that the various factors discussed in this and the previous two chapters in relation to involvement weave the motivational framework within which a member's emotions, inclinations, choices, and commitments arise: they do not arise fully formed from the individual. Even prior dispositions and inclinations must be seen in their broader context (Poulet 2010). Indeed, I would argue that the various attractions described, and problems highlighted, go a long way toward unpacking the ideal-typical involvement motivations of Freemasons today.

Furthermore, if curiosity and—by extension—other kinds of motivation noted herein can be socially evoked, constructed, and expanded, they can also be socially stifled, short-circuited, undermined, and dissolved. In some respects, for example, the various factors discussed may foster a greater curiosity and a desire to dig deeper, all the while opening up other motivational pathways (e.g., friendship, status). In other cases, the social framework may suck the very life out of motivation, facilitating a sense of disappointment where "the big secret is that there's no secret," punctuated with a medley of "boring business meetings" and a lingering sense of "disconnect with the reading." Combined in various ways, the social construction of curiosity, along with other motivations, may continue for some to facilitate involvement over time; in others, motivation may begin to decay much more quickly and raise question for members about why they bother at all.

Finally, a careful perusal of the matters expounded above will help to differentiate factors that motivate volunteers to join from those that motivate them to stay (Renauer 2001; Ilsley 1990, 15–32), suggest strategies to diversify and maximize the satisfactory engagement of differing types of motivation (Batson, Ahmad, and Tsang 2002), and highlight motivational differences between younger versus older volunteers (Omoto, Snyder, and Martino 2000).

DISCUSSION: ANALYTICAL TYPOLOGY

Respondents' comments in this and the previous two chapters about factors that facilitate and discourage involvement in the Craft have been both voluminous and detailed. Now that these have been outlined in depth, it is time to pull everything together in a comprehensive analytic model in relation to the literature at hand. Following classical sociologist Max Weber (1949), this section will do so by constructing a system of ideal types. I utilize the involvement factors above to outline an idealized series of polar opposites—one group illustrative of the ideal lodge and social context facilitating long-term involvement, the other group one that ideally encourages the quick exit of its members. While these are extremes drawn for analytic purposes and any real lodge will undoubtedly fit somewhere on the continuum between these two poles, such an analytic exercise enables us to represent more clearly elements critical to Masonic involvement today.

Beginning with the key element of social atmosphere, the ideal lodge that fosters long-term involvement is characterized by the following traits: (1) good "fit" between members' prior background and the social atmosphere of the lodge (this involves sufficient similarity between members' prior interests, perception of the lodge as a social "sanctuary" that offsets the stresses and strains of members' day-to-day lives and concerns, and remaining relevant in both regards in order to comprehensively maximize a "fruitful balance" between traditional and contemporary members); (2) close friendships (both prior and those developed within the lodge); (3) close family ties to the lodge; (4) good fellowship, with a strong emphasis on welcoming new members and attempting to develop personal connections through shared, relevant, and enjoyable social activities for them and their families; (5) an emphasis on providing attention and recognition to members when due, quasi-altruistically when they need support, as well as through extraordinary, meaningful gestures; (6) a membership carefully balanced in terms of equality and status such that there is a healthy, productive tension between internal and external referents of equality and status, between "brotherhood" and the alternate status hierarchy; and (7) the existence of a reverse onus of social bonding and trust developed through working together in meaningful activities and pursuing valued goals, and a normative emphasis on what is shared, culminating in the development of a Masonic identity.

Such an idealized social atmosphere can be readily perceived through its opposite: a lodge exhibiting a negative social atmosphere that drives members away. Such a lodge is characterized by (1) a poor "fit" between members' prior background and the social atmosphere of the lodge, whether measured in terms of interests, relevance, or expectations (rather than maintaining a fruitful balance in these respects, such a lodge is out of sync, not a sanctuary but a burden, representing more a meaningless obligation than anything else); (2) no close friendships; (3) no family ties to the lodge; (4) poor fellowship (few social events, members are not made to feel welcome, they are often left alone or ignored or left out of the loop by cliques, and perfunctory interactions are characterized by a feeling of ritualism and insincerity); (5) little (or negative) attention and recognition, taking the forms of either ignoring or criticizing members in light of a moralistic perfectionism; (6) an imbalance of emphasis on status, whether externally or internally referenced, related to "professionalization" or the "workplace model," such that there is a perceived breach between the rhetoric of equality and the apparent hypocrisy of those climbing the alternate status hierarchy; and (7) social divisions, few shared activities, and negative interactions resulting in little social bonding or reverse onus of trust—hence poor ground for a Masonic identity to grow.

Turning now to organizational factors, the second major area herein, the ideal lodge fostering long-term involvement has the following characteristics:

(1) a membership policy productively balanced between (a) bringing in enough members to offset attrition and efforts to involve and retain current members, (b) secrecy and openness, and (c) emphasis on quantity and on quality; (2) a dues structure of sufficient cost to emphasize the importance and status of Masonry, while nevertheless providing options for those on fixed incomes; (3) the right of new brethren to participate in the business of the lodge immediately after receiving their first degree; (4) leaders' tactful, fair encouragement of brethren to become involved in existing office opportunities, with support along the way as needed, facilitating a willingness to take part; (5) a strong emphasis on the lodge experience itself, including good meeting content, efficient meeting management, and accoutrements of exclusivity; (6) interactions with the wider community that involve working together for a common, worthy goal, openness about Masonic charity, and creative integration in other forms of community engagement; (7) no conflict or contentious dynamics, with a strong ability for the lodge to solve and cope with such things when they emerge; (8) a good, supportive relationship with the Grand Lodge reflective of accessibility, a sense of being heard, and the ability to get things done, coupled, again, with a productive balance between equality and status; (9) a good relationship with the local Shrine with few issues over recruitment; and (10) a demographic/generational balance whereby there is a good working relationship between younger and older members, a productive division of labour, and a sense of mutual input and respect.

Such an organizationally productive lodge may again be highlighted against its opposite. The organizationally problematic lodge has the following traits: (1) an ineffective membership policy that (a) neither brings in enough new members to offset attrition nor effectively re-engages existing members, (b) is characterized by an imbalance between secrecy and openness, and (c) stresses quantity or quality to the virtual exclusion of the other; (2) a dues structure that "sells Masonry too cheap," rendering it relatively meaningless to members; (3) restrictions on members such that they may not attend and take part until after they have their third degree; (4) few brethren willing to take part, pressure to take offices, lack of support for current officers, poor ritual work, poor administrative leadership, and burnout due to too few people taking on too many responsibilities; (5) boring, poorly managed business meetings characterized by the workplace model, bureaucratization, an emphasis on externalities such as the Grand Lodge, minutiae, and boring education (if any), all serving to provide a "disconnect with the reading," that is, with both Masonic teachings and many members' expectations and understandings of what the Craft is all about; (6) few, if any, interactions with the wider community in favour of an insular focus on the group; (7) conflict, contentious dynamics, and infighting over hot-button issues; (8) a poor relationship with the Grand Lodge in relation to bureaucratization, a problematic, unresponsive administrative structure, and a contentious perception of elitism out of sync with today's more egalitarian social ethos; (9) a problematic relationship with the Shrine and its overlapping membership, particularly in relation to recruitment; and (10) either an aging, declining membership that is not being replaced or demographic/generational divisions (if the latter, this generation gap involves older members resisting change, claiming they are doing all the work, and gradually dying off, while younger members see them as an obstacle to advancement and programming that could be culturally relevant to today's Masons).

Thirdly, the ideal lodge can be seen reflected in its orientation toward Masonic education. Such a lodge is characterized by (1) good, relevant mentoring of candidates, both informally (including by proposers) and formally through mentoring programs; (2) the willingness of a relatively high proportion of brethren to "learn by doing," whether through taking an office, taking part in the ritual, conducting research in line with their personal interests, or providing interesting educational talks and presentations; and (3) educational initiatives that bridge the gap between the end of mentoring and "learning by doing" by focusing attention on members involved in neither. This involves targeting uninvolved brethren through screening prior interests and individual brethren providing informal venues for sharing common issues and topics in a relaxed, convivial social atmosphere. This can be neither forced nor bureaucratically administered, but must begin socially and develop organically, with the lodge serving as but a facilitator.

Lodges with such a productive orientation toward Masonic education can be readily contrasted with their opposite, lodges where (1) proposers and other brethren do not provide informal mentoring, formal programs are non-existent or poorly implemented, and there is a stress on getting candidates through their third degree so they can be put in an office; (2) learning by doing is typically experienced as a "baptism of fire," where lack of support for members' efforts is frequently seasoned with criticism; and (3) there is neither screening of interests nor informal venues provided for sharing common issues and topics. In such lodges, Masonic education, if it exists at all, either consists of boring, monotone lectures on arcane subjects that are of interest to few (if any), or members being left to learn essentially on their own.

Fourth, ideal-typical lodges are characterized by a complementary relationship between their activities and programs and members' other commitments and involvements. Their members have relatively few other social involvements, activities, or commitments; they experience support for (or at least indifference about) their Masonic activities from others in their social milieu; and both members and their associates are able to effectively accommodate contemporary gender issues. Such lodges, moreover, exhibit a willingness to creatively accommodate members' other commitments, involvements, and orientations in a fruitful way. On the other hand, lodges facing difficulties have a membership facing many other involvements, whether in relation to work, family, or other activities and interests, that allow them little time to commit to Freemasonry. Such lodges must also deal with opposition to member involvement from significant others (whether spouses, family members, friends, religious leaders, or others in the members' social milieu), whom the lodges are either unable or unwilling to creatively address. In such lodges, gender issues are seen as problematic not only by others but by many members themselves, reducing the legitimacy of their involvement.

Fifth, ideal-typical lodges are seen by their members as providing moral and ethical benefits. They are often seen by members as providing a firm foundation, a moral haven in relation to society at large, benefits to character, and a means of fostering self-improvement and identity. Conversely, less-than-ideal lodges are seen as falling considerably short of such an image by their members, being rife with perceptions of hypocrisy, nepotism, and other forms of unethical behaviour less than conducive to both positive Masonic identity and members' long-term involvement.

Finally, ideal-typical lodges build on members' original curiosity behind joining and diversify motivations over time, thereby providing unforeseen benefits to brethren. Such lodges strategically diversify and balance activities and programs to provide a broad range of productive motivations for involvement (Batson, Ahmad, and Tsang 2002) by diverse categories of participants—for example, younger and older members (Omoto, Snyder, and Martino 2000) and new and seasoned volunteers (Ilsley 1990). They simultaneously position themselves well for changing motivations over time. Conversely, problematic lodges neither build on members' original motivations nor kindle new ones. Leaders do not strategically diversify their activities and programs in a balanced fashion, nor are they able to sufficiently meet changing motivations; members' original motivations to join are undermined, and the opportunity to present other motivations that might have encouraged them to stay is wasted.

The above contrasting characteristics of the ideal-typical and ideally problematic lodge in relation to member involvement are graphically outlined in Table 6.1, one side suggesting potential ways forward for the Craft, the other depicting clear paths to atrophy, loss of legitimacy, and environmental entropy—what Richard Hall (1987, 205) called "organizational death."

It occurs that much of the above may be conceptualized in terms of what Hirschi (1969) refers to as social bonding. He argues that, when our bonds to others are meaningful, we are forced to take their opinions into account when we act. If, however, we are detached from others, we are more free to leave. Hirschi attempts to further specify several dimensions of the social bonding process that, when underdeveloped or disrupted, increase the likelihood of deviation (which may be reconceptualized here as leaving the

Table 6.1   Ideal-Typical Lodges/Members Compared in Relation to Long-Term Involvement

PRO-INVOLVEMENT	ANTI-INVOLVEMENT
Social Atmosphere	Social Atmosphere
Good "fit" between members/atmosphere	Poor "fit" between members/atmosphere
Close friendships, prior and developed	No close friendships in lodge
Close family ties in lodge	No family ties in lodge
Good fellowship (welcoming/activities)	Poor fellowship (ignored/meaningless)
Attention/recognition for members	Little or negative attention to members
Productive tension between equality/status	Imbalance between equality/status
Social bonding/trust in shared activity	Little social bonding/trust: negativity
Reverse onus of trust between members	External social standard of trust
Development of Masonic identity	No Masonic identity
Organizational Factors	Organizational Factors
Balanced/diversified membership policy	Imbalanced/narrow membership policy
Dues structure reflecting significance	Selling Masonry "too cheap"
New initiates can attend/vote on business	Cannot attend/vote until after third degree
Tactful/fair encouragement to take office	"Arm-twisting" to take office; burnout
Strong emphasis on the lodge experience	Boring, poorly managed business meetings
Common activities/community integration	Insularity/little community integration
Little conflict; ability to solve if emerges	Conflict and contentious dynamics
Good relationship with the Grand Lodge	Poor relationship with the Grand Lodge
Good relationship with the Shrine	Poor relationship with the Shrine
Complementary intergenerational relations	Aging/dying members and/or generation gap
Educational Issues	Educational Issues
Effective informal and formal mentoring	Mentoring neglected or poorly implemented
Effective approach to "learning by doing"	"Baptism of fire" seasoned with negativity
Targeting interests; informal venues for rest	No informal venues; boring speeches
Other Commitments/Involvements	Other Commitments/Involvements
Complementary relationship	Conflicting relationship
Much free time in members' social context	Little free time in members' social context
Support/indifference of significant others	Opposition from significant others
Support for men-only policy	Opposition to men-only policy

Continued

Table 6.1 continued

PRO-INVOLVEMENT	ANTI-INVOLVEMENT
Moral and Ethical	**Moral and Ethical**
Lodge as firm foundation, moral haven	Perceptions of immorality and hypocrisy
Lodge as venue for self-improvement	Lodge not conducive to self-improvement
Motivational	**Motivational**
Original motivations addressed/extended	Original motivations undermined
New/emergent motivations encouraged	New/emergent motivations undermined
Diverse motivations balanced strategically	Diverse motivations poorly addressed
Changing motivations addressed	Changing motivations not addressed

order). There are both inner and outer dimensions. The inner dimensions are characterized by socialization into a set of conventional *beliefs* about how one should act—and where, when, and toward whom (which, in Freemasonry, occurs during initiation, education, and participation in the lodge, its ritual, business, and social activities) (Hirschi 1969, 23–26). Yet these do not always operate successfully to prevent deviation (i.e., leaving). Hence, Hirschi also considers what he refers to as the outer dimensions of social bonding. He sees these bonds to the group as made up of three distinct but related bands: (1) *attachment*—the degree to which individuals are sensitive to the expectations of others representing the world of the group; (2) *commitment*—investments of time and energy made to valued lines of activity in the group (investments which may be put at risk or lost); and (3) *involvement*—the extent to which time and energy are used up by non-group pursuits, limiting time for group ones (1969, 16–23). Taken as a whole, Hirschi's theory permits us to imagine more concretely, in a social psychological fashion, how many of the above factors may operate, in various ways, to foster attachment or detachment from the Masonic order. To the extent that these operate to closely bond brethren to the lodge, the greater is the chance of the inner dimension of social bonding, a Masonic identity, being reinforced by the outer.

Beyond this broad conceptualization, several key themes emerged from the data that must be noted. Significantly, these cut across a number of the factors discussed in the table above. Thus, the changing external social context, particularly the changes in gender relations over the past half century and the neo-liberal reorganization of work and family life, looms large in relation to things like "fit" between one's external life and the social atmosphere of the lodge, member motivations, morality, and the role of other commitments, activities, and involvements. Lodges that are, for example, attuned to both the differing structure of employment relations today (Ryle 2002; Rotolo and

Wilson 2003; Ryle 2000) and the need for both spouses to work (Becker and Hofmeister 2000) and that are adaptable enough to creatively accommodate and work with the responsibilities and ideals surrounding these new realities stand a much better chance of fostering involvement than those who do not. Similarly, respondents' comments suggest that a two-pronged approach would be best for the Masonic order: on the one hand, creatively target and engage men who are traditionalists alienated by changing structures and the "disappearance of the sacred" (Meštrovi 1997, 101–22), including the relative absence of emotionally meaningful rites in the Durkheimian sense, and, on the other hand, be open, interesting, and engaging to a greater diversity of men than in the past. What this adds up to are lodges that remain traditional in ways that work yet are nimble and adaptive in relation to a changing society at large.

Secondly, the theme of status versus equality was notable in a number of the above contexts. While Masonic ritual, the structure of offices, and the level and system of honorary titles all contain elements of both, there appear to be problems when these are not carefully balanced. While status attainment can contribute to involvement (Poulet 2010; Mahmud-Abdelwahib 2008; Welser 2006), whether discussed in terms of the economy of attention and recognition, emphasis on the Grand Lodge as opposed to the lodge experience, motivation, or other issues, these data show that an alternate status hierarchy can be both productive and destructive to member involvement if not carefully balanced. Moreover, given that today's society has a much more egalitarian ethos than the past and that Freemasonry recruits fewer members of high social rank, this balance must be set differently than in the days where titles, social rank, and deference to authority were the social norm. Lodges that do not recognize this and adapt, or that adhere uncritically to the way that it's always been done, risk perpetuating a maladaptive, imbalanced approach that increasingly risks alienating rank-and-file members.

Third, many of the issues above can be related to the demographics of lodges today. Due to the "lost generation" (baby boomers who largely did not become involved in Masonry), many of the factors in the above table are exacerbated by cultural differences between generations. Social activities, the way meetings are run, styles of education, motivations, moralities, and understandings surrounding other commitments and involvements often mean very different things to younger and older Masons, who in some cases fail to understand each other, while the lodge bleeds members from either deaths or demits. Constructive ways to bridge this gap must be found, particularly in urban areas where it is most notable, in order to bump up long-term involvement by those who will be the future of the Craft.

Finally, in all of these respects, there is a need to consider the important principle of balance. Lodges today should respect the Masonic landmarks, yet be willing to shake off the restrictive encrustations of those unnecessary traditions often premised with the words "This is how we've always done it here." Rather than perpetuate the bureaucratic "business model," itself largely a development reflective of the mid-twentieth-century focus on big business and organized philanthropy (Tabbert 2007), lodges need to be nimble, adaptive, and better able to balance necessary traditions with a rapidly changing society. Keeping an eye on the original, broad Masonic ideal of self-improvement, lodges must balance attention to the various motivations for joining and those that emerge, equality and status, young and old, Masonic culture and the culture at large. They must balance business and ritual for all with greater emphasis on informal, convivial groupings of shared interests.

Ultimately, the factors noted in the table must be considered in light of members' social contexts today, maintaining a fruitful tension between status and equality, facilitating productive engagement between generations, and carefully balancing involvement initiatives on several dimensions. In effect, to encourage involvement, lodges today must break out of the restrictive bindings of the past and, within the landmarks, get input and experiment, see what works for their membership and what does not, and facilitate both the growth of Hirschi's social bonds and strong Masonic identities among their members. As noted earlier, volunteer involvement has not so much declined as changed in recent decades. What is needed is a pragmatic willingness to use the working tools provided herein to try once, to try again, and to see what works to build the temple in today's society. This is the Freemasonry of the future.

CHAPTER 7

CLAIMED LIFE CHANGES SINCE BECOMING A FREEMASON

I n the discussions thus far on recruitment, rites of passage, and involvement in the Masonic order, issues of identity have never been far from the surface. To help unpack these further, in what follows I outline in detail the typical thematic claims that emerged about the changes, if any, in respondent's lives that they feel have resulted from their Masonic activities. First, I consider those few responses that address the issue of whether there have been changes or not. Second, I will consider the various changes in their social lives claimed by respondents, most notably the dimensions of (1) expanded social contacts and (2) the multi-faceted experience of "brotherhood." Finally, I turn to outline the typical impacts on their character and abilities claimed by respondents, specifically those relating to (1) morality generally, (2) tolerance, (3) altruism, (4) confidence, (5) memory, and (6) inquisitiveness. Since one of the basic tenets of sociological social psychology is that self is a social construct in continual development in mutual interaction with others (Hewitt 2003; Mead 1934), *to the extent* that respondents' comments herein reflect more than mere claims but actual life changes occurring in ritual social interaction, one may consider their involvement in Freemasonry a *transformative practice in relation to self.*

OVERALL CHANGES (IF ANY)

Before getting into the patterned claims surrounding the impact of respondents' Masonic activities on their lives, it is important to note that there were a few respondents who qualified their statements beforehand, at times initially utilizing "disclaimers" (Hewitt and Stokes 1975) before going on to articulate the various claims outlined below. Fourteen respondents asserted that, in the words of one, there had been "no major, dramatic changes" in their lives since becoming a Mason, while another six claimed to be "unsure" as to whether any changes had been the result.

Beyond such slippery statements, there was a second broad group, primarily represented by seventeen respondents, who agreed with one man who claimed that becoming a Mason "reaffirmed my prior morality." Ten in this group tended to emphasize the ethical aspect of Masonic teachings, particularly how they were "brought up," with statements like "I was already a Mason in spirit." Relatedly, there were seven additional respondents who more broadly denied that Masonry had "changed" them but also paradoxically claimed it had somehow "enhanced" them:

> I've become more of what I already was.
>
> Freemasonry has added richness and meaning to my life. It has allowed a fuller expression of who I really am.

Despite the logical difficulties of such statements, and the implications of a core self in the latter, such claims again largely illustrate tentativeness about commenting on having changed as a result of their associations with others. Whether this contains a gender component relating to traditional male individualism and strength in relation to implications of external influence or is merely a way of buying time to think before commenting, it is sufficient to indicate at this point that all such respondents soon went on to make one or more of the thematic claims below as the interviews progressed—to which I now turn.

CLAIMED SOCIAL CHANGES IN RESPONDENTS' LIVES

One of the major areas in which respondents claimed life changes since becoming a Freemason was in their social lives. While there were a variety of dimensions to these claims, they primarily revolved around two broad themes: (1) expanded social contacts and (2) brotherhood, both of which suggest *Freemasonry as social engagement*. A third, interrelated group of claims, revolving around changes to respondents' character and abilities, will be discussed in the section following.

Expanded Social Contacts

Scholars have pointed to the important role of friendship in Freemasonry (Kaplan 2014), and Freemasonry as a means of meeting others was also commented on by a great many respondents. Perhaps the most common comment, articulated by forty-one respondents, was that after becoming a Mason "I met a wide group of friends that I otherwise never would have met." Beyond this, there were eight men who claimed to have met their "best friend" at lodge, and four more who stated, "A lot of the people I'm friends with now are Masons."

Indeed, one man became emotional during his discussion of this aspect, then simply stated, "I started to meet incredible people." Hence, Freemasonry as a means of meeting friends stands as a very prominent social claim, testifying to the continued role today of Freemasonry in promoting sociability, as scholars have noted it did in the past (Hoffman 2001; Carnes 1989; Bolle de Bal 1989).

Similarly, eight respondents commented on the expansion of their network of acquaintances:

My circle of acquaintances has grown beyond imagination.

You can get in and meet folks that you wouldn't otherwise know. And it's so true, but, again, only true in retrospect—but I bet that I know a thousand men in this town that I wouldn't have known under any other circumstances—and I've lived my life here. I'm committed to this town. But here's probably a thousand folks—these two characters here included—who I just wouldn't have known. But now I know them and I feel they're part of my community.

Interestingly, the data revealed two competing, but mutually reinforcing aspects to such claims. On the one hand, with a tip of the hat to the various commonalities or pre-existing dispositions in the respondents' social background, interests, roles, and emotional makeup (Poulet 2010), twenty-one respondents emphasized how involvement in the Craft served as a way for them to meet "like-minded" others with similar moral outlooks and "common interests" (e.g., history or religion)—four adding that they'd "never met a bad person" as a result. This corroborates work on earlier periods suggesting that Freemasonry has a select appeal to certain segments of the population (Doan 1993; Combes 1989). On the other hand, and in line with Jacob's (1981, 1991) work on the Enlightenment (to give but one example), sixteen respondents claimed that Freemasonry served as both a ritual forum and a catalyst for smoothing out social boundaries:

Now I have a common reason to associate with a diverse group of people.

There's more diversity in this lodge than there is on the streets of this town.

In this latter respect, eleven variously claimed that Masonic topics "opened the door for communication," served as an "icebreaker," gave them "something to talk about," and provided "an opportunity to discuss things with people of that background." Whether, like three respondents, they "spot the ring and introduce myself," using this as a "starting point," or simply get to know local members of the Craft in lodge, respondents often claimed, in one way or another, that Freemasonry provides a vehicle to converse freely with men with whom they otherwise would have little in common. As one man put it, "It's just great having all of these people to talk to." Respondents also occasionally drew a comparison with their existing social milieus, such as the workplace, where they had "little in common" with others, or even the home—one father of small children relishing the "opportunity to be out and converse with adults for a change."

Whether the predominant claim was that respondents met like-minded people in the Craft or that involvement gave them the opportunity to meaningfully engage diverse others, both are partially reflected in the Craft and in the lives of individual respondents themselves, and both lead to the same destination: claims of a broader friendship network and a more meaningful social life through the social outlet provided by Freemasonry.

Brotherhood

Going hand in hand with Freemasonry's ability to facilitate meeting new people is the second primary set of social changes related by involved respondents: brotherhood. This was a multi-faceted concept that, for the purposes of analysis, may be broken down into five interrelated components: bonding, social support, trust, travelling, and status associations.

First and foremost in this respect, respondents spoke of the "*bond*" that they experienced with their "brother" Freemasons. Twenty-one respondents laid emphasis on "the whole brotherhood, fellowship, handshaking-when-you-meet kind of bonding that's there," while another fourteen simply stated that "socially, there's a bond with your brothers." Some of these men spoke of a sense of "belonging" or of "family" that they had found in the Craft, while another five simply claimed that they felt "embraced" by a "larger community." Such themes were echoed in comments like the following:

> I like the concept of a permanent, ongoing brotherhood. With the guys, I don't have doubts.

> If you hang out with Masons, you pick up a sense of well-being. I felt an acceptance that I could pass on to others.

Interestingly in this regard, some related this brotherly sense of bonding to other people and events in their lives:

> I developed a closer, more special relationship with my father by practising Freemasonry together.

> The feelings I get in the lodge seem like those people get in military-type relationships.

You don't seem to appreciate these things until you go through a lot of grief and crap.

This updates, in the twenty-first century, historical studies indicating that Freemasonry provides one of the ultimate opportunities for male bonding in society (Morrison 2012; Hoffman 2001; Jacob 1991; Carnes 1989; Clawson 1989), a place where gender and emotional dynamics extend bonds of loyalty and obligation beyond the family (Clawson 1989, 15).

Second, picking up on the last quote above, this sense of bonding was related by many respondents to a strong sense of *social support*, of feeling supported in various ways by their "brothers" in the Craft. Beyond the seventeen respondents who simply claimed a vague sense of "support" from their fellow Masons and seven who claimed that they felt "encouraged" by others, more specific types of support were recounted. Twelve respondents specifically expressed thankfulness for the support and encouragement they received in relation to their activities in the Craft itself (e.g., while on their way to becoming Master of the lodge or a Grand Lodge officer). There were respondents who spoke of feeling supported "even if you make a mistake," those who felt encouragement "to do better," men who noted how brethren "helped steer you in the right direction if you have questions," and several who indicated how others helped them "learn." Indeed, two respondents gave heartwarming stories of how shy, uneducated, elderly men were both encouraged, over time, to become Master and were supported by the entire lodge during their tenure in office. This support in their Masonic activities can reasonably be related to the increased sense of "confidence" noted by brethren, as will be discussed below.

Yet, beyond this internally focused support, respondents also spoke of receiving meaningful support from the Craft when facing stressful, difficult situations in their lives. Twenty-seven spoke of receiving support when they faced a difficult personal crisis or problem. For example, five men indicated that their involvement in Freemasonry helped them in their struggle with alcoholism; two spoke of how involvement in the Craft helped them cope with a disabling illness; and a series of individuals recounted the support they received during a spouse's illness, after a divorce, during a bereavement, or when very ill in hospital.

Masonry helped me in my struggle with alcoholism. It's almost like a back church for sharing, teaching tolerance and honesty. It's taken me from being down in the depths to feeling respected again. Not only does it cross back and forth with the skills and lessons I've learned in 12-step organizations, the support is great. The brethren help keep me on the straight and narrow. They helped save my life.

For seventeen years after my divorce, Masonry was my life.

After my illness and subsequent disability, I think Masonry saved my sanity.

There appear to be three key aspects to this type of support as experienced by the brethren: (1) providing an outlet or venue for one's concerns; (2) ongoing, organized activity to keep one focused; and (3) organized responses by the brethren when necessary. In the first respect, sixteen respondents variously spoke of the lodge and its brethren as a "comfort zone," a "safety blanket," "a safe environment," "a sanctuary," "a place to share," and "a place where people will hear your story and allow it to be expressed."

As for the second aspect, fifteen respondents claimed their Masonic activities provided an "outlet" or "focus" that they could concentrate on to help them stop dwelling on their problems. In the words of one man, "Being busy and studying helps take your mind off other things." Masonry as a gendered method of emotion management looms large here (Hochschild 1983, 1990). In this way, for example, one business executive, previously hard-working and extremely active, who had experienced disability after coming down with a debilitating disease, and another previously busy organizational leader, who had suffered a stroke, found a way to focus their mental energies—the latter even referring to it as "ritual therapy." Indeed, five respondents variously noted that the common ritual in various lodges enabled them to "feel at home," "distance myself," and "get a break from everyday life, reflect, and recharge," suggesting the continuing ability of "liminal rituals" to not only cathartically address members' anxieties (Carnes 1989) but also be a means of facilitating a "controlled decontrolling of emotions" (Elias 1994).

Finally, there was the actual, organized support brethren provided to respondents when they needed it. Beyond the emotional and, sometimes, financial assistance received, fifteen respondents spoke of the interest shown in them by the brethren, how, for example, "these people cared and took an interest in me and my well-being like an extended family." Indeed, two of these referred to "unsolicited support" received, three spoke of how "support comes together in lodge when you need it" (e.g., "at a low point in my life"), and five likened it to a "lifeline" that, in the words of one man, is "always open whenever you need it."

The upshot of these various facets of support when engaged in and experienced by the respondents was that they claimed to experience less stress in their lives. Eleven claimed that they were "less stressed" or "more calm," two of these even claiming a greater sense of "peace." Moreover, four additional respondents reported that they had overheard Masons' wives claiming that their husbands were "less stressed" after meetings. Thus, one cannot underestimate the importance of social support in facilitating calmness and coping among Masons facing adversity. Indeed, all of the above comments testify to the continuing ability of Freemasonry in the twenty-first century to provide solace and social support during stressful periods of change (Summers 2003; Hoffman 2001; Hetherington 1997; Carnes 1989; Clawson 1989). Considering the social inputs above, to the extent that these supportive strategies and responses claimed by respondents are valid, they may not only be interactive methods for respondents to reconstruct themselves in a more coping form but contemporary reflections of the adage that "you get out of it what you put into it."

The third component of brotherhood is related to the above dimensions of bonding and support: namely, *trust*. Significantly, eighteen respondents, in one way or another, articulated that knowing another man was a Mason "reverses the onus of trust" when meeting and/or dealing with others, four adding that this is because they, in the words of one man, "realize that the person has travelled the same path you have, and you can identify with that." Respondents spoke of other Masons being "vouched for beforehand," of "feeling differently about them," even of experiencing an "instant connection" with them—quite unlike when dealing with the general public.

> *You've got a common, instant bond. I think that's important.*

In effect, knowing that someone is a Mason provides a different set of typifications or indexical resources with which to approach them (Schutz 1962; Garfinkel 1967).

Indeed, several respondents articulated precisely the same sentiment to me when they were approached to be interviewed for this research (i.e., my formal assurances of confidentiality and anonymity were often brushed off as redundant). Yet perhaps the best example in the data of this sense of trust was seen in the case of one man who, when preparing for a degree in costume, left his billfold on the table of the dressing room, followed by others. He went on to say, when participating with other Masons in a group interview for this study,

> *I wouldn't be scared to leave my wallet here either, unlike any-where outside.*

Moreover, beyond such respondents who "look on Masons differently than men I meet at other clubs and social gatherings," three more added that they had become "more trusting generally," even "less cynical about people"—not surprising for a group that teaches "the brotherhood of man." This corroborates today Hetherington's (1997, 103) comment about lodges historically creating a space ... of trustworthiness."

Fourth, brotherhood was claimed important for brethren when they were *travelling*, visiting, or even moving to another location. Twenty-four respondents pointed to how being a Mason was helpful when they were away from home:

> *You now have friends all over.*
>
> *I can travel anywhere now. The world is a smaller place. I'll never be alone anywhere I am.*
>
> *I feel a great sense of family and community when I'm away from home.*
>
> *My wife and I developed a social network right across the country.*

Indeed, the ready trust noted above, along with the vouching provided by the symbol or the setting, was said to encourage social interaction:

> *People spotted my ring and that provided me with contacts and buddies in various places.*
>
> *I make a point to introduce myself and meet new people I see in lodge.*
>
> *There's no member in regular attendance in this district that I can't walk up to and know by name.*

This was particularly important when respondents moved to a new area. Twelve respondents spoke of the help they received from brethren who had been informed that they were coming: some showed up to help with moving, while others greeted them on the street, introduced them around, and helped them get to know the area. Indeed, I can vouch for this personally in my own case.

The final aspect of brotherhood revolves around issues of *equality and status*. Basically, thirteen respondents articulated how important it was for brothers to interact as equals. As noted earlier, this is a complex issue, but *symbolic* equality was nevertheless meaningful to respondents from different directions. On the one hand, this opened doors and enabled members to interact socially with a more diverse group of people that they would not have otherwise, where "your background doesn't matter, and everyone is met on the level." In the latter sense, it served to facilitate a greater sense of status:

> *I got to meet the elders of my community.*
>
> *I was able to associate with the movers and shakers, even to pick up their characteristics.*

Thus, it would appear that this symbolic equality, encapsulated in the term "brotherhood," may have different emphases for different people: for relative equals, diversity; for relative unequals, status. While more will be said about this in the next chapter, at this point it will suffice to say that, when the tension between these two principles is meaningfully balanced between people of varying internal and external statuses, it can serve more as a way to bring subordinates up than to bring the others down—a means to gain status by association. The data also reveal that, in today's more egalitarian social ethos, when there is too much emphasis on social status or rank, it can be counterproductive to the sense of brotherhood noted above—as evidenced by respondents' recriminations about who gets ahead, the Grand Lodge hierarchy, and so on:

> [There are] *guys who are aching, just aching to have someone drop a Right Worshipful title on them, or Right Excellent, or Right Illustrious. Ah, what they wouldn't give for that!*

In other words, an alternative status hierarchy may be a meaningful symbolic realm for some, but it shouldn't be too vulgar or obvious today or it undercuts the sense of brotherhood that respondents found so important about the Craft.[1]

CLAIMED CHANGES IN RESPONDENTS' CHARACTER AND ABILITIES

Beyond the primary themes of expanded social contacts and brotherhood, there was a third broad group of changes claimed in relation to respondents' character and abilities. The former were primarily moral in nature, relating to increases in traditional virtues such as tolerance, altruism, and the like. The latter, while related to character traits such as confidence or inquisitiveness, also involved the acquisition of transferable abilities such as, for example, the ability to speak in public, leadership skills, and the capacity to memorize and understand complex texts. With regard to these claimed changes in respondent's character and abilities, I will outline the various aspects as follows: (1) morality, (2) tolerance, (3) altruism, (4) confidence, (5) memory, and (6) inquisitiveness.

Morality

Respondents spoke extensively of a relationship between involvement in Freemasonry and moral character, a theme that has been much discussed in relation to the past, whether as a means for moral improvement; as a place for civilizing members (and, through them—the "moral elect"—for improving society) (Hoffman 2001); as a space for performing moral stability in a society where the normative order was in a state of flux (Hetherington 1997); as a realm of expressive idealism, for teaching civility and morality (Jacob 1991); as a means of inculcating and enacting masculine morality in a world where it was under threat (Carnes 1989; Rich 1997); as a kind of perpetual morality play that is chiefly middle-class, male, WASP, and segregated (Wilson 1980); even as a civil religion fostering a common set of moral understandings (Jolicoeur and Knowles 1978).

Much in line with the above, by far the largest group of respondents claimed Freemasonry to be a means of moral development and action (i.e., as something that helps improve and regulate one's ethical actions and moral character, something that gives men a core or standard to live up to). Thirty-six respondents claimed that their involvement in Freemasonry was beneficial in that the moral obligations they swore to uphold helped to improve their "character," "outlook," or "moral actions" over time. Respondents spoke variously of "learning a lot about myself"; of "changing"; of becoming "less volatile," "less materialistic," "more selfless," and "more considerate." They claimed that, as "historically lodges were about fair dealing," "now my word is my bond." Indeed, twenty-two respondents explicitly referenced the common phrase that "Freemasonry takes a good man and makes him better," some going on to elaborate that the Craft is about "self-improvement" and "personal development" and is a "character builder." Ten claimed that it gave them a good moral "framework" or "foundation" upon which to live and raise a family, three stating that they had experienced "personal growth over time" and two reporting "a different outlook on life."

> It's amazing when you find something to believe in, and to give some expression in your life in what you do.
>
> The Masonic principles represent an ideal I strive for, a beacon for how I should live my life.
>
> Masonry made me better as a man, better with my family—and you're supposed to be.
>
> If you can live up to the obligations in Masonry, you've lived a saint's life.

Such comments were often linked to the current social order. Eighteen respondents contrasted the morality taught in Masonry with the state of contemporary Western society, seeing the Craft as beneficial in that it "provides a firm foundation to live by in today's crazy world." Indeed, such respondents saw Freemasonry as a meaningful "balance" for "negative social forces" such as anomie:

> For me, Freemasonry provides grounding in this world of uncertainties and watered down morality. It's attractive in a

*disposable world going down the tubes. It is the opposite of
people wasting time on the Internet, playing video games, going
to bars three times a week and blowing money, and so on.
Many people are lost today. Freemasonry gives purpose, walking on real rather than superficial ground.*

In some respects, such comments may reflect the "disappearance of the
sacred" (Meštrović 1997, 101–22), a search for moral authenticity or for
"collective effervescence" in today's mass-mediated cultural terrain, where
emotionally meaningful rites in the Durkheimian sense are relatively absent
and where interpersonal hazing rituals and rites of passage are making a comeback as ways to set groups apart and make members feel special (1997, 113).

Thus it was not surprising to find respondents drawing upon Masonic
symbolism when discussing moral incidents or dilemmas (e.g., someone not
acting "on the level," or engaging in "square dealing"). One man said:

*Many Masons wear a Masonic ring, and it was expressed to me
at one point that you wear it so that the square and compasses
are facing you, not the other way around, because it's not to
show other people that you are a Mason necessarily. It's for you
to be aware of the moral lessons that are taught by those two
symbols in your day-to-day activity and your life.*

Another comment was that "the symbols can jump up like flags or prompters
in day-to-day life." For example, eight respondents claimed that considering
the tenets of the Craft and their obligation "makes me catch myself once in a
while," four said that they try to "practise the tenets of Freemasonry out of
the lodge," and four others indicated how these tenets interact with specific
observations of social life: "That's not something that we would accept."

Such respondents often contrasted this image, in broad ways, with their
prior and present character, indicating degrees of progress along the way:

*I don't know if I was ever good. I wish that I could say that my
background is really pure.*

*I was sort of half-good before I started. I was a half-decent
person.*

I have a lot more to do.

*I'm still learning to subdue my passions. But now I'm on the
right path.*

Added to this were claims about how "personal" some of their comments were, how "special" making a lifelong promise was for them, how

"deeply" they have come to feel about "their" Masonry, how they have come to "embrace the Masonic code" as "knights of morality," and how "thankful" they are to have been "prodded" to "do things better."

Beyond respondents' claims of specific improvements in how one "treats others" (six respondents); of becoming more "balanced" by "sorting out my priorities in life" (four); and of becoming "less materialistic" (two), "less temperamental" (two), and "more spiritual" (two), there were also several dramatic stories of moral improvement, such as situations where former adversaries had been able to make peace with one another, even to become friends, due to their mutual involvement in Masonry. Thus, beyond those individuals discussed above who claimed to be dealing with their problems (e.g., with alcohol) in part through their involvement in the Craft, there were three accounts of men who claimed to have known brethren who since refrained from "immoral behaviours" as a result of the obligation that they have sworn, often through fear of losing the respect of their brothers should they do anything improper. I include one such claim at length:

> I know a couple that are not good friends of mine but they are pretty close, and I became aware a few years ago, just from private conversations and jokes, that he was messing around with another woman. And I mean, I knew the married couple well, and the marriage looked like it was going to go down the drain. And I kind of watched this quietly, without getting involved in any way, for I suppose a year, maybe. And then he told me how that ended; this is the story. He was kind of in a mid-life crisis—and I happen to know the other woman. The other woman was very attractive [laughing]. So this guy went along, and then suddenly he became aware of what he did not know, that the husband of the other woman was a Freemason. And he broke off that relationship as quickly as he could [chuckling]. And to the best of my knowledge never got involved in another one again. And what strikes me about that story, it perfectly illustrates the power of Masonic oaths and obligations. Because it was not his marriage vow that brought him to his senses, and it was not the moral teaching of his parents, or even the church. It was his Masonic obligation [bangs fist on table], and we can all quote it! And he told me when he suddenly realized it, his blood just about congealed in his veins when he realized that potential of what might have happened, and I think that's a perfectly illustrated story of how our obligations and what we learn in the lodge are perhaps the most important ones we'll make in our lives.

Such elaborate claims, if true, serve to dramatically underscore the "moral improvement" claimed as a result of Masonic activities.

But how is this claimed moral impact said to come about? Respondents' claims addressed this issue. Beyond the ritual impact of the degrees and their obligations noted above, ten claimed that there was a moral socialization process underway that operates "like multiplication," where "goodness rubs off" and "just keeps growing" (e.g., "There's an energy there. It's like when you put two candles together and the flame is three times as big"). Beyond this, five made explicit reference to the metaphorical symbolism of chipping away the rough parts of a stone to render it perfectly square:

> *It's like the difference between the rough and perfect ashlar. Over time, you're not adding things, but chipping away the bad or imperfect. In that respect, less is always more.*

> *As time goes on, you become part of each other and those bad parts are disappearing.*

Whether or not it is quite that simple, there can be no doubt that long-term involvement, interaction, and identification with the ethos of any organized group does have some degree of impact upon one's self, identity, and approved courses of action, whether or not it translates quite as directly as claimed above.

Yet, it must be pointed out that there was a second broad group that claimed a different relationship between their involvement in Freemasonry and their moral state. Twenty respondents, rather than claiming that Freemasonry improved their prior morality, claimed that it simply ratified it:

> *Becoming a Freemason reaffirmed my prior morality. I was already a Mason in spirit.*

> *It didn't really change me morally. I look back at the way I was raised as a kid. There was always a line that you didn't cross.*

Other comments in this respect included those of respondents who claimed that the Craft "consolidated my beliefs and principles," "provided a forum and expression of prior principles," and "confirmed that I was at least internally on the right track." All such respondents, while they undoubtedly have been impacted in some way, usefully point out that Masonic moral socialization, despite some of the more dramatic claims, is far from the entire story—indeed, that it interacts significantly with one's prior moral traits.

Finally, there is a third group whose claims are difficult to place in either the moral socialization or ratification camps: those twenty-seven respondents who claimed merely to "identify" with the moral tenets and traditions of Freemasonry:

I've embraced the Masonic code.

Freemasonry provides a system, a subtext, and an infrastructure to practise moral imperatives in the community.

Rather than get into a chicken-and-egg debate over the priority of these claims or attempt to evaluate the veracity of respondents' claimed moral improvements—which the nature of the data do not answer in any event—I simply conclude that there appears, from the three groups of claims above, to be some sort of interactive relationship claimed between one's prior moral state, the socialization one experiences during one's activities in the Craft, and one's moral *claims* at a later time. In some cases, the Masonic socialization element may be stronger; in other cases, one's prior socialization may prevail. Regardless of which is predominant in any given case, however, it is clear that, at least in a moral sense, respondents claimed that their involvement in Freemasonry provided them with both a valued moral "identity" and a "way of life."

Beyond bringing the relationship between Masonic involvement and morality noted in earlier literature into the present, respondents' claims in this section in particular resonate with the ideas that the Craft continues to represent (1) moral improvement (Hoffman 2001); (2) a space for performing moral stability in a society where the normative order was in a state of flux (Hetherington 1997); (3) a realm of expressive idealism, for teaching civility and morality (Jacob 1991); (4) a kind of perpetual morality play that is chiefly middle-class and male (Wilson 1980); and (5) a living civil religion for some that fosters, among this group, a common set of moral understandings (Fozdar 2011; Jolicoeur and Knowles, 1978).

Tolerance

The most common thematic variation on respondents' claims of having become more moral involved claims of increased tolerance, a theme that has been noted historically (Hetherington 1997). Twenty-seven respondents claimed to have generally become "more tolerant" as a result of their involvement in the Craft. Beyond the most general claims, however, there were several significant additional dimensions. First, there were thirty additional respondents who claimed that they had become more appreciative of others' differences:

I'm more willing to appreciate differences as contributions.

I'm more open to consider others' opinions and points of view in decision making.

Now I don't look for why I don't like a guy, but "I want to like this guy because …"

I've become more tolerant of other faiths after meeting people of different backgrounds and seeing the different books on the altar.

Relatedly, there were an additional fifteen respondents who asserted that they now attempted to focus on what they had "in common" with others:

I now see that we're all the same, the same blood, on the same level, with nobody better than the other.

I'm more willing to look at commonalities than differences, then use these as a nucleus to build around in groups.

It's taught me to think more of my fellow man. We look at the better part of the person that we meet and become a part of.

Third, there were forty respondents who claimed to be less "judgmental" or "critical" of others. Variations included those who claimed to have become more "patient" and less "volatile," "aggressive," and "manipulative" when dealing with problematic others. Some variations include the following:

Freemasonry helped me improve the bad attitude I once had. I don't have unrealistic expectations of others.

I don't gossip or try to climb over them like before—or I try not to.

Now I fight over issues. I never make it personal.

Even if I don't like the person, I'm very conscious of treating them fairly. I hesitate before I do or say something negative.

Fourth, there were respondents whose claims to increased tolerance were expressed in terms of being more "considerate," "understanding," even "forgiving." Comments by the thirty respondents who articulated such themes included the following:

I'm more willing now to build bridges with people who have problems.

I'm more willing now to consider others' situations, where the other side is coming from.

I see now that, as humans, we all have our failings. I appreciate people for their abilities.

Rather than criticize, I ask, "If I were in his shoes, what would I do different?"

Finally in this respect, there were two interesting comments articulated by spouses in relation to tolerance and its related actions. As one wife reported,

> I've seen more forgiveness in my husband since he became a Freemason.

And a respondent stated,

> My wife said to me once, "You're always so much more loving when you come home from lodge."

Thus, there were a variety of ways in which tolerance was claimed to translate into Masons' character and actions today as a result of their involvement in the Craft, updating and fleshing out historical work in this respect (Hetherington 1997).

Altruism

Another thematic variation that respondents articulated in relation to morality related to altruism: seventeen respondents claimed to have broadly become more "altruistic" as a result of their involvement in the Craft. In addition, nine said that they had become "more charitable"; seven that they "felt encouraged to contribute" to their community, culture, or society in contrast to "the way things are in society today"; and seven that they had become "more genuinely concerned for others."

> I found myself becoming more charitable in thought, word, and deed, and I've practised small acts of charity. That lecture [in the first degree] really struck home. There were things in the community where I remember sometimes I'd be out and I'd see people there saying, "Oh, would you like to buy a ticket? Would you like to buy a ticket to support our thing?" Before I became a Freemason, I was kind of like, kind of grumbly about that. I sort of felt in my head, "Get lost" and "Go away," you know, "Stop bugging me," and then I thought, you know, one example comes to mind. It wasn't long after I was made an Entered Apprentice, over at the mall there were some kids there selling tickets and raising money to go to a basketball camp. And I thought, you know, "Do I really need this cup of coffee, or do I buy two bucks' worth of tickets for their basketball camp?" And it was, you know, I bought tickets for the camp. But, prior to becoming a Freemason, I wouldn't have thought about things in that kind of a way.

> I think that I feel more compassion and caring for my fellow man than I otherwise would have had.

Whether as a reflective response to a key lesson in the first degree, to the general injunction "to practise out of the lodge those great moral duties inculcated in it," to reciprocity for assistance previously provided, or simply to socialization with other Masons over time, respondents claimed an impressive list of specific altruistic actions and an ability to do more collectively than they would be able to alone. Beyond the well-known work of the Shriners with burned and disabled children (noted by many respondents), and a variety of other organized charities associated with the other concordant bodies (e.g., the Scottish Rite's support of Alzheimer's research), respondents mentioned, among other things, volunteering with youth or the Abilities Foundation; raising money for cancer research; assisting widows, orphans, and the elderly; visiting the sick in hospital; buying glasses for a woman who couldn't afford them; buying heating oil for individuals on fixed incomes; and befriending or otherwise assisting local women who had been harassed or abused. Interestingly, while most such respondents were quite willing to discuss the charitable actions of the Craft, there were three who eschewed the limelight, taking the more traditional stance that "you don't look for recognition" because "charity is its own reward."

Such claimed altruistic changes in respondents' character and actions were undoubtedly, along with tolerance, significant underpinnings of the positive moral identity that many nurtured in relation to their involvement in the Craft. As well, unlike studies of much earlier periods, these findings likely reflect historical developments in the Craft. By the mid-twentieth century, with the development of big government, big business, and big labour, plus the popularity of "service clubs" such as Rotary and Kiwanis, Freemasonry, particularly in the United States, had shifted from a fraternity primarily emphasizing ritual and self-improvement to a highly organized, institutionalized, even bureaucratic group focused on supporting or coordinating various Masonic philanthropies (Tabbert 2007). The above comments should be seen in this context.

Confidence

Up to this point, the changes claimed in respondents' character and abilities have tended to predominantly emphasize the former. While there may be skills and abilities exercised in activities related to becoming more tolerant and altruistic, these remain primarily matters of moral character actively developed in interaction with others. At this point, however, the emphasis begins to shift more to respondents' abilities and skills. This shift becomes evident in dealing with claims surrounding confidence.

Thirty-three respondents claimed that they had become "more confident" since becoming a Freemason:

> *I have a feeling of self-confidence I probably wouldn't have otherwise.*
>
> *I'm more assertive now. I'll stand up for myself more.*

In addition, twenty-nine respondents credit their involvement in the Craft with overcoming previous shyness:

> *I got over my shyness.*
>
> *I'm more comfortable meeting new people.*
>
> *I'm less of a loner now.*

When asked about the mechanism behind these changes, responses focused squarely on interactive involvement and support. Fourteen respondents attributed the changes to the various administrative and ritual offices that they had held in the lodge and to developing and exercising increasingly complex skills as they advanced with the support of others. For example, one shy eighty-one-year-old man was encouraged, and developed the skills, to become Master of the lodge with the encouragement and support of the brethren. Similarly, ten respondents attributed their increased confidence to memorizing part of the ritual and performing it before the lodge, while five more recent initiates put emphasis on "proving up" in open lodge prior to taking their next degree. The similarities between all of these mechanisms involve responsibility, memorization, practice, support, a safe environment, successful completion, and the emerging knowledge that one can handle it—even repeat it again if necessary.

In perhaps the most notable outcome of these ritual actions, twenty-three respondents claimed that their involvement in Freemasonry had helped them to overcome their fear and to learn to speak in public. Given their claim to feel "supported if I make a mistake," there seemed to be a progression as follows:

> *That was the first time I ever spoke in public.*
>
> *I no longer stammer and stutter.*
>
> *I've become a better communicator.*
>
> *Now I do it with style.*
>
> *I'm more outspoken now.*

The upshot of all this was that, in the words of one man,

> *It's easy to have courage to do a part when people support and assist you. It gave me confidence eventually to take on Masonic leadership roles.*

Yet this involvement in Masonic activities, respondents claimed, did more than simply help them within the Craft. As with public speaking, it helped provide them with useful, transferable skills that they could use in business, even to advance in their career:

> As a result of Freemasonry, I learned how to organize things, to be organized and involved.

> The Craft is where I really learned leadership skills. These helped me eventually move up in my job to deputy [fire] chief, to effectively handle the media at fire scenes, and so on.

> Once I wouldn't say a word, but recently I sat on a public panel where I competed against a professor.

Beyond this, respondents claimed that the confidence they had developed from their time in the Craft enabled them to better deal with their personal situation, including making important decisions:

> Freemasonry helped me gain the inner strength to make a tough decision. I quit my job, went back to school, and changed careers. Now I've opened my own business.

> I learned more about what I can handle personally and found a growing sense of purpose. It enabled me to move from "going with the flow" to "taking control" of my life.

But perhaps the most significant impact that such involvement and responsibility, coupled with support, had was on men from modest backgrounds. There were nine general comments in this regard. One man, who previously saw himself as a lowly "grease monkey," felt "moved" when his work resulted in his being elevated to the position of Master of the lodge. Another respondent observed:

> Freemasonry really helps guys who have had limited education. I know guys who were functionally illiterate who underwent an amazing transformation. One guy developed an amazing memory and is such a quick study he can take on just about any part on just a few minutes' notice. He's so much more confident now that he's gone through the Master's chair and beyond.

Indeed, it was among such men that were primarily found multiple comments such as claims to "increased self esteem" (seven respondents), "self-respect" (four), "recognition" (three), and "status" (three).

Thus, in several respects, Freemasonry may be seen as administrative practice. For the individual seeking transferable administrative skills, Masonry may provide a private, supportive environment to overcome shyness, learn to speak publicly, increase confidence, participate in offices and committees, develop organizational and leadership abilities, and facilitate decision making. Moreover, it may also be that, when practised by those from modest social backgrounds, such men are given a "charge," even a "boost" of recognition on an alternate status hierarchy—providing a meaningful, perceived alternate source of social power that they do not have outside.

Memory

Closely intertwined with the above claims of increased confidence and transferable life skills are respondents' claims of improved memory. Given the requirement in most lodges to perform the ritual orally from memory, such claims are hardly more surprising than assertions from those who exercise that they gain strength and muscle tone.[2] Seventeen respondents asserted that their mnemonic abilities had grown as a result of their involvement in Masonic activities. For example:

> Without becoming a Mason, I would never have known my abilities. Since going through the chair and serving with Grand Lodge, I can recite the whole installation ceremony without the book!

Others spoke of having the words "in my brain so that I can access it later," and "almost slipping into the rhetoric learned in lodge" when asked a question.

Respondents' mnemonic abilities are first exercised as they "prove up" while taking their degrees, and there are numerous opportunities for them to be further practised over time as they are asked to do small parts, take an office, maybe even eventually become Master or get involved in the activities of the Grand Lodge. Insofar as respondents did these things, they exercised an ability—a trained memory—that was once highly prized by orators (Yates 1966) but has fallen into disuse in modern times. Practising and working up one's abilities in this regard, when done in a safe and supportive environment, is interrelated with claims of increased confidence and may help foster another valuable and transferable skill of use in other social contexts.

But there is more. Three respondents indicated that their memory exercises "reminded me of principles to live by," harkening back to the moral element discussed above. Finally, and more germane to the section that follows, four added that memorization "helped me to understand it," suggesting an interpretive, intellectual function. It is thus to that final group of claimed changes that I now turn.

Inquisitiveness

The final group of changes respondents claimed in relation to their involvement in the Craft involves aspects of both character and ability: increased inquisitiveness. This testifies to how curiosity can continue to be manufactured through Masonic activity. Thirteen respondents claimed to have found an increased impetus to learn: to have become, in the words of one man, "more inquisitive." As one man commented:

> Masonry provided a catalyst for reading up on stuff that I wouldn't have [read otherwise]. It branched me out further, stimulated an interest that wasn't there.

Twenty-nine respondents also broadly claimed that their involvement in Masonry, in the words of one man, "helped me to educate myself." Hence there were comments such as the following:

> Beyond the mere mechanics, I've learned a lot from studying the ritual.

> I've learned more from Masonry than all of my university years or any service club I've been involved in.

> I realized quickly that this was setting me off on a lifelong learning process.

Respondents who made such comments discussed both the *content* that they had become drawn to unravelling and the *means* and abilities that they utilized to do so. These must be seen in light of how one's life and activity impact one's interpretation of Masonic imagery. I have previously argued (Kenney 2008) that at least three things have to be added together for an interpretation of Masonic material to emerge: (1) what is in the ritual (and there are different versions); (2) the level and/or type of Masonic activity (and memorization) in which the Mason is involved; and (3) the individual Mason's personal and social background. The first aspect was noted by Masons who travel to other lodges and jurisdictions and observe familiar things being done differently, often remarking that they get something different out of it as a result. The second factor was noted in the often differing experiences of active lodge officers versus "benchers" (the latter more often "social Masons" taking basic moral meanings, except for some who were once quite active but are now stepping back). It was also seen in comments that working/memorizing different offices, such as Senior Deacon or Worshipful Master, can be instrumental in helping different perspectives on the ritual emerge. Yet it is the third factor, the Mason's background, that may be of much more importance than many believe. Masonic activity always takes place in one's personal and social context. Thus, respondents were often quietly willing to recognize that educational background may have an impact on how Masons interpret the ritual, draw parallels, and read in analogies, at least initially (since some pointed out that there were less-educated brethren who had developed a deep knowledge over time). Fewer considered that cultural, religious, or occupational background might play a part (e.g., immigrants, Catholics, bomber pilots, prison guards),[3] though the role of analogical reasoning and tacit pedagogy have certainly been noted elsewhere (Poulet 2010; Mahmud-Abdelwahib 2008). Most respondents would deny, however, that things like class and race were significant to the active interpretation of the ritual, despite the fact, for example, that respondents reported that traditionally (i.e., "in the old days") Masons were largely prominent people like bankers and lawyers, and that part of the membership draw was to be "on the level" with them. As for neglecting race, this overlooks striking examples, such as the African-Canadian man who, unlike anyone else in his lodge, struggled over the term "freeborn" when joining Masonry. Thus, beyond what is internalized in memorization, when engaging the interpretive element of this faculty, it is very important to be cognizant of the Mason's social background when considering the meaning, the interpretation actively constructed through ritual memorization. Interpretation is a two-way street.

But beyond such hermeneutic considerations, respondents spoke of changes in their specific interests as a result of their involvement. Twenty-four respondents claimed that they had become "more philosophical," particularly in their newfound willingness to "consider big questions" in life. Regarding their "fascination" with dissecting the "system of allegory," comments such as the following emerged:

> The "wisdom of the ages" I found has helped me to improve my own understanding and enjoyment of life.

> While I understand myself better, I could spend a lifetime and still not piece it all together.

Relatedly, twenty respondents specifically claimed to have become more interested in "spiritual" or "religious" matters. In this respect, it appears that the mnemonic practices that persist throughout one's Masonic career can interact with Masonic imagery and gradually sedimentize, as it were, from the "surface" to the "deep" phenomenological level of one's emotional self (Denzin 1985, 232). Hence respondents spoke of the ritual as being "almost like a mantra," where practitioners can "really take it to heart." Beyond members drawing upon Masonic symbolism when discussing moral incidents or dilemmas, others added how "personal" some of their comments in these respects were, how "deeply" they have come to feel about "their" Masonry, especially how Masons attempt to "maintain contact with the inner self" and apply the lessons in other areas of their lives.

Within this group, ten claimed a deeper "spirituality" in relation to Masonic imagery, while another ten claimed that Masonry deepened their existing religious faith:

> Masonry is all about "getting in touch with the centre," your inner self, seeing yourself symbolically organized as the lodge and reflecting that ideal back in yourself to others. Not only have I become more spiritual as a result, it's all given me a better appreciation of other religions.

> Freemasonry has enriched my faith and made me a better Christian. It's stimulated an interest in the Old Testament and forced me to understand and explain Christianity better. I not only understand the Trinity in a new way now, I really feel that I have a deeper relationship with Christ.

Finally in this respect, six respondents specifically claimed to have either developed or deepened an interest in history through their involvement in the Craft:

> I found myself becoming interested in history, where I wasn't at all before.

> I became much more interested in history since joining the lodge. I became like a detective in local Masonic stuff, digging through old minutes of the lodge and so on. It was almost like I was reading a secret book that enabled me to piece together an alternative history of our community. It was fascinating, almost an obsession.

Yet such results were not obtained without effort, time, and the exercise of the emerging abilities outlined earlier as respondents progressed through the offices. Thirteen respondents claimed that the meaning comes "from working at it":

> The more that you work at it, the more it's going to affect you.

> You go along for some time just attending meetings, and it's pretty basic. You see more as you're doing different parts and taking offices, but, for me, there was an amazing transformation when I became Master. It was like the flower blossomed and suddenly a whole world opens up.

Part of the story here also involves challenging interactions with other
Masons:

> *You can really learn a lot of life lessons from the diverse others*
> *and viewpoints that you encounter in the Craft.*

> *I've picked up so much from dealing with other Masons who*
> *challenged me intellectually.*

Indeed, nine respondents claimed, in the words of one man, that "the
meaning comes in time." Thus:

> *It took me a while to really start understanding things, after*
> *getting up to speed for the first few years.*

Nine more respondents related the emergence of meaningful understandings to their circumstances in life:

> *The meaning comes when you're ready, when you need it. I*
> *found that as I got older I got more contemplative, more recep-*
> *tive to the wisdom of the ages that was being passed down.*

In the end, claims of increased inquisitiveness, and the changes in character that go with its exercise, illustrate the fecundity of the interaction between
Masonic socialization and involvement. This is amply illustrated in the comments of two respondents who claimed to see an evolution in the meaning of
their involvement:

> *My involvement in the Craft evolved over time. At first, I was*
> *just in it for the social aspect, for a "boys' night out." I moved*
> *on to study the technical, "how-to" aspects as I took offices,*
> *and the meaning started coming. Ultimately I found myself*
> *becoming more charitable in and out of lodge.*

> *For me, Masonry went from being about belonging to a sense*
> *of personal achievement, developing personal knowledge, and*
> *finally towards more of a sense of balance between brotherhood*
> *and self-improvement.*

Thus, for those willing to do the work, respondents' comments suggest
that Freemasonry may serve as a vehicle for exploration, providing symbolic
tools for a spiritual/philosophical/historical journey (e.g., "You can get an initial meaning, but spend the rest of your life expanding on it"). The multi-faceted, interconnected strands of the Masonic ritual can be taken far deeper than
the basic moral lessons that are apparent on the surface. Indeed, for those who

want to privately move beyond the "how-to" aspect and to delve beneath the surface moral meanings, the ritual provides an interesting and almost endless set of possibilities for free spiritual and philosophical investigation. This is because the extensive memory work inevitably involves more than repetition. To a greater or lesser extent, consciously or unconsciously, it involves *digestion* as well. In each of these cases, it is not so much what members *do* to *make sense* of the Masonic ritual. Rather, *Masonry is the method*. Such freedom, despite the practice of apparent rote learning, is, of course, one of the great ironies of the Craft.

Before closing this section, however, it must nevertheless be noted that, likely due to the historic shift from a fraternity primarily emphasizing ritual and self-improvement to a highly organized, institutionalized, even bureaucratic group focused on supporting or coordinating various Masonic philanthropies (Tabbert 2007), aside from those brethren who make the effort, who take active parts, or who have had the benefit of a strong mentor program of Masonic education, an increased share of responsibility for deriving these meaningful insights now falls on individual Masons. There were five respondents who complained that such meaningful discussion was largely absent and "you have to do the work yourself." Moreover, I attended meetings of two separate, informal groups of Masons who meet regularly to have a drink, to discuss Masonic themes, and to challenge each other—most crediting their Masonic knowledge more to that informal group than to their encounters in lodge. Both my personal experience and comments from respondents indicate that such informal gatherings are quite rare today, crowded out by formalities, "boring business meetings" and bureaucratic concerns. In the absence of meaningful venues for such encounters, understandings either remain basic or motivation and responsibility for learning fall back much more heavily on the individual.

CONCLUSION

In contrast to the plethora of historical research on the social meanings of Masonry for its members, this chapter has outlined various thematic claims made by contemporary Freemasons about changes in their lives since joining the Craft. Clearly, these are *claims* that one cannot test for veracity given the nature of the data. Yet, even taking self-presentation (Goffman 1959) and a highly committed sample into account, there remain present strong thematic patterns that shed light on much-neglected areas of both Masonic and sociological research. Indeed, to the extent that these shed light on what respondents find *meaningful* about the Craft, these provide numerous continuities with—and extensions of—historical studies (e.g., claims of Masonry as a place of refuge and morality in a rapidly changing society in relation to the former; and administrative, mnemonic, and inquisitive claims for the latter).

Second, to the extent that these claims are valid, they may be reflections of a transformative practice in relation to self (Hewitt 2003; Mead 1934), of ritualized social interactions where older, less-desired aspects of the social self (e.g., those that were variously isolated, administratively unskilled, coping poorly, spiritually uncertain, or in need of moral work) are sacrificed in ritual social interaction, at a pace and to an extent largely chosen by each. Meanwhile, at the same time, new selves, new identities—indeed, new individuals—are continually rebuilt from within and without. These are selves that are claimed to be, among other things, more morally and socially engaged, charitable, administratively skilled, spiritually aware, and capable of coping with a greater variety of difficulties. Ultimately, however these aspects develop—and what their relative weighting is in an individual case—such claims bear further investigation by sociological researchers in relation to the rapidly changing social landscape today.

Third, the social changes and developments in personal character and abilities claimed here are inextricably tied to involvement, to matters that respondents claim deepen or deter their active participation in the Craft. Thus these comments must be considered in the broader context of those factors that are both conducive to, and corrosive of, involvement in order to balance out the often positive claims here.

Fourth, researchers would do well to examine whether these thematic patterns hold or differ in important respects across jurisdictions, in lodges that meet in different cultural settings, in areas where Masonry represents the social elite versus a neglected or persecuted group, and in co-Masonic or women's lodges, to name but a few.

In the end, there is much more work to be done, and the above merely scratches the surface of the potential research agenda. Nevertheless, it is hoped that the findings reported herein serve as both a foundation and a springboard for further sociological investigation of contemporary—not just historical—Freemasonry in the twenty-first century.

CHAPTER 8

CONTEMPORARY FREEMASONRY
The Direction Forward?

T his study represents a detailed look at what remains a moving picture. It is a snapshot in time of an old and venerable institution in flux—and one very much in reciprocal evolution with society at large. While the ultimate path the "regular" Freemasonry of the Anglo-Saxon world will take remains somewhat unclear, the previous chapters do contain clear hints of emergent issues involved in the Craft today—often hidden, at other times more open—with important implications for the future direction of the order. In this final chapter I will sketch out, in broad outlines, the principal factors and social dynamics at play—both within Freemasonry and in relation to broader society—to suggest possible, perhaps even probable, directions the Craft may evolve as time goes on. In so doing, my goal is to help analytically highlight the key sociological dynamics to be considered for both future researchers and members of the Craft.

Based upon available information, I contend that regular twenty-first-century Freemasonry may evolve in two broad directions. In one possible future, it may become increasingly responsive to the rapidly evolving diversity of contemporary society, attempting to more effectively integrate its ideals, practices, members, and organization in parallel with broader social developments. In the second, it may remain something socially, ideologically, drama-turgically, and organizationally set apart. In this latter case, it will continue on doing things the way they have "always been done," and, in response to declining numbers, pitch its appeal to a select demographic group attracted to traditional ideals and forms. The former, more liberal, and convergent path holds the potential benefits of greater relevance to a broader demographic, but risks watering down long-standing traditions and alienating both senior and more traditional members. The more traditional, divergent path holds out the potential for success among a smaller, select group alienated by various aspects of rapid social change, but it risks irrelevance to a wider demographic, will likely turn off potential recruits (especially younger ones), and effectively turns the Craft into an aging, increasingly "deviant" subculture, at least as perceived by the wider society.

This does not imply that these two possible futures are pure, mutually exclusive alternatives. Indeed, the present situation can fairly be characterized as a precarious, evolving balance between aspects of each. What I am suggesting is that these scenarios are much like two points on a continuum. Nevertheless, rapid social change, evolving demographics, and economic and structural changes will likely make this balancing act more precarious over time, such that the Freemasonry of the future will probably be characterized by a predominant emphasis closer to one or the other end of this spectrum. The Craft will likely survive, as it has through the vicissitudes of past centuries, but its size and the predominant form it will likely take are the question.

In what follows, while highlighting the contributions of this study, I sketch out the argument as follows. First, I return to the social and demographic composition of the Craft in relation to society and what this can tell us about where things may be heading. Next, and relatedly, I turn to issues of social stratification, noting that the makeup and organization of the Craft today in relation to the social structure suggest very different—and at times conflictual—dynamics in relation to social ideals than in the past. Third, given the concerns raised above, I turn to ritual, including the method or means of facilitating social bonding and integration of members across social boundaries, raising questions about its liminal flexibility and its ability to do so equally well for all groups, which may, along with the matters above, be ultimately reflected in form. Fourth, I integrate each of these factors into an analytical model representing the possible impact of each on the potential outcomes at each end of the continuum. Finally, I discuss the relevance of all of these matters for future research.

SOCIAL DEMOGRAPHICS: THE CRAFT VERSUS CONTEMPORARY SOCIETY

If the Craft ultimately depends on the wider society to provide members, and, in various ways, to sustain its relevance in their lives, then it becomes important to consider whether this is a mutually beneficial relationship or one fraught with problems. One significant way to approach this is by building upon the demographic issues discussed in the chapters above. In effect, the key questions are (1) Who are Masons today? and (2) How well integrated are they with ongoing changes in today's society?

To some extent the first question can be answered by commenting on the sample in this study. In chapter 1 it was noted that the subjects were largely

White, middle-class, Christian men in their sixties and seventies, many with post-secondary education, and with more of an emphasis on white-collar rather than blue-collar occupational backgrounds. They exhibited relatively little ethnic or religious diversity, although this was less true of the urban dwellers. In addition, because membership statistically declined from the early 1960s until a slight uptick in interest in the new millennium, the "missed generations" have resulted in a significant "generation gap" between a relatively small number of new members and a much larger group of seasoned members, as outlined in chapter 5. Considering that today we have moved away from a more traditional society of widely shared social traditions, status hierarchies, and high social capital to one with greater diversity, greater stress on equality, and lower social capital, in many instances current demographic composition and generational divides do not bode well for a broadly meaningful interface between the Craft and society at large.

Against this backdrop, one might also consider the social characteristics respondents claimed lay behind their recruitment. In chapter 2 it was noted that predisposing factors included (1) long-standing personal or family connections with Freemasons; (2) congruent personal traits or interests (e.g., religion or history); (3) unfulfilled social needs (e.g., friendship, status); and (4) experiencing a state of anomie or alienation in relation to society at large. On balance, these factors further point in the direction of heritage and tradition, and, while it may be that unfulfilled social needs and anomie affect a broader group in today's socio-economic climate, many individuals may find ways to deal with such issues other than by joining the Masons. These predisposing factors largely suggest demographic congruency between the Masonic order and a select subset of the wider population.

Indeed, none of this is inconsistent with the discussion in chapter 4 where statistics revealed that the number of Masons has dropped throughout North America for decades and that Masonry is characterized by an aging membership, retention problems, and decreasing periods of involvement—all in the context of a society with a much larger population than in the past and changing, rather than declining, patterns of civic and volunteer involvement.

Given these matters, and regardless of promotional campaigns, one might reasonably question the breadth of the meaningful interface between regular Freemasonry and contemporary society. Which social groups would be most interested in Freemasonry today? Which would be more likely to be indifferent? To mount opposition? Which social backgrounds are most conducive to "getting it," to "having it click?" Which are not? Which recruits are more likely to drift away? Of course, the data here cannot completely answer these questions, but several reasonable suppositions can be made on the basis of attractive and repelling factors noted by respondents.

One supposition flows from the discussion of "fit" in chapter 4, where it was noted that those who relish tradition, roots, history, religion, or spirituality may find "sanctuary" in the lodge, as may some who have a sense of anomie or alienation from contemporary society in the context of rapid social change and a stressful, neo-liberal work environment.

In contrast, chapter 2 discussed various "hurdles" to joining, supplemented in chapter 6 by a discussion of factors that inhibited involvement. Beyond lack of information and presumed membership requirements, these included the many negative stereotypes that have been circulated by conspiracy theorists in popular culture, as well as religious opposition, spousal opposition, family opposition, and a variety of other matters such as regulatory constraints, friends' opposition, secular ideals, and comments from disillusioned former members. Along with an increase in alternative recreational opportunities, changes in gender relations, ethnic diversity, and the rise of two-job families in a neo-liberal, consumer economy, these factors may dissuade many and stand in social tension with the select group predisposed or attracted to Masonry as noted above.

Such tensions were further manifested in members themselves, revealed by discussions about the "generation gap," by questions about remaining true to old ways of doing things versus "rebranding" and promotion to make the lodge more relevant to, and better "fit," a greater diversity of potential members, and by comments about whether the traditional "male-only" membership requirement is problematic. Indeed, intertwined with the above were respondents' doubts, revealed in comments about "unmet expectations"; a "disconnect with the reading"; the social irrelevance of language, music, and social activities; "boring business meetings"; and the like.

In effect, both socially and within individuals themselves, there is clearly tension as to whether involvement in the Craft makes sense in relation to their lives in the broader society. For men of some social backgrounds (e.g., those with busy lives and few congruent interests, who face opposition and other hurdles), the answer is likely to be no. For those exhibiting many of the predisposing factors and the better "fit" as described herein, the answer—against the backdrop of our larger society—seems to be more of a qualified yes.

Such demographic and social issues, and the apparently shrinking breadth of the relevance interface between the Craft and contemporary society, may be usefully contrasted with the way that things operated in the past. In chapter 1 it was noted that Freemasonry in the nineteenth century helped ritually resolve social contradictions of class and gender for members in a changing society, integrating members of somewhat differing backgrounds into a shared symbolic order of solidarity, even emotional intimacy. While there is some evidence of bonding and integration in the current data (e.g., claims of increased "tolerance," "trust," and the ability to socially engage with a network of "more diverse" others through the shared symbolic vehicle of Masonic talk), in chapter 7 it was noted that this exists in tension with an attraction to "like-minded" individuals sharing common interests. Hence, the overall impression is that this bonding dynamic operates more effectively for a relatively select group in a narrowing relevance interface with society at large.

True, Masonry is not as much of an "elite thing" as in the past, and there does seem to have been some broadening of the membership in terms of class (more on this below). However, today it is not as socially acceptable to bond across certain social divisions using others (e.g., gender) as the foil, as noted in the generational split on the issue of remaining a male-only order in chapter 6. Such a "generation gap," if it existed in the past, was of relatively little consequence as the overall membership profile was much younger in those days. Further, while the slight uptick in new members may reflect less the culture of contentment of the baby boom than the economic and social uncertainty of the new millennium, one might question who these new members are. Could they show at one and the same time a fluctuating range of economic achievement and social devaluation in a rapidly changing cultural and moral landscape? Despite some claims using societal buzzwords like *diversity*, this is often more rhetoric than reality, suggesting that what we are largely seeing is the recruitment and integration of a few younger, like-minded people with older, more traditional members, and the attrition of those who don't fit the mould. Freemasonry is notoriously resistant to change, so we are likely witnessing the integration of that relatively small, socially congruent group of people in society to an existing order of authenticity and relevance ("conservatives who wanna find a place to be") rather than the adaptation of a group rich in symbolic diversity to the great bulk of a changing society. In effect, links between Freemasonry and society seems to be occurring where it is easiest, and Masonry is not adapting itself quickly enough to the vast social changes that have occurred in past decades. For now, from the demographic standpoint at least, Freemasonry effectively appears to be headed in the direction of a traditionalist subculture, and this is unlikely to change so long as the old guard remains relatively dominant in terms of both numbers and authority.

CLASS AND STATUS ISSUES: COMPLEMENTARY EVOLUTION OR DEVOLUTION?

Implicit in the above are a series of interrelated issues surrounding the social class and status of Freemasons relative to the surrounding society. As noted in chapter 1, historically Freemasonry frequently found success as an elite organization in stratified societies where the "civilizing process" often placed great cultural emphasis on status groups (e.g., royalty, aristocracy, sophisticated elites, professionals, and political and business leaders). Meanwhile, the higher social classes often significantly overlapped, or attempted to associate themselves with, these status groupings.[1] Correspondingly, not everybody got in, and, in such instances, much of Freemasonry's membership draw involved individuals of relatively more diverse social standing seeking to be "on the level" with the elite.[2] Under such circumstances Freemasonry served as an alternate status hierarchy,[3] a means of symbolically integrating select individuals across social inequalities into meaningful groupings.

Yet Western society has changed significantly since those days, and, while today social class no doubt remains highly stratified, some historical status groups have gone through considerable devolution and been replaced by others in relative social esteem, all in a context where there is much more emphasis on social equality as a primary cultural value. Given such changes, it is valid to question whether the alternate status hierarchy that operated historically can work in the same fashion in today's social landscape.

In the current study, on the one hand, membership demographics certainly revealed a picture of a moderately high social class grouping vis-à-vis the surrounding society—although it was far from the virtual who's who of community bankers, lawyers, business magnates, and politicians who comprised Masonic membership in many communities in the past. Meanwhile, lodges have become significantly less selective in class terms than they once were. With regard to membership, it would thus be fair to say that there has been both a relative devolution in class terms and a relative democratization in recruitment. The overall membership frame has moved downward in stratification relative to the society at large.

Perhaps this has something to do with the cultural turning away from deference to traditional elites in the direction of egalitarianism, or perhaps Freemasonry is simply not as popular as it was in the past and needs to broaden recruitment. In any event, the order now exists in a society where the emphasis on diversity above is found alongside a strong cultural, institutional, and moral emphasis on *equality*, which at least partially undermines the historic dynamics identified in the literature. Meanwhile, the devolution and downward movement of the membership frame partially undermines the motivation of those who still retain the earlier outlook. Put bluntly, in a society that places less cultural value on traditional status elites, there is likely to be less desire among a broad swath of the general public to emulate or associate with them—and for those that do, the membership is not quite as elite as it used to be. In this sense, the symbolic vehicle of the skilled craftsman that formerly served to foster bonds between relative unequals increasingly becomes *irrelevant from two directions at once*.

I would suggest that this historic shift—from a scenario where class and status show relative structural and ideological convergence to one where they show, at the very least, more ideological separation in favour of a cultural fetishization of equalities—cuts the traditional draw of Freemasonry in favour

Table 8.1   Historical Comparison: Masonic Social Stratification Issues

	Eighteenth/Nineteenth Centuries	Twenty-first Century
Membership	Relative class/status convergence	Relative class/status disavowal
Ideology	Relative deference to traditional elites; status by association	Egalitarianism; emphasis on promoting social justice as marker of esteem/status
Society	Legitimation by traditional authority	Legitimation by rational/legal authority
Freemasonry	External legitimation by traditional authority	Struggle between legitimation by traditional/rational legal authority

of volunteer recruitment and involvement in more fashionable, expressive, "social justice" groups that are more in line with prominent societal values (as noted in chapter 4). A further difficulty here is that Freemasonry often still articulates its legitimation in favour of what Max Weber referred to as "traditional authority" for a shrinking demographic, while newer groups tend to more strongly emphasize concern over culturally favoured issues in terms of the rhetoric of "rational legal" authority.

These developments are represented graphically in table 8.1.

How has Freemasonry responded? In some cases, it has not, while in other instances, it has struggled over various internal issues related to recruitment, retention, and attempts to become more socially relevant. Yet one thing stands out: the emergence of bureaucratization. Historically there seems to have been a move from the lodge being primarily a local group, with a minimal internal officer hierarchy, to one that is more and more bureaucratically organized and geographically spread out, containing an extensive ladder of Grand Lodge and District Grand Lodge officers, along with numerous committees and their associated paraphernalia. Many of the issues and debates over offices, tasks, dues structures, the Grand Lodge, and the like that were noted earlier must be seen in this context. While likely reflecting a broader societal trend toward bureaucratization, Freemasonry has, at least in part, effectively attempted to replace its traditional elite status vis-à-vis society by *compensating* with a more extensive *internal* status hierarchy. Where the external status referencing is breaking down, the internal hierarchy is, in theory at least, taking up the slack.

This is a tricky balancing act, one that, as noted in chapter 4, requires maintaining a productive tension between meaningful social inclusiveness and the recognition/acceptance of the rank and file by high-status members (in both internal and external terms). If this is not carefully handled (for example, if there is too much emphasis on Grand Lodge officers and neglect of the rank and file), members may grumble about elitism; if there is too little emphasis—formally and informally—on internal hierarchies, lack of recognition may similarly undermine the motivation, or even retention, of those seeking to move up.

The overall picture here is of an organization struggling to find itself in the changed landscape of class and status in the twenty-first century. While the membership scores relatively high in class terms, that score is not as high as in the past. Meanwhile, status referents have changed significantly in tandem with culture, moving away from the status groups historically associated with the Craft, while traditional authority has somewhat given way to rational-legal authority in a culture emphasizing equality. Freemasonry has lost status—indeed, it has retained a membership with more class than status yet often does not want to admit even its class context in the current cultural milieu. It struggles to remain culturally relevant through various internal programs, all the while importing bureaucratization from the surrounding society to, among other purposes, effectively compensate for these disconnections.

In effect, Freemasonry has moved from being an elite group to a culturally marginalized one, a group that is often treated with indifference. To the extent that it still serves as an alternate status hierarchy, it does so among a relatively small, select group of traditionalists, conservatives, and alienated individuals as noted above, often seeking to support one another and construct an alternate status hierarchy within an alternate subculture, thus enabling recognition and a sense of identity standing in contrast to their relative devaluation by the wider society. Yet, even then, problems remain.

I would suggest that one of the major problems here is that, unlike those Masons in the past who faced persecution in hostile societies and thus found meaning and integrative solidarity in the tightly knit brotherhood of the lodge, many Masons today are not so much persecuted as neglected, not so much faced with hostility as cultural indifference. The risk involved in being a Mason is often not great in the West today. Meanwhile, the social class position of Masons makes it relatively hard to claim marginalization, other than, perhaps, in terms of cultural status and esteem. In the end, the alternate status hierarchy that worked so well in the past is in the process of fragmenting, and only time will tell whether the Masonic order will be able to meaningfully reconstruct it in the changing social and ideological landscape of the twenty-first century.

RITUAL ISSUES: THEORETICAL EXPANSION AND INTEGRATIVE COMPLICATIONS

As this is the first major study to qualitatively examine the lived experienced of contemporary Freemasons, the historic role played by ritual suggests a very important theoretical frame for understanding the interrelation of the Craft with society today. Indeed, as we have seen, its relevance has been empirically extended by employing the theoretical tools of symbolic interactionism, dramaturgy, ethnomethodology, and the sociology of emotion outside of the lodge itself—for example, in relation to ritualized processes of formal and informal recruitment. In tandem with these, it has facilitated an empirical elaboration of the work of ritual theorists like Van Gennep and Turner in relation to the liminalities within liminalities revealed in Masons' experience of the degrees, among other things. Moreover, in the multi-faceted evolution of respondents' experiences in the Craft over time, whether through taking an office, participating in degree work, performing administrative tasks, or variously engaging with society in their day-to-day lives, formal and informal ritualized interactions can serve as both gendered forms of emotion management and transformative practices in relation to self, helping to construct both meaningful and less-than-congruent identities over time. In all of these ways, the concept of ritual has made a contribution by informing, yet being theoretically extended through, this exercise.

Given the previous two sections, however, important questions necessarily arise. How *flexible* is ritual? How far can the rites of passage that frame liminality be stretched and still operate effectively? Given the increasing demographic and ideological diversity of society and the evolving social stratification issues noted above, can the formal and informal rituals surrounding Masonry serve to attract and form bonds between society and the order as effectively as in the past? Can it do so equally as well for all groups, or are some more prone to find the ritualized interactions associated with Masonry more meaningful? Are ritually constructed identities better grounded and more durable for some than for others? Is this reflected in retention? While the present data do not enable a complete answer to all of these questions, cutting through all of them is a common theme: is the social bonding that occurs in ritual occurring primarily among those who are *similar*, or is it predominantly integrating those who *differ* from one another in a host of ways?

From the available evidence, it seems reasonable to assert that today there is undoubtedly *some* meaningful integration of diverse individuals across social boundaries. Nevertheless, on balance, *more* bonding seems to be occurring among those who are relatively similar to one another on a number of measures. It would suggest that those who are already predisposed on the basis of their social background are most susceptible to the bonding offered by Masonic ritual; those who are socially dissimilar face a steeper curve, or indeed, may find that, rather than meaningful integration to a relevant group, these processes are short-circuited by a relative lack of social relevance such that they experience mere ritualism, a sense of bonding to anomie, cognitive dissonance, and irrelevance.

While more research is undoubtedly needed, the general thrust of this conclusion is not only congruent with the two sections above but supported by a number of matters discussed in previous chapters. Social bonding is supported, in part, by the discussion about the development of close friendships between individuals who would never otherwise have met, "brotherhood," the sense of purpose involved in common activities, the ready availability of common topics and discourse, and particularly the reverse onus of trust that occurs for some brethren. The somewhat greater demographic diversity of brethren in urban areas also provides some evidence for both this "bridging" effect of ritual and some fruitful interface with the broader society. For that matter, the split over the gender issue shows that, for *some* at least, gender effectively serves as the ritualized foil that, in part, fosters integration across other social boundaries. Indeed, it may, in part, interact with the male gender in a ritualized, masculine form of emotion management to help bridge the gap between old and young—traditionalists and younger members of various stripes who are alienated by social change—and help them find a place of sanctuary in today's society.

But this somewhat limited bonding *across* boundaries needs to be seen against the backdrop of a far more pronounced bonding *within* already congruent groups. Thus, beyond the broad demographic similarity of contemporary Masons, both in the sample and the research literature, the fact is that bonding often occurs between family, friends, and acquaintances. Such connections are supplemented by shared interests, like-minded people, common activities and topics, and the ritualized development of new (often traditionally masculine) skills and abilities, enabling relatively narrow differences to be overcome among relatively similar individuals. Indeed, the claimed "moral improvement" in chapter 7, while not necessarily showing differences between generations, often tends to stress traditionalist ethical concerns. Taken together, when supplemented by social support and building trust, such bonding can be meaningful for those relatively predisposed to it.

What this all suggests is that "fit" remains important. As noted earlier, the ritualized bonding process above may be externally short-circuited along the way by a number of cumulative factors, including lack of family connections, differing backgrounds or beliefs, social opposition, contemporary work schedules and family structures, the generation gap, or a particular lodge's inability to remain socially relevant. In such cases, Hirschi's bonds of belief, attachment, commitment, and involvement are already far more connected *externally* and leave little room or relevance for the lodge. Meanwhile, *within* the lodge, even relatively congruent individuals may experience irrelevance or lack of meaningful common activities, poor ritual work, excessive emphasis on status, politics, or filling up meetings with boring business rather than something interesting and engaging for members. Under such circumstances, ritual becomes drained of meaning and becomes ritualism—a "disconnect with the reading"—and bureaucracy forms the organizational structure of meaninglessness. Whether out of social irrelevance or the perceived uselessness of anomie linking with anomie, meaningful social bonding is undermined. In other words, for ritual to facilitate social bonding, the best results are likely to occur when there is meaningful bonding *within* the lodge that is simultaneously connected to *congruent* individuals and social groups *outside* of the lodge (i.e., those whose existing social bonds do not so readily get in the way). The better the "fit," the narrower the social gaps between potential members and the lodge. The better job the lodge does on these internal measures, the more likely it is that the ritual bonding process will successfully take hold and facilitate a strong Masonic identity.

All of this raises the issue of both getting and keeping members, as reflected in the literature on declining membership and reduced periods of retention as well as in the various involvement factors detailed in chapters 4 through 6. As noted in chapter 4, in order to have a broadly based membership it is necessary for an organization to play to, and remain relevant to, prominent societal values. In today's world, this introduces a tension between the ability of leadership to maintain a healthy "balance"—that is, to adaptively remain on top of the moving target of change—and a conservative tendency toward maintaining things as they are, doing things the way they have "always" been done, and circling the wagons. For the Craft at least, this tension is being predominantly settled in one direction. Despite room in the ritual to be interpreted more broadly, the generation gap and the relatively small proportion of younger, more diverse members means that the Craft remains relatively more traditional in its orientation than the broader society. Barring a radical reorientation in stance, in an organization already notoriously resistant to change, this points to the Craft drawing from, and ritually integrating, a narrower and narrower pool of alienated traditionalists, effectively maintaining itself as a traditionalist subculture. In terms of congruency, such bonding may be easier in rural areas with few young people and a membership drawn mostly from the same generation, but such lodges face the problem of few new members and existing ones dying off. The congruency gap is wider in cities, and bonding more difficult when there is a more pronounced generation gap—but that is where the new blood is to be found. As such, the Craft may still prosper for a time by targeting its recruitment to congruent demographics as they are variously found throughout society, engaging—in effect if not intent—in *selective bonding*. It may stave off "organizational death" for some time. Yet, the Craft will be smaller, and its ritual bonds relevant to more limited segments of society.

ANALYTIC MODEL: CONVERGENCE OF DEMOGRAPHICS, SOCIAL STRATIFICATION, AND RITUAL

The previous three sections provide different yet closely interrelated vantage points on the state of Freemasonry today. Indeed they suggest a series of important analytic dimensions for understanding the Craft—and, perhaps, to some extent, other community organizations—in the context of a rapidly changing society. Moreover, they point to a *convergence* on these dimensions that bears significant implications for the Craft in the future. In this section, these frames will be unpacked and arranged in an analytic model. Following this, the current state of the Craft will be discussed and various conclusions drawn.

It is my contention that it is useful to understand Freemasonry, both historically and today—in relation to three interrelated sociological dimensions: (1) the *lateral/compositional*, (2) the *vertical/hierarchical*, and (3) the *interactional/processual*. Each of these is analytically implicit throughout this book.

The *lateral/compositional* dimension stresses the social makeup of the Craft in terms of its relative structural homogeneity or diversity and how this compares to the rest of society. It comprehends issues of relative convergence or divergence between these populations, as well as in corresponding social beliefs and ideologies. All of this speaks to the relative breadth or narrowness of the social interface between society and the Craft—that is, to whether there is a high degree of congruence or relative inconsistency between the membership and society. The answer to this question, in any historical context, will have much bearing on the relative success of the Craft, or its marginalization, in any specific social context.

The *vertical/hierarchical* dimension, in contrast, emphasizes issues of internal versus external social stratification between the Craft and society, particularly on the analytically distinct, but closely related, issues of class, status, and predominant type of legitimacy/authority. Freemasonry has historically operated as an alternate status hierarchy in relation to these, but this dynamic, and the membership frame, has been changing along with society in more recent times. This dimension attends to the way in which these changes can serve as either a fruitful evolution or a discordant devolution in this important historical dynamic.

The *interactional/processual* dimension, finally, turns away from these primarily structural issues to stress the role of ritual, particularly the processes and interactions that individuals engage in and are subject to in their time in the Craft. In particular, this dimension addresses the relative flexibility of ritual, the potential impact that this may have on the meaningfulness of the social bonding process and identity formation, and how this is reflected in the social bonds formed both within the lodge and between the lodge and outside individuals, groups, and society at large. A summary of the characteristics of these dimensions is shown in table 8.2.

It is my contention that each of these dimensions can be usefully represented analytically in a series of ideal types to illustrate various possibilities for the relationship between the Craft and its social environment. Thus, on

Table 8.2   Sociological Dimensions Relevant to Freemasonry

Lateral/Compositional	Vertical/Hierarchical	Interactional/Processual
Homogeneity/diversity	Alternate status hierarchy	Ritual flexibility
Internal/external makeup	Class, status, and legitimation	Internal/external bonds
Congruence of interface	Frame evolution/ devolution	Meaningfulness/identity

the *lateral/compositional dimension*, one can usefully compare a situation of relative social homogeneity within and outside the Craft to one where there is much more divergence between the two (i.e., more social diversity in society than in the Masonic order). Furthermore, couple this with a greater ideological emphasis on promoting diversity in the wider society versus its toleration in the Craft alongside widespread veneration of heritage and tradition. The former situation would likely be one with a much wider, more comfortable interface with society at large; the latter's social and ideological divergence would *narrow* the congruence interface, resulting in the greater social marginalization of Freemasonry. Of course, when looking at any actual lodge, Grand Lodge, or jurisdiction, one will usually find examples closer to one or the other end of this continuum, but the current situation would likely find these more frequently clustering closer to the latter rather than the former end of this frame. (See table 8.3.)

Next, on the vertical/hierarchical dimension, one might usefully contrast the operation of an alternate status hierarchy in a society where class, status, and traditional legitimation often intersect in an elite group to one where social class, the cultural basis of status, and basis of legitimation diverge, the membership frame moves downward relative to society, and bureaucratization compensates by constructing an internal status hierarchy. Again, while any actual group may find itself with features at various points, on the basis of the available evidence, I suspect that many lodges and Grand Lodges today find themselves closer to the latter end of the continuum. (See table 8.4.)

Table 8.3   Lateral/Compositional Continuum

Traditional	Contemporary
Internal/external member homogeneity	Internal/external member divergence
Ideology valuing heritage/tradition	Ideology valuing social diversity
Congruence of interface	Narrowing of interface

Table 8.4 Vertical/Hierarchical Continuum

Traditional	Contemporary
Alternate status hierarchy external	Alternate status hierarchy internal
Class, status, and legitimation intersect	Class, status, and legitimation diverge
Elite social membership frame	Devolved social membership frame

As for the interactional/processual dimension, one may draw a distinction between, on the one hand, social contexts where ritual is flexible enough and congruent enough that it fosters meaningful bonding both among the vast majority of members within the lodge and between the lodge and those outside it and, on the other hand, social contexts where liminality is stretched too far and ritual is seen by most of the members as increasingly rigid, irrelevant, and meaningless,[4] with the result that they are less able to form either meaningful bonds within the lodge or close connections with those outside (many of whom are already more closely bonded in other ways). Today the picture painted here is, again, likely to bear more of a resemblance to the latter scenario, one where the ritual is not flexible enough, or at least is perceived as irrelevant, to people more externally bonded to other ideas, groups, pastimes, and obligations. Here, for many, meaningful ritual devolves into ritualism, identity to nothingness, and bonding to something that evokes anomie and seems both meaningless and pointless at the same time. (See table 8.5.)

At the outset of this chapter I asserted that contemporary Freemasonry has the potential to evolve in two broad directions: either it could become increasingly responsive to social change and the nature of society today or it could increasingly become something set apart. Either of these possibilities still remain, but it is nevertheless the case, based on the three sections above, and the analytic dimensions identified here, that Freemasonry today has already moved quite far along the road toward the latter scenario. Whether looking at it from the lateral/compositional, vertical/hierarchical, or interactional/processual dimensions, contemporary Freemasonry is diverging in many respects from society at large, and, while not actively persecuted, faces significant issues nonetheless. Unless things change radically, Freemasonry is likely to

Table 8.5 Interactional/Processual Continuum

Traditional	Contemporary
Sufficient ritual flexibility/liminality	Insufficient ritual flexibility/liminality
Internal/external bonds productive	Internal/external bonds inconsistent
Meaningfulness/fostering identity	Ritualism/anomie/identity deficit

diminish in the near term, to remain potentially successful only among a small, select group alienated by various aspects of rapid social change, and thus to become an aging, traditionalist, perhaps even "deviant" subculture—at least as perceived by many in society. Indeed, it may even find success by targeting individuals and groups most likely to fit in.

In this case, it is possible that the outcome constructed through Masonic ritual could emphasize the idea of "haven" and "sanctuary" in an oppositional fashion, essentially grafting a "deviant identity" onto Masonry and using shared, ritualized action as a masculine form of emotion management by a marginalized, traditional subculture in the face of a rapidly changing society. In this sense, emotion-as-doing would take precedence over expressiveness, and Masonry itself would become the method.

Then again, Masonic leaders still have time to read the writing on the wall, to make relevant adjustments and position the Order in a manner that aligns it more meaningfully with an evolving society. For example, the Craft's multivalent ceremonies could be articulated in a style that places more emphasis on their openness—and compatibility—with diverse multicultural groups and emotional styles, building sanctuary while building bridges. Perhaps even gradually opening to *informal* ties with European women's lodges (many of which are themselves quite keen on traditional forms) on select issues or at specific events—such as through participation in academic conferences—might, in time, help lay a subcultural foundation for something more. While there are, of course, considerable difficulties here, time will tell if history is eventually made or merely repeats itself.

Aspects of both approaches are still at play now in regular Freemasonry, partly driven by different generations, which, as with gender and race in the past, remain glossed over by shared ritual. While one approach is apparently in the ascendant, how these ultimately play out for the Craft in the future is an empirical question for future researchers to discern. All I have done here is map out key issues to be considered along the way.

FUTURE RESEARCH AND IMPLICATIONS

As one of the first sociological investigations of contemporary Freemasonry, this study undoubtedly raises as many questions as it answers. That was the plan from the beginning. Any in-depth qualitative investigation of relatively uncharted social terrain is bound to shed light on some matters and simultaneously raise a bumper crop of questions requiring further investigation. In a sense, this is an exploratory investigation highlighting specific theoretical and empirical issues for future researchers to follow up. If it has been successful in doing so, it has already more than served its purpose.

In what follows, I highlight what I see as the most significant matters that researchers might want to consider in the future.

First, and most broadly, it will be important to investigate whether the structural and demographic patterns, social processes, analytic typologies, and key issues raised in this study hold true elsewhere or need to be modified and empirically extended in other contexts. This calls for comparative study of other Masonic jurisdictions, particularly those with more diverse demographic, age, ethnic, and cultural profiles. It suggests cross-cultural comparisons, especially when there are variations in ritual, language, organizational structure, and local culture. Given that there are women's and co-Masonic lodges in many countries, it will also be important to make comparisons between them and what has been revealed here in relation to the larger, male orders. Indeed, future researchers will want to consider the relevance of the issues raised here to wider social and organizational contexts including, for example, volunteer organizations; community groups; service clubs; religious, political, and educational organizations; and various other bureaucratically organized institutions.

Employing a more diverse array of methodologies will also be helpful in these respects. While the primarily inductive, qualitative approach utilized here is useful for generating in-depth data about a variety of issues, it cannot do everything. Other qualitative methods, such as ethnographic observation, content analysis of documents, media, even historical methods applied to recent years may help shed further light in these respects. Yet the "deep but narrow" insights gleaned here must be followed up using a wider variety of methodological tools. In particular, future researchers may want to take some of the issues raised in this exploratory study and build them into more quantitative, survey-based methods. This will provide easier comparisons and facilitate better generalization and broader conclusions in some of the contexts noted above. In particular, such methods will more readily enable comparing individuals who never joined with those who did, and those who joined with those who left. Further, adding longitudinal analysis to this methodological toolbox will enable future researchers to better examine key issues across time, discuss significant trends, and make better attributions of causality. All of these will help future researchers check, broaden, and deepen the initial understanding of issues raised here.

In a more theoretical sense, this research has empirically reiterated the relevance of interpretive sociological traditions such as symbolic interactionism, dramaturgy, phenomenology, ethnomethodology, and the sociology of emotion when employed to study organizations. These, when combined with ritual theory, are particularly relevant to the study of processes of member attraction and the various rituals of initiation. In relation to the former, future researchers may wish to compare the relative effectiveness of the role played by confidentiality gerrymandering and strategic information leakage in traditionally closed versus currently more open information contexts. Indeed, it would be interesting to see how these processes play out, if at all, in other social joining contexts.

Going hand in hand with this, future researchers will want to follow up on the role played by formal and informal ritual. Does the dramaturgical interplay between teasing and support, for example, deepen curiosity in all social contexts? In what circumstances can the social construction of curiosity in this fashion either fail or result in premature satiation? Are the liminalities within liminalities identified earlier more effective for some groups than for others? How does today compare to the past, to different jurisdictions, different cultures, age groups, social statuses, and so on? How do these practices intersect most productively—and most problematically—with the surrounding culture? As that culture evolves? How do variations on traditional degree work, like the "one-day, three-degree" programs, affect this? How does quality of degree work fit in? In all of these, one might ask who finishes their degrees, and who does not, and why?

Gender is another area where future researchers could make a contribution. In several places I have characterized Freemasonry as a *method*, a traditionally masculine form of emotion management where emotion-as-doing takes precedence over emotional expression. Yet emotion norms have changed somewhat in recent decades, with several respondents—particularly younger ones—much more open in their emotional expressiveness. This raises the question of whether the relatively silent/active approach to ritualized emotion management traditionally embodied in Freemasonry is as relevant to young men today, something that future researchers might want to follow up.

A matter that emerged much more strongly than expected in this study was involvement. In the three chapters devoted to this issue, many factors were highlighted that could be followed up by researchers in other Masonic and wider organizational contexts. I will not reiterate them all here; suffice it to say that the ideal-typical model of pro- and anti-involvement lodges outlined in chapter 6 is something that may be relevant not only to Freemasonry but to any number of other organizations. I would invite both Masonic researchers and organizational sociologists to use this comparatively in a variety of other contexts, using multiple methods, to determine its relative utility, all while refining and extending its constituent elements in an evolving society.

A fifth matter that suggests follow-up involves the claimed life changes of members discussed in chapter 7. The current methods did not enable one to determine whether these were largely self-presentational or whether some deeper transformation in self and identity was occurring—hence the stress on "claimed." It would be most interesting if future researchers were able to do a longitudinal study measuring quantitative indices of self and identity before joining, after taking the degrees, and among Masons with varying years and degrees of involvement in the order. Such harder data on this, and also on the claimed changes in character and ability, would be a welcome contribution to the interactionist study of self and identity, and of ritual theory more generally.

Finally, this final chapter has developed an analytical model focused on the evolution of key internal versus external relationships between the Craft and society, outlining how these three theoretical vantage points converge to paint a distinct picture of contemporary Freemasonry as a traditionalist subculture. Nevertheless, it must be remembered that the lateral/compositional, vertical/hierarchical, and interactional/processual dimensions exist on a historical continuum, and the above discussion provides clues as to how things could evolve. Examining these issues in broader Masonic, social, and organizational contexts, utilizing a variety of methods, will not only help glean a deeper theoretical and empirical appreciation of a variety of organizations and groups, it may ultimately help provide clues to building the Freemasonry of the future.

NOTES

NOTES TO CHAPTER 1

1 See their website at http://www.therooseveltcenter.org. The Masonic Research Centre at the University of Sheffield and the Canonbury Masonic Research Centre in London were important representatives of this academic movement but have since closed due to budget cuts.

2 *It is important to emphasize that not everything in Freemasonry is secret.* Not only have the alleged secrets of Freemasonry been repeatedly published since the Craft went public in 1717, one can quite readily purchase the ritual at bookstores, and the Internet has made exposing Freemasonry a virtual growth industry. Moreover, it is quite clear that the only secrets Masons are *specifically* sworn to uphold relate to certain passwords and modes of recognition, nothing more (Pietre-Stones 2005). This is the position that I have taken in discussing the Masonic ritual throughout this book.

3 In an earlier paper, I also outlined in detail how contemporary Freemasons symbolically reconstruct the past for present ends. See Kenney 2010. As it has been dealt with elsewhere, and does not fit the logical flow of this book, it has been omitted.

4 Freemasons are quick to point out, however, that one of the key things that they are sworn to do is to care for women, particularly "widows and orphans," and, in recent years, have expanded this traditional obligation to providing funding for women's shelters, implementing identification programs for lost children, and so on. I would add that, in my experience, there are currently significantly differing ideas on women's participation by generation. Many older, traditional men I have met (who often dominate the Craft) still hold to this "landmark," while younger Masons tend to hold more egalitarian views. I expect that, as the younger generation supplants the elder—and if there is agitation by women seeking admittance—there may be interesting developments worthy of study.

5 Freemasonry is similar to other historic institutions, such as churches, that have often been effectively segregated despite no scriptural justification for this practice. Some societies have been more tolerant of multi-race lodges (e.g., in parts of Britain and Continental Europe), while much of the United States has been traditionally segregated (e.g., Black "Prince Hall" Masonry was first officially recognized by the Grand Lodge of England, but not by American Grand Lodges).

Even today, despite the impact of the civil rights movement, Freemasonry, like other institutions, is much more racially integrated in some jurisdictions than others. This largely reflects varying degrees of racial integration in broader areas of the surrounding society, not membership stipulations in the ritual. Nevertheless, in some instances, Freemasonry is *more* racially integrated than in the surrounding locale. Thus, while Masonry may *reflect* societal racial schisms in places, in others it may serve, in some small part, as a vehicle to heal them—by providing a forum for interracial interaction often missing elsewhere.

6 On occasion, I also draw upon my observations and experiences over more than fifteen years as a practising Freemason.

7 Note that potential candidates are not eligible to become Masons until they reach the age of twenty-one (nineteen in some jurisdictions). Some Grand Lodges also permit the son of a Mason to be initiated at eighteen.

8 "White-collar" includes professionals and those engaged in clerical and administrative work. Retired individuals who gave their former occupation are coded as either "blue-collar" or "white-collar." Individuals who did not give their current occupation and retired individuals who did not give their former occupation are listed as "unknown."

9 Please note that the higher ranks are inclusive of the lower, so they will not be counted more than once. Thus, a Past Grand Master must have previously served as a Grand Lodge officer, be a Past Master, have served as a lodge officer, and have received all three degrees in Masonry.

NOTES TO CHAPTER 2

1 In the case of women, such as grandmothers, aunts, and wives, they often—though not always—belonged to the associated Order of the Eastern Star.

2 A good example would be Christopher Hodapp's *Freemasons for Dummies* (Hoboken, NJ: Wiley, 2005).

3 Anti-Masonic materials and conspiracy theories have been around for hundreds of years, probably reaching their previous zenith following the 1826 William Morgan affair and the subsequent formation of the Anti-Masonic Party in the United States. However, for most of the past three centuries at least, such materials have been popular only among a small fringe. Nor were they as readily available as they are today on the Internet. Nothing compares historically to today's technologies of dissemination combined with a broader cultural fascination with conspiracy theories, whose growth we have witnessed in the past several decades.

4 School lodges, particularly at universities, were once a significant tradition in the United Kingdom and elsewhere.

5 Given the above discussion, and the number of respondents in this study, I would not agree with such a blanket statement. However, there is a grain of truth in these observations, and the statement might be usefully rephrased as to "who" or "which groups" might find Freemasonry to be of value today. Respondents' comments in this chapter, along with the demographic profile of the sample, give us a reasonable indication of who they are.

6 Before closing this segment on paths to Masonry, this is perhaps as good a place as any to mention respondents' assessment of their decision not to join the craft earlier. Twenty-three respondents stressed that they "regret missing out on it before." In particular, given the strong family connections that were associated with those joining, there were also six respondents who expressed "regret that I did not do this while my father was alive," one even claiming that it "helped me to know him better in retrospect."

7 In this, respondents again commented on the need to carefully screen members, seven stressing that this is not a "numbers game" because there is a need to pick "quality members." Despite such claims, however, it has been the author's experience that most applicants, if they are not avowed atheists or obviously people of bad character, will pass this investigation stage.

NOTES TO CHAPTER 3

1 While technically "initiation" refers only to the first degree in Masonry, here I am using the word in its broader sense to encompass the entire rite of passage involved—the process of one passing from the state of being a mere candidate for initiation to becoming a third-degree Master Mason.

2 Interestingly, one thing that runs through the data as a whole is that the often younger respondents here—quite unlike what one would expect to see given traditional male gender roles—are often openly speaking about their feelings. This takes bearing in mind throughout the sections that follow.

3 While some of the rougher aspects of the initiation process are undoubtedly waning today in most places, and Grand Lodges frown on "roughness" and "horseplay" as well (often due to insurance regulations), it is telling that only three respondents felt that there has been a corresponding decrease in the ritualized teasing of candidates before initiation.

4 In some jurisdictions, these penalties are no longer given, nor even stated quite as vividly. Yet there are those who feel, as did one respondent, that they still should be explained, as the degree "loses something" otherwise.

5 Perhaps the most dramatic apron presentation involved a friend of mine who, upon being presented his apron, was suddenly told that it had belonged to his deceased grandfather in another country.

6 This lecture may be done on a separate night, but is usually done immediately following the initiation. One respondent explicitly favoured doing the lecture on a separate night to "break things up and improve candidates' attention."

7 One man recounted how the Grand Master left the lodge room with him to keep him company while the lodge closed (an unusual occurrence). He only later realized that this was a great honour bestowed upon him.

8 These impressions are not necessarily exclusive of one another as, for example, partial understanding of an experience may exist in addition to confusion or lack of complete understanding of the ritual.

9 The "catechism" facing candidates in Nova Scotia is considerably longer than the one in Newfoundland and Labrador.

10 Traditionally, when the candidates finish "the usual questions," the Master asks if anyone in the lodge wishes to put further questions to the candidates. This provides a little scare, but in my experience no one has ever ask further questions, and only one respondent said it happened to him (and the questioning was quickly shut down by the Master).

11 The phrase "give [someone] the third degree" has, in fact, entered the English language to signify an ordeal one endures at the hands of others. Lesser known is that this term also was also used to signify one grade of medieval torture, of which the "third degree" was the most severe.

12 Interestingly, it is only this obligation where respondents commented on a substantive detail, particularly the line that they "not violate the chastity" of another Mason's wife, daughter, sister, mother, and so on.

13 There are a few lodges that use a ritual similar to that used in Nova Scotia, but the rest use some variation on English Emulation ritual, where the drama is not

enacted. Newfoundland and Labrador lodges under the District Grand Lodge of
Scotland use a variety of rituals, some closer to Emulation, others to that used in
Nova Scotia in certain respects.

14 Technically, this does not represent a symbolic resurrection; it is the recovery of
the remains of a good man who had suffered injustice so that he can receive a
proper burial in an honoured place close to the temple. However, many Masonic
commentators have drawn parallels between the raising and numerous historic
myths of death and resurrection.

15 Respondents recounted that, in the past, in some places, they had to pay for the
meal and the bar afterwards. While only one respondent mentioned this as a
requirement, it is certainly the case that much celebration and very late nights are
not uncommon.

16 It is possible that the outcome constructed through these degrees could emphasize
the idea of "haven" and "sanctuary" in an oppositional fashion, essentially grafting a deviant identity onto Masonry (Rubington and Weinberg 1987) and using
emotion as shared, ritualized action as a masculine form of emotion management
by a marginalized, traditional subculture in the face of a rapidly changing society.
In this sense, emotion-as-doing would take precedence over expressiveness, and
Masonry itself would become the method. Conversely, it is possible that these
multivalent ceremonies could be articulated in a manner that emphasizes their
openness—and compatibility—with diverse groups and emotional styles, building
sanctuary while building bridges. Both hold the potential to deal with anomie,
with loss of social capital, in different ways. Both approaches are at play now,
partly driven by different generations; yet, as with gender and race in the past
(Hoffman 2001; Clawson 1989; Carnes 1989), they remain glossed over by shared
ritual.

NOTES TO CHAPTER 4

1 While religious involvement has traditionally been the key predictor of volunteer
participation (Bekkers and de Graaf 2002), and, unlike youth sports and social
cultural activities, youth religious activity has been linked to adult participation in
community service (Perks and Haan 2011; Van Horn 2002), it remains important
to consider that the impact of religious involvement varies by denomination, and
that volunteering to help others solve community problems depends on type of
theology (Wilson and Janoski 1995). Indeed, some have asserted that, beyond
specifically religious volunteerism, religiosity has only a small "spill-over" effect
on other forms of civic involvement (Smith and Peyrot 2008).

2 For example, volunteering in religious orders. Of course, given Freemasonry's
insistence on belief in a Supreme Being, the massive decline in religious participation, particularly among youth, might be considered more worrying than for
secular, expressive organizations.

3 While one might suggest that this question could have been better dealt with by
seeking out lapsed or demitted Masons to compare with the range of members
interviewed herein, that is a difficult methodological order to fill. It is one thing
to write to lodges and seek interested members, quite another to approach current
or former members unsolicited. Masonic membership rolls are treated as strictly
private information by lodges. Indeed, given Masonic vows of secrecy and various
controversies surrounding the order, such individuals might not take kindly to their
involvement in the order being revealed to strangers. Thus, ethical problems pose
significant hurdles to overcome in implementing such a methodological design.
Moreover, while imperfect, the current data—involving new Masons, seasoned

veterans, and spouses—enable us to observe the views of a range of respondents as they identify issues and work through their own questions about involvement. Indeed, many seasoned brethren have repeatedly observed the struggles, questions, and comings and goings of others as well. Thus, while imperfect in some respects, carefully cross-comparing such responses nevertheless enables a great deal to be gleaned from this exercise that bears serious consideration.

4   Since the sample was somewhat (and unavoidably) weighted toward senior Masons with a history of involvement in the Craft, these kind of comments may reflect a certain degree of self-selection, telling us less about maintaining the involvement of brethren with differing backgrounds. Conclusions must be qualified on that basis.

5   The first three items are not mutually exclusive, watertight categories so much as points on a continuum between, at one end, positive attention that respondents feel has been earned in some way and, at the other, attention that they feel was extraordinary in relation to their self-image.

6   However, as noted in the introductory chapter, there was greater ethnic and religious diversity in urban areas.

NOTES TO CHAPTER 5

1   Many older members were opposed to, even "shocked," by this last practice.

2   Of course, the same thing could be done by simply improving the monthly lodge notice or having a good website. Regardless of the medium utilized, however, if effectively disseminating such information did actually have an impact on which meetings—and which lodges—were better attended, such a strategy would hold the potential to encourage friendly *competition* among lodges for more interesting meetings. Such a potential change would be a far cry from what was observed in the two jurisdictions herein, where lodges are supposed to "officially visit" each other based on a bureaucratic "visitation schedule"—which does absolutely nothing to foster interesting meetings, attendance, or involvement.

3   Undoubtedly, lodge policies that foster involvement deal with many more things than are addressed in this section. Many of these matters are specifically dealt with in the various sections herein.

4   The internal status hierarchy has other restrictions on participation as well, such as when only Past Masters are allowed to participate in the "inner work" when a new Master of the lodge is being installed. There are also additional Masonic orders ("concordant bodies") that restrict participation to third-degree Masons, as well as the Grand Lodge bureaucracy that restricts certain types of participation to, for example, Master Masons, board members, or office holders. Many of the comments in this section could be applicable to these as well. However, the concordant bodies are not the subject of this study, and issues surrounding the Grand Lodge will be addressed in a later section.

5   Although the idea was not mentioned by respondents, one wonders whether willingness to participate might be better fostered by adding—or enhancing—stipends for various offices (Tang, Morrow-Howell, and Choi 2010), such as those that currently exist for some lodge secretaries.

6   Issues surrounding restrictions posed by other activities and involvements will be dealt with in detail in the next chapter.

7   Not all lodges were equally characterized by this situation. Generally, rural lodges had a much smaller group of relatively new, younger members, if any. As such, they more generally faced the problem of recycling officers from the shrinking

pool of an aging and declining membership. In urban areas, on the other hand, the generation gap tended to be more salient in respondents' minds.

NOTES TO CHAPTER 6

1 For example, by the Master initiating discussions, employing Past Masters, or having "lodges of instruction."
2 This is not entirely determinative, however, given the fact, noted in the literature review, that certain forms of volunteer activity have maintained involvement and others have not.
3 This shows the danger, noted by Scott (1987), that one's involvement in a group can "engulf" one's other social identities.

NOTES TO CHAPTER 7

1 While Jacob (1991) noted the historical importance of emotional bonding and identification with exclusive status, and Clawson (1989, 255) noted how Free-masonry constructed bonds of loyalty across class lines, picturing "a society in which everyone began symbolically at the bottom, on an equal footing, and rose as a matter of course to the top," this comforting myth faces problems in a society where, on the one hand, the ethos is more egalitarian and, on the other, the more traditional ideal of equality of opportunity faces stiff headwinds in the contemporary neo-liberal era.
2 Indeed, beyond the respective abilities that each Mason is endowed with—either by birth or as the result of a good education—there have always been various methods, aside from mere rote learning, that Masons have used to artificially train their memory. For example, I have heard of brethren who swear by speaking their parts out loud, performing their charges in front of a mirror, studying together with a friend who "prompts" them, and so on. There are books that have been written specifically for Masons in this respect (e.g., David Royal's *Masonic Mnemonics*) as well as a plethora of material on the Internet containing advice on improving one's memory (e.g., an article by Tamin Ansary entitled "12 Memory Tricks").
3 For example, a Mason who had served as a bomber pilot during the Second World War interpreted the three degrees as reflective of (1) basic military training; (2) the technical knowledge imparted in flight training; and (3) aerial combat, where one is unsure about one's survival. He would be unlikely to have constructed this interpretation without his background in the air force.

NOTES TO CHAPTER 8

1 This is in keeping with Max Weber's classic distinction between social class (based in economic production) and status (based in consumption, lifestyle, relative social esteem, and honour).
2 It was this status principle, and the inability to get in, that historically led, in part, to the formation of groups like the Oddfellows (a.k.a. the "poor man's Masons") and other fraternal organizations in the nineteenth century.
3 Indeed, many of the concordant bodies in Masonry emerged as a result of the inability of lower status members to move up in the internal ranks.
4 Indeed, it is questionable whether the symbolic tools can be properly understood by many in today's technological culture.

GLOSSARY

Adoptive. A term commonly used to denote one—but not all—of the major female Masonic orders. Originating in France, such lodges claimed legitimacy by residing under the guardianship of the established French order. Other women-only Grand Lodges, such as La Grande Loge Féminine de France, grew out of adoptive lodges but have had a full-fledged non-adoptive structure for many years. Neither type is officially recognized by mainstream Freemasonry.

Ancient Charges. Traditional regulations for the government of the Masonic order, rooted in historic, constitutional, and, at times, apocryphal records.

Anti-Masonic. Refers to both (1) an American political movement in the nineteenth century, and (2) opposition to Freemasonry more generally.

Applicant. A person who has filled out an application for initiation and had it signed by two Freemasons (the Proposer and the Seconder).

Application. A form that an applicant fills out, either requesting to be initiated as a Freemason or (for existing Freemasons) requesting to become a member of an additional lodge.

Apron. To be appropriately dressed, all Freemasons are supposed to wear either a white leather or cloth apron (a.k.a. "badge") when in open lodge. These vary in their ornamentation and colour depending on one's current degree, jurisdiction, and Masonic rank.

Ashlar. In stonemasonry, an ashlar is a rough stone as it is hewn out of the quarry. In Freemasonry, this term is taken in a symbolic sense, the rough ashlar (which has just been quarried) representing the Mason in his infant, unpolished state, and the perfect ashlar (a finished stone, ready for building) representing a mature Mason who has spent years in Masonic work and education to improve himself in moral dealing with others and fitting well into society.

Benches, Bencher. Slang terms used to denote a Mason who comes to meetings but sits on the sidelines, not taking an office or participating in degree work.

Blackball. A negative vote against a proposed member of the lodge that is registered secretly by placing a black ball (or cube) into the ballot box. Varying numbers are required in different jurisdictions to reject an applicant, but rarely more than one or two.

Board of General Purposes. The key administrative body of the Grand Lodge in any given jurisdiction. Roughly equivalent to the board of directors of a corporation.

Brethren. More than one Freemason.

Brother. An individual Freemason.

Brotherhood. Both Freemasonry in general and the feeling of camaraderie found among brethren.

Business. A collection of administrative matters typically dealt with in the lodge, usually including minutes, accounts, applications, ballots, committee reports, motions, and so on.

Bylaws. A set of written rules for the governance of a particular lodge as approved by both its members and its Grand Lodge.

Cable Tow. A rope used during initiation.

Candidate. A person who has submitted a duly proposed and seconded petition for initiation, met with the investigating committee, been given a favourable report in open lodge, and approved by ballot to be initiated at some time in the future.

Chair. The Master of the lodge, who runs meetings from a chair situated in the symbolic East of the lodge room.

Chairs. The three principal officers of the lodge, namely the Worshipful Master (who sits in the East), the Senior Warden (in the West), and the Junior Warden (in the South).

Co-Masonic. Used to denote a type of Masonic organization that admits both men and women.

Co-Masonry. A form of Masonry that admits both men and women. Not officially recognized by mainstream Freemasonry.

Concordant Bodies. Masonic organizations that a Mason can join after receiving the third degree. The two main ones are the York Rite (composed of Chapter, Council, and Preceptory) and the Scottish Rite (composed of Lodge of Perfection, Chapter, and Consistory). Each take Masons through a further set of rituals that expand upon the lessons learned in the first three degrees.

Conductor. A person who assists and guides a candidate as they go through the first degree.

Constitution. The legal document that establishes a Grand Lodge and governs it and the actions of its constituent lodges in a given jurisdiction.

Craft, The Craft. A synonym for Freemasonry.

Craft Lodge. A Masonic lodge that confers the first three degrees in Masonry.

Craft Masonry. The ritual system and fraternal organization built around the first three degrees in Masonry.

Craftsman. A term typically used to refer to a Mason who has received the second degree.

Deacon. An officer who is responsible for the floorwork of the lodge, most notably in opening and closing, as well as for ritually conducting candidates around the room during degree work. There are two Deacons (Senior and Junior), each of whom have different duties in these respects.

Degree. A Masonic rite of passage during which candidates are both taught lessons and incorporated into the group.

Degree Team. A group of lodge officers and other brethren involved in performing a degree.

Degree Work. The practice of putting on a Masonic degree.

Demit, Demitted. Terms used for formally withdrawing from the lodge in good standing, or having done so. A document is issued to this effect.

DeMolay. A Masonic organization for youth.

District. A geographic area within a Grand Lodge jurisdiction.

District Grand Lodge. For Grand Lodges with widely dispersed members (e.g., the Grand Lodge of England, the Grand Lodge of Scotland), a separate body governed by a District Grand Master who, in turn, reports to the Grand Master. For example, in Newfoundland and Labrador, there is a District Grand Lodge of Scotland that reports to the Grand Master in Edinburgh.

Dues. An annual amount that a Mason pays to his lodge to remain a member.

East, The East. That part of the lodge where the Master and various dignitaries sit. A symbolic place of honour and status.

Eastern Star, Order of the. An auxiliary Masonic organization for women. Unlike adoptive or co-Masonic organizations, it does not attempt to utilize or adapt Masonic rituals.

Emulation, English Emulation. A form of Masonic ritual that originated in England in the early 1800s that is widely practised there and in other jurisdictions formerly under the United Grand Lodge of England.

English Mason. In this text, a term used by Masons in lodges under the Grand Lodge of Scotland to refer to those in the Grand Lodge of Newfoundland and Labrador, which was formed in 1997 from lodges formerly operating as part of the District Grand Lodge of England.

Entered Apprentice. A Mason who has been initiated into the first degree. The ritual process is analogous to birth; it also stresses basic morality.

Fees. Money paid by a candidate for items not covered by dues, such as applications, the cost of initiation, an apron, and so on.

Fellowcraft. A Mason who has received his second degree.

Festive Board. A Masonic banquet involving food, drink, speeches, and toasts.

First Degree. The first ritual drama that a candidate goes through (a.k.a. initiation). See *Entered Apprentice.*

Floorwork. Ritual work that involves symbolic movement around the lodge, most often by the Deacons, especially during a degree.

Fraternalism. A term that includes Freemasonry and a wide variety of other initiatic organizations based upon the ideas of mutual support and brotherhood.

Fraternity. An organization based upon the ideas of mutual support and brotherhood.

Freeborn. A term used in some old Masonic rituals that stipulate that a candidate must be free to make his own oaths when joining the Craft, a historical reference to the potential existence of binding prior medieval feudal obligations.

Freemason. A member of the Masonic order. Technically, one can be called a Freemason upon receiving the first degree.

Freemasonry. A fraternal organization, based upon the historic stonemason's trade, that uses rituals and metaphorical understandings of the trade's working tools and practices to teach moral and spiritual lessons. See also *The Craft*; *Masonry*.

Grand Bodies. Administrative, umbrella organizations that manage specific Masonic organizations within a particular geographic area (e.g., the Scottish Rite, Grand Chapter, etc.). These are analogous to the Grand Lodge but for various concordant bodies.

Grand Lodge. An administrative, umbrella organization that manages Craft Masonry within a particular geographic area.

Grand Master. The executive and highest-ranking Mason in a particular Grand Lodge.

Grip. A secret handshake by means of which one Freemason can recognize another.

Handshake. See *Grip*.

Higher Degrees. Various Masonic degrees that a Mason can take once they join one or more of the concordant bodies. This term is somewhat controversial, though commonly used, as the third degree is supposed to be the highest degree, and these others merely elaborations.

Hiram Abiff. The central character in the story of Freemasonry, particularly in the second and third degrees. Based on an elaboration of a biblical story, Hiram was the chief architect of Solomon's Temple and was murdered as a result of his fidelity in not revealing the secrets of Masonry when threatened by conspirators seeking personal gain.

Hoodwink. Blindfold.

Horseplay. A term used to describe some of the rougher hazing practices involved in Masonic rituals in the past. These are now widely frowned upon and rarely practised.

Immediate Past Master. A Mason who finished his term as Master of the lodge during the previous year; the last Master of the lodge before the current one was installed.

Initiate. A Mason who has received the first, or Entered Apprentice, degree.

Initiation. The ritual process of receiving the first, or Entered Apprentice, degree.

Inner Work. A specific ritual for installing the new Master of a lodge. Only members who have previously served as a Master can be present and participate.

Installation. A ceremony, usually held yearly, where the old lodge officers vacate their positions and new ones are sworn in to replace them.

Investigation. The process whereby a committee is appointed to meet with a petitioner to see if he is likely an appropriate member of the Craft, then reports back to the lodge before a ballot is taken.

Investigation Committee. The committee appointed by the Master to meet with a petitioner. See *Investigation.*

Jewel. A Masonic medal signifying a degree, membership, status, or rank.

Junior Warden. One of the three principal officers of the lodge. The Junior Warden is situated in the South and is responsible for the lodge at refreshment (i.e., social events).

Landmark, Masonic Landmarks. Traditional requirements and rules in Freemasonry that supposedly cannot be changed without rendering an organization un-Masonic or clandestine (e.g., it is a landmark that atheists cannot be admitted into Masonry). Lodges not adhering to landmarks risk losing recognition.

Lecture. A speech given at the end of each degree elaborating on the story and lessons involved for the benefit of candidates.

Lewis Jewel. A Masonic medal that can be worn by a Mason who is the son of a Mason.

Level, On the Level. Terms that refer to treating others as equals, a symbolic elaboration of the tool used to prove flat surfaces in the building trade.

Lodge. A term used to describe an individual Masonic group, its members, and the place where it meets.

Lodges of Adoption. Female Masonic lodges that operate in some jurisdictions. Not officially recognized by mainstream Masonry. See *Adoptive.*

Master. The leader of a specific Masonic lodge.

Master-Elect. The person who has been elected Master of a lodge for the upcoming year but has not yet been formally installed in his office. In this capacity, the Master-Elect typically visits other lodges to invite officers and brethren to attend his installation ceremony.

Master Mason. A Mason who has received the third degree.

Mason. A term referring to both individual stonemasons and Freemasons. Within Freemasonry, it commonly refers to a person who is a member of the organization.

Masonic. Of, or referring to Freemasonry.

Masonic Restoration Foundation. An American organization that seeks to revive Freemasonry by taking the emphasis off the administrative and business aspects and re-emphasizing the ritual and fraternal ones.

Masonry. A term referring to the organizational aspect of both operative stonemasons and Freemasons. Within the Masonic order, it is often employed as a synonym for Freemasonry.

Meeting. A monthly gathering where, in between the rituals of opening and closing the lodge, members of a Masonic lodge conduct business and do degree work.

Mentoring. A process whereby designated individuals ("mentors") help candidates and new Masons to learn about the Craft and its practices, etiquette, history, and lore. A form of Masonic education.

Middle Chamber Lecture. A lengthy lecture in the second degree, in some jurisdictions.

Modes of Recognition. Secret handshakes, words, and gestures ("signs") whereby one Mason may recognize another.

Morgan Affair. An 1826 murder case in Upstate New York, in which a man who had published an exposé of the Craft was allegedly killed by Masons. It resulted in considerable controversy at the time (and even the formation of an anti-Masonic political party). It is frequently mentioned by anti-Masonic critics even today.

Mother Lodge. The lodge in which a Mason is initiated and receives his degrees.

Obligation. The oath that one swears in each of the three degrees not to reveal the secrets of the order (i.e., the signs and modes of recognition).

Ode. A Masonic song or hymn. Various odes may be sung at various points in rituals, such as those performed during the opening and closing of the lodge or during degree work. This practice is not as widely observed as it was in the past.

Officer. An individual who is formally invested with a specific role in the rituals and in running the affairs of the lodge during a given year.

Office, Offices. A formal role or collection of roles in the ritual and administrative operation of the lodge, filled by specific individuals on an annual basis.

Open Lodge. When a lodge has performed the ceremony of opening at a monthly meeting, it is said to be open. Business or degree work can then be conducted.

Operative. A term that refers to stonemasons, those whose work actually involves working with stone.

Order of the Eastern Star. See *Eastern Star, Order of the*

Passing. A term used for the ritual of the second degree.

Past Master. A Mason who has served as Master of the lodge in the past.

Penal Sign. A ritual gesture signifying the symbolic punishment imposed for revealing the secrets of a given degree. Ritually employed as a salute.

Penalty. The symbolic punishment imposed upon a Mason who reveals the secrets of a given degree.

Petitioner. A person who has filled out an application for initiation and had it duly proposed and seconded by two members of the lodge.

Preparation. The process of readying a candidate for a degree, which involves specific ritual clothing and props.

Preparation Room. The room adjacent to the lodge room where candidates are made ready for a degree.

Prince Hall Freemasonry. An African-American form of Freemasonry that first emerged in Massachusetts at a time when African-Americans were not admitted into other lodges, just as they were not admitted into many mainstream religious institutions.

Proposer. A Mason who signs a petition ("proposes") on behalf of an applicant for initiation or joining a lodge.

Prove. Ritually demonstrate that one is a Mason to another, using various symbolic signs and gestures. See *Modes of Recognition.*

Prove Up. A formal process whereby candidates recite ritual questions and answers from memory in open lodge before they can receive their next degree.

Raising. A term used to describe the third degree.

Rank. One's formal status in the Grand Lodge hierarchy. For example (from lowest to highest), Worshipful, Very Worshipful, Right Worshipful, and Most Worshipful.

Recognition. The legitimacy of a particular Grand Lodge is based upon other Grand Lodges seeing it as valid. If others do not recognize it as such, it is deemed clandestine, and members from other jurisdictions cannot officially visit or have anything to do with it.

Regalia. The various items of symbolic attire worn by a Mason (e.g., an apron). May include jewels, a collar, and so on, depending on rank.

Right Worshipful. A high Masonic rank in the Grand Lodge, one level lower than the highest in a given jurisdiction.

Right Excellent. A high Masonic rank in one of the concordant bodies.

Right Illustrious. A high Masonic rank in one of the concordant bodies.

Ring. Many, though not all, Masons wear a ring bearing an image of the square and compasses, the symbol of the order.

Ruffians. The three offenders who conspired to murder Hiram Abiff; these characters subsequently appear as roles performed during the ritual of the third degree.

Second Degree. The ritual a Mason "passes through" between their initiation ("first degree") and their raising ("third degree"). It emphasizes the importance of education and work in personal growth.

Seconder. The person who signs a petition ("seconds") on behalf of a petitioner after the proposer has done so, thereby formally vouching for the petitioner after the proposer.

Secretary. The officer who handles the administrative paperwork for a lodge.

Scottish Rite. One of the two routes that a Master Mason can take in the concordant bodies. It involves a set of thirty-two degrees.

Secret Society. An organization that, while it draws members from the wider society, operates in a hidden fashion, its purpose, practices, and membership remaining concealed, known only to members. Freemasonry's members, practices, charity, and meeting places have been too widely publicized for it to fit this definition, and Masons widely deny that it is a secret society for these reasons, often preferring the phrase "a society with secrets."

Secrets/Principal Secrets. The modes of recognition, words, and penal signs of the three degrees. None of these have been mentioned in this book.

Senior Warden. One of the three principal officers of the lodge. The Senior Warden is situated in the West and is responsible for helping the Master open and close the lodge. The Senior Warden is usually next in line to become Master.

Service Club. A community organization that engages in fundraising and charity work. While Freemasonry does these things, its ritualistic focus and moral lessons lead many to deny that Masonry is simply another service club.

Shrine. A spinoff organization founded by Masons in the nineteenth century. It focuses on fun and raising money for children's hospitals.

Sign, Signs. See *Modes of Recognition*; *Penal Sign*.

Soliciting. The practice of proactively seeking out new members, as opposed to the reactive strategy of attracting them. Soliciting has been traditionally frowned upon in Freemasonry, though less so in recent years.

Sponsor. Another term for proposer.

Square. Traditionally a construction tool used to prove a right angle, in Masonry it is said to symbolize morality when dealing with others (hence the traditional phrase "square dealing" in business).

Square and Compasses. The most common symbol or emblem of Freemasonry.

Solomon's Temple. The biblical temple constructed by King Solomon of Israel. It provides much of the legend, symbolism, and story of Freemasonry.

Steward. A lodge officer responsible for helping the Junior Warden in preparing the food and refreshment before or after a meeting.

Temple. The lodge represents Solomon's Temple, as does (symbolically) the individual Mason.

Testing. See *Prove Up*.

Third Degree. The final degree in Craft Masonry. Its ritual centres on a symbolic death and the meanings thereof.

Tracing Board. A visual chart or diagram for each degree. The lecture given during the degree ritual is largely based upon this chart.

Trestle Board. The Master's agenda for a particular lodge meeting.

Tyler. The officer who guards the door of the lodge.

Warden. A term referring to two of the principal officers of the lodge. See *Junior Warden*; *Senior Warden*.

Work, At Work. After the lodge has been ritually opened and before it is closed, it is said to be "at work." This is when business can be conducted and degree work performed.

Working Tools. A box of tools, taken from the building trade, that are symbolically explained in the various degrees.

Worshipful Master. The formal title of the Master of the lodge.

York Rite. One of the two routes that a Master Mason can take in the concordant bodies. It involves three separate, linked organizations: the Royal Arch Chapter, the Council of Royal and Select Masters (Cryptic Rite), and the Preceptory (Knights Templar).

WORKS CITED

Alban, Dean R. 2007. "The Future of the Scottish Rite." *Scottish Rite Journal* (March-April). http://www.scottishrite.org/ee/php?/journal/pastarticles/the_future_of_the_scottish_rite/.

Allen, James S. 2003. "Sisters of Another Sort: Freemason Women in Modern France, 1725–1940." *Journal of Modern History* 75(4): 783–835.

Ansary, Tamim. 2008. "12 Memory Tricks." *MSN Encarta*. http://wasthu.blog spot.ca/2008/04/12-memory-tricks-msn-encarta.html.

Arcadia Entertainment. 2004. *Inside Freemasonry*. Halifax, NS: Arcadia Entertainment/Vision TV.

Auge, Axel. 2007. "The Solidarity of Political Elites in Gabon: Between Ethno-Community Logic and Social Networks." *Cahiers internationaux de sociologie* 123 (July): 245–68.

Batson, Daniel, Nadia Ahmad, and Jo-Ann Tsang. 2002. "Four Motives for Community Involvement." *Journal of Social Issues* 58 (3): 429–45.

Beaurepaire, Pierre-Yves. 2006. "Le temple maçonnique: Un espace de paix religieuse et de dialogue interconfessionnel dans l'Europe du XVIIIᵉ siècle" [The Masonic Temple: An Environment of Religious Peace and Interfaith Dialogue in 18th-Century Europe]. *Socio-anthropologie* (April) 17–18. http://socio -anthropologie.revues.org/466.

Becker, Penny Edgell, and Heather Hofmeister. 2000. "Work Hours and Community Involvement of Dual-Earner Couples: Building Social Capital or Competing for Time?" Paper presented at the Annual Meetings of the American Sociological Association, Washington, DC, August 12–16.

Beito, David T. 2000. *From Mutual Aid to the Welfare State: Fraternal Societies and Social Services, 1890–1967*. Chapel Hill: University of North Carolina Press.

Bekkers, René, and Nan Dirk de Graaf. 2002. "Shifting Backgrounds of Participation in Voluntary Associations in the Netherlands." *Mens en Maatschappij* 77 (4): 338–60.

Belton, John L. 1999. "The Missing Master Mason." Installation inaugural address to Internet Lodge 9659. http://www.themasonictrowel.com/leadership/management/membership_files/the_missing_master_mason_by_belton.htm.

———. 2004. "Masonic Membership Myths Debunked." In *Freemasonry in Context: History, Ritual, Controversy*, edited by A. des Hoyos and S. B. Morris, 313–34. Lanham, MD: Lexington Books.

Belton, John L., and David Harrison. 2007. "Masonic Fraternalism: Two Centuries of Membership Fluctuations Examined." Paper presented at the International Conference on the History of Freemasonry, Edinburgh, UK, May 25–27.

Belton, John, and Kent Henderson. 2000. "Freemasons: An Endangered Species?" Address to Quatuor Coronati Lodge No. 2076, London, 14 September. First published in *Ars Quatuor Coronatorum* Vol. 113.

Berger, Peter L., and Thomas Luckmann. 1966. *The Social Construction of Reality: A Treatise on the Sociology of Knowledge*. New York: Doubleday.

Best, Joel, and David F. Luckenbill. 1982. *Organizing Deviance*. Englewood Cliffs, NJ: Prentice Hall.

Bickel, Jean-Francois, and Christian Lalive d'Epinay. 2001. "The Evolution of Participation in Voluntary Associations: A Comparison of Two Cohorts." *Schweizerische Zeitschrift für Soziologie* 27 (1): 31–60.

Blum, Alan F., and Peter McHugh. 1971. "The Social Ascription of Motives." *American Sociological Review* 36: 98–109.

Bolle de Bal, Marcel. 1989. "At the Centre of the Temple: An Experience of Reliance, or the Tribe Rediscovered." *Societies* 24 (July): 11–13.

Bonjean, Charles M., William T. Markham, and Patrick O. Macken. 1994. "Measuring Self-Expression in Volunteer Organizations: A Theory-Based Questionnaire." *Journal of Applied Behavioral Science* 30 (4): 487–515.

Broese van Groenou, Marjolein. 2010. "Formal and Informal Social Participation of the 'Young-Old' in the Netherlands in 1992 and 2002." *Ageing and Society* 30 (3): 445–65.

Brown, Dan. 2003. *The Da Vinci Code*. New York: Doubleday.

Bryon-Portet, Céline. 2011. "The Tension in the Heart of the Anthropological Research: The Dialectic Inside/Outside, Theory/Practice, a Necessity for the Study of Closed Institutions." *Anthropologie et Sociétés* 35 (3): 209–31.

Bullock, Steven C. 1998. *Revolutionary Brotherhood: Freemasonry and the Transformation of the American Social Order, 1730–1840*. Chapel Hill: University of North Carolina Press.

———. 2007. "Creative Destruction: The Cycles of American Masonic History." Paper presented at the International Conference on the History of Freemasonry, Edinburgh, UK, May 25–27.

Burke, Janet M. 1989. "Freemasonry, Friendship and Noblewomen: The Role of the Secret Society in Bringing Enlightenment Thought to Pre-Revolutionary Women Elites." *History of European Ideas* 10 (3): 283–93.

Canepa, Andrew M. 1990. "Profile of the Italian-Language Masonic Lodge in California (1871–1966)." *Studi Emigrazione/Etudes Migrations* 27 (97): 87–107.

Cano, Gilberto Loaiza. 2009. "Sociability and Public Life in Colombia in the 19th Century: Liberal Political Clubs." *Revue des sciences sociales* 41: 170–81.

Carnes, Mark C. 1989. *Secret Ritual and Manhood in Victorian America*. New Haven, CT: Yale University Press.

Chacon, Fernando, Maria Louisa Vecina, and Maria Celeste Davila. 2007. "The Three-Stage Model of Volunteers' Duration of Service." *Social Behavior and Personality* 35 (5): 627–42.

Clark, Candace. 1987. "Sympathy Biography and Sympathy Margin" *American Journal of Sociology* 93 (2): 290–321.

———. 1990. "Emotions and Micropolitics in Everyday Life: Some Patterns and Paradoxes of 'Place.'" In Kemper 1990, 305–33.

Clark, Roland. 2012. "Anti-Masonry as Political Protest: Fascists and Freemasons in Interwar Romania." *Patterns of Prejudice* 46 (1): 40–57.

Clawson, Mary Ann. 1989. *Constructing Brotherhood: Class, Gender and Fraternalism*. Princeton, NJ: Princeton University Press.

———. 2007. "Masculinity, Consumption, and the Transformation of Scottish Rite Freemasonry in the Turn-of-the-Century United States." *Gender and History* 19 (1): 101–21.

Coil, H. W. 1996. *Coil's Masonic Encyclopedia*. New York: Macoy.

Collins, Randall. 1990. "Stratification, Emotional Energy, and the Transient Emotions." In Kemper 1990, 27–57.

Combes, Andre. 1989. "Notes on a Sociology of the Grand Orient of France." *Societies* 24 (July): 23–24.

Cook, Judith A. 1988. "Dad's Double Binds: Rethinking Fathers' Bereavement from a Men's Studies Perspective." *Journal of Contemporary Ethnography* 17 (3): 285–308.

Cools, Marc. 2012. "Freemasonry and Criminalization during the Vichy Regime: A Criminological Approach to the 'Forces Occultes.'" *Tijdschrift Over Cultuur & Criminaliteit* 2. http://search.proquest.com/docview/1494748766?accountid=12378.

Cox, Eva. 2002. "Australia: Making the Lucky Country." In *Democracies in Flux: The Evolution of Social Capital in Contemporary Society*, edited by Robert D. Putnam, 333–58. New York: Oxford University Press.

Curtis, James E., Douglas E. Baer, and Edward G. Grabb. 2001. "Nations of Joiners: Explaining Voluntary Association Membership in Democratic Societies." *American Sociological Review* 66 (6): 783–805.

Curtis, James, Douglas Baer, Edward Grabb, and Thomas Perks. 2003. "Estimating Trends in Voluntary Association Activity over Recent Decades in Quebec and English Canada." *Sociologie et sociétés* 35 (1): 115–41.

Davis, Matthew Reid. 2000. "Nineteenth-Century Rhetorics of American Brotherhood." PhD thesis, University of Washington.

de Hoyos, Arturo, and S. Brent Morris. 1997. *Is It True What They Say about Freemasonry? The Methods of Anti-Masons*. Washington, DC: Supreme Council, Ancient and Accepted Scottish Rite of the Southern Jurisdiction.

de Los Reyes, Guillermo, and Antonio Lara. 1999. "Civil Society and Volunteerism: Lodges in Mining Communities." *Annals of the American Academy of Political and Social Science* 565 (September.): 218–24.

Denzin, Norman K. 1982. "A Note on Emotionality, Self, and Interaction." *American Journal of Sociology* 89 (2): 402–9.

———. 1984. *On Understanding Emotion*. San Francisco: Jossey-Bass.

———. 1985. "Emotion as Lived Experience." *Symbolic Interaction* 8 (2): 223–40.

———. 1990. "On Understanding Emotion: The Interpretive-Cultural Agenda." In Kemper 1990, 85–116.

Derber, Charles. 1979. *The Pursuit of Attention: Power and Ego in Everyday Life*. Boston: G. K. Hall and Co.

———. 2000. *The Pursuit of Attention: Power and Ego in Everyday Life*. Oxford: Oxford University Press.

Dierickx, J. 1989. "The Ritual Dimension: Regarding the Language of Masonic Rituals." *Societies* 24 (July): 28–30.

Doan, R. Stephen. 1993. "Origins of Masonry." *Education* 114 (1): 24–26.

Douglas, Jack D. 1977. "Shame and Deceit in Creative Deviance." In *Deviance and Social Change*, edited by Edward Sagarin, 59–86. Beverly Hills, CA: Sage.

Dunbar, Paul L. 2012. "Hidden in Plain Sight: African American Secret Societies and Black Freemasonry." *Journal of African American Studies* 16 (4): 622–37.

Durkheim, Émile. (1912) 1965. *The Elementary Forms of the Religious Life*. Reprint, New York: Free Press.

Egel, Daniel Peter. 2011. "Social Institutions and Development." PhD thesis, University of California, Berkeley.

Elias, Norbert. 1994. *The Civilizing Process*. Oxford: Blackwell.

Erickson, Bonnie H. 1981. "Secret Societies and Social Structure." *Social Forces* 60 (1): 188–210.

Fine, Gary A., and Lori Holyfield. 1996. "Secrecy, Trust and Dangerous Leisure: Generating Group Cohesion in Voluntary Organizations." *Social Psychology Quarterly* 59 (1): 22–38.

Fozdar, Vahid. 2011. "'That Grand Primeval and Fundamental Religion': The Transformation of Freemasonry into a British Imperial Cult." *Journal of World History* 22 (3): 493–525.

Garfinkel, Harold. 1967. *Studies in Ethnomethodology*. Englewood Cliffs, NJ: Prentice Hall.

Glaser, Barney, and Anselm Strauss. 1967. *The Discovery of Grounded Theory: Strategies for Qualitative Research*. Chicago: Aldine.

Goffman, Erving. 1959. *The Presentation of Self in Everyday Life*. Garden City, NY: Doubleday Anchor.

Gramsci, Antonio. 2007. "Gramsci in Parliament." *Cultural Studies* 21 (4–5): 784–95.

Greene, Thomas M. 2002. "Clubs, Secret Societies, and Male Quest Romance (Rudyard Kipling, H. Rider Haggard, Bram Stoker)." PhD thesis, University of Massachusetts, Amherst.

Griggs, Clive. 1994. "The Influence of British Public Schools on British Imperialism." *British Journal of Sociology of Education* 15 (1): 129–36.

Hackett, David G. 2014. *That Religion in Which All Men Agree: Freemasonry in American Culture*. Berkeley: University of California Press.

Hall, Peter A. 2002. "Great Britain: The Role of Government and the Distribution of Social Capital." In *Democracies in Flux: The Evolution of Social Capital in Contemporary Society*, edited by Robert D. Putnam, 21–57. New York: Oxford University Press.

Hall, Richard H. 1987. *Organizations: Structures, Processes, and Outcomes*, 4th ed. Englewood Cliffs, NJ: Prentice Hall.

Harland-Jacobs, Jessica. 2007. *Builders of Empire: Freemasonry and British Imperialism*. Chapel Hill: University of North Carolina Press.

Harland-Jacobs, Jessica Leigh. 2000. "The Essential Link: Freemasonry and British Imperialism, 1751–1918." PhD thesis, Duke University.

Hazelrigg, Lawrence E. 1969. "A Reexamination of Simmel's 'The Secret and the Secret Society': Nine Propositions." *Social Forces* 47 (3): 323–29.

Hellman, John. 2001. "Memory, History and National Identity in Vichy France." *Modern and Contemporary France* 9 (1): 37–42.

Hetherington, Kevin. 1997. *The Badlands of Modernity: Heterotopia and Social Order*. London: Routledge.

Hewitt, John P. 2003. *Self and Society: A Symbolic Interactionist Social Psychology*, 9th ed. Boston: Allyn & Bacon.

Hewitt, John P., and Randall Stokes. 1975. "Disclaimers." *American Sociological Review* 40 (February): 1–11.

Hirschi, Travis. 1969. *Causes of Delinquency*. Berkeley and Los Angeles: University of California Press.

Hochschild, Arlie R. 1983. *The Managed Heart*. Berkeley: University of California Press.

———. 1990. "Ideology and Emotion Management: A Perspective and Path for Future Research." In Kemper 1990, 117–42.

Hodapp, Christopher. 2013. "Boring Our Members to Death." http://www.masonicdictionary.com/boredom.html.

Hoffman, Stefan-Ludwig. 2001. "Civility, Male Friendship, and Masonic Sociability in Nineteenth-Century Germany." *Gender and History* 13 (2): 224–48.

Holstein, James A., and Jaber F. Gubrium. 2000. *The Self We Live By: Narrative Identity in a Postmodern World*. New York: Oxford.

Ilsley, Paul J. 1990. *Enhancing the Volunteer Experience: New Insights on Strengthening Volunteer Participation, Learning, and Commitment*. San Francisco: Jossey-Bass.

Jacob, Margaret C. 1981. *The Radical Enlightenment: Pantheists, Freemasons and Republicans*. London: George Allen and Unwin.

———. 1991. "The Enlightenment Redefined: The Formation of Modern Civil Society." *Social Research* 58 (2): 475–95.

Jeremy, David J. 1984. "Anatomy of the British Business Elite, 1860–1980." *Business History* 26 (1): 3–23.

Jolicoeur, Pamela M., and Louis L. Knowles. 1978. "Fraternal Associations and Civil Religion: Scottish Rite Freemasonry." *Review of Religious Research* 20 (1): 3–22.

Jones, Bernard E. 1950. *Freemasons' Guide and Compendium*. London: Harrap.

Kaplan, Danny. 2014. "The Architecture of Collective Intimacy: Masonic Friendships as a Model for Collective Attachments." *American Anthropologist* 116 (1): 81–93.

Karpiel, Frank J. 1998. "Mystic Ties of Brotherhood: Freemasonry, Royalty, and Ritual in Hawaii, 1843–1910." PhD thesis, University of Hawaii.

Kemper, Theodore, ed. 1990. *Research Agendas in the Sociology of Emotions*. Albany: State University of New York Press

Kenney, J. Scott. 2007. "Ritual Actions and Meaning among Freemasons: A Sociological Approach." In *Freemasonry and Initiatic Traditions*, edited by R. A. Gilbert, 80–114. Vol. 4 of *The Canonbury Papers*. Hersham, UK: Lewis/Ian Allan.

———. 2008. "Social Research on Freemasonry: Some Initial Impressions." http://www.Freemasons-Freemasonry.com/Freemasonry_social_research.html.

———. 2010. "Pragmatic Constructions of History among Contemporary Freemasons." *Journal for Research into Freemasonry and Fraternalism* 1 (2): 159–85.

Knight, Stephen. 1984. *The Brotherhood: The Secret World of the Freemasons.* London: Dorset Press.

Lammers, John C. 1991. "Attitudes, Motives, and Demographic Predictors of Volunteer Commitment and Service Duration." *Journal of Social Service Research* 14 (3–4): 125–40.

Lemert, Edwin M. 1951. *Social Pathology.* New York: McGraw-Hill.

Mackey, Albert G. 1925. *Encyclopedia of Freemasonry.* New York: Masonic History Company.

Mahmud, Lilith. 2012. "In the Name of Transparency: Gender, Terrorism, and Masonic Conspiracies in Italy." *Anthropological Quarterly* 85 (4): 1177–1207.

Mahmud-Abdelwahib, Lilith. 2008. "The Brotherhood of Freemason Sisters: Knowledge, Subjectivity, and Discretion in Italian Masonic Lodges." PhD thesis, Harvard University.

Mangham, Iain L., and Michael A. Overington. 1987. *Organizations as Theatre: A Social Psychology of Dramatic Appearances.* Chichester, UK: John Wiley and Sons.

Marcello, Melissa K., and Robert Perrucci. 2000. "Small Groups and Civic Engagement." *The Responsive Community* 10 (3): 67–73.

Marshall, Alison R. 2009. "Everyday Religion and Identity in a Western Manitoban Chinese Community: Christianity, the KMT, Foodways and Related Events." *Journal of the American Academy of Religion* 77 (3): 573–608.

Masonic Service Association of North America. 2004. "It's About Time." http://www.msana.com/aboutime_intro.asp.

———. 2014. "Masonic Membership Statistics: Membership Totals since 1924." http://www.msana.com/msastats.asp.

The Masonic Trowel. 2012. "10 Steps to Lodge Renewal." http://www.themasonic trowel.com/leadership/management/management_files/10_steps_to_lodge _renewal.htm.

McBride, Harriet W. 2000. "Fraternal Regalia in America, 1865 to 1918: Dressing the Lodges; Clothing the Brotherhood." PhD thesis, Ohio State University.

Mead, George H. 1934. *Mind, Self, and Society.* Chicago: University of Chicago Press.

Merton, Robert. 1968. *Social Theory and Social Structure.* New York: Free Press.

Mesch, Gustavo S., and Ilan Talmud. 2010. "Internet Connectivity, Community Participation, and Place Attachment: A Longitudinal Study." *American Behavioral Scientist* 53 (8): 1095–110.

Meštrović, Stjepan G. 1997. *Postemotional Society.* London: Sage.

Mills, C. Wright. 1940. "Situated Actions and Vocabularies of Motive." *American Sociological Review* 5 (October): 904–13.

Morris, S. Brent. 2007a. "The Six Stages of the Evolution of Freemasonry in the United States of America." Paper presented at the International Conference on the History of Freemasonry, Edinburgh, UK, May 25–27.

———. 2007b. Personal email to author May 30, containing statistics and commentary re: Masonic membership in the United States.

Morrison, Heather. 2012. "Making Degenerates into Men by Doing Shots, Breaking Plates, and Embracing Brothers in Eighteenth-Century Freemasonry." *Journal of Social History* 46 (1): 48–65.

National Treasure. 2004. Burbank, CA: Walt Disney Pictures.

Omoto, Allen M., Mark Snyder, and Steven C. Martino. 2000. "Volunteerism and the Life Course: Investigating Age-Related Agendas for Action." *Basic and Applied Social Psychology* 22 (3): 181–97.

Ormières, Jean-Louis. 2011. Review of *Women's Agency and Rituals in Mixed and Female Masonic Orders*, by Alexandra Heidle and Jan A. M. Snoek. *Archives de sciences sociales des religions* 56 (156): 174–76.

Ortiz, Hector Luis. 2010. "Disruption and Stability: A Study of the Effects of Inter-Community Mobility on Political Participation." PhD thesis, Syracuse University.

Osborne, Katy, Anna Ziersch, and Fran Baum. 2008. "Who Participates? Socioeconomic Factors Associated with Women's Participation in Voluntary Groups." *Australian Journal of Social Issues* 43 (1): 103–22.

Papademas, Diana. 1991. "Patriarchy and Philanthropy." Paper presented at the August meetings of the American Sociological Association, Cincinnati, OH.

Perks, Thomas, and Michael Haan. 2011. "Youth Religious Involvement and Adult Community Participation: Do Levels of Youth Religious Involvement Matter?" *Nonprofit and VolSector Quarterly* 40 (1): 107–29.

Perren, Kim, Sara Arber, and Kate Davidson. 2003. "Men's Organizational Affiliations in Later Life: The Influence of Social Class and Marital Status on Informal Group Membership." *Ageing and Society* 23 (1): 69–82.

Petitat, Andre. 1998. "Symbolic Reversibility and Social Forms." Paper presented at the 14th ISA World Congress of Sociology, Montreal.

Pietre-Stones Review of Freemasonry. 2005. http://www.Freemasons-Freemasonry .com.

Poulet, Celia. 2010. "Recognizing and Revealing Knowers: An Enhanced Bernsteinian Analysis of Masonic Recruitment and Apprenticeship." *British Journal of Sociology of Education* 31 (6): 793–812.

Prus, Robert. 1997. *Subcultural Mosaics and Intersubjective Realities: An Ethnographic Research Agenda for Pragmatizing the Social Sciences.* Albany: State University of New York Press.

Putnam, Robert D. 2000. *Bowling Alone: The Collapse and Revival of American Community.* New York: Simon and Schuster.

Quiroz, Alfonzo W. 2007. "Freemasonry and Nation: Masonic and Political Networks in the Construction of Cuban Identity (1811–1902)." *Journal of Latin American Studies* 39 (4): 876–78.

Ren, Yuqing, Robert Kraut, and Sara Kiesler. 2007. "Applying Common Identity and Bond Theory to Design of Online Communities." *Organization Studies* 28 (3): 377–408.

Renauer, Brian C. 2001. "Why Get Involved? Examining the Motivational, Identity, and Ideological Aspects of Resident Involvement in Place-Based Organizations." PhD thesis, State University of New York, Albany.

Rich, Paul. 1997. "Female Freemasons: Gender, Democracy and Fraternalism." *Journal of American Culture* 20 (1): 105–10.

Rotolo, Thomas, and John Wilson. 2003. "Work Histories and Voluntary Association Memberships." *Sociological Forum* 18 (4): 603–19.

Royal, David. 2008. *Masonic Mnemonics.* Lewis Masonic.

Rubington, Earl, and Martin S. Weinberg. 1987. *Deviance: The Interactionist Perspective*, 5th ed. New York: Macmillan.

Ryle, Robyn R. 2000. "Unstable Careers and Community Involvement Effects of Job Insecurity, Local Economy and Work." Paper presented at the annual meeting of the Southern Sociological Society. http://search.proquest.com/docview/61756856?accountid=12378.

———. 2002. "Work and the Salience of Community Involvement in the Shadow of Deindustrialization." Paper presented at the annual meeting of the Southern Sociological Society. http://search.proquest.com/docview/61779179?accountid=12378.

Scanlan, Matthew D. J., ed. 2002. *The Social Impact of Freemasonry on the Modern Western World*. Vol. 1 of *The Canonbury Papers*. London: Canonbury Masonic Research Centre.

Schmidt, Alvin J. 1987. "Sexism in Fraternal Organizations." Paper presented at the annual meeting of the American Sociological Association, Chicago, October.

Schutz, Alfred. 1962. *Collected Papers 1: The Problem of Social Reality*. Edited by Maurice Natanson. The Hague: Martinus Nijhoff Publishers.

Scott, W. Richard. 1987. *Organizations: Rational, Natural, and Open Systems*, 2nd ed. Englewood Cliffs, NJ: Prentice Hall.

Scott, Marvin B., and Stanford M. Lyman. 1968. "Accounts." *American Sociological Review* 33 (February): 46–62.

Simmel, Georg. 1908. *Soziologie*. Berlin: Duncker and Humblot.

Simpson, Charles R. 1994. "A Fraternity of Danger: Volunteer Fire Companies and the Contradiction of Modernization." Paper presented at the annual meeting of the American Sociological Association, Los Angeles, August.

The Simpsons. 1995. "Homer the Great." http://simpsons.wikia.com/wiki/Homer_the_Great.

Skocpol, Theda. 2003. *Diminished Democracy: From Membership to Management in American Civic Life*. Norman: University of Oklahoma Press.

Smith, Douglas C. 1996. "Working the Rough Stone: Freemasonry and Society in Eighteenth-Century Russia." PhD thesis, University of California, Los Angeles.

Smith, H. Lovell, and Mark Peyrot. 2008. "Examining the 'Spill-Over' Effect of Religiosity on Civic Involvement and Efficacy." *Research in the Social Scientific Study of Religion* 19: 143–62.

Stevenson, David. 1990. *The Origins of Freemasonry: Scotland's Second Century 1590–1710*. Cambridge: Cambridge University Press.

Summers, Martin. 2003. "Diasporic Brotherhood: Freemasonry and the Transnational Production of Black Middle-Class Masculinity." *Gender and History* 15 (3): 550–74.

Summers-Effler, Erika. 2004. "Humble Saints and Righteous Heroes: Sustaining Intense Involvement in Altruistic Social Movements." PhD diss., University of Pennsylvania.

Sykes, Gresham M., and David Matza. 1957. "Techniques of Neutralization: A Theory of Delinquency." *American Sociological Review* 22 (December): 667–70.

Tabbert, M. A. 2007. "The Development of 20th Century American Masonic Philanthropies." Paper presented at the International Conference on the History of Freemasonry, Edinburgh, UK, May 25–27.

Tang, Fengyan. 2006. "What Resources Are Needed for Volunteerism?" *Journal of Applied Gerontology* 25 (5): 375–90.

Tang, Fengyan, Nancy Morrow-Howell, and Eunhee Choi. 2010. "Why Do Older Volunteers Stop Volunteering?" *Ageing and Society* 30 (5): 859–78.

Taylor, Laurie. 1979. "Vocabularies, Rhetorics and Grammar: Problems in the Sociology of Motivation." In *Deviant Interpretations*, edited by D. Downes and P. Rock, 145–61. Oxford: Oxford University Press.

Thoits, Peggy A. 1990. "Emotional Deviance: Research Agendas." In Kemper 1990, 180–203.

Tschorn, Adam. 2008. "Freemasons in Midst of Popularity, Membership Boom." *Los Angeles Times*, May 18. http://www.latimes.com/features/lifestyle/la-ig-masons18-2008may18,0,562412.story.

Turner, Victor. 1967. *The Forest of Symbols*. Ithaca, NY: Cornell University Press.

———. 1969. *The Ritual Process: Structure and Anti-Structure*. Chicago: Aldine.

Uribe-Uran, Victor M. 2000. "The Birth of a Public Sphere in Latin America during the Age of Revolution." *Comparative Studies in Society and History* 42 (2): 425–57.

Van Gennep, Arnold. 1960. *Rites of Passage*. Chicago: University of Chicago Press.

Van Horn, Beth E. 2002. "Youth, Family, and Club Experiences and Adult Civic Engagement." PhD thesis, Pennsylvania State University.

van Ingen, Erik, and Matthijs Kalmijn. 2010. "Does Voluntary Association Participation Boost Social Resources?" *Social Science Quarterly* 91 (2): 493–510.

van Ingen, Erik, and Tom van der Meer. 2011. "Welfare State Expenditure and Inequalities in Voluntary Association Participation." *Journal of European Social Policy* 21 (4): 302–22.

Wade, John. 2002. "The Centre for Research into Freemasonry, University of Sheffield." Lecture presented at Lodge Chimera No. 160 on the rolls of the Regular Grand Lodge of Italy, Arezzo, Italy, November 21. http://www.freemasons-freemasonry.com/wadesheffield.html.

Walker, Corey D. B. 2008. *A Noble Fight: African American Freemasonry and the Struggle for Democracy in America*. Champaign-Urbana: University of Illinois Press.

Wallace, Maurice O. 1995. "Constructing the Black Masculine: Identity and Ideology in African-American Men's Literature and Culture." PhD thesis, Duke University.

Wallace, Ruth A., and Alison Wolf. 1980. *Contemporary Sociological Theory*. Englewood Cliffs, NJ: Prentice Hall.

Weber, Max. 1949. *The Methodology of the Social Sciences*. New York: Free Press.

Welser, Howard T. 2006. "A Theory of Status Achievement." PhD thesis, University of Washington.

Wilmshurst, Leslie. 1922. *The Meaning of Masonry*. New York: E. P. Dutton & Co.

Wilson, John. 1980. "Voluntary Associations and Civil Religion: The Case of Freemasonry." *Review of Religious Research* 22 (2): 125–36.

Wilson, John, and Thomas Janoski. 1995. "The Contribution of Religion to Volunteer Work." *Sociology of Religion* 56 (2): 137–52.

Yates, Frances. 1966. *The Art of Memory*. London: Routledge and Kegan Paul.

Yronwode, Catherine. 2002. "Freemasonry for Women." LuckyMojo. http://www
.luckymojo.com/comasonry.html.

Zurcher, Louis A. 1982. "The Staging of Emotion: A Dramaturgical Analysis."
Symbolic Interaction 5 (1): 1–22.

———. 1985. "The War Game: Organizational Scripting and the Expression of
Emotion." *Symbolic Interaction* 8 (2): 191–206.

INDEX

225; Craft as alternative, 55, 215, 247–48, 250; Craft as enforcing, 33, 266n2; and involvement, 140–43, 144; and restrictions on participation, 265n4. *See also* status, and equality
Stevenson, David, 3
Strauss, Anselm, 29
support. *See* conductors; mentorship; social support; sponsors
symbolic interactionism: introduction to, 11; dramaturgical analysis, 12–14; emergent meaning, 11–12; and individual interpretation and action, 26
symbolism. *See* ritual
sympathy biography, 135

teamwork, 92
teasing, 61, 63, 70, 73–74, 98, 263n3
"10 Steps to Lodge Renewal" program, 116
theatre: of organizations, 13–14, 63, 68
third degree. *See* degree, third
third degree, giving someone the, 263n11
Thoits, Peggy, 17, 18
tolerance, 230–32
traditional authority, 249
travelling, 223–24

trust, 223
Turner, Victor, 251

universities, lodges at, 262n4
urban lodges, 31, 179, 265n7

Van Gennep, Arnold, 9, 251
vocabularies of motive, 207
volunteerism: available time for, 195–96; changing nature of, 117, 216; and employment issues, 118; fit for, 118; and Freemasonry, 120–21, 266n2; motivations for, 119; and organizational dynamics, 120; and organizational identity, 119–20, 145–46, 205; and religious involvement, 117, 264nn1–2; and social contexts, 117–18; and status attainment, 141; and workplace model for organizations, 167
vulnerability, organizational, 121

Weber, Max, 38, 208, 249, 266n1
Welser, Howard T., 174
women: admittance of, 2, 257, 261n4; and charitable work, 261n4; exclusion of, 14; mentioned in degree work, 263n12; Order of the Eastern Star, 50–51, 132, 262n1; perceived problems from admitting, 201–2; studies on, 6. *See also* spouses

CPSIA information can be obtained
at www.ICGtesting.com
Printed in the USA
BVOW07s0913070416

443205BV00007B/5/P